D1376583

WITHDRAWN

Lives of Their Own

Lives of
Their Own

Blacks, Italians, and Poles in
Pittsburgh, 1900-1960

John Bodnar, Roger Simon,
and Michael P. Weber

University of Illinois Press   *Urbana   Chicago   London*

LIBRARY OF CONGRESS CATALOGING IN PUBLICATION DATA

Bodnar, John E., 1944-
  Lives of their own.

  (The Working class in American history)
  Bibliography: p.
  Includes index.
  1. Minorities—Pennsylvania—Pittsburgh.
2. Afro-Americans—Pennsylvania—Pittsburgh.
3. Italian Americans—Pennsylvania—Pittsburgh.
4. Polish Americans—Pennsylvania—Pittsburgh.
5. Pittsburgh (Pa.)—Social conditions.   6. Pittsburgh (Pa.)—Economic conditions.   I. Simon,
Roger D.   II. Weber, Michael P.   III. Title.
IV. Series: Working class in American history.
F159.P69A22   974.8'86004   81-3382
ISBN 0-252-00880-4   AACR2

For the Blacks, Italians, and Poles
Who Lived This Experience

Contents

List of Tables

Acknowledgments

During the lengthy process of writing this book we became indebted to countless numbers of people. Colleagues offered encouragement and shared our enthusiasm; public officials opened doors, enabling us to secure vital information; foundations provided funds, and our own institutions permitted us the time to complete our work. We are grateful to too many individuals to thank each one publicly, but we appreciate their efforts nonetheless.

Several individuals, however, made major contributions, and their mention here is our small way of expressing our sincere gratitude. As with most historical studies this one depended in important ways on the work of competent research assistants. Cynthia Tonia, Theresa Woodruff, Mindy K. Small, and Bernard Ulozas patiently and carefully assisted in gathering and codifying quantitative data. Peter Gottleib, Gregory Mihalik, and William Simons conducted the majority of the oral interviews. Gerald Weber provided valuable aid at several crucial moments. Undergraduate and graduate students at Carnegie-Mellon University made small but important contributions throughout the past four years. We thank them all.

Every librarian whom we encountered, whether with the National Archives in Washington, D.C., or with our own institutions, willingly tolerated our most unusual requests and often refused to rest until they had secured the desired information. Several, in particular, however, deserve special mention. Frank Zabroski and Joseph Rishel of the Pittsburgh Archives of Industrial Society were personally interested in our work; the reference librarians of the Allegheny Branch of the Carnegie Library, in particular Stephan Padgajny, went out of their way to secure important records. They also helped make our countless library hours pleasant as well as useful.

Our colleagues, with whom we discussed our work, provided intellectual stimulation and important ideas. Several read and commented upon earlier versions of this work. The constructive but gentle criticisms of Peter Stearns, Joel Tarr, William Shade, and Charles Tilly significantly improved the manuscript. Reginald Baker prepared the quantitative data for computer analysis and performed all statistical operations. We are grateful for their willingness to contribute their valuable time and perceptive ideas.

Officials at our home institutions also provided encouragement. Ludwig Schaefer at Carnegie-Mellon University, Lawrence Leder at Lehigh University, and William Wewer at the Pennsylvania Historical and Museum Commission, in particular, supported our work and provided the time needed to complete this project. To them we are deeply indebted.

We thank, too, the Rockefeller Foundation and the Pennsylvania Ethnic Heritage Study Center. The major grant provided by the Rockefeller Foundation gave continuing support throughout most of the project. The Ethnic Heritage Study Center gave small but needed financial assistance at a most opportune moment. Without the generous assistance of both organizations this work could not have been completed.

We also thank the editors of the *Journal of American History* for permission to reprint portions of our earlier article, "Migration, Kinship, and Urban Adjustment: Blacks and Poles in Pittsburgh, 1900-1930" from volume 66 (1979): 548-65.

Many individuals who transformed our barely legible scrawls to the typed page deserve thanks. This heroic task was performed by Ellen Parkes, Debbie Miller, Joanne Bornman, Terry Racosky, and Betty Macadam. Our special gratitude goes to Eunice Hench who tirelessly and patiently served as the major typist for the entire project. Susan L. Patterson of the University of Illinois Press was our highly capable and efficient editor.

Finally, we wish to acknowledge the hundreds of blacks, Italians, and Poles who willingly submitted to our probing questions. They opened their homes, their private lives, and occasionally their wine bottles to outsiders so that we may all better understand their worlds. To them this work is dedicated.

Introduction

In the winter of 1890 a young Polish immigrant from the village of Rypin, Kajetan Kuczmarski, wrote to his father to assure him that he was "doing quite well" with his job of pulling steel beams on the Southside of Pittsburgh. Kuczmarski also inquired if his brother had grown large enough to work in an American mill. He cautioned his family not to worry about educating their younger son much longer, for "if he wants to earn a living here with a pen that is not for America. America does not like writers but hard working people."[1] While he probably had little time to reflect on such matters, Kuczmarski was part of a much larger movement of "hard working people" who began to look toward expanding industrial cities such as Pittsburgh for solutions to mounting economic and social problems proliferating in their homelands. Throughout less industrialized regions such as the American South, southern and central Italy, and Congress Poland, Prussia, and Galicia, ordinary individuals turned their attention to the mills and the factories of the place contemporary observers called "capitalism's key city." What people from these particular regions brought with them to Pittsburgh, how they entered the city, and what they encountered during the first half of the twentieth century are matters that define the shape and direction of this study.

Most inquiries of a scholarly nature begin with several assumptions, and this one is no exception. In this case the urbanization of preindustrial people is viewed not as a common experience but as one that progressed differently for various groups of newcomers. While southern-born blacks, Poles, and Italians all moved to the "steel city" between 1890 and the 1920s, they ultimately displayed divergent occupational paths, outlooks, and behavioral strategies. Their experiences in Pittsburgh differed widely. Consider three who did make the move. Joseph Maszak left Russian Poland in 1908 and settled in Pittsburgh's Strip District, an early area of Polish settlement along the Allegheny River. Like many of his friends and relatives he obtained work in a mill. By the early 1920s, however, illness forced him to abandon his physically demanding job in the mill. Unable to secure steady work thereafter, he resorted to helping his teenage son deliver newspapers. He performed this task somewhat disheartedly until he died in 1926.

Opportunities seemed somewhat limited for Henry Brown as well. Childhood ended rather abruptly at age fourteen when his father died on the family's Virginia farm, and he was forced to live with relatives and work in Washington, D.C. By 1918 he found himself in Pittsburgh, looking after a sister who had moved there earlier but was now ill. Brown decided to stay when he obtained one of the few jobs that was open to him, a labor gang position at the Jones and Laughlin steel mill, and to make a life in the "steel city." He remained at Jones and Laughlin until he retired in 1958.

Events went somewhat better for Ray LaMarca. After the sulfur mines closed near Villa Rosa, Sicily, in 1909, his father followed a relative to Pittsburgh to earn a living as a barber, a trade he had acquired in Italy. After seven years, Ray and his mother were able to join the elder LaMarca. Not surprisingly, his father's barber shop provided the necessary contact to help Ray find a steady job at the Fort Pitt Spring Company, a position that allowed him to build a base for a small entrepreneurial venture later in life.

For all three men Pittsburgh promised employment and a solution to their immediate need to make a living, which was growing more difficult to accomplish in their homelands. But they were — despite the similarity of their general predicament — different men from varying backgrounds moving toward divergent futures. Whether immigrant or black, the larger historical processes of industrialization and urbanization would not treat them all alike.

Comparisons of the experiences of blacks and European immigrants have stirred controversy in the academic community and among the public at large for several decades. Particularly at issue has been the question of whether blacks should properly be viewed as the latest in a long succession of identifiable minorities to migrate to the industrial city from rural areas.[2] It seemed that European immigrant groups assimilated into the wider society after several generations, enjoying considerable social mobility and leaving behind unskilled jobs and old neighborhoods for the next wave of workers. The implications of this view was that blacks would in time achieve similar progress. However, sociologists such as Herbert Gans, Nathan Glazer, and Daniel Moynihan demolished the notion of easy and rapid assimilation of immigrants.[3] In addition, they suggested that mobility followed no clearly discernible chronological pattern. Nonetheless, the issue of relative deprivation and hardship for blacks and immigrants persists.[4]

But the preoccupation of historical inquiry with progress and success, matters that may not have been paramount to most working-class immigrants and migrants in the first place, deflected scholars away from more fundamental lines of inquiry. Beyond the somewhat narrow models of ethnic succession and mobility, real people were attempting to create lives for themselves in the midst of numerous, countervailing forces. Immediate problems of leaving home, moving to a strange city, finding work, and maintaining families loomed so large as to obscure the larger concerns of scholars — status, success, and succession. This study developed from the belief that a more accurate understanding of the urbanization of migrants could result from a microscopic analysis of individuals in the process of fabricating life strategies in response to specific urban and industrial conditions. While we did not attempt to investigate every facet of individual and group adjustment, we did concentrate on issues that seemed to preoccupy the historical actors themselves: migration, employment, family, and housing. Arguments could easily be made that additional concerns existed. Religion, politics, leisure, and labor conditions all affected newcomers deeply and surely deserve more extended treatment. But we do not pretend to claim that this study is exhaustive. Rather, we seek ultimately to move the entire subject of urbanization and industrialization beyond simple quantitative measurements and sweeping generalizations to perspectives that acknowledge the reality of disparate individuals attempting to survive in a specific time and place. We further viewed urban adjustment and the lives of working-class families in a comparative framework that promises to illuminate the patterns of blacks, Italians, and Poles through comparison and contrast.

Certainly historians in recent years have made important strides toward dealing with these difficult issues and appreciating the complexity of urban settlement. They have begun to make careful distinctions among ethnic groups, especially the eastern Europeans, and to evaluate separately the strategies and achievements of each. Josef Barton, Thomas Kessner, and Caroline Golab have each used a comparative framework in their studies.[5] However, studies of black migra-

tion and urbanization have tended to be more institutional and aggregate in their scope and analysis. This is particularly the case with the
work of Allan Spear on Chicago and Gilbert Osofsky on Harlem, but
it is also true of Kenneth Kusmer's more recent, outstanding study of
Cleveland.[6] Researchers on blacks and immigrants have not always
asked the same questions.

One partial attempt to compare blacks and immigrants in a single
community was Stephan Thernstrom's *The Other Bostonians*. This
analysis was conducted within the framework of the last-of-the immigrants thesis. Thernstrom could not fully identify the ethnic background of the foreign-born groups. He did find that over the course of
a century Boston's blacks were heavily concentrated in the most servile
occupations. Comparing first- and second-generation blacks and immigrants, he argued that the blacks continued to lag behind in mobility.
The similar experiences of northern- and southern-born blacks in Boston tended to reinforce this conclusion. Black workers, regardless of
origin, suffered from limited occupational opportunity. He concluded
that blacks were not merely the newest of the migrant groups but
were different in kind because of the pervasive discrimination they
suffered.[7]

Although further research may support these findings, Thernstrom's
analysis is not entirely satisfying. The conclusions are based largely on
aggregate data that obscure subtle but important factors in the adjustment process. Furthermore, while occupational mobility is an
essential element of accommodation to the city, it is only one of
several dimensions of adjustment. A detailed analysis of individuals,
tracing them through time, provides the prospect of greatly increasing
our understanding of the larger adjustment process. Comparing blacks
with late-arriving European immigrants, those from eastern and
southern Europe, in a single city provides the possibility of holding
the variables of time and place somewhat constant and making comparisons more meaningful.

Existing interpretations of urban migration and adaptation for blacks
and immigrants generally fall between two generalizations. For some
historians the urban environment was essentially destructive and resulted in poverty, familial disorganization, a separation between work
and family interests, and the abandonment of premigration behavioral
patterns. The theory of ethnic succession, a widely employed model in
explaining the adaptation of various ethnic groups to urban America,
rested partially upon this assumption. It saw a direct correlation between adaptation and length of residency in the city. Recent arrivals
would fill the lower jobs and the homes of older residents who moved

upward and outward.[8] Urbanization would in time inevitably eradicate premigration cultures and effect an accommodation of the migrant with the urban society. This model implied that adjustment and integration, for better or for worse, were inevitable. Sociologists who accepted this model frequently noted the special difficulties of blacks but resorted to the recency of their arrival from preurban settings as an explanation. Some felt they would eventually experience the same accommodation that previous immigrants had. However, more recently historians have suggested that the earlier immigrants benefited from the pervasive racism of society and advanced occupationally and socially in American cities only at the expense of blacks.[9] The findings of the Philadelphia Social History Project have especially emphasized the destructive impact of the urban experience as an explanation of black behavior and persistence in poverty. Black families, for instance, suffered in the city because of high mortality among males. Black workers, moreover, were unable to overcome racial hostility and pass job skills to their children. Urban racism and structural inequality were also found to have a greater impact upon blacks than the preindustrial legacy of slavery.[10]

An alternative interpretation of movement and adaptation to urban America rests upon the assumption that premigration culture and values persisted in the cities and withstood the disintegrating impact of city life. This widely held approach emphasized race and ethnicity as independent variables that accounted for dissimilar patterns of urban adaptation. Barton, in a recent study of Cleveland, explained the divergent patterns of immigrant mobility among Slovaks, Rumanians, and Italians in terms of their respective ethnic backgrounds and orientation. Victor Greene's account of Poles in Chicago interpreted Polish behavior on the basis of a search for "traditional objectives" of religion and land. Helena Lopata argued that Polish behavior in America is to be understood in terms of status competition that originated in peasant Poland. Thus, for instance, young Poles would be eager to get a mill job because of the value placed upon hard work within the Polish community. Herbert Gutman has emphasized the continuity in the black family during migration from the rural South to the urban North. Gutman in particular stressed the persistence of black kinship ties, but neither he nor the others closely examined the manner in which immigrants and their families functioned during migration and initial settlement in the city. Similarly, a study of New York City concluded that the cultural backgrounds of Italian and Jewish immigrants explained their differential patterns of mobility.[11]

A more balanced portrait of urban adaptation — one that acknowl-

edges the complexity of the process — is found in the work of Robert
L. Crain and Carol Sachs Weisman. Basing their analysis on detailed
survey interviews, they found that the view of the unstable black
family in northern ghettos was overly simplistic. To be sure a high rate
of marital instability was found among blacks, but no evidence of
intergenerational transfer of such instability was discovered. For instance, daughters from broken homes were not more likely to initiate
divorce in their own homes. In other words the urban experience, at
least for blacks, was not simply a question of destruction or cultural
persistence but involved complex and specific reactions to particular
circumstances. Data in recent historical works offer even more sug-
gestions that adaptation was considerably more involved than the
sweeping generalizations of the past have indicated. Research has
demonstrated that Jews were more upwardly mobile than Italians.
Rumanians manifested higher educational aspirations than Slovaks,
and women were less likely to work outside the home in an Italian
than in a Polish family. Dissimilarity was no more evident than when
immigrants were compared with blacks. The intensity of racism directed toward blacks was unparalleled, although immigrants encountered a degree of hostility themselves. Precisely how both these groups
interacted with a racially biased urban society is still unclear, however.
Few examinations exist that attempt to go beyond "ethnic succession"
or "premigration culture" as explanations for the process of urban
adaptation and confront the complex interplay of migration and the
city they encountered.[12]

This particular work views the urbanization of working-class families within an interactional framework in which traditional cultures
and structural realities confront each other to produce distinct patterns
of adjustment. We shall attempt to test previous assumptions about
adjustment of blacks and immigrants by focusing on several areas of
major concern to the workers themselves: migration and job procurement, family organization and neighborhood formation, and occupational mobility and homeownership. In these areas we shall analyze
the respective experiences of blacks, Italians, and Poles against the
backdrop of the industrial environment in order to understand the
process of urbanization; to identify and explain the varied patterns of
group adjustment; and to test widely held theories and assumptions
about immigrant-black differences.

We compare the experiences of two generations of Poles, blacks, and
Italians living in the city of Pittsburgh between 1900 and 1960 and
suggest that the family and premigration attitudes played a major
role in the migration patterns, occupational choices, and housing ac-

commodations of both first- and second-generation Poles and Italians. Our findings also suggest that the black family was just as important, if not more so, as the immigrant family in providing information about migration and in securing lodgings in the city. However, blacks were less successful in aiding kin in finding work, especially in Pittsburgh's basic industries, which could have offered long-term stable employment. Both generations of blacks were unable to establish occupational beachheads in any major local industry. Black family patterns and child socialization practices, therefore, encouraged a greater self-reliance among progeny, while Polish and Italian practices emphasized strong familial relationships.

The occupational experiences and the disparate family roles of each group exercised a strong influence on homeownership and neighborhood development. The location of their work and the continued reliance on family by Poles and Italians contributed to the creation of strong ethnic neighborhoods and a reliance on homeownership as an important element in family relations. Ownership also became a vital form of stability for both groups. Black families, on the other hand, hampered for various reasons by an inability to acquire either better jobs or occupational security, remained geographically mobile. Neither stable neighborhoods nor homeownership played a crucial role in their lives in Pittsburgh through 1960.

This study combines three major types of historical data for its analyses. Data on the first generation consist of a 20 percent sample derived from the 1900 manuscript census (6,059 individuals organized into 2,829 families), subsequent city directory traces at five-year intervals through 1930, housing deed and mortgage data, and testimony offered through more than 200 oral interviews. Second-generation data (1930-60) were derived from a microanalysis of the residents of seven Pittsburgh neighborhoods (each approximately six blocks square – 1,595 individuals, 1,037 households), city directory traces, and the body of interview information. Second-generation data sources also included church records, voter registrations, and census block and tract data. (A discussion of sources and methodology appears in Appendix A.)

Because the analytical nature of the entire work rested essentially upon a comparative framework, some concern existed that in using disparate sources from different points in time the validity of our attempt would be weakened. The year 1900, selected as a baseline for our analysis, presented certain problems. Some blacks, for example, lived in Pittsburgh long before that year, and a large proportion came after 1915. Poles and Italians continued to migrate to Pittsburgh for some years after 1900. Fortunately, the 1900 manuscript census provided information that enabled us to separate northern-born from southern-born blacks, and we did this throughout the study. The 1900 manuscript census, however, did record blacks in Pittsburgh somewhat before the massive migration after 1915. These blacks may have been less comparable to European peasants than those who came later from the deeper South. To an extent this is a problem, even though our evidence did not indicate any measurable qualitative differences between blacks coming to Pittsburgh in 1900 and those who arrived later. In fact, Poles in 1900 were also part of an initial wave from the Prussian and Russian sectors and not fully representative of the Galician peasants who came later. Thus, we cannot totally resolve potential discrepancies with existing sources of data. The 1900 baseline, however, does present some advantages. It was the last decade interval during which the Pittsburgh economy was thriving and still attracting newcomers. By 1910, unemployment was becoming a problem, and migration toward Europe exceeded that toward Pittsburgh. The 1900 baseline enabled us to catch our three populations shortly after their arrival in Pittsburgh, to observe them in the process of job procurement and community development. The disparate sources consulted throughout the study enabled us to examine changes in these processes over several generations. The integration of quantitative data with oral testimony, along with information from more traditional historical resources, demonstrated striking points of consistency and convergence. Thus, for example, the 1900 quantitative data, which show a greater reliance on boarders for income during midlife stages among black families than among other ethnic groups, strongly reinforced oral data from later arrivals, which indicated that black children were raised to meet the demands of survival on their own. Historical inquiry that compares slightly different groups from various sources may lack a degree of precision, but it does offer an opportunity to penetrate the interior of lives and processes that have long remained obscure to scholars.

Naturally the use of these methodological tools is not without drawbacks. Manuscript census data are essentially "snapshots" of a point in time. While efforts were made to achieve a longitudinal perspective through the use of cross-sectional methods such as the reliance on family-stages, the census is largely a record of a point in time and invariably a product of some degree of underenumeration. City directories suffer from a similar distortion, and oral history is a somewhat controversial research tool. The problem of potentially faulty memories was muted a bit by the use of standard questionnaires, which enhance prospects for comparability. And quite clearly those who remained in Pittsburgh in the 1970s were persisters. Certainly many of their friends and kin left the city at some point, although it is equally certain that persistence cannot simply be equated with economic gain or successful adjustment. Many could not afford to leave the city, others cared not to sever work or friendship routines. Among those who did depart, many returned home better off than when they left; some returned broken in spirit and health, and of course, others died. While we cannot be specific about the character of those who stayed or those who left, we feel strongly that oral data, when collected systematically and focused on specific research questions, can contribute vital information and perspectives that would otherwise have been unobtainable. Integrated with other data, a portrait of the life strategies of ordinary men and women emerges that at the very least warrants careful consideration in the attempt to explain the early adjustment period of the urban working class and its divergent standards of behavior. Finally, obvious source materials such as the black or immigrant press were not relied upon extensively because they did not offer substantive information on most of the questions addressed in the study. *Pittsburgczanin,* for instance, a widely read Pittsburgh Polish newspaper, and the black *Pittsburgh Courier* were essentially middle-class ventures that had little to say about the concerns and behavior of working people.

Thus this study of immigrants and blacks in Pittsburgh is not without its drawbacks. All potential questions are not pursued, and limitations exist in the historical sources used here — as is true with any historical record. But like the lives it seeks to understand, we attempt to deal with complex problems in a logical and reasonable manner. And we argue ultimately that the adjustment of working people to the industrial-urban structure was an intricate process that was not the same for all newcomers. Beyond the cultural determinism of immigrant historians, the class determinism of labor historians, and the structural determinism of urban historians lies the multifaceted workings of a social system[13] that was a product of ordinary men and women from disparate backgrounds interacting with a sprawling economic complex in an attempt to construct lives for themselves. That the patterns and life courses of blacks, Italians, and Poles differed is not a total surprise. But the causes of those differences and their long-term effects can only be understood in the context of an interactional framework that we seek to advance in this book.

NOTES

1. Kajetan Kuczmarski to Jozef Kuczmarski, Dec. 7, 1890, in Witold Kula, Nine Assoroddoraj-Kula, and Marian Kula, eds., *Listy Emigrantowz Brazylii i Stanow Zjed Noczonych, 1890-91* [Emigrant Letters from Brazil and the United States, 1890-91] (Warsaw, 1973), 314.
2. See, for example, *The Report of the National Advisory Commission on Civil Disorders* (Washington, D.C., 1968), ch. 9.
3. Herbert Gans, *Urban Villagers* (New York, 1962); Nathan Glazer and Daniel P. Moynihan, *Beyond the Melting Pot* (Cambridge, Mass., 1959).
4. Nathan Glazer, "Blacks and Ethnic Groups: The Difference, and the Political Difference It Makes," in Nathan Huggins, Martin Kilson, and Daniel Fox, eds., *Key Issues in the Afro-American Experience*, 2 (New York, 1971), 193-211.
5. Josef Barton, *Peasants and Strangers: Italians, Rumanians and Slovaks in an American City* (Cambridge, Mass., 1975); Caroline Golab, *Immigrant Destinations* (Philadelphia, 1977); Thomas Kessner, *The Golden Door: Italian and Jewish Immigrant Mobility in New York City, 1880-1915* (New York, 1977).
6. Allan H. Spear, *Black Chicago: The Making of a Negro Ghetto, 1890-1920* (Chicago, 1967); Gilbert Osofsky, *Harlem: The Making of a Ghetto* (New York, 1966); Kenneth Kusmer, *A Ghetto Takes Shape: Black Cleveland, 1870-1930* (Urbana, Ill., 1976).
7. Stephan Thernstrom, *The Other Bostonians: Poverty and Progress in the American Metropolis, 1880-1970* (Cambridge, Mass., 1973), ch. 8.
8. The classic statement of this view is Paul F. Cressey, "Population Succession in Chicago, 1898-1930," *American Journal of Sociology*, 44 (July 1938), 61. This view is modified by Kessner, *The Golden Door*, 156-60, who felt Cressey's view of ethnic settlement was too static. He stressed continual turnover within immigrant communities. Humbert Nelli, *The Italians in Chicago, 1880-1930: A Study in Ethnic Mobility* (New York, 1970), 45-48. See also W. Lloyd Warner and Leo Srole, *The Social System of American Ethnic Groups* (New Haven, Conn., 1945), 2; Thernstrom, *The Other Bostonians*, 176-77; Thomas Sowell, *Race and Economics* (New York, 1975), 149-50.
9. See Thernstrom, *The Other Bostonians*, 177, 186-87.
10. Frank Furstenberg, Theodore Hershberg, and John Modell, "The Origins of the Female-Headed Black Family: The Impact of the Urban Experience," *Journal of Interdisciplinary History*, 6 (Fall 1975), 232; Hershberg, "Free Blacks in Antebellum Philadelphia: A Study of Ex-Slaves, Freeborn, and Socioeconomic Decline," *Journal of Social History*, 5 (1972), 192-204.
11. Barton, *Peasants and Strangers*, 54, 89-90; Victor Greene, *For God and Country: The Rise of Polish and Lithuanian Ethnic Consciousness in America* (Madison, Wis., 1975), 35-36; Herbert Gutman, *The Black Family in Slavery and Freedom, 1750-1925* (New York, 1976), 450-52; Elizabeth Pleck, "The Two-Parent Household: Black Family Structure

in Late Nineteenth Century Boston," *Journal of Social History*, 5 (1972), 3-31; Sowell, *Race and Economics*, 144-45. See also Helena Znaniecki Lopata, *Polish Americans: Status Competition in an Ethnic Community* (Englewood Cliffs, N.J., 1976), 4; Kessner, *The Golden Door*, 24-43; Virginia Yans-McLaughlin, *Family and Community: Italian Immigrants in Buffalo, 1880-1930* (Ithaca, N.Y., 1977), 55-81.

12. Robert L. Crain and Carol Sachs Weisman, *Discrimination, Personality, and Achievement. A Survey of Northern Blacks* (New York, 1972), 10-18, 103-8; Kessner, *The Golden Door;* Barton, *Peasants and Strangers*, 48-63; Yans-McLaughlin, *Family and Community*, 203-10; Thernstrom, *The Other Bostonians*, 176-77; John Bodnar, *Immigration and Industrialization: Ethnicity in an American Mill Town, 1870-1940* (Pittsburgh, 1977), 73, 136-37. For other comparisons of the black and immigrant experience, see Joseph Roucek and Francis J. Brown, "The Problem of the Negro and European Immigrant Minorities: Some Comparisons and Contrasts," *Journal of Negro Education*, 18 (July 1939), 299. Roucek and Brown argued that immigrants were more optimistic than blacks. John J. Appel, "American Negro and Immigrant Experience: Similarities and Differences," *American Quarterly*, 18 (Spring 1966), 95-103. Charles H. Wesley, *Negro Labor in the United States, 1850-1925* (New York, 1965), 75-76, 199; Timothy Smith, "Native Blacks and Foreign Whites: Varying Responses to Educational Opportunity in America, 1880-1950," *Perspectives in American History*, 6 (1972), 309-11; John R. Commons, *Race and Immigrants in America* (New York, 1907), 147-52. Comparisons of Irish and blacks can be found in Oscar Handlin, *Boston's Immigrants: A Study in Acculturation* (Cambridge, Mass., 1959), 133, 205, 216; Niles Carpenter, *Nationality, Color, and Economic Opportunity in the City of Buffalo* (Buffalo, N.Y., 1927), 190-91. J. Iverne Dowie, "The American Negro: An Old Immigrant on a New Frontier," in O. Firtof Ander, ed., *In the Trek of the Immigrants* (Rock Island, Ill., 1964), 241, 260, called blacks America's oldest immigrants who were held down until they moved northward; Osofsky, *Harlem*, 34-40.

13. See James H. Henrietta, "Social History as Lived and Written," *American Historical Review*, 84 (Dec. 1979), 1293-1322.

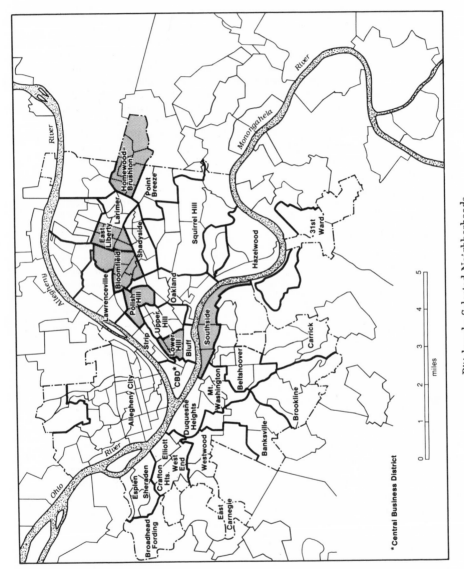

Pittsburgh: Selected Neighborhoods

*Central Business District

miles
0   1   2   3   4   5

1

Pittsburgh in 1900

Pittsburgh is the quintessential symbol of the American industrial city. Long identified as smoky, dirty, and grimy, only recently has it undergone a renaissance of sorts. The foundation of the city's economy—and the determining factor in its physical quality—has been the iron and steel industry. At the turn of the century it was the nation's largest steel-producing center. In the city and its immediate environs, in the first decade of the century, 150,000 people worked for 105 firms producing a wide range of iron and steel products.[1] This smoky inferno with its vast work force of unskilled labor was a magnet for many of the migrants from southern Italy, Poland, and the American South. The environment that they encountered, to a large degree, shaped their lives in the "steel city." Premigration values and patterns interacted with those existing in Pittsburgh to produce distinctive modes of adjustment. An analysis of those methods thus requires some understanding of the occupational and living conditions available to newcomers. The alternatives, as this chapter shows, were severely limited.

Pittsburgh emerged around a wilderness fort at the point where the Monongahela and the Allegheny rivers join to form the Ohio. This strategic position at the headwaters of the Ohio–Mississippi river system made it a major supply point for westward pioneers and a commercial entrepôt early in the nineteenth century. The mineral resources tapped by the river system—coal, limestone, and iron ore—spurred industrial activity from an early date. The first iron foundry opened in 1806. In the following decade steam engines and steamboats were built in the city. By the 1830s it had already earned its unenviable reputation for smoke and soot.[2]

As early as 1860 nearly half of the city's workers engaged in the production of industrial goods. A diversified economy produced a wide range of products, including textiles, engines, glass, pottery, paper, tobacco products, and steamboats, but the dominant role of the iron industry was already evident. Thirteen rolling mills and more than thirty foundries employed 5,000 men and produced a variety of metal products valued in excess of $6,000,000.[3]

During the next forty years the production of heavy industrial goods replaced the earlier diversity. Cotton production declined after 1870 and disappeared altogether in 1885. Oil refining and the manufacture of paper goods and wood products also declined. The economy concentrated on a small number of basic manufacturing products that required large amounts of heat: iron and steel, aluminum, and glass. Other heavy industries, primarily by-products of this group, included fabricated steel products, machinery, and electrical equipment.[4]

Of paramount importance in this transition was the role played by the region's vast quantity of high-quality coking coal. As long as the cost of coking coal represented the major price difference in the production of a ton of steel, Pittsburgh held a natural advantage. *The American Manufacturer* explained the importance of coal to the Pittsburgh region:

> If you would see what coal can do for the people who turn it to full account, look at Pittsburgh. . . . Possessing in its coal the creative power, it stretches out its mighty arms and gathers the wealth of half a continent into its lap. It brings to its furnaces and forges the iron and copper of Lake Superior; glass sand from New England, Missouri and Illinois; lead from Wisconsin and Missouri; zinc, brass and tin from beyond the seas. You pass through its gigantic establishments, and are amazed at the variety and extent of their perfected productions. Yet, all these, from the most delicate fabric of glass to the ponderous cannon and steam engine, are in the coal which underlies the smoky hills of Pittsburgh.[5]

Coke production, begun in the Connelsville district in 1860, soared following the economic depression of 1873. By 1886 the Henry Clay Frick Company alone owned nearly 210,000 acres of land from which coal could be mined and operated 12,000 coke ovens in the region.[6] The short distance from the coke region to Pittsburgh enabled the city's iron and steel firms to purchase coke at one dollar less per ton of iron in Pittsburgh than in the rest of the country. The Carnegie-Frick merger in 1881 produced even greater advantages, permitting the Carnegie Steel firm to purchase coke at cost while selling it to competitors at high market prices.

Technological innovation also contributed to the dominance of heavy industry in Pittsburgh. Carnegie introduced the Bessemer process to the area in 1868. Open-hearth production began at the Homestead Works in 1888, and the Edgar Thomson Works in Braddock introduced the continuous-operation process the same year, becoming the prototype for the industry. Three years later the Jones and Laughlin Iron Works dismantled most of its 110 puddling furnaces, converting to open-hearth production. Furnace capacity at the same time continually increased, growing from 150 tons weekly in 1870 to 450 tons per day in 1896. Production and profit records were set almost monthly. In 1891, for example, the Homestead Works established a new record, producing 8,000 tons of steel in a month. Eight years later Carnegie's 33rd Street mill produced 20,501 tons monthly, while the district norm exceeded 16,000 tons per month.[7]

Aggressive cost-cutting practices supplemented these basic technologies. Andrew Carnegie usually took the lead, but his competitors followed quickly. Cost accounting, for example, introduced at the Edgar Thomson Works in the 1880s, produced a savings of $40,000 a year within the first few years of operation. "Show me your cost sheet," Carnegie exhorted his managers. "It is more interesting to know how well and how cheaply you have done this thing than how much money you have made, because the one is a temporary result ... but the other means a permanency that will go on with the works as long as they last."[8]

The use of recycled waste products within the mill enabled the firm to cut costs further. Carnegie's willingness to rely upon the judgment of technical experts and chemical analysis led to the purchase of less expensive, but higher grade ores. Competitors, for a time, relied upon more expensive, lower quality ores. The firm was also quick to replace obsolete machinery when improvements became available. Horizontal integration, made possible with the purchase of the Homestead Works in 1891, led to important economies of scale and continued to push costs downward while increasing the city's dominance of the industrial market at the same time.[9]

The advantages of location, technological innovations, and aggressive cost cutting accounted both for the high level of profit and the substantial growth of the iron and steel industry in the late nineteenth century. Even during the depression of the mid-1890s, the Pittsburgh firms showed a profit. The Carnegie Works earned $3 million in 1893 and $4 million in 1894.[10] By 1900 the region produced 64 percent of the country's structural steel, 57 percent of its crucible steel, half of its coking coal, almost half of its Bessemer steel, and 26 percent of its steel rails.[11]

By the end of the nineteenth century, a relatively small number of large firms, concentrated in a few basic industries, dominated the economy of Pittsburgh. In 1870, 167 iron and steel firms employed an average of ninety workers each. By 1899 the number of metal firms fell to forty-seven, employing an average work force of 1,600; thirty-two firms employed between 1,000 and 10,000, and four firms in the district each employed more than 10,000 workers. Carnegie Steel, the city's largest company, employed 23,000 workers. Philadelphia County, in contrast, with one-third more people, had no firm with more than 10,000 workers and only twenty-five with more than 1,000.[12]

While Pittsburgh's industrial power grew during the last half of the nineteenth century, blue-collar workers as a group experienced a gradual but continuous weakening of economic and social position. The shift from iron to steel production, the relentless drive for economy within the industry, technological innovation, and the demise of the union movement undermined the skills of an earlier generation of iron and steel craftsmen. Puddlers, heaters, catchers, and rollers, for example, dominated the iron and steel industry prior to 1880. Possessing skills acquired over long periods of time, these men manipulated small batches of molten pig iron and cinder at the puddling furnaces or manually prepared and moved hot steel through the rolling mills. By 1900 their skills were virtually obsolete. The number of puddlers in the Pittsburgh district declined from 1,400 to less than 200 during the twenty-year period. Heaters, catchers, and rollers decreased by more than 50 percent between 1890 and 1900 as mechanical devices were installed in mill after mill. By 1907 nearly 75 percent of the men employed in basic steel in Pittsburgh held semiskilled or unskilled jobs.[13]

Mechanization within the industry also affected the demand for unskilled labor as electric chargers (lorries), cranes, and other devices replaced large numbers of men and increased production dramatically. The Carnegie Works in Homestead, for example, reduced its work force by 25 percent during the eight years following the unsuccessful strike of 1892. Immigrants arriving in Pittsburgh in 1900 could expect stiff competition for jobs in the steel industry. Even if one found work quickly, keeping on the job and staying healthy required luck and fortitude.

The high rates of European immigration, the intense competition within the industry, and the relentless pressure on foremen to cut costs all worked to keep wage rates low while the hours of work remained long. Prior to the introduction of mechanical devices, metal workers received wages on a tonnage basis. Mechanization, however, increased production by 10- and 12-fold. One's wages could no longer reflect one's output. Hourly wages replaced the tonnage rates, and workers were subjected to the variables of the economy and the labor supply. Conn Strott, a soaking pit heater, explained the deteriorating wage condition of skilled workers: "Before 1892 I made $10 and $12 a day. After the strike wages went down to $7 and by 1903 they were $3. At the same time, the work load increased and my hours of work were increased."[14] The cost of living during the same period increased by 12 percent.[15]

Managers, following Carnegie's admonition to watch costs not profits, systematically reduced wages during business slowdowns. (Unskilled laborers received only $1 per day during the 1893-97 depression.) Job furloughs were also introduced as a means of controlling costs. During the 1893-97 depression, nearly 40 percent of all steel workers experienced some unemployment. Even in a prosperous business year, 1900, almost one-fourth of the city's male work force faced at least one month's unemployment, and 11 percent were laid off more than three months.[16] Workers seeking economic security frequently left the city for employment elsewhere. A typical article in the *Pittsburgh Leader* in 1900 reported that "25 of the best skilled men ... have left for Granite City, Indiana, to operate a new tin plate mill established at the latter place. The reason given by the men to make the change is the uncertain operation of the mills."[17] The *Leader* estimated that at least one-fourth of Pittsburgh's skilled labor force left the city between 1895 and 1900.

The cost-cutting methods of Pittsburgh's entrepreneurs also affected working conditions within the mills. In 1877 the Carnegie Company abandoned its experiment with the eight-hour day. Other companies quickly fell into line, introducing the twelve-hour day, usually without a corresponding increase in wages. By 1895 the twelve-hour day was established in most steel mills and had become the standard in the entire industry by 1910.[18]

In addition to long hours at low pay, unskilled workers in the steel industry were exposed to extremely hazardous conditions in the mills. Newspaper articles announcing "Two Dozen Men Injured in Furnace Disaster: Two Will Die," or "Five Workmen Injured, Three May Die: Boiler Blew to Pieces," or "Death in the Pit" became so common they were relegated to a regular entry on page five.[19] Pittsburgh firms refused to release accurate data on serious accidents. Thus one can only speculate about the annual accident rate. In her examination of work accidents for the Pittsburgh Survey, Crystal Eastman analyzed injuries requiring hospitalization. She concluded that the Pittsburgh district annually produced "45 one-legged men; 100 hopeless cripples; . . . 45 men with a twisted useless arm; 30 men with an empty sleeve; 20 men with but one hand; . . . 70 one-eyed men—500 such wrecks in all."[20] In the first such survey of industrial deaths in Pittsburgh, Eastman recorded 526 fatalities between July 1, 1906, and June 30, 1907. Nearly 40 percent of these deaths occurred in the steel industry.[21]

The pace of work within the industry also changed, intensifying dramatically by 1900. The continuous-operation process put pressure on each man to match the pace of the fastest, strongest man on the labor crew. Company officials provided substantial bonuses to foremen and superintendents as a reward for increased production. Intermill competition pitted foreman against foreman in the race to set monthly production records, while powerless workers struggled to maintain the ever increasing pace. Predictably, the foremen replaced aging workers with younger stronger men. One British visitor to Pittsburgh reported: "The bosses drive the men to an extent that employers would never dream of in this country [England] getting the maximum work out of them, and the men do not have the inclination or the power to resist the pressure."[22] Tom Crockett, a charger at the Duquesne Works, provided an excellent illustration of the relationship between record production levels and wage rates: "Twice a year the Carnegie mills have a record month. Any month of 31 days is selected, and the mills do not stop from end to end of the month. Sundays and Saturday nights they run full blast. The best material is saved for this month, and an attempt is made to break the [output] record. If wages are changed at the end of the year, the new scale is based on the output of the record month."[23]

The impotence of the worker resulted partly from the collapse of the union movement following the 1892 Homestead Steel strike. Many participants in the Homestead disturbance were fired by the Carnegie Corporation. Owners circulated blacklists of labor agitators throughout the industry. Jacob Rushe, who sought work elsewhere, revealed that "the mills in Chicago were in need of men, but they sent back here and asked if there was anything against these men before they would employ them."[24] The obvious weakness of the Amalgamated Association of Iron and Steel Workers prompted other firms to follow Carnegie's example. By 1900 the steel companies in the district presented a united front in refusing to recognize the Amalgamated Association. The union survived, but largely outside of the steel industry. Labor spies, company unions, and "iron clad agreements" became the order of the day. As one worker noted: "All the steel companies have effective methods of learning what is going on among the workmen. The

Jones and Laughlin Company has some organization that keeps it sufficiently informed as to the likelihood of sedition breaking out, and the U.S. Steel Corporation has regular secret service departments."[25]

By the turn of the century market conditions and the decisions of the industrialists controlled the wages, hours, and working conditions of men in the Pittsburgh steel industry. Workers unwilling to accept the terms of employment could seek work elsewhere.

Working conditions for unskilled labor outside of the steel industry were marginally better than inside the mills; at least there were fewer risks to life and limb. The advantage of the mills was that during prosperous years the work was steady, although the hourly rate was not significantly higher than in other sectors. It was for that reason that so many men took the considerable risk of working in the mills. In the early twentieth century common labor in the steel mills paid 16.5¢ per hour or $1.98 for a twelve-hour day.[26]

The other major opportunities for unskilled labor included working on streets or in construction, hauling, and personal service. As the city expanded, there were numerous jobs available in street and construction work, although the work was more seasonal than work in the steel mills. At the turn of the century the city had 500 miles of streets and 250 miles of sewer lines to maintain. Common laborers working for the city earned between $1.50 and $1.75 for an eight-hour day. In addition to city work on the sewers and streets, large numbers were employed by the gas, streetcar, electric, telephone, and railroad companies, extending those networks. Street work for the gas company paid around 13.5¢ per hour early in the century.[27]

The rapid growth of Pittsburgh around the turn of the century also brought a building boom in both residential and commercial construction. Between 1893 and 1906 over 350 commercial buildings went up in the central business district alone. Nearly 2,000 residential structures appeared during the same period. Laborers on these jobs often earned slightly more than those in the mills, partly because of the strong unions among the skilled building tradesmen and because of the seasonal work. Hod carriers, for example, earned $3 per day in 1907, but these jobs were often restricted to native-born workers and Irish, English, or German immigrants.[28]

Driving a hack or a freight wagon required a knowledge of horses and usually a command of English. The position provided little status, and a disproportionate share of these jobs in early twentieth-century Pittsburgh went to blacks. Teamsters usually worked a ten-hour day and earned between $10 and $12 per week. The cab companies paid $9 to $10 per week for a longer day until a successful strike in 1905 raised the rate to $14. Blacks also found employment in hotels and other areas of personal service where the wages tended to be even lower.[29] In general, unskilled labor in early twentieth-century Pittsburgh earned between $8 and $12 per week. Such earnings proved insufficient to support a family.[30]

In spite of these low wages the industrial and financial growth of the city attracted thousands of new residents. The population, reflecting the city's dynamic quality, nearly doubled between 1880 and 1900, reaching 451,000. To compete for the new jobs thought to be available for workers lacking skills, southern and eastern European immigrants and a growing number of southern blacks flocked to the "steel city." By 1900 the recent arrivals among the foreign born, mainly from Polish territories and from Italy, constituted nearly one-third of the city's foreign-born population. The city's Polish and Italian communities both became the country's sixth largest in 1900. Pittsburgh's black population grew simultaneously, to 20,355, the sixth largest of any large northern city. That Pittsburgh attracted all three groups attests to its strong pulling power. Only Chicago and New York, both much larger in population, provided a similar attraction for all three migrant groups. (See Table 1.)

Table 1. Black, Italian, and Polish Populations of Northern Cities with Total Populations of 250,000 or More in 1900

	Blacks			Italians			Poles		
City	Number	Rank	% of Total	Number	Rank	% of Total	Number	Rank	% of Total
Baltimore	79,258	1	15.6	2,042	10	0.4	2,811	11	0.6
Philadelphia	62,613	2	4.8	17,830	2	1.4	7,554	8	0.6
New York	60,666	3	1.8	145,443	1	4.5	32,873	2	1.0
St. Louis	35,576	4	6.2	2,227	9	0.4	2,857	10	0.5
Chicago	30,150	5	1.8	16,008	3	0.9	59,713	1	3.5
Pittsburgh[1]	20,355	6	4.5	6,495	6	1.4	11,892	6	2.6
Cincinnati	14,482	7	4.4	917	11	0.2	471	13	0.2
Boston	11,591	8	2.1	13,738	4	2.5	3,832	9	0.7
Newark	6,694	9	2.7	8,537	5	3.5	1,913	12	0.8
Detroit	5,988	10	0.3	905	12	0.3	13,631	5	4.8
Cleveland	4,111	11	0.8	3,065	8	0.8	8,592	7	2.3
Buffalo	1,698	12	0.4	5,669	7	1.6	18,830	3	5.3
Milwaukee	862	13	0.3	726	13	0.2	17,027	4	6.0

SOURCE: U.S. Bureau of the Census, *Twelfth Census Population*, 609-46, 796-803.

[1]Pittsburgh data include Allegheny City. Pittsburgh and Allegheny City merged in 1907, but in the interest of consistency and clarity the two cities are treated as one throughout the study. Land areas in 1900 have been adjusted to conform to the post-1907 neighborhood and political boundaries.

The growth of population and industry stimulated the physical expansion of the city in all possible directions (see map). The patterns of land use, shaped by the unique topography and geography of the site, continued along the lines established during the earliest decades of settlement. The area around the mouth of the Ohio River was exceptionally hilly except for narrow flood plains along the river banks and near the point where the Monongahela and Allegheny rivers came together. The rivers served as the primary transportation arteries and also provided water for industrial uses and a receptacle for industrial wastes. From an early date, factories clustered along the river banks. The flood plain also served as convenient and economical routes for railroad lines.[31]

By 1900 nine major shipping lines carried nearly 11 million tons of commercial and industrial goods into and out of the city and sixteen rail lines brought almost 5,000 freight cars a day into Pittsburgh. The choice flat terrain along the rivers was wholly given over to the railroads and to heavy industry. For example, large firms along the north shore of the Allegheny River included the Pressed Steel Car Works (2,725 employees), Pittsburgh Machine Company (1,082 employees), the Ft. Wayne Railroad shops (1,043 employees), and American Steel and Hoop Company (575 employees). The south banks of the Allegheny River featured ten iron and steel firms with over 10,000 employees, several brick yards, Armstrong Cork Company (606 employees), and the extensive yards of the Pennsylvania Railroad. The banks of the Monongahela were dominated by similar firms. The huge Jones and Laughlin steel works occupied nearly 30 blocks along the river and employed over 8,000 people. Farther east on the river, just outside the city limits, were the Carnegie steel works at Homestead and Braddock.[32]

The central business district of Pittsburgh emerged in the narrow triangle behind the original fort in the area of first settlement. By 1900 the 200-acre site was almost exclusively commercial and governmental. The special financial district containing the Pittsburgh Stock Exchange, thirty banks, and several investment firms developed around Fourth Avenue in the 1870s. The city's business district grew around the financial section during the next decade and a commercial district, complete with multistoried warehouses, occupied twenty blocks along Penn and Liberty streets near the Allegheny River. The governmental district opened in the late 1890s with the completion of the H. H. Richardson Courthouse and the county jail along Grant Street.

Changing population densities, land costs, and building construction resulted in specialized land uses within the city's core. Residential population in the central business district decreased by more than

one-third between 1890 and 1900.[33] At the same time land costs within
the central city began to soar. The average cost per square foot of
city land increased by $10 between 1899 and 1902. Six parcels of land
scattered throughout the central city, for example, were sold in 1899
and again within the next three years. Buyers paid $392,000 for these
six parcels in 1899; three years later this same land brought $660,000,
an increase of 68 percent. One lot at 534 Fourth Avenue changed
hands three times during the three years. It brought $40,000 in 1899,
$50,000 in 1901, and $70,000 in 1902. Henry W. Oliver paid $333 per
square foot for land at the corner of Sixth Avenue and Smithfield
Street in 1902.[34]

The dramatic increase in land prices led to the initiation of the
high-rise building in Pittsburgh. Thirteen buildings, ranging from
twelve to twenty-five stories, were built in the core between 1895 and
1905, and several streets were widened to accommodate the increased
daytime activities in the city. Property assessments in the central core
reached $80 million in 1900; the assessments were $104 million in all
other wards combined.[35] "The heart of the town," commented one
British industrial investigator in 1906, "is not so bad. There are fine
shops and fairly good public buildings and the main streets do not
lack dignity though they are much too narrow to carry the swarming
traffic. . . . The congestion is greater than in N.Y., Philadelphia or Boston and is only surpassed by London. In the pollution of the atmosphere by smoke Pittsburgh beats the world . . . Pittsburgh is at least
twice as smoky as Sheffield or Manchester and London cannot compete
at all except in a bad fog."[36]

The availability of public transportation, the density of the central
city, and the rising cost of land contributed to the development of
Pittsburgh's suburbs.[37] Equally important was the ribbonlike location
of the industrial factories along the city's rivers. By 1900, with the
exception of several small slum areas at the point and along Second
Avenue, few people resided in the core of the city.

Uneven transportation patterns and the rugged topography also
influenced the development of residential suburbs in Pittsburgh. Public
transportation as well as highway construction always followed the
line of least resistance, and so easy access developed along the natural
corridors formed by valleys and plains. Crosstown (north-south) streetcar service was poor, and neighborhoods were separated by rivers and
sharp hills, and transportation among these was inadequate.[38] In addition, Pittsburgh's unique topography facilitated the division of residential areas along social, racial, and ethnic lines.

The Pittsburgh elite, mostly native-born steel manufacturers and bankers of Scotch-Irish or German ancestry, began to establish exclusive residential areas during the mid-1870s. By the turn of the century they dominated two areas within the city's boundaries. The earliest of these residential developments began before the Civil War in Allegheny City, just across the Allegheny River from the city's central core. By 1900 three avenues within this area — Ridge, Western, and Lincoln — contained 22 percent of the city's iron-and-steel elite. Twenty-seven families, identified as elite, resided on Ridge Avenue, ten on Western Avenue, and twenty-two on Lincoln Avenue.[39] The second major area, the East End, began to attract wealthy families in the 1870s and contained one-half of the city's elite by the turn of the century. The proportion subsequently rose to two-thirds in 1915.[40] Less concentrated than the elite Allegheny City neighborhood, small isolated villages developed. A "Carnegie colony," for example, located at the intersection of Homewood and Lexington avenues contained a dozen wealthy families associated at one time or another with the Carnegie enterprises. Other elite areas contained clusters of Negleys and Mellons — along Penn Avenue — and the Bissel, Howe, and Laughlin families on Woodland Road.[41] Land sales on the newly opened Beechwood Boulevard area averaged $86,000 per parcel in 1902 and 1903.[42]

Middle-class neighborhoods also began to develop as early German, Irish, and English residents left the core in the 1880s and 1890s. More dependent than the elite upon streetcar transportation, a growing middle class settled along transportation lines. Neighborhoods opened east of Pittsburgh in Oakland, Squirrel Hill, Shadyside, and in the third-class city of Wilkinsburg. Other neighborhoods developed to the north in Allegheny City and to the south in Mt. Washington and Mt. Oliver. These streetcar suburbs were characterized by moderate single-family dwellings separated by a distance of several miles from large places of employment. Some, as one visitor noted, were "even free from smoke."[43]

The development of blue-collar neighborhoods began in the 1880s, and the older homes of the Hill District and other areas adjacent to the core became major blue-collar clusters by 1900. Although these areas were not ethnically homogeneous, they did contain large numbers of blacks and recent immigrants. Other blue-collar neighborhoods developed along the flood plains by the yards and mills. When these narrow strips of land filled with row houses, the workers' homes began to climb the hillside along both banks of the Monongahela and Allegheny. Analysis of the wards for 1900 indicated a wide distribution of ethnic and racial groups. The index of dissimilarity between blacks and whites for Pittsburgh and Allegheny combined was 42, meaning that 42 percent of the black population would have to be redistributed to other wards for the percentage of each race in each ward to be the same. The index of dissimilarity between foreign-born whites and native whites of native parentage was 28. Although blacks and immigrants could be found all over the city, the development of some neighborhood clusters was already apparent. Blacks were overrepresented relative to their share of the total population in wards 3, 5, 8, 11, 12, and 22. Those six wards contained more than half of the black population. The greatest concentration was in the Hill District, which was within walking distance of the core and hence provided access to a variety of service employments.[44]

Recent European immigrants also displayed tendencies to cluster in certain areas, notably near the central business district and close to the mills and factories along the river banks. Russian Jews settled near established German-Jewish residents in sections of the core and the Lower Hill around Center Avenue. Hungarians, Croatians, and other eastern Europeans established small enclaves near the Jones and Laughlin mill in Hazelwood (15th Ward), in company homes in "Painter's Row" on the Southside, and in the industrial satellite communities of Homestead and Braddock.[45]

Italians first settled in Virgin Alley (Oliver Avenue) in the business district in 1880. During the 1890s the colony shifted to the lower hill, which had an extensive Italian community by 1910. "Through the heart of this area," one researcher explained, "runs ... what might be termed the professional and intellectual center of Pittsburghers of Italian stock. Here are congregated the majority of Italian doctors, lawyers, a bank or two, an Italian picture shop, a book shop and the publishing house of an Italian newspaper. Here too are Italian Protestant Missions, a large Italian Catholic Church and two parochial schools."[46] Later Italian arrivals opened new neighborhoods in Bloomfield (8th Ward) and East Liberty (12th Ward). A small but densely settled cluster also occupied the hollow in Schenley Park.[47]

Poles entered Pittsburgh in successive waves from provinces under control of Germany, Russia, and Austria; by 1900 nearly 12,000 lived within the city. Seeking industrial work, they settled in close proximity to the factories along the river banks. The earliest arrivals came from the Prussian sector and, like Poles in other cities, settled in German sections because they had some familiarity with that language. Thus Pittsburgh's early Poles moved into the Strip District, a narrow flood plain along the south bank of the Allegheny River. Here they could look for work at Heppenstall's Forge, Pittsburgh Machine Company, Carnegie Steel, and smaller industrial shops. In the 1880s they began to establish their own churches and neighborhoods on the steep north slopes of Herron Hill (6th Ward, Polish Hill), and on the Southside (16th and 17th wards), near the Oliver Iron Works and the Jones and Laughlin mill. In the 1890s and early twentieth century Russian Poles displaced the older German and Irish workers in the Strip District and in Lawrenceville, which lies just beyond it (6th and 9th wards). Austrian Poles from Galicia joined the larger German and Russian communities.[48]

By 1900 Pittsburgh possessed many of the patterns associated with the modern city. The growth of population and the extension of the streetcar system led to the separation of work and residence into specific areas. Neighborhoods were segregated by occupation and ethnic background. After a two-year exhaustive study of the community, the editors of the famous Pittsburgh Survey condemned the startling contrasts between the wealth of the economy and the poverty of so many of the producers:

> the prosperity on the one hand, of the most prosperous of all the communities of our western civilization, with its vast natural resources . . . the human energy, the technical development, the gigantic tonnage of the mines and mills, the enormous capital . . .; and on the other hand the neglect of life, of health, of physical vigor, often of the industrial efficiency of the individual. Certainly no community before in America or Europe has ever had such a surplus and never before has a great community applied what it had so meagerly to the rational purposes of human life. Not by gifts of libraries, galleries, technical schools, and parks, but by the cessation of toil one day in seven and sixteen hours in twenty-four, by the increase in wages, by the sparing of lives, . . . and by raising the standards of domestic life should the surplus come back to the people of the community in which it is created.[49]

It was to this community of prosperity and poverty that thousands of Polish, black, and Italian migrants came seeking work and a better way of life. Each group was distinct in many ways, but they shared similar dreams. How they adjusted to the realities of the city, found work, sought economic security or advancement, established their own neighborhoods and, in short, realized those dreams will be examined in detail in succeeding chapters.

NOTES

1. U.S. Department of Commerce and Labor, Bureau of the Cer trial Districts: 1905, *Manufactures and Population*, Bullet (Washington, D.C., 1909), 38-45.
2. Carroll Pursell, *Early Stationary Steam Engines in America* ton, D.C., 1909), ch. 5.

3. George Davis, "Greater Pittsburgh Commercial and Industrial Development, 1850-1900" (Ph.D. diss., University of Pittsburgh, 1951), 232.

4. Ibid., 220ff.

5. *The American Manufacturer*, Feb. 18, 1873.

6. Davis, "Greater Pittsburgh," 232.

7. *Pittsburgh Leader*, Oct. 9, 1899.

8. Harold Livesay, *Andrew Carnegie and the Rise of Big Business* (Boston, 1975), 112.

9. Ibid., 117, 118.

10. David Brody, *Steel Workers in America: The Non-Union Era* (Cambridge, Mass., 1960), 55.

11. Davis, "Greater Pittsburgh," 195, 236; U.S. Bureau of the Census, *Statistics of Manufacturers, Supplement for Pennsylvania* (Washington, D.C., 1910), 747-49; *The American Manufacturer*, May 31, 1900; Roy Lubove, *Twentieth-Century Pittsburgh: Government, Business, and Environmental Change* (New York, 1969), 2.

12. Caroline Golab, *Immigrant Destinations* (Philadelphia, 1977), 42.

13. Brody, *Steel Workers in America*, 55; John A. Fitch, *The Steel Workers*, The Pittsburgh Survey, ed. Paul U. Kellogg (New York, 1910), 14.

14. Fitch, *Steel Workers*, 39. Fitch conducted interviews with 145 men between 1907-8. These field notes are currently in the possession of his grandson, Mr. Charles Hill. We are indebted to Mr. Hill.

15. Fitch, *Steel Workers*, 161.

16. Peter Shergold, "The Loan Shark," *Pennsylvania History*, 14 (July 1978), 197.

17. *Pittsburgh Leader*, "New Tin Plate Mill," Apr. 23, 1900.

18. Fitch, *Steel Workers*, 112-15, 119.

19. *Pittsburgh Leader*, Apr. 13, 1900; *Pittsburgh Press*, Apr. 7, 1900; *Pittsburgh Commercial Gazette*, Jan. 3, 1900.

20. Crystal Eastman, *Work, Accidents and the Law*, The Pittsburgh Survey, ed. Paul U. Kellogg (New York, 1910), 12.

21. Ibid., 14, 51.

22. James Kitson as reported in Fitch, *Steel Workers*, 195.

23. Fitch, ms. field notes, p. 187.

24. Ibid.

25. Fitch, *Steel Workers*, 219.

26. Margaret Byington, *Homestead: The Households of a Mill Town*, The Pittsburgh Survey, ed. Paul U. Kellogg (New York, 1910), 40; Paul U. Kellogg, ed., *Wage-Earning Pittsburgh*, The Pittsburgh Survey (New York, 1910), 119.

27. Kellogg, ed., *Wage-Earning Pittsburgh*, 119-20; *Pittsburgh Press*, Nov. 2, 1900.

28. Kellogg, ed., *Wage-Earning Pittsburgh*, 119-20; Joel Tarr, *Transportation Innovations and Changing Spatial Patterns in Pittsburgh, 1850-1934* (Chicago, 1978), 18-19; William F. Smith, *The Greater Pittsburgh Real Estate Reference Book* (Pittsburgh, 1903).

29. Kellogg, ed., *Wage-Earning Pittsburgh*, 121-22.

30. Byington, *Homestead*, ch. 1 and appendices; Kellogg, ed., *Wage-Earning Pittsburgh*, 182-84.

31. Tarr, *Transportation Innovations,* 3-4.
32. *Pittsburgh Press,* Nov. 2, 1900; Pennsylvania Department of Factory Inspectors, *Eleventh Annual Report of the Factory Inspector for the Year 1900* (Harrisburg, 1901). G. M. Hopkins, *Real Estate Plat-Book of the City of Pittsburgh* (Philadelphia, 1903).
33. Smith, *Greater Pittsburgh Real Estate,* 10-12.
34. Ibid., 33-35, 41-47, 78-85.
35. *Pittsburgh Leader,* Feb. 27, 1900. These data exclude assessments for rural and agricultural land. The second highest assessed wards were those along the two rivers and reflected the concentration of iron and steel mills and other heavy industries within these wards.
36. Arthur Shadewell, *Industrial Efficiency: A Comparative Study of Industrial Life in England, Germany and America,* 1 (London, 1906), 325.
37. By 1902 the Pittsburgh region had approximately 400 miles of streetcar track. In addition, nearly 300 commuter trains ran into and out of the city daily. Eighteen inclines also operated to carry passengers up and down the steep hills to and from work.
38. See Tarr, *Transportation Innovations,* 2ff.
39. John N. Ingham, *The Iron Barons: A Social Analysis of an American Urban Elite, 1874-1965* (Westport, Conn., 1978), 108.
40. Ibid., 113.
41. Ibid., 114.
42. Smith, *Greater Pittsburgh Real Estate,* 143, 148, 152, 154.
43. Shadewell, *Industrial Efficiency,* 327.
44. U.S. Bureau of the Census, *Twelfth Census of Population, 1900 Population* (Washington, D.C., 1902), sample data; Jacqueline Wolfe, "The Changing Pattern of Residence of the Negro in Pittsburgh" (M.S. thesis, University of Pittsburgh, 1964), 10. The cities of Pittsburgh and Allegheny merged in 1907, and all political wards were renumbered. To avoid confusion and insure comparability, post-1907 boundaries and ward numbers will be used throughout this study.
45. Russian Jews constituted 58 and 42 percent, respectively, of the foreign-born whites in the 3rd and 5th wards in 1910. Approximately 20 percent of the foreign born in each ward were born in Italy.
46. Ella Burns Myers, "Some Italian Groups in Pittsburgh" (M.S. thesis, Carnegie Institute of Technology, 1920), 23.
47. Hilda Becker, "Statistical Analysis of the Census Reports on the Distribution of the Foreign White Population in Pittsburgh, 1890-1930" (Ph.D. diss., University of Pittsburgh, 1932), 85. The Italian group that settled in the Schenley Park hollow was recruited via the padronè system to work on railroad and utility construction gangs. It was the only Italian cluster attracted to Pittsburgh in that manner.
48. The extent of succession in this area may be seen by the fact that 65 percent of all the real estate transactions in the Lawrenceville area between 1905 and 1910 involved a non-Slavic seller and a Slavic buyer. Another 20 percent of the sales involved Slavic buyers and sellers. See R. F. Hill, "Exploring the Dimensions of Ethnicity" (M.S. thesis, University of Pittsburgh, 1975), 47. See also *Historja parafji SW. Wojciecha BM* (Pittsburgh, 1933); *Pamietnik of St. Adalbert's Parish* (Pittsburgh,

1915); W. X. Kruseka, *Historya Polska W. Ameryce,* 8 vols. (Milwaukee, Wis., 1905-6), 2: 6-7; "Audit of International Institutes, Material on Pittsburgh's Nationality Communities," American Council for Nationalities Services, Shipment 4, Box 2, Archives of Industrial Society, University of Pittsburgh.

49. Edward T. Devine, "Pittsburgh: The Year of the Survey," in Paul U. Kellogg, ed., *The Pittsburgh District: Civic Frontage,* The Pittsburgh Survey (New York, 1914), 6.

2

Backgrounds and Expectations

During the first two decades of the twentieth century, Pittsburgh's population increased by nearly one-third. Such an increase was not the result of growth in all sectors of its population, however, but resulted basically from a massive infusion of unskilled and semiskilled workers and their families from largely agricultural areas. City residents emanating from Poland increased 39 percent from 1900 to 1920; Italians saw their ranks more than double, and blacks expanded their ranks by 85 percent. It is true that the increase in immigrant population took place largely during the century's first decade, and the foreign-born count declined somewhat between 1910 and 1920 when war in Europe restricted emigration. Indeed, black expansion exceeded that of any immigrant group after 1914. But overall it was from the ranks of this aspiring proletariat that Pittsburgh could count its new citizens.[1] Simultaneously, the flow of newcomers from the areas of migration in the nineteenth century — Germany, Ireland, and England — declined considerably. Between 1890 and 1910 the number of residents from the older immigrant stock declined 10 to 20 percent. In effect the German, English, and Irish stock consisted mainly of second and third generations as the pioneers were slowly dying out.[2] See Table 2.

While these newcomers all perceived certain benefits to be derived from the jobs that were available to them in the industrial city, an easy assumption should not be made that they pursued common objectives or possessed similar experiences before emigration. Generalizations about destitute individuals abandoning a rural world in

Table 2. Population Distribution: Pittsburgh, 1890-1920

Group	1890[1]	1900[1]	Percentage Change	1910	Percentage Change	1920	Percentage Change
Native-born white	235,547	316,063	34.2	387,851	22.7	429,995	10.9
German	36,646	33,224	- 9.3	29,438	-11.0	16,028	-45.5
Irish	26,643	23,690	-11.0	18,872	-20.0	13,889	-26.4
English	12,408	11,079	-10.7	9,525	-14.0	7,374	-22.6
Black	10,357	20,355	96.5	25,623	26.0	37,725	47.2
Pole	2,840	11,892	318.0	20,606	73.5	15,537	-24.6
Italian	2,035	6,495	219.0	14,120	117.0	15,371	8.9
Total population	343,904	451,512	31.3	533,905	18.2	588,343	10.2

SOURCE: U.S. census population schedules for the years 1890, 1900, 1910, and 1920.
[1] Includes Allegheny City.

search of golden opportunity in growing cities have pervaded both scholarly and popular thinking about American urbanization in the twentieth century. But such abstractions have obscured the complex origins of urban newcomers and the attitudinal posture they carried from their ancestral homes. Certainly similarities existed. Blacks were clearly dissatisfied with political exclusion in the South, and Poles resented their subservience to Germans, Austrians, and Russians. But such similarities should not obscure fundamental differences that characterized the experiences of blacks, Italians, and Poles prior to their arrival in Pittsburgh. Without acknowledging the specific condition of preurban existence, a full understanding of later developments in the industrial city is simply not possible.

Industrialization not only weaned ordinary people away from the land, but also it altered the nature of the workplace. The need to acquire specific skills before entering factory work lessened as corporations sought ways to improve efficiency and production. Mechanization and streamlined production modes, in fact, opened up thousands of manual operations that could be quickly learned by newly arrived workers from rural or considerably less industrialized regions. Factory and mill production also undercut the household and traditional manufacturing in agricultural areas and began to force land dwellers to supplement their wages in industrial areas rather than at home. Landholding itself became a growing problem as various factors conspired to make it more difficult to own land in sufficient quantities to support agricultural activities. This was particularly true in Russian Poland and Galicia, where agriculture suffered from an uncontrolled parcelization of estates. On the other extreme, blacks and Italians had difficulty in obtaining land at all. When industrialization began dislocating the worker in the countryside, the stage was set for the black, Italian, and Polish movement to Pittsburgh.[3]

Like most assumptions about urban migration, the movement of blacks has been subjected to numerous opinions but little empirical testing. Scholarship concerning early black migration from the South is a good example. Observers such as Carter G. Woodson thought the initial wave of blacks were composed mostly of "talented" individuals who were "higher" in education and aspirations than the mass of poor blacks who composed the bulk of migrants before World War I. A later study of Detroit concluded that early migrants were primarily those disillusioned by the deprivation of black political rights in the South. Some investigators have modified Woodson's views, but nearly all agreed with Gunnar Myrdal that a desire for economic and social betterment was the chief motive for migration.[4]

Among the few studies that have probed the stirrings of black migration deeply, Clyde Kiser's work suggested an important framework for understanding the beginnings of the movement. Kiser demonstrated that black migration began neither as a movement of exceptional individuals nor as a reaction to political oppression. He detected a more complicated process whereby southern-born blacks gradually moved in wider and wider circles to earn supplemental wages. In his study of St. Helene's Island, South Carolina, he discovered that permanent migration to New York City was preceded by temporary migration to nearby cities such as Savannah. Usually a father or other family member would seek temporary work outside the island in order to supplement agricultural income and allow most of the family to remain intact at home. These short-term movements not only provided additional income but familiarized blacks with wage labor and broader possibilities beyond farming.[5]

The gradual movement of southern blacks from farms, rather than an escape of the "talented tenth," as an explanation for early black migration was confirmed in oral interviews conducted for this study among migrants who came to Pittsburgh before 1917.[6] Most blacks interviewed in Pittsburgh were raised on small farms in Alabama, Georgia, and Virginia. Migrants recalled their parents working as sharecroppers for larger farmers who were in a few instances black. About one-fifth of the respondents came from farms owned by their fathers.

Common to most personal histories was the inevitable, temporary departure of the male from the household in search of supplemental wages. Carrie J. recalled that her sharecropper father was frequently cheated by a white owner when cotton was sold. Several times he was denied his extra bale of cotton at Christmas. Such exploitation created economic difficulties that forced him to obtain a garbage collection job in Fitzgerald, Georgia.[7] The father of Olive W. first left sharecropping in Georgia to tap turpentine. Several years later he moved to a neighboring town to work in a sawmill. William H. recalled that his father, who owned his own farm, traveled from Alabama to a Georgia sawmill when farm work was "slack." Floyd T. had a father who left their family-owned Virginia farm to earn wages "driving" in Roanoke. Ben E. remembered his father leaving their Alabama farm to work on the railroad for "long periods of time." His father even spent some time in Pittsburgh before returning from one trip. It was no accident that Ben, who moved to the "steel city" at age eighteen, or other respondents eventually came North. Their parents had already provided a glimpse of industrial wages and broader horizons.[8]

Often temporary toil stretched into periods of longer duration. Hezikiah M. was born in Louisa County, Virginia, in 1886. His parents had been slaves in Louisa County and by 1880 had only twenty acres of "poor land" on which they grew mostly vegetables for the consumption of their fourteen children. When his father heard of "higher and regular" wages in West Virginia coal mines, he temporarily left his wife and children. Hezikiah recalled his father returning about twice annually to bring much needed wages. In the meantime, his mother raised the children and earned extra money by taking in laundry work. At age thirteen Hezikiah and his brothers were taken by their father to Sunswitch, West Virginia, to load coal. Living in shanties with older men, Hezikiah worked the mines for four years and then left for a series of jobs in hotel kitchens that eventually brought him to Pittsburgh.[9]

A small stream of Pittsburgh's blacks originated initially in the Southwest and worked in the steel mills of the Midwest before arriving in Pittsburgh. Similar to other migrants, family members experienced temporary moves for industrial wages. Freeman P. was raised in Parish, Texas, where his father was recruited to Gary, Indiana, by a real estate developer. Freeman recalled a number of blacks leaving for Gary and Chicago. The men had previously left small farms in Texas to work in cotton mills and railroad shops in Parish before leaving for the North. Freeman followed his father to Gary in 1909 and eventually joined a brother in Pittsburgh.[10]

Herbert Gutman has demonstrated that various aspects of black kinship endured during slavery. The adversity blacks faced during the late eighteenth and early nineteenth centuries continued to nurture a reliance on kin. A similar dependence upon kin was clearly evident in the migration process. While black settlement in western Pennsylvania was frequently attributed to the importation of blacks as strikebreakers, nearly all blacks interviewed for this study came to Pittsburgh on their own volition as part of an expanding migratory process that had no other foundation than friends and kin. Essential services such as information about wage rates and job selection were provided by fellow blacks already in the city. An important distinction, however, was evident. While black migrants were able to supply information concerning wages and jobs, they appeared unable to assist other migrants in obtaining work regularly.

The movement of friends and kin from southern farms generated informal dissemination of knowledge about industrial employment. As a teenager Jean B. began working at a sawmill near Mobile, Alabama, while living on his parents' farm. It was at the sawmill that he heard mention of Philadelphia, New York, and Chicago. Such conversation prompted him to come north. He decided upon Pittsburgh because two friends were already there. After saving $45, he took a train from Mobile through Cincinnati to Pittsburgh, where his friends obtained a room for him.[11] William H. was working for a railroad in Alabama. His wife's uncle, who had worked in coal mines near Pittsburgh, informed him of higher wages. Although he initially intended to seek employment in the mines, a friend in Pittsburgh drew him to the Jones and Laughlin plant where wages appeared even "better." Another black, who preferred to remain anonymous, told how his father became dissatisfied with his career of "hiring out" from farm to farm in Virginia. He decided to come to Pittsburgh in 1902, where he gained "permanent" work and later brought his family. Several relatives "on his mother's side" followed his father to Pittsburgh, lived with him until they found work, and then moved out.[12]

Similar experiences were related by other migrants. James N. learned of larger opportunities and wages while periodically working as a "sawmill man" and in an Alabama steel mill. James eventually followed a younger brother to Pittsburgh's Hill District, where he recalled a neighborhood teeming with Jews, Italians, and blacks. Another black woman recalled following brothers to Pittsburgh and settling in "Jewtown."[13] Olive W. settled in the Mt. Washington section because her husband had relatives there. She eventually brought a sister to Pittsburgh to live with her in 1920.[14]

It should not come as a complete surprise that blacks were not tied wholly to the land and were beginning to loosen the ties they had. Black migration was not simply a direct transfer of people from an agricultural to an urban environment. Even prior to migration blacks were being weaned from the land and slowly being drawn into a wage-labor economy. To be sure, the vast majority of blacks still lived on farms, but a discernible trend away from agriculture had begun in the South in the late nineteenth century. By 1900 about 18 percent of all southern blacks were living in southern towns and cities. Among the remainder still living on the land only about 17 percent were owners; the rest were tenants or sharecroppers despite government programs such as the Southern Homestead Act that attempted to stimulate black land ownership.[15] Compounding the problem of deriving a living from the land was the overall decline in southern agriculture, including the reduction in sizes of farms in the five decades following the Civil War and the difficulties blacks encountered in securing farm loans and mortgages. By 1900 blacks owned only about 8 percent of all farms and about 6.5 percent of all farmland in the five major cotton-producing states. Small gains made in ownership prior to 1892 were halted by 1900 because of depressed cotton prices. The resulting ties of most blacks to the land were based upon a system of sharecropping that facilitated further exploitation of black farmers by owners who alone knew the amounts crop sales brought and could easily distort the percentage earned by black and white tenants.[16]

Already in the South by the 1870s the blacks were manifesting an outlook toward wage labor and a disposition to quit the land. Northern industrial firms such as the Pennsylvania Railroad did not begin active recruitment of blacks until 1917, an indication that much of the impetus for "quitting the land" came from blacks themselves. This should not be surprising in light of their tenuous ties to the land in the first place. By 1890 over one-quarter of the nonwhite males in the five largest cotton states worked in nonagricultural pursuits; among females the figure reached 34.8 percent. In the same year over 46 percent of Alabama coal miners were black. The U.S. Department of Labor also noted the heavy migration of blacks who had either worked in sawmills or lived in towns.[17] Published letters of migrants reveal further that blacks were not coming directly from farms. Blacks migrating to Chicago claimed they were "first class laundresses" or employees on the Florida East Coast railroad. One man wrote the *Chicago Defender*, indicating that he was mechanically inclined and trained in automobile repair. Another individual from Fullerton, Louisiana, indicated that he had done "moulding work" and had been around machinery for a decade. Other prospective migrants revealed expertise in furniture repair, plumbing, and blacksmithing and as stevedores, ironworkers, carpenters, insurance salesmen, and bookkeepers.[18]

But beyond the economic and social difficulties, which intensified the desire to quit the land, blacks were developing specific goals and aspirations that caused them to pursue eagerly what Arna Bontemps and Jack Conroy described as the "lure of the North." Again Kiser's findings are relevant. Kiser discovered that after 1890 young blacks had higher outlooks than their parents and viewed farming as "stagnant" and "monotonous."[19] Woven through numerous accounts of black migration northward was an indication of high motivation and hopes for the future. Blacks were clearly enthusiastic about their move. W. E. B. DuBois noticed it in his study of the *Philadelphia Negro* in 1898. Everett J. Scott observed the same enthusiasm two decades later. In 1919 the *Chicago Defender* reported on fifteen black families who left Huntsville, Alabama, for Pittsburgh because they had received letters from friends in the city who had already "made good." Similar inclinations have been found in recent studies of black workers in western Pennsylvania. And a study of black migration to Boston found high hopes that the author attributed to the influence of middle-class values of northern-born blacks, but clearly expectations had been elevated even before contact with the urban-born.[20]

The high hopes blacks possessed for social improvement expressed themselves most cogently in their school attendance rates. An examination of blacks moving to Chicago, for instance, stressed the widespread desire of black parents to place their children in better schools as a reason for abandoning the South. By 1920 in Pennsylvania 84.5 percent of black males aged fourteen and fifteen enrolled in school compared to only 72 percent of adolescent males of foreign-born parents. Among females, blacks were more likely to be in school by their midteens than were immigrant girls. In New York and New Jersey black attendance rates also exceeded those of immigrant children. Among black high school students in Pittsburgh in 1928, moreover, occupational goals were anything but modest with over 43 percent indicating a desire to enter teaching, dentistry, pharmacy, law, or some other profession.[21]

Expectations were equally high among blacks coming to Pittsburgh before 1917. Explanations that blacks simply abandoned the political oppression of the South seem less viable in the face of evidence that suggests they were slowly being weaned away from farming by industrial opportunities. Jasper A. left a farm near Albany, Georgia, at age twenty because his father and a job at a cotton seed mill simply did not "give me enough of everything I should have." Harrison G. initially aspired to be a "bigger farmer" than his father. Eventually, however, he grew tired of "bad years" and "bad raps" and decided to see if work could be better somewhere else. At age sixteen he began a search that took him to Tennessee, Cincinnati, and ultimately to the Oliver Steel plant in Pittsburgh. The father of Harrison G. urged his son to go to Pittsburgh because men who remained in Georgia "were not accomplishing anything." Roy M. left Brinkley, Arkansas, because he felt he could "get a good job" and live in the better homes "where you couldn't live before." After a visit to New Jersey, Olive W. "couldn't stand" Georgia anymore. William S. recalled assisting his father in constructing a roof for the first time and vowing to himself never to have a similar occupation but "to live better." William learned bricklaying and later started his own contracting company.[22]

Black aspirations were not simply vague dreams, moreover, but consisted of specific occupational goals that were anything but modest. Sadie A. came to Pittsburgh to become an interior decorator. Freeman P. hoped to become a physical education instructor and even managed to attend Wilberforce University before his financial resources were exhausted. Harrison G. came to Pittsburgh to open a grocery store. John W. intended to become a social worker. Numerous migrants expressed a desire to become teachers, although Pittsburgh would not hire black (or even Slavic) teachers before the 1930s.[23] That socioeconomic obstacles frustrated black goals made their initial intentions no less real.

Closely related to the high expectations of southern migrants was the importance attached to formal schooling and education. One scholar has even detected a black "folk tradition" that linked schooling and personal advancement. In fact, by 1910 a larger proportion of blacks than of American-born children of immigrants between the ages of fourteen and eighteen were in school.[24] Pittsburgh was no exception to this trend. At age fifteen, 48 percent of immigrant children were in school as compared with 63 percent of black children. By age sixteen only 30 percent of immigrant children remained in school; the figure for blacks was 41 percent. A decade later, black attendance still exceeded that of foreign-born and second-generation children in Pittsburgh. Middle-class black publications like the *Pittsburgh Courier* reinforced this sentiment. The *Courier,* for instance, continually urged black youth to seek "educational advantages" and criticized the exclusion of black teachers from the public schools.[25]

Black migrants were explicit when it came to education. William H. recalled that his farming parents stressed the importance of acquiring as much education as possible. Indeed, his father wanted William and his two sisters to become teachers and sent them away for training. Although William was forced to leave school to work in a sawmill, his sisters did become teachers. William later left the sawmill and returned to a school in Florida. He articulated his motives: "I felt I would be better prepared to land the job I wanted. I figured that a person with enough education would always be able to get a nice easy job."[26]

Other migrant memories supported the general emphasis on education. Sadie A. related that her mother insisted that her sister attend business school. "We were a poor family," Sadie related, "but we always aspired to higher things." Freeman P. remembered that one of the reasons his parents brought their children northward was to secure a "better education" for them. One migrant from Virginia related how his father would not allow any of his eleven children to leave high school. As a young girl Olive W. wanted to attend Morris Brown College in Atlanta because several of her friends were there already. Several blacks related being sent to a boarding school in Albany, Georgia, by parents who could have used the extra income.[27]

Like southern American blacks, Poles also began to loosen their ties to the land by the late nineteenth century. Population pressure on existing landholdings increased in all three divisions of Poland but especially in the Russian controlled sector (Congress Poland), which experienced a population growth of 179 percent in the four decades before 1900. Villages were overpopulated and one Polish source estimated that the Polish territories had a surplus population of four to eight million.[28] Consequently, the migration of Polish workers on both a seasonal and permanent basis intensified as families sought to supplement their income. Migrants traveled to Prussia, Bosnia, and Brazil as well as the United States, often returning with their earnings to purchase additional land. In Galicia associations of returned emigrants were formed to buy large estates with earnings from abroad. Not all migrations, of course, resulted in economic success. Jozef Sepek, an agricultural worker and later a miner under Austrian rule, described how his father eventually deserted the family: "It was difficult to subsist on a little plot of ground. I had to work. Father was a wanderer, so to speak. From his early years he had traveled around looking for work where he took all sorts of jobs, on farms or in factories. After having married my mother, he went to work in Germany and remained there for whole years, visiting his home only during the important holidays. At first he sent money home, but with time he forgot his wife and children, leaving them to the mercy of fate."[29] Many Poles like Sepek found it more convenient to move to larger Polish towns and villages to supplement their incomes. When the growth of the textile industry in Congress Poland eroded much of the household weaving trade and Russian attempts to conscript young Poles for the czar's army drove many to America, districts holding the highest density of villages such as Kalisz supplied most of the newcomers. Additional evidence suggests that these villages were growing crowded by 1900 with destitute farm laborers. Between 1893 and 1901, for instance, former farmhands, servants, and day laborers grew from 13.2 percent to 43.7 percent of village populations in districts such as Kalisz, Kielce, Warsaw, and Piotrkow that supplied most of the emigrants. Prussian Poles had also moved to Berlin, the Ruhr basin, and numerous villages prior to emigration and were, perhaps, the most familiar of all Polish groups with industrial society. In Bottrop they held some of the best jobs in the Prussian mining industry.[30]

Like blacks coming at the same time, Poles were obviously mobile before movement to Pittsburgh. A popular poem by Walenty Rozdziewsky, a Polish foundry worker, perhaps best illustrates the tradition of mobility among Polish workers.

> Freedom is our sole delight, the sole reward
> Of our misery, not treasures, not money!
> Since the Cyclops time we have never been
> Slaves to any tyrant, free to come
> And go as we please, after one year
> In one place we can move to another. . . .[31]

Industrial Silesia, Polish cities such as Poznan and Warsaw, and even Russia attracted temporary wage earners by the 1870s and the 1880s.[32] The father of Joseph C. worked on the family farm near Vilna but also "hired himself out to owners of larger estates." John S. and his father worked a market in the nearby town to gain additional wages. Valerian D. recalled while growing up in Poland that his peasant father had mined coal in Germany. Joseph B. was sent to Pittsburgh to earn wages for his family and eventually returned to settle in Poland and see his own son John leave for America. Over half of the families of Russian Polish origin interviewed for this study were started by immigrants who had served several years in the Russian army in Asia.[33]

Land reform and emancipation of the peasantry also influenced the social and economic position of workers in Polish-occupied lands. In Prussian Poland, for example, emancipation and the right to own land began earliest, with peasants on state-owned lands gaining rights to their landholdings as early as 1807 in Pomerania, Silesia, and Poznania. Subsequent development in Prussia, however, led to a gradual polarization of peasant society rather than a wide distribution of land ownership. Wealthier peasants purchased so much land that by 1880 a full 80 percent of the agricultural population were wage earners working for larger estates or migrating to the industrial areas of Silesia. The gradual monopolization of land by a few made it increasingly difficult for most farming families to pass land to progeny or survive. After nearly seventy years of steadily losing their ability to live off the land, this rural proletariat had little choice but to move. Traveling largely in family units they settled in midwestern agricultural areas such as Wisconsin. Some, however, settled in cities as early as the 1870s and became the least likely of all Polish groups to return to Europe.[34]

Emancipation and land reform came later in Russian Poland but also led to heightened social stratification, although not as extensively as in Poznania. Because laws allowed peasants to divide their holdings primarily among their children, a somewhat wider distribution of land ownership occurred. Emigration began in the 1880s when systematic Russian oppression intensified growing economic difficulties caused by unequal land distribution and an increasing surplus labor force. Since land could be inherited, however, emigration was more typical of individuals than family units. As in Prussia, the emigrant came from families who had owned land for several decades and were faced with further declines in status if additional land or wages were not obtained.[35]

If land reform and emancipation led to varying degrees of polarization in Prussian and Russian areas, Galicia (or Austrian Poland) experienced pervasive pauperization after emancipation. Small holdings proliferated in this most impoverished of Polish lands, and landholding quickly became a common tradition. Between 1850 and 1890 the amount of peasant-owned tilled land increased by 750,000 acres. Inevitably, parents could not pass sufficient land to their sons to support agriculture. Obsessed with the value of land, these sons emigrated as individuals to Brazil and America after 1890 to earn wages that would allow them to return to Galicia to purchase additional acreage. It was no accident that more money was sent from America to Galicia than to any other section of Poland. These immigrants left home to stave off a decline in status by acquiring the means to purchase more land.[36] Indeed, the widespread ownership of land in Galicia and the encounter with land ownership experienced by so many Poles in the Russian and Prussian sectors offered a sharp contrast to southern blacks in America, 17 percent of whom were landowners by 1900.[37] If blacks had glimpsed an opportunity to abandon their position at the bottom of southern society, Poles, despite their various regional origins, had already flirted with social improvement after various emancipation acts. While emancipation benefited some, however, others grew disillusioned and sought to avoid any further decline in economic status. If blacks coming to Pittsburgh exhibited some hope for what they might find, it should seem reasonable that Poles were considerably more skeptical.

While mobility was not unfamiliar to Poles prior to emigration, they did not appear to acquire the range of nonagricultural skills characteristic of blacks and, as shown below, Italians. Those who had migrated to Prussian Polish villages did acquire some expertise in mining and textile production. But those moving overseas were typically neither established very well nor long in either industrial, village, or agricultural sectors. Rather they were recent refugees from areas where agriculture was in decline. They had never really had the opportunity to learn a skill or, for that matter, own land for any length of time, although many still harbored notions of eventual proprietorship. Looking at the structural position of emigrants, a portrait is discernible of individuals who were unskilled and landless. In 1908 about two-thirds of all Polish males leaving Galicia were either agricultural workers or day laborers; only 6.6 percent were trained craftsmen. About one-half of all emigrants leaving Congress Poland four years later were landless. While about one in five had worked in a factory or acquired a skill, only 27.1 percent were peasant landowners. It should be stressed, of course, that many in the landless category came from families that held property and that they sought someday to become owners themselves. Nevertheless, like blacks leaving the American South, Polish emigrants did tend to be unfamiliar with proprietorship and skills and somewhat detached from their agricultural moorings.[38]

But if migration of blacks to Pittsburgh originated within a framework of gradually rising expectations and individualism, Polish newcomers were considerably more tentative about the promise of the "steel city" and still susceptible to the larger claims of their families of origin. To be sure the same pattern of periodic transiency that characterized rural blacks prior to migration to Pittsburgh existed in late nineteenth-century Poland. Little justification remains to cling to the view that immigrants were leaving "isolated villages." But if blacks were rapidly becoming aware of new possibilities and seeking survival largely on their own, Poles were reluctantly realizing that continued existence on the land was becoming more difficult. Their initial experiences in industrial work, however, underscored their precarious economic situation. The working day, normally twelve or more hours, sustained life but gave little cause for rising expectations. Jakub Bajorski, whose family abandoned a small plot for industrial work in Warsaw, recalled conditions under Russian rule. "My parents occupied a small . . . apartment on the ground floor. It was always uncomfortable for our large family because of its small size. I remember that we slept four in one bed, two at the head and two at the foot. The apartment was always cold . . . and the subsistence of the whole family was pitiful."[39] If blacks had even a hint of an elevation in social status, Poles were desperately trying to resist what seemed a precipitous decline.

As in most instances of urban migration, kinship was an essential element. This was as true for Poles as well as blacks. The mother of Joseph D. was brought from Gdansk (Prussia) to "Polish Hill" by an uncle who ran a grocery store. Indeed Polish migration from Prussia consisted heavily of family units as opposed to the more individualistic migration from Galicia, Georgia, Alabama, or Virginia. Valerian D. was brought to McKeesport, Pennsylvania, by his father in 1906. Peter L. avoided service in the Russian army by following a brother to the "steel city." The parents of Joseph B. were brought from Russian Poland by relatives. With two sisters and a brother already working in the city, the father of Stephanie L. left German Poland in 1899 with his wife and Stephanie herself. Joseph B. sent passage for two brothers and a sister to come to the Southside. Joseph Z. attracted two brothers to the Oliver Steel plant.[40]

The extent of the influence of the kin migration may be seen in the early settlement patterns of each group of Poles. Generally they entered Pittsburgh in successive waves from provinces under the control of Germany, Russia, and Austria. Beginning in the early 1870s German Poles began settling in the Strip District along Penn Avenue. Russian Poles settled along Penn Avenue and further north in Lawrenceville. Those from German-held territories predominated in Herron Hill (Polish Hill) and the Southside before 1900. After the late 1890s Austrian Poles from Galicia joined German Poles on the Southside and Russian Poles in the Lawrenceville section.[41]

Perhaps most important, kin and friends could supply vital, practical information on migration to perspective newcomers. Especially descriptive is the letter Stanislaw Zielinski wrote to his brother who was planning on joining him in Pittsburgh. He advised:

> Now prepare yourself for the trip in the following way. Take rubles for spending. Take a suit with you because you will need it in Prussia. Buy sugar and vinegar and a bottle of vodka. The day when you will be leaving for the ocean don't eat anything cooked or boiled on the ship because they are adding powder to make you throw up. Eat only dry bread and vodka and then maybe you will be well. And when you arrive in New York you will leave the station so send me a telegram, and I will wait for you in Pittsburgh. . . . And now write me what day you are leaving

the country and whatever papers you get from the agent take
them with you, because in Berlin the agent will ask you for them
and tell him we already bought the ticket for you from Bremen to
New York. . . . We pray that God will help you with your passage
through the ocean.[42]

If black migrants left for Pittsburgh with positive occupational
goals, Poles were considerably less optimistic. The goal of most immigrant Poles was simply "to get a job, any job." The variety and spe-
cificity of occupational goals expressed by black migrants were nowhere to be found among the Polish newcomers. The Polish pattern
was consistent. Mike B. entered a Southside mill because he felt the
nature of a job was unimportant as long as he was working. "You've
got to work because you've got to live whether you like it or not," he
reasoned. Walter B. did not particularly like his work on a labor gang,
but it satisfied his major occupational goal: "to stay out of debt." Joe
R. kept a position finishing freight cars because it allowed him to play
in a band on weekends. Mike M. took the first job that seemed "steady"
because "there was no other way out." Women such as Stephanie W.
sought only employment that would allow her to "walk to work and
bring home money."[43]

Once a job was secured, it was not easily abandoned. While blacks
would frequently walk away from a job over personal dissatisfactions,
Poles endured — unless economic dislocations necessitated a move or
enough funds were accumulated to return to their homeland. As Ignacy
M. exclaimed, "When you're in the mill, where are you going to go?"
Thus, Joseph B. related that his father was a boiler mechanic at the
Jones and Laughlin plant for fifty years. John K. estimated that his
father worked in the same rolling mill near Polish Hill for over fifty
years. A number of Polish laborers at the Heppenstall plant in Lawrenceville reported similar patterns of longevity. Several immigrant
children described their fathers as believing in "work, work, and more
work." Joseph B. described his father, a railroad inspector, as content
simply with a "steady income." Incisively the son concluded, "He died
on the job."[44]

The modest thrust of Polish orientations and the high value placed
upon steady work within the status system of the Polish community
did not foster strong support of extensive secular education. To be sure,
religious instruction was important, and a few Polish children progressed through the American educational system. But Polish support
for secular education seemed less pronounced than that of blacks. In
the hierarchy of Polish values, work and family came before educational nourishment of the individual. Even the priesthood was some-

times discouraged. Etched in the memory of Francis P. was the disappointment on his parents' faces when he informed them of his desire to pursue a religious vocation. "The old time people looked for you to get a job and help out," he explained. Other Poles echoed this theme. Stephanie W. was removed from school by her father at age thirteen to work and remembered only two of ten brothers and sisters completing high school. Stanley N. left high school because his teachers continually made him self-conscious and uncomfortable by erroneously pronouncing his name. "That was one of the things that bothered me and caused me the hell to drop out," he emphasized. Another immigrant child described his parents' views on schooling: "Well, to tell you the truth most of the old people came from the old country and all they believed was in sending their children to work. . . . I had only one brother that finished school and no sisters."[45]

Subsequent observers of Pittsburgh Poles reinforced the view that work was valued over education. A 1928 survey by the American Council for Nationalities Services in Pittsburgh witnessed considerable complaints among the "better educated" Poles about the lack of educational appreciation among young Poles. A later survey in 1942 quoted a Pole who pointed out that youth on the Southside went into the mills before finishing high school because "even when they're small, they get the feeling that some day they'll be filing out one of them [mill] gates on some shift. I guess maybe it's their parents that give 'em that feeling."[46] The residue of this early period of Polish settlement was evident in a 1973 survey by the Pittsburgh Catholic diocese, which found 60.7 percent of the adults at a Southside Polish church without a high school degree and 33 percent who never entered high school.[47] Among 995 Polish adults on the Southside the median year of school was 9.5; according to the federal census of 1970, the median figure among Pittsburgh blacks was 10.6.[48]

Poles and blacks certainly did not represent the full range of premigration experiences. Italians as well showed similarities and differences in their prior experiences that would influence their settlement in the "steel city." If the decline of feudal arrangements heralded widespread land ownership in most areas of Poland, the result in southern Italy was significantly different and more nearly resembled that of the American South. Most land in the Mezzogiorno, which included Abruzzie Molise, Campania, Puglia, Basilicata, Calabria, and Sicily, had been in the possession of royalty or government. An 1806 law finally encouraged the division of public land among serfs, but the edict was rarely enforced. Consequently, a small group of independent landowners obtained land that was inferior in quality. Lacking the necessary capital needed for improvement, the peasants or "contadini" eventually sold their large pieces to wealthier owners. The result was that by the late nineteenth century large estates (latifondi) were increasingly significant.[49]

The implications of the inability of southern Italian peasants to cultivate the soil profitably and to own land led to patterns of survival that differed from those of both the American South and Poland. The counterpart of the black tenant or the small Polish landowner was usually a villager who tended to walk several miles daily to perform his agricultural tasks in the fields of a large owner. Challenging the view of historian Oscar Handlin, who characterized immigrants as land-oriented peasants, Virginia Yans-McLaughlin asserted that Italians were distinguished by the relatively complex socioeconomic structure of the towns they lived in and by the fact that they were in reality "farmer-laborers." The classic, self-sufficient farmer rarely appeared in the Mezzogiorno. Rather, as Yans-McLaughlin writes, villages held small owners, day laborers, and even tenants who made the daily trek to the fields. Emotional attachments to land and work were giving way to economic ones. Not surprisingly, after 1882 land ownership among south Italian peasants declined.[50]

The growing inability of the small landowner to retain his property and the evolution of his status as a laborer dependent upon an employer initiated gradual changes in southern Italian society. As with blacks and Poles, Italians began moving in a wider area for supplemental wages, especially because agriculture was seasonal and unpredictable. Some followed the harvests in other regions of Italy. Others migrated much further. As early as 1858 an Italian government official noted considerable movement to the Americas. Writing for the *Annuario Statistico Italiano,* he commented: "The number of Italians who are settled abroad or wandering there is large. . . . Italian refugees, adventurers, tradesmen, and doctors are scattered in all parts of the East. On the Algerian coast about 15,000 Italians have settled in the last ten years. The United States has received 10,000 immigrants, and three times that number of peddlars, laborers, and tradesmen have located in Argentina, Uruguay, Brazil and other South American countries."[51] Contadini entered sulphur mining, quarrying, and construction work. By the late nineteenth century, men from Abruzzi, an area that supplied many Pittsburgh Italians, were toiling in French metal works, railways, and mines.[52] Diminishing opportunities in agriculture particularly intensified the desire to acquire a skill or trade that could provide either additional income or regular employment by itself. In addition, the social structure of southern Italy already pos-

sessed a significant class of artisans and wage laborers, including fishermen, peddlers, shoemakers, tailors, carpenters, and masons. With
the periodic uncertainty of agricultural employment and declining
child mortality after 1890, more individuals were competing for wages
offered by these alternative forms of employment. This search would
eventually take many abroad.[53]

Because of their experience with wage labor and skills, Italians who
were eventually forced to extend their job search to America were more
than simply impoverished, tradition-bound peasants. Invariably they
came from the middle or upper reaches of the Italian working class
and were eager for capital to acquire more land in Italy or to assist
their sons in entering a business or trade.[54] An observer of migration
to Buffalo concluded that Italians came from the "higher echelon" of
peasants and workers. Historian John Briggs, in studying movement
to Kansas City, Rochester, and Utica, found that those most likely
to emigrate were agriculturalists or townsmen who had a stake in
society such as a skill or a parcel of land and confidence in their ability
to influence their futures. Briggs felt that those in the lowest stratum
of Italian society, the day laborers, were the least likely to leave. In a
sample of Sicilian passports Briggs found that 54 percent of the adult
male passports between 1901 and 1914 were in nonagricultural operations, including 18 percent town laborers, 12 percent fishermen, and
17 percent skilled tradesmen.[55] Italian census statistics indicate that
between 1911 and 1921 in Abruzzi, Basilicata, Calabria, and Sicily the
proportion of individuals engaged in agriculture increased, an indication that emigration from nonagricultural sectors of the occupational
spectrum had been heavier.[56] And where the movement of people
from agriculture was taking place, the heaviest flow came from areas
characterized by a wide distribution of land ownership — that is, in
regions where landholdings were small and widespread and residents
were more inclined to seek supplemental wages and skills. In regions
of vast inequality of holdings, large estates usually employed the
landless, day laborer.[57]

The exact nature of the goals and expectations of Italians leaving
for America is still debated. Older interpretations stress that immigrants hoped to avoid a "slow decline in status by pursuing industrial
wages even in areas where language and culture were unfamiliar,"
much like the Polish model.[58] Recent accounts have indicated that
Italians were ready for improvement and had high expectations of
social mobility. Briggs stated unequivocally that they were intent on
individual advancement and proprietorship in America.[59] What is clear
is that despite a heavy incidence of return migration, Italians' associa-

tion with the land had been severely reduced by 1900. Italian workers
seemed intent on improving their social condition, whether in Italy or
America, by avenues other than farming. Many crossed the ocean semiannually in search of suitable work. In 1907 the Italian Commissariat
of Emigration reported that

> transoceanic emigration is ... assuming an increasingly temporary
> character.... Even emigrants to America can return to Italy to
> see their families and their native land for two or three years,
> then leave again to take part in new work. Actual currents of
> periodic emigration are being formed in some transoceanic coun-
> tries. Southern peasants, as well as workers from Piedmont, the
> Veneto and other regions of Italy ... emigrate about March or
> April to the United States to do outside construction work, and
> then they return to Italy at the beginning of the winter season.[60]

To the extent that Italians had loosened their ties to the land and had
elevated their future expectation, they more nearly resembled blacks
coming to the "steel city" than Poles.

Interviews with Italians in Pittsburgh,[61] conducted mostly with
families emanating from Abruzzi, suggest that Italians saw Pittsburgh
as a definite opportunity for improvement. Most of those interviewed
indicated little intention ever to return. Since interviews were conducted only with those who did persist in the city, this is not unusual.
Thousands, of course, did return to Europe with savings that enabled
them to improve their life in Italy. In Abruzzi so many returned to
buy additional land that a usury industry emerged because men had
excess money to loan. The *Banco de Napoli* through which all emigrants were to transmit savings from America reported receiving an
average of 21 million lire annually between 1903 and 1909. The average jumped to 54 million during the 1910-14 period.[62] Nevertheless, the
interviews with Italians were noticeably different from those of persisting Poles, who invariably indicated an initial desire to return.
Nicholas R. had no intention of returning because he felt Pittsburgh
afforded "greater opportunity" than Italy. The father of Felix D. came
to Saffire Alley in the city because he was "mad" that as an apprentice
in Italy he was only allowed to sweep floors. In disgust he left for
America, "where everyone was making money." As a young woman
in Abruzzi, Domenica M. was impressed by letters from Pittsburgh
that described the earnings and acquisitions of emigrants. "The people
were smart," she reasoned. "They saved the money. They built the
houses. They got what they need."[63]

Like blacks and Poles coming to the city, Italians structured their
entire migration around kinship. Beginning in the late 1880s a steady

stream of Italians poured into four blocks bounded by Sixth Avenue, Smithfield Street, Fifth Avenue, and Grant Street in downtown Pittsburgh. Business expansion into the area forced both Poles and Italians outward, with Poles moving to the Lawrenceville section, where they were concentrating in factory jobs, and Italians moving into Bloomfield and especially East Liberty, where many found employment in the erection of the city's new filtration plant in 1905. It was in East Liberty that the first Italian Catholic church was opened in 1897.[64] In Bloomfield, the site of the majority of Italian interviews, settlement concentrated around Liberty Avenue and Pearl, Juniper, and Edmund streets in the 1890s while the area was still heavily German. While small settlements from Calabria and Sicily appeared, most of Bloomfield's Italians were from Abruzzi.[65]

The Italian community in Bloomfield was built on a foundation of friends and kin already in the city by the 1890s. Most of the neighborhood's Italians came from a half-dozen villages in Abruzzi, especially Castel di Sangro, Rocca Cinque Miglia, Ateleta, and Pesco Costanza. The father of Michael M. settled in the Strip District around 1911, lived with a brother, and worked in his brother's small produce business. Eventually another brother and sister followed them to the city. Precisely because all of his brothers and sisters settled in the city, Michael's father reluctantly abandoned his intention of returning to Italy in 1925 to open a dry goods store. Felix D. had worked in Pittsburgh between 1888 and 1890 before returning to Abruzzi. After marrying a girl from his village in 1890, he contacted relatives in Bloomfield, who secured a construction job that allowed him to return to Pittsburgh with his bride. Tom B. was brought to the city in 1912 by a grandfather who had worked in Wisconsin a decade before with Tom's father. After Tom's father died from an illness that he contracted while loading coal barges, his grandfather brought three other grandchildren, Tom's mother, and several uncles and aunts to Bloomfield. Vincent L. was sent from Ateleta to Pittsburgh at sixteen years of age to live with an aunt. His father had already worked in the "steel city" in 1900 and felt it was "rough" but provided an opportunity to earn additional wages. The father of Nicholas R. had made five trips to Pittsburgh before Nicholas joined a brother in 1914. The father of Leo G. came to Pittsburgh in 1910 rather than anywhere else because he had a brother and a sister in Bloomfield. They later brought Leo's grandparents and an uncle and provided them with a place to live on Liberty Avenue. Because he was an only son, Frank A. disappointed his father when he decided to sail from Naples to New York in 1914. He sought to escape the approaching war in

Europe and live with one of three sisters already in Pittsburgh, earn higher wages, and return after the war had ended.[66]

All Italians, of course, were not coming to Pittsburgh in a feverish search for improvement. Once immigrant networks were established, they offered solutions to familial and economic problems that existed at the time. A surprising number involved young girls whose parents had died and who were in need of a place to live. In many instances these female immigrants married as soon as possible, often before the age of eighteen, to stabilize their lives and secure their position in America. Albina B. came to an aunt in 1913 and one year later married an Italian laborer who was living across the street. Domenica M. came to Bloomfield at the age of fourteen after her mother died in 1910. She lived with an aunt whom she assisted in caring for boarders until she married in 1914. Lidwina P. came to Pittsburgh to live with her father after her mother's death.[67]

Clearly newcomers to Pittsburgh had much in common. Blacks, Italians, and Poles had encountered a gradual loosening of their ties to the land, which allowed them to become familiar with various forms of wage labor. All groups, moreover, relied essentially on friends and kin in moving to the industrial city and finding a place to live. But important distinctions emerged in the evolutionary process of transforming agricultural laborers into industrial toilers. Leaving at a time when their ties to the land were still meaningful, most Poles looked upon Pittsburgh as a temporary necessity in achieving the larger goal of proprietorship in the homeland. Blacks and Italians, on the other hand, had never experienced widespread proprietorship and were rather optimistic about entering the "steel city." Italians, in particular, even brought numerous skills that promised to serve them well. What would happen to these newcomers in the crucible that was Pittsburgh, however, remained to be seen.

NOTES

1. U.S. Bureau of the Census, *Abstract of the Twelfth Census of the United States, 1900* (Washington, D.C., 1902), 107; U.S. Bureau of the Census, *Thirteenth Census of the United States, 1910. Abstract of the Census with Supplement for Pennsylvania* (Washington, D.C., 1913), 630; U.S. Bureau of the Census, *Fourteenth Census of the United States, 1920, III: Population* (Washington, D.C., 1922), 900-1.
2. *Annual Report of the Executive Departments of the City of Pittsburgh,* 1910. The growth of native-born white residents accounted for the bulk of Pittsburgh's population before the 1890s.
3. U.S. Bureau of the Census, Manuscript Census for Pittsburgh, 1900,

Carnegie Library of Pittsburgh. A 20 percent sample of black, Italian, and Polish families was derived for this study, hereafter identified as 1900 sample data.

4. Carter G. Woodson, *A Century of Negro Migration* (New York, 1969), 11, 21, 46-91; David M. Katzman, *Before the Ghetto: Black Detroit in the Nineteenth Century* (Urbana, Ill., 1973), 64; Florette Henri, *Black Migration: Movement North, 1900-1920* (New York, 1975), 152-53, 352; Gunnar Myrdal, *An American Dilemma*, 2 vols. (New York, 1964), 1: 193-97; U.S. Department of Labor, *Negro Migration in 1916-1917* (Washington, D.C., 1919).

5. Clyde V. Kiser, *Sea Island to City* (New York, 1969), 149-52.

6. The oral histories in this study were obtained from a series of interviews conducted between 1974 and 1978 with blacks, Polish-Americans, and Italian-Americans living in Pittsburgh and born before 1920. The personal histories were based on a common questionnaire that was developed by the oral history program of the Pennsylvania Historical and Museum Commission. The consistent use of a questionnaire insured comparability of all data generated. A copy of the questionnaire and all tapes are available for inspection at the Historical and Museum Commission, Harrisburg. In addition to Bodnar, the majority of the interviews were conducted by Peter Gottlieb, Gregory Mihalik, and William Simons.

7. Interview with Carrie J., July 30, 1976, Pittsburgh Oral History Project (POHP).

8. Interviews with Olive W., July 23, 1976; William H., June 17, 1976; Floyd T., May 11, 1976; Ben E., July 31, 1974, POHP.

9. Interview with Hezikiah M., Oct. 8, 1976, POHP.

10. Interviews with Freeman P., July 11, 1974; Roy M., July 9, 1974, POHP.

11. Interview with Jean B., June 29, 1976, POHP.

12. Interviews with William H., June 17, 1976; Anonymous southern-born black, Aug. 11, 1977, POHP.

13. Interviews with Queen W., Oct. 8, 1976; Anonymous, Sept. 2, 1976, POHP. Many black women did "day work" for Jewish families in the city. See also interview with James N., June 28, 1976, POHP.

14. Interviews with Olive W., July 23, 1976; Willie S., July 10, 1976, POHP. The importance of kinship in the urban migration process is emphasized more fully in Charles Tilly and C. Harold Brown, "On Uprooting, Kinship, and the Auspices of Migration," *International Journal of Comparative Sociology*, 8 (1967). See also Arthur F. Raper, *Preface to Peasantry: A Tale of Two Black Belt Counties* (New York, 1968), 71, for a discussion of black migration in the 1930s from Georgia. Although covering a later period than this study, Raper noticed the continuing relationship between kinship and migration.

15. Henri, *Black Migration*, 26; Robert Higgs, *Competition and Coercion: Blacks in the American Economy, 1865-1914* (Cambridge, 1977), 40-41.

16. Roger Ransom and Richard Sutch, "The Ex-Slave in the Post-Bellum South: A Study of the Economic Impact of Racism in a Market Environment," *Journal of Economic History*, 33 (Mar. 1973), 136-37;

Joseph Reed, "Sharecropping as an Understandable Market Response: The Post-Bellum South," ibid., 106-7; Higgs, *Competition and Coercion*, 131; Henri, *Black Migration*, 28.

17. Roger Ransom and Richard Sutch, *One Kind of Freedom: The Economic Consequences of Emancipation* (Cambridge, Mass., 1977); Robert D. Ward and William W. Rodgers, *Labor Revolt in Alabama* (Birmingham, Ala., 1965), 21; U.S. Department of Labor, *Negro Migration*, 18.

18. Emmett J. Scott, ed., "Letters of Negro Migrants of 1916-1918," *Journal of Negro History*, 4 (July 1919), 290-340; Scott, ed., "Additional Letters of Negro Migrants of 1916-1918," ibid., 4 (Oct. 1919), 432-65.

19. Arna Bontemps and Jack Conroy, *They Seek a City* (New York, 1945), 89-91; Kiser, *Sea Island to City*, 131-44. See also George E. Haynes, *The Negro at Work in New York City* (New York, 1912), 27. U.S. Department of Labor, *Negro Migration*, cited "lower wages" as a cause of black migration. For implications of optimism among black migrants see Andrew Buni, *Robert L. Vann of the Pittsburgh Courier* (Pittsburgh, 1974), 24-28; Kenneth Kusmer, *A Ghetto Takes Shape: Black Cleveland, 1870-1930* (Urbana, Ill., 1976), 219, discussed optimism among the black middle class.

20. W. E. B. DuBois, *The Philadelphia Negro: A Social Study* (Philadelphia, 1898), 168; Everett J. Scott, *Negro Migration during the War* (New York, 1920), 40-41. *Chicago Defender*, Jan. 19, 1919, quoted in Chicago Commission on Race Relations, *The Negro in Chicago: A Study of Race Relations and a Race Riot* (Chicago, 1922), 89; Philip S. Foner and Ronald L. Lewis, *The Black Worker during the Era of the National Labor Union*, 2 vols. (Philadelphia, 1978), 2: 342-51; Dennis Clark Dickerson, "Black Steelworkers in Western Pennsylvania, 1915-1950" (Ph.D. diss., Washington University, 1978), 35-43; Elizabeth Pleck, *Black Migration and Poverty: Boston, 1865-1900* (New York, 1979), 201.

21. Chicago Commission, *The Negro in Chicago*, 82; U.S. Bureau of Census, *School Attendance in 1920* (Washington, D.C., 1924), 240-57; Floyd Covington, "Occupational Choices in Relation to Economic Opportunities of Negro Youth in Pittsburgh" (M.A. thesis, University of Pittsburgh, 1928), 31.

22. Interviews with Jasper A., July 12, 1976; Harrison G., Aug. 23, 1974; Roy M., July 9, 1974; Sally S., June 18, 1976; William S., Mar. 11, 1977, POHP. See "The Negro in Pittsburgh," WPA Papers, RG-41, Box 1, Folder 4, Pennsylvania Historical and Museum Commission. Peter Gottlieb has concluded from oral interviews with black migrants in Pittsburgh and Homestead that newcomers came from the South with expectations higher than industrial work in the city could meet; see his "Migration and Jobs: The New Black Workers in Pittsburgh, 1916-1930," *Western Pennsylvania Historical Magazine*, 61 (Jan. 1978), 1-15.

23. Interviews with Sadie A., June 21, 1976; Freeman P., July 11, 1974; Harrison G., Aug. 23, 1974; John W., June 28, 1974; Olive W., July 23, 1976, POHP. A 1928 study of 434 black high school students in Pittsburgh found teaching to be the most preferred occupation (14.5 percent) among the students. Over 60 percent of the respondents aspired to professions, such as physician, accountant, or a business position.

Covington, "Occupational Choices of Negro Youth in Pittsburgh," 31.

24. Ralph Ellison, "An American Dilemma: A Review," in Joyce Lander, ed., *The Death of White Sociology* (New York, 1973), 84. Ellison also suggested that black attitudes were not always the product of a "social pathology" but were often the result of a rejection of "middle class values." Timothy Smith, "Native Blacks and Foreign Whites: Varying Responses to Educational Opportunity in America, 1880-1950," *Perspectives in American History*, 6 (1972), 309-19.

25. U.S. Bureau of Census, *Thirteenth Census of the United States, 1910, Vol. 1: Population* (Washington, 1913), p. 1159; U.S. Bureau of the Census, *School Attendance in 1920*, 276-77. *Pittsburgh Courier*, July 1, 1911, p. 4; June 24, 1911, p. 4; Aug. 6, 1911, p. 1.

26. Interview with William H., June 17, 1976, POHP. Philip Klein, *A Social Study of Pittsburgh: Community Problems and Social Services of Allegheny County* (New York, 1938), 37, found that in 1928 teaching was a frequent aspiration for young black women.

27. Interview with Sadie A., June 21, 1976; Freeman P., July 11, 1974; Anonymous, July 17, 1974; Floyd T., May 11, 1976; Gertrude D., Nov. 3, 1976; Olive W., July 23, 1976; Carrie J., July 23, 1976, POHP.

28. Jozef Poniatowski, "Excess Population in the Village" (Warsaw, 1936) quoted in Feliks Gross, *The Polish Worker: A Study of a Social Stratum* (New York, 1945), 36.

29. Zygmunt Myslakowski and Jozef Sepek, Document no. 75 (in Polish) Warsaw, 1938, p. 323, in Gross, *The Polish Worker*, 82.

30. U.S. Congress, *Reports of the Immigration Commission, Emigrant Conditions in Europe*, 61st Cong., 3rd sess., Senate Document 748, Serial 5870 (Washington, D.C., 1911), 386; Celina Bobinska and Andrezej Pilch, *Employment Seeking Emigration of the Pole World Wide XIX and XX Century* (Krakow, 1975), 39-40, 47-49, 67, 79; Witold Kula, Nine Assorodobraj-Kula, and Marian Kula, eds., *Listy Emigrantowz Brazylii i Stanow Zjed Noczonych, 1890-91* [Emigrant Letters from Brazil and the United States, 1890-91] (Warsaw, 1973), 241-330; Richard C. Murphy, "Polish In-Migrants in Bottrop, 1891-1933: An Ethnic Minority in a German Industrial City" (Ph.D. diss. University of Iowa, 1977); Z. Daszynska-Golinska, "L'Accroissement de la Population in Pologne," in *La Pologne au VIIIe Congres International des Sciences Historiques*, 1 (Warsaw, 1933), 115-22.

31. Walenty Rozdziewsky, *Officina Ferraria* [The Foundry and Workshop with Smithies of the Noble Iron Craft], first published in 1642, in Gross, *The Polish Worker*, 14.

32. See Laurence Shofer, "Patterns of Worker Protest: Upper Silesia, 1863-1914," in Peter N. Stearns and Daniel J. Walkowitz, eds., *Workers in the Industrial Revolution* (New Brunswick, N.J., 1974), 325-26; William I. Thomas and Florian Znaniecki, *The Polish Peasant in Europe and America*, 5 vols. (New York, 1920), 5: 19. V. E. McHale and E. A. Johnson, "Urbanization, Industrialization, and Crime in Imperial Germany," *Social Science History*, 1 (Fall 1976), 50.

33. Interviews with John S., Sept. 30, 1976; John B., Mar. 3, 1976; Valerian D., July 8, 1974; Stanley P., Nov. 11, 1976; Carl M., Nov. 11, 1976; Stanley E., Sept. 9, 1976; Walter K., July 2, 1974, POHP.

34. Stefan Kieniewicz, *The Emancipation of the Polish Peasantry* (Chicago, 1969), 58-65, 190-94. Prussian areas such as Silesia, which were already industrialized, supplied almost no immigrants since surplus labor could be absorbed; Silesia did supply emigrants to Texas in the 1850s who had little intention of returning; see Lindsay Baker, *The First Polish Americans* (College Station, Tex., 1979), 33; Bobinska and Pilch, *Employment Seeking Emigration of the Poles*, 64-65; St. *Osada Historia Zwiazko Narodowogo Polskiego* (Chicago, 1905), 100-5.

35. Kieniewicz, *Emancipation of Polish Peasantry*, 180-84.

36. Ibid., 203-14; Victor Greene, *For God and Country: The Rise of Polish and Lithuanian Ethnic Consciousness in America* (Madison, Wis., 1975), 18-20; Emily Greene Balch, *Our Slavic Fellow Citizens* (New York, 1910), 135-38, pointed out that the decline of weaving and other home industries in Galicia by the 1870s, especially from competition in industrial areas like Silesia and even Warsaw, caused the loss of additional means of supplementing agricultural income and necessitated finding other ways of preventing further declines in status. The increasingly poor land-farmer ratio in Galicia is documented in Folke Dovring, *Land and Labor in Europe, 1900-1950* (The Hague, 1960), 672.

37. Henri, *Black Migration*, 26.

38. Bobinska and Pilch, *Employment Seeking Emigration of the Poles*, 43-49, 84-87.

39. Myslakowski and Sepek, Document no. 75, p. 323, and Jakob Bajorski, Document no. 5, p. 213, both in Gross, *The Polish Worker*, 82, 84, respectively.

40. Interviews with Joseph D., Sept. 17, 1976; Valerian D., July 8, 1974; Peter L., Sept. 17, 1976; Joseph B., May 13 and 20, 1976; Stephanie W., Mar. 24, 1976; John B., Mar. 24, 1976; John B., Mar. 3, 1976; Francis P., Jan. 16, 1976, POHP.

41. *Historja Parafji SW. Wojciecha BM* (Pittsburgh, 1933); *Pamietnik of St. Adalbert's Parish* (Pittsburgh, 1915). W. X. Kruszka, *Historya Polska W. Ameryce*, 8 vols. (Milwaukee, Wis., 1905-6), 2: 6-7. "Audit of International Institutes, Material on Pittsburgh's Nationality Communities," American Council for Nationalities Services Papers, Shipment 4, Box 2, Archives of Industrial Society, University of Pittsburgh.

42. Stanislow Zielinski to [brother], Feb. 17, 1891 in Kula, Assorodobraj-Kula, and Kula, eds., *Listy Emigrantow z Brazylii i Stanow Zjednoczonych*, 418.

43. Interviews with Mike B., June 24, 1974; Walter B., June 11, 1974; Joe R., July 21, 1974; Bernard G., June 20, 1974; Peter H., June 26, 1974; Mike M., June 24, 1974; Stephanie W., Mar. 24, 1976; Stanley N., Sept. 22, 1976; Josephine B., Mar. 3, 1976; Francis P., Jan. 16, 1976, POHP.

44. Interviews with Ignacy M., July 2, 1974; John B., Mar. 3, 1976; John K., Sept. 13, 1976; John S., Sept. 30, 1976; Stanley N., Sept. 22, 1976; Francis P., Jan. 16, 1976; Joseph B., May 13 and 20, 1976; Walter K., July 2, 1974, POHP.

45. Interviews with Francis P., Jan. 16, 1976; Stephanie W., Mar. 3, 1976; Stanley P., Nov. 11, 1976; John K., Sept. 13, 1976, POHP.

46. "Audit of International Institutes, Material on Pittsburgh Nationality Communities," Shipment 4, Box 2. Bert Gold, "Our South Side," manu-

script in the "Audit of International Institutes." See also Anthony Kuzniewski, "Bootstrap and Book Learning," *Polish-American Studies,* 22 (Autumn 1975), 5-26.

47. "South Side Survey Report, 1973," manuscript on file in Office of Planning, Catholic Diocese of Pittsburgh, and in possession of J. B. We are grateful to Sister A. Hoppul for allowing us to use this report. The entire study consisted of a sample of 7,096 Southside residents.

48. U.S. Bureau of the Census, *1970 Census of the Population, Pennsylvania* (Washington, D.C., 1972), 40-436–40-440.

49. Leonard Covello, *The Social Background of the Italo-American School Child: A Study of the Southern Italian Family Mores and Their Effect on the School Situation in Italy and America* (Leiden, 1967), 46-47, 61-63. This is a reprint of Covello's 1944 study, which was based largely on oral interviews with Italians in New York City. See also Edward C. Banfield, *The Moral Basis of a Backward Society* (Glencoe, Ill., 1958), and Phyllis H. Williams, *South Italian Folkways in Europe and America* (New Haven, Conn., 1938).

50. Virginia Yans-McLaughlin, *Family and Community: Italian Immigrants in Buffalo, 1880-1930* (Ithaca, N.Y., 1977), 26-27; Constantine Panunzio, *The Soul of An Immigrant* (New York, 1928), 76-88; Covello, *Social Background of the Italo-American Child,* 65-71; Gaetano Zingali, *Liberalismo e Fascismo mel mezzogiorno d'Italia,* 2 vols. (Milan, 1933), vol. 1, passim.

51. Cesare Correnti, *Annuario Statistico Italiano, 1854-58* (Turin, 1858), 441.

52. Williams, *South Italian Folkways,* 24-26; Robert F. Foerster, *The Italian Emigration of Our Time* (Cambridge, Mass., 1919), 139; Yans-McLaughlin, *Family and Community,* 27.

53. Williams, *Italian Folkways in Europe and America,* 25-26; Yans-McLaughlin, *Family and Community,* 33; Covello, *Social Background of the Italo-American Child,* 92.

54. Rudolph J. Vecoli, "Contadini in Chicago: A Critique of the *Uprooted*," *Journal of American History,* 51 (Dec. 1964), 407.

55. Yans-McLaughlin, *Family and Community,* 35; John W. Briggs, *An Italian Passage: Immigrants to Three American Cities, 1890-1930* (New Haven, Conn., 1977), 2-12; Foerster, *Italian Emigration,* 38-39, 529.

56. Zingali, *Liberalismo e Fascismo,* 1: iii.

57. Josef Barton, *Peasants and Strangers: Italians, Rumanians, and Slovaks to an American City* (Cambridge, Mass., 1975), 32.

58. Foerster, *Italian Emigration,* 416-20.

59. Briggs, *Italian Passage,* 7-10, 68. See also Barton, *Peasants and Strangers,* 77-78.

60. Commissariato Generale dell' Emigrazione, *Annuario Statistico della Emigrazione Italiana dal 1876-1925* (Rome, 1925), 1647-48, in Betty Boyd Caroli, *Italian Repatriation from the United States, 1900-1914* (New York, 1973), 59 (Table XXIV).

61. Interviews with Italian-Americans in Pittsburgh were conducted between 1975 and 1977. All interviews are on tape at the Pennsylvania Historical and Museum Commission. Interviews among Italians were based on the same questionnaire as those among blacks and Poles and

were conducted by Bodnar, Gregory Mihalik of the University of Pittsburgh, and Williams Simons of the State University of New York at Oneonta. While the bulk of Italian interviews were conducted in the Bloomfield section of the city, some were completed in the East Liberty area, which was heavily Sicilian.

62. Commissariato Generale dell' Emigrazione, *Bollettino dell' Emigrazione,* no. 11 (1907), 20, in Caroli, *Italian Repatriation,* 55.

63. Interviews with Nicholas R., June 23, 1977; Albina B., Mar. 19, 1977, POHP. Foerster, *Italian Emigration,* 452.

64. Salvatore Migliore, "Half-Century of Italian Immigration into Pittsburgh" (M.A. thesis, University of Pittsburgh, 1928), 20-21, 37-38.

65. Interviews with Frank D., May 19, 1977; Martin D., Mar. 15, 1977; Don C., Mar. 31, 1977, POHP.

66. Interviews with Michael M., July 16, 1977; Mary I., May 13, 1977; Frank D., May 19, 1977; Don C., Mar. 31, 1977; Vincent L., June 21, 1977; Nicholas R., June 23, 1977; Leo G., May 11, 1977; Frank A., May 16, 1977; Tom B., July 7, 1977, POHP.

67. Interviews with Albina B., Mar. 19, 1977; Domenica M., Mar. 18, 1977; Lidwina P., May 26, 1977, POHP.

3

Work and Residence

Whatever goals or traits were brought to Pittsburgh by newly arrived settlers from disparate homelands, they alone could not and would not define the course of subsequent adjustment to working-class life in the city. Premigration experience mattered greatly, but adaptation was an evolving process not subject to any one overriding variable. Whatever the past had been, two realities confronted newcomers immediately upon arrival. One could not remain in Pittsburgh long without a home or a job, and effective measures had to be devised quickly to secure both. Unfortunately for the newly arrived job seeker, the fullfilment of their immediate needs was complicated by existing arrangements in the city's occupational and residential patterns. Pittsburgh, like the rest of industrial America, was in the midst of a steady decline in its skilled trades and possessed an inadequate supply of decent low-rent dwelling units. Better paying tasks and superior residential units were made even more inaccessible by the hold earlier immigrant and native-born workers had upon them. Thus newcomers would be forced to formulate occupational and housing strategies to conform to urban realities. Again, all three groups would display similarities, but ultimately all three groups would be differentiated by important discrepancies in obtaining employment and housing.

Nowhere was the existing urban-industrial structure more unrelenting than in its hierarchy of jobs. Whatever skills had been acquired before moving to industrial America, they were of limited use in early twentieth-century cities such as Pittsburgh, where generally the skilled sectors of the work force were shrinking. This was especially true in the steel industry, where mechanization and efficiency schemes were turning most workers into what one scholar has called "machine tenders." Even with the transformation in work, however, it was not uncommon for the supply of unskilled and semiskilled workers to exceed industry's need. Companies such as the Pittsburgh Consolidated Traction Company, the Pennsylvania Railroad, and most construction firms secured help on a day-to-day basis. Individuals seeking more secure employment turned to the large, established industries, intensifying the competition for steady work and creating an inverse relationship between the flow of European immigration and black migration, a connection noted by Charles S. Johnson nearly one-half century ago.[1]

Faced with competition for a limited number of work opportunities in Pittsburgh's basic industries, migrants sought assistance where they could get it and resorted to specific strategies. Most effective was the aid provided by kin and friends. Such networks operated to inform newcomers about occupational opportunities in Pittsburgh before and after arrival in the city.

Relying on friends and relatives, Poles established occupational beachheads at the Jones and Laughlin and Oliver mills on the Southside, Heppenstalls and the Pennsylvania Railroad in Lawrenceville, and at the Armstrong Cork Company and the H. J. Heinz plant. Valentine G. gained his first job in America through his brother. Brothers also assisted Peter H. in obtaining employment in a foundry making castings for mines. Ignacy M. left Russian Poland in 1912 and relied on his brother to get him a position piling steel beams at the Jones and Laughlin plant. Joseph D. left Prussia for a job in a mill that was procured by his wife's uncle. A cousin found Edward R. work at a machine shop. John S. followed friends from Galicia in 1909, but he needed relatives to acquire machinists' work for him. Charles W. relied on a friend to transform him from a shepherd in Russian Poland to a moulder at the Crucible Steel Company. And women such as Mary K. and the mother of Francis P. relied upon relatives to help them gain access to domestic employment, working for Americans or performing boardinghouse tasks among the Poles. John K. underscored the importance of the kin network in securing work for Poles:

> Work was around ... you had the cork factory [Armstrong] here
> — you had all kinds of factories here. The only way you got a job
> [was] through somebody at work who got you in. I mean this

application, that's a big joke. They just threw them away. No matter how many ... to get a job with the railroad, my brother-in-law got it for me. My job at the hospital, my dad got it for me. I got the job at this meat place ... the boy I used to play ball with, he got it for me. So in other words, so far as your application goes, that was a big joke.[2]

Italians, similar to their Polish counterparts, inevitably relied on kin associations for providing essential contacts for jobs. If the Pittsburgh experience is any indication, the widespread notion that they relied extensively on padroné or labor agents to find employment must be modified. Older interpretations maintain that the padroné was indispensable for newcomers who failed to understand the English language. In Pittsburgh, however, in only one small area of Oakland—east of downtown—did Italian immigrants rely on labor agents for obtaining work. In almost every instance Pittsburgh Italians counted on kin and close friends to persuade foremen or other supervisors to hire them. Where a relative had already established a trade or business, a position was usually waiting.[3]

The dependence on other Italians for helping one gain an initial job in Pittsburgh was nearly total. Foremen's opinions of Italian workers were usually similar to those held toward Slavs. Contemporary stereotypes portrayed them as "docile, submissive, amenable to discipline and willing to work without a murmur."[4] Italian newcomers seldom had to explore a number of occupational alternatives but moved unimpeded into a task secured for them. Consequently, men like the father of Nicholas R. could travel back and forth between Pittsburgh and Abruzzi as often as five times, each time securing work, before deciding to remain in the "steel city" or return to his native village. Occupational and kinship networks facilitated job procurement and narrowed the employment search considerably. Thus both the father and brother of Nicholas R. relied on friends to gain employment on the railroads in 1904. When Nicholas himself arrived in America, his father asked the foreman to "give him a break." Nicholas joined his kin in laying tracks. While the father of Nicholas R. eventually returned to Italy, Antonio S. worked in the "steel city" on three different occasions before deciding to remain and reunite his entire family in Bloomfield. He was able to board and obtain work on the railroad through cousins from the same village. That Leo G. worked for the Pittsburgh Railway Company, laying stone base for street car tracks, was almost inevitable. His grandfather, father, brother, and uncle were all employed by the company. Frank D. recalled that his father agreed to house three cousins from Abruzzi and get them jobs as stone masons in 1911. Similarly, Palfilo C. came to Bloomfield in 1900, lived with his sister, and relied on a brother-in-law to find employment on a pipe-laying gang.[5]

A striking example of the ability of Italians to use kinship to thrust themselves into a particular occupational sector was the accomplishment of newcomers to the Bloomfield section from the village of Ateleta, Abruzzi. From the 1890s to the 1930s, repeated instances surfaced of men from the village bringing "paesano" to the pipe line construction department of the Equitable Gas Company. This entire process was structured around the Ateleta Beneficial Association, which provided for the "welfare and mutual assistance" of its members as well as job contacts. One of the earliest to gain work was Anthony B., a farmer in Italy, who found work with the gas company, informed several friends in Ateleta about job possibilities, and brought his wife and son to Pittsburgh. Amico L., who arrived initially in 1890, returned to Ateleta three times. Upon each return to Pittsburgh he brought a friend or relative from the village and secured work for them on the "pipe-line gang." Vincent L. came to the city around 1900 and obtained his job laying pipe through an uncle already here. After two more trips to Pittsburgh he returned to Ateleta permanently in 1911. He later sent a son who was hired by sewer contractors at the request of friends already working with the firm.[6]

It was not uncommon to find an Italian immigrant leaving his initial job after several years. Often, of course, he returned home. If he decided to remain longer, however, he frequently changed jobs because of dissatisfaction with the work or a disagreement with the foremen. Even when moving to a second job in America, he invariably could rely on kin as did Vincent L., who moved from sewer construction to the Ford Motor Company assembly plant. Frank A. left Italy and became a candy maker through the aid of a friend in 1912. Three years later he followed a cousin to a spring making shop. A final change was made shortly thereafter, when his brother-in-law helped him to find employment with the Pennsylvania Railroad. Antonio S. left his first job in America, which was with the railroad in Bloomfield, and relied on a brother-in-law to help him enter a glass factory in Jeannette, Pennsylvania. When the glass works closed, cousins provided board and job contacts with the railroad, enabling him to return to Bloomfield.[7]

Blacks, like the Poles and Italians, successfully employed kinship and friendship ties in migrating northward. These devices, however, were considerably less effective in helping the newly arrived acquire industrial jobs. This is not to say that blacks were completely unable to aid each other in getting work with various firms or wealthy families. The Pittsburgh Survey described an exceptional cluster of black steel-workers at the Clark Mills of the Carnegie Steel Company. This group had worked as hod carriers or on the railroad before coming to Pittsburgh. That over 61 percent of the group was from Virginia suggested the existence of a form of chain migration. Nevertheless, these examples were far from pervasive, primarily because of the attitudes of white foremen, usually of native or old immigrant stock, who were the key contact in gaining industrial employment. Nearly every investigation of early twentieth-century Pittsburgh, in fact, depicted the stereotypical outlooks of these influential men. Southern-born blacks were particularly disliked because they were thought to be "inefficient, unsuitable, and unstable" for the heavy pace of mill work. By contrast Slavs were preferred because of their assumed docility and "habit of silent submission, their amenability to discipline, and their willingness to work long hours and overtime without a murmur." One foreman, interviewed by the Pittsburgh Survey, commented, "Give [Slavs] rye bread, a herring, and a beer and they are all right." Whether any validity could be attached to these views is not as important as their existence. Both immigrants and blacks were the objects of a condescending racism, but Slavs and even Italians benefited from such views by being allowed to enter the expanding industrial sectors of the city's economy and to bring their friends and relatives with them. By 1910 busy foremen were relying almost totally on white ethnic networks to meet their demands for laborers and factory operatives.[8]

Oral testimony underscored the inability of blacks to overcome racial barriers and rely on kin in obtaining industrial employment and the necessity of seeking jobs on their own over a wide area. Leroy M. correctly recalled that Jones and Laughlin hired few black men, while Jasper M. complained that Frank and Seder's and other department stores prohibited blacks from sales positions. "At that time," he noted, "black people couldn't think about waiting on no customers or things like that. The biggest we could do was porter work and run the elevators, that's all."[9] Ben E. followed his father to a coal mine and, after six months, decided to move to Pittsburgh. Although he had friends in the city, he was forced to find work on his own as a limestone loader at the American Steel and Wire Company. When work was slack, he successively obtained employment for himself in a Kentucky coal mine and, after returning to the city, at the Jones and Laughlin plant's boiler department. His experience was not unique. Jean B. simply persisted in talking a foreman into hiring him on a labor gang.

Some started businesses of their own. Gertrude D. testified that her husband began by contracting his own work as a plasterer. Another migrant hired himself out to contractors as a cement finisher, wallpaper hanger, and plasterer. Floyd T. started a small trucking and hauling concern with his brother. Hezikiah M.'s brother opened a small print shop.[10]

Without other means of assistance black migrants developed strategies for dealing with white foremen, the key person in hiring new labor, which frequently included boastful claims of work abilities. Harrison G. left Georgia for Pittsburgh and encountered a long line of potential employees at the Jones and Laughlin plant. When his turn arrived, he told the foreman he could perform better than anyone else. Harrison explained that such boasting was part of his "strategy" for getting a job. Other blacks promised potential employers that they would "play it straight and go home when the job was done," "stay out of mischief," and "remain on the job for a long time." Forced to project himself as an individual, James N. approached prospective employers and asserted he was "a good man whom the company could use." Ernest F. received no assistance at all in obtaining a job in a brick plant; he simply approached the foreman on his own. Harrison G. secured a position at a Southside plant by showing a foreman he could load scrap even faster than a "bunch of hunkies."[11] Certainly this analysis casts doubt upon the interpretation that black migrants were "idle loafers" who sought "easy money."[12]

The combination of differences in their premigration experiences and the ability or inability of kin to assist in securing work produced dramatically different work experiences for incoming Poles, blacks, and Italians. Polish workers, for example, clustered in a single industry — metal production. Italians clustered in a variety of occupations, and blacks were widely distributed throughout the blue-collar occupational spectrum (Table 3).

The inability of blacks to establish occupational networks in the steel industry was apparent. Only 1.6 percent of southern-born blacks and 10.8 percent of those born in the North held jobs in the metal industries. The greater proportion of northern-born blacks in the metal industry is no doubt related to their longevity in the city. Many were born and raised in Pittsburgh, but even this advantage was slight, as only 507 blacks were found among the 19,686 men working in Pittsburgh's blast furnaces and rolling mills. This disparity continued for the next decade. A survey of industrial plants conducted in 1917 revealed that, except for the Carnegie and Jones and Laughlin plants, sixteen major metal firms in Pittsburgh employed a total of 425 black

Table 3. Industrial Employment by Ethnicity in Pittsburgh, 1900

Industry	Black Southern-Born	Black Northern-Born	Russian	Austrian	German	Italian
Labor	24.1	39.9	54.8	42.4	34.8	60.9
Apparel	2.6	....	1.2	....	....	6.3
Metal	1.6	10.8	19.1	47.5	43.7	2.0
Food production	3.7	2.0	....	....	....	2.7
Construction	2.3	2.6	1.6	2.0	2.6	6.3
Commerce	1.6	1.4	4.2	....	4.1	6.5
Transportation	17.9	12.3	3.6	4.0	2.6	6.9
Public service	17.9	7.2	0.6	1.0	1.5	1.2
Domestic service	18.3	11.0	0.5	....	0.7	0.8
Miscellaneous	10.0	12.8	14.4	3.1	10.0	6.4
N	264	1,134	560	99	289	507

(Header spans: "Black" over Southern-Born and Northern-Born; "Pole" over Russian, Austrian, German)

SOURCE: A 20 percent sample of black, Italian, and Polish families derived from the Manuscript Census for Pittsburgh, 1900 (U.S. Bureau of the Census). All data are given as percentages and include only adult males. Dots = no record of employment in that category.

workers.[13] The self-reliance required by blacks in securing jobs is clearly reflected in their wide distribution in a variety of occupational categories. Nearly four of ten held general laboring positions such as hod carrier, janitor, or day laborer. A substantial number also found jobs in public service (barber, waiter, hairdresser) and in transportation (teamster, draymen). The number in transportation grew so rapidly that by 1903 fully half of the city's teamsters were black.[14] A small group of forty blacks worked as patrolmen on the city police force. Others found work in domestic service (porter, servant, gardener), and by 1910 nearly one-third of all the city's black males were employed in this category.[15] Few, however, held white-collar positions. Of the nearly 10,000 clerks in the city, only 87 were black. Not surprisingly, a federal survey several years later noted that blacks in Pittsburgh were distributed among "a variety of occupational enclaves." The report mentioned "hundreds" of blacks in business as printers, grocers, hairdressers, and restaurant owners as well as those in transportation, domestic service, and construction.[16] One contemporary observer even thought such variety was encouraging and a sign of advancement.[17] Contrasting signs, however, rest on the inability of black migrants to secure work in the metal industries. Exclusion from steel production in Pittsburgh was characteristic of the general exclusion of blacks from industrial occupations throughout the North. In New York City, for example, less than 15 percent of the black male population held jobs in manufacturing.[18] Similar situations prevailed in other northern industrial cities. Detroit's auto industry employed only 17 blacks in 1910.[19] In Boston even third-generation blacks clustered disproportionately in nonmanufacturing occupations, while fewer than 10 percent of the black population held industrial jobs in Chicago.[20] Thus while a considerable number of blacks migrated to the industrial North, few could take advantage of the wide variety of manufacturing occupations. Prior to 1915 both the recent black migrants and those born in the North were excluded from the opportunities industrial America had to offer.

Poles, in contrast to blacks, were clearly able to funnel their incoming migrants into metal production. Nearly one-half of the Austrian- and German-born Poles were recorded as metal workers by the 1900 census. In addition, many of those listed as laborers also worked in the metal industry. While it is difficult to document, other sources and the oral interviews suggest that perhaps as many as two-thirds of Pittsburgh's Poles worked in the iron and steel industry.

The ethnic occupational network operated selectively, not only securing work in specific mills in the city but also laboring positions within certain departments inside the mill. The Pittsburgh Survey, for example, reported entire construction shops staffed by Italians, blast furnaces by Poles, and Slovenians on the open-hearth floor. Most departments, according to Joe R., a Polish immigrant, were dominated by particular national groups. "You take in the erection department — it was the hardest and noisiest and everything. — It was mostly all Slavs . . . Not Slovaks, it was Polish. . . . We didn't have Lithuanians there and the Russians were not involved there." Joe R. explained how the process operated. "Now if a Russian got his job in a shear department . . . he's looking for a buddy, a Russian buddy. He's not going to look for a Croatian buddy. And if he see the boss looking for a man he says, 'Look, I have a good man,' and he's picking out his friends. A Ukrainian department, a Russian department, a Polish department. And it was a beautiful thing in a way."[21]

Italians were equally as successful as Poles in securing blue-collar work upon their arrival in the city. The results, however, were different. As noted earlier, Italians coming to Pittsburgh had considerable experience in nonagricultural and skilled blue-collar work. These experiences enabled them to secure work in a variety of occupations while the successful operation of the kin network at the same time funneled Italian workers into clusters within certain industries. Nearly 60 percent of all adult male Italians were classified as laborers in the 1900 census. Oral interviews and the Pittsburgh Survey of 1907 uncovered several distinct groupings of Italian day laborers. Italians in the steel industry dominated the carpentry, repair, and rail shops. Others worked on the Italian construction gangs of the Equitable Gas Company, the Pittsburgh Railways, or the city of Pittsburgh. Many worked for the Pennsylvania Railroad despite the low wages — 13.5 cents per hour — paid by that company.[22] Michael M., a resident of Pittsburgh's Strip District, told of boarding the Pennsylvania Railroad car at 5:00 A.M. each day to travel to the city's East End for work on the railroad section gang. "By the time we arrived at the job the train was filled with Italian workers."[23] When the city of Pittsburgh constructed its filtration plant in 1905, most of those employed as diggers and hod carriers were Italians.[24]

Italian-born workers, particularly those living in the East Liberty section of the city, also clustered in four other industrial classifications. Approximately one-fourth of all Italian workers held jobs in construction, apparel, commerce, or transportation by 1900.

Poles and Italians who arrived in Pittsburgh at the turn of the century apparently held several advantages over their black southern-born counterparts. They received the valuable assistance of kin and friends in securing their initial job in the city. They also worked side by side with their brothers, fathers, or friends during the most crucial period of adjustment. These contacts, no doubt, assisted the immigrant, providing a sheltered apprenticeship as he became acclimated to drastically new work and living environments. Blacks, on the other hand, were forced to seek work on their own and often endured substantial periods of unemployment before securing their initial job. The work they did find, moreover, often denied them the extended work associations enjoyed by the Poles and Italians. Blacks most often worked alone or in small groups. They received little assistance in adjusting to the demands of new occupations. Thus, while they arrived in the city at the same time and in much the same manner as did immigrant workers, they would begin their working careers one step behind.

The ability of immigrant groups to channel their kin into particular industries or the rapidity with which these positions were secured, of course, provided no guarantee of easy or rewarding work. Excluding the northern-born blacks, most of whom were born and raised in Pittsburgh, more than half of each group of workers in Table 4 held unskilled jobs.

In 1907 the authors of the Pittsburgh Survey characterized the immigrants in Pittsburgh as "the hewers of wood and drawers of water . . . the bulk of the unskilled labor in the city — the digging and carry-

Table 4. Vertical Occupational Structure of Selected Adult Male Workers
in Pittsburgh, 1900

| | Black | | Pole | | | | |
Category of Job	Northern-Born	Southern-Born	Russian	Austrian	German	Italian	Entire City
Unskilled	38.6	58.5	86.8	90.0	81.0	72.2	32.2
Semiskilled	43.2	28.9	3.2	2.2	5.5	3.2	24.0
Skilled	14.7	9.8	6.4	4.4	9.0	22.7	19.4
Low white collar	3.0	1.0	3.0	2.2	4.4	1.9	17.9
High white collar	0	0	0	0	0	0	6.5
N	264	1,134	560	99	289	507	107,902

SOURCE: A 20 percent study sample derived from the Manuscript Census for Pittsburgh, 1900 (U.S. Bureau of the Census). Data are given as percentages.

ing in the street, the heavy labor in the mill, the loading and unloading of raw material on railroad and river, the rough work at forge and foundry . . . is performed by them."[25] Recent data from the 1900 census reveal the essential correctness of that conclusion. Polish immigrants, in particular, obviously went from one kind of menial labor in Europe to another type in Pittsburgh. Nearly nine of every ten Austrian- or Russian-born immigrants performed unskilled work in Pittsburgh in 1900. The one exception was a small proportion of German-born Poles who managed to secure skilled or low white-collar occupations. Italians also performed unskilled labor (72 percent), although as noted above they clustered in different industrial groups than did Poles. In addition, more than one-fifth were able to take advantage of their prior training to secure craft positions in Pittsburgh.

Black workers generally fell between the two immigrant groups with clusters in all three blue-collar classifications. Their occupational class distribution clearly reflects their wide dispersion among several industrial groups. Black overrepresentation at the semiskilled level, however, largely reflects the type of occupation in which they engaged and represented no real difference in status or income. The city's 1,500 black teamsters, for example, worked ten-plus hours per day, six days per week. They normally received $10 per week, slightly less than unskilled steel workers. In addition, they seldom received overtime pay. Steel workers, conversely, could usually depend on several hours of overtime pay per week. The semiskilled occupations of the black workers may have provided better working conditions than mill work — relatively clean air and a measure of independence — but they proved only slightly more satisfying. If one combines both unskilled and semiskilled classifications, the distribution of blacks more nearly resembles those of the Poles, with more than four-fifths clustered at the bottom of the occupational hierarchy.

A small proportion of black workers (between 10 and 15 percent) did manage to secure skilled jobs, mainly in construction or the service trades such as barbering, printing, and shoe repair. By 1910, 244 black workers held skilled positions as carpenters, masons, painters, and paperhangers. The majority of these occupations, the Pittsburgh Survey reported, were provided by small entrepreneur–operated businesses and usually served the black community or provided household services to affluent whites.[26] Northern-born blacks were slightly better off than their southern-born counterparts. The differences, however, were marginal, with only 5 percent more in skilled work and a 1 percent increase in white-collar occupations. Stephan Thernstrom noted a similar miniscule difference among first- and second-generation blacks in Boston. He concluded that for blacks, the length of stay in the community held little significance.[27] While our northern-born group contains both first- and second-generation Pittsburghers, the evidence points toward a similar conclusion.

It was originally suspected that the ages of workers may have had an impact on job procurement, but this was not the case. Age had only a marginal effect on the level of skill of those within each sample group. While older workers in each ethnic group tended to hold slightly better jobs than their younger counterparts, none of the differences was statistically significant. A Polish worker in his twenties, for example, was neither more nor less likely to hold a particular job than those in any other age group claiming the same birthplace. Only among the unemployed did age seem to make a difference. The proportion of unemployed increased in each age cohort from 2 percent of those in their twenties and thirties to 10 to 21 percent of those in their fifties and sixties. The reasons for this increase in employment for aging workers are not clear, but it seems reasonable to speculate that the arduous nature of occupations in Pittsburgh had a negative effect on older workers. Advancing age brought a decline in health and strength. Few workers in their fifties and sixties could withstand the long twelve-hour day or the "long turn" of twenty-four hours required every two weeks of those in the Pittsburgh steel mills.

Time of migration, however, did seem to influence occupational differences among the various Polish groups. On the average, Poles from Prussia arrived in America six years before the Russian Poles and eight years before those from Austrian territory. Moreover, fully one-third arrived before 1885. This group had been in Pittsburgh for at least fifteen years by the 1900 census. Their ability to secure better

occupations no doubt contributed to their longevity in the community.
A number of the less successful may have already left the community,
thus presenting a slightly biased sample. The dominance of the German Polish in the higher level occupations nevertheless suggests that
their Pittsburgh experience would be somewhat different from the
other European-born migrants.

Poles, blacks, and Italians all nurtured strong kinship associations
before moving to the "steel city," and many had worked in nonagricultural pursuits. The premigration employment of Poles and blacks,
moreover, usually consisted of jobs as unskilled or semiskilled laborers.
While some were able to acquire skills such as carpentry or tailoring,
they were fewer in number and were seldom able to use those trades
in Pittsburgh. This, of course, should prove no surprise, since even immigrants who came to America with artisan or industrial skills had
little choice but to abandon their old trades. Labor historian David
Montgomery points out, for example, that the number of immigrants
engaged as shoemakers, curriers, blacksmiths, bookbinders, and cabi-
netmakers declined in America from 1900 to 1910. The immigrant
population, at the same time, increased dramatically.[28]

The experience of Italians in Pittsburgh, however, suggests that if a
migrant group did possess skills in a particular profession in sufficient
numbers, it was possible that they could gain a modest foothold as
craftsmen in specific areas of the city's occupational spectrum. Nearly
one-fourth of the Italian migrants to Pittsburgh held skilled occupations by 1900. An earlier analysis of economic backgrounds had revealed that Italians tended to seek out supplemental skills in the
Mezzogiorno because of lessening opportunities in agriculture. Interviews with Pittsburgh's Italians uncovered the extensive familiarity
these newcomers had with nonagricultural skills such as shoemaking
or stonecutting. In fact, nearly one-half of all Italian immigrants identified in the interviews worked in such endeavors prior to their arrival
in America. Guiseppe D., before he came to Pittsburgh in 1889, was a
stone mason. The brother of Domenica M. was a shoemaker; Domenica
herself was encouraged by her mother while still in Abruzzi to attend
a school that taught embroidery. Charles D., who was born in Abruzzi
in 1884, studied tailoring as an apprentice before coming to Pittsburgh. Vincent K. recalled that in his village of Ateleta the number
of young men learning building trades increased after the onset of
emigration. Migrants who returned from America, Switzerland, and
Germany used their earnings to expand their homes and consequently
created a growing demand for construction skills. Frank A. testified
that a number of young men in his village learned to be bricklayers,

stonecutters, and tailors so they could find suitable employment in Italian cities. An early historian of Pittsburgh's Italians, Salvatore Migliore, noticed in a 1928 study that a "good percentage of the peasants knew some kind of trade." He estimated at least one-third were stonecutters, mechanics, mariners, masons, barbers, seamstresses, and shoemakers.[29]

Italians were frequently able to implement this Old World familiarity with skills in the "steel city." To an extent even greater than Poles, they were able to move beyond a reliance on kinship and to use their skills to earn a living. Unlike blacks, they enjoyed the advantages of being able to rely both on kinship and skills. The father of Michael M., for instance, was a "commercial fisherman" in Sicily before coming to Pittsburgh in 1904. Shortly after arriving in the city, he put his commercial experience to work. Because it cost him nearly as much to buy two pairs of work gloves as he earned in a week at a Pittsburgh glass factory, he quit, purchased a cart, and began selling fruits and vegetables. Nicholas R. and his brother received training as shoemakers in Italy and then established a shop in the "steel city." Similarly Ray L. was sent to Rome from his native Palermo as a boy to learn barbering. Both he and an uncle opened barber shops in western Pennsylvania before 1918. Martin T. affirmed that his father became a chef in this country because he had learned such a skill in Italy.[30]

The largest concentration of Italian workers was in the construction trades. Although the clustering resulted partially from kinship and ethnic ties, premigration skills were again a factor. Migliore found thirty-eight Italian building contractors, fourteen cement contractors, and six marble-cutting establishments, all of whom employed mostly Italians with skills such as bricklaying and stonecutting that were learned in Italy. Frank D. indicated that his father was a blacksmith in Italy and was consequently hired by an American contractor to make steel forms. In turn his father was responsible for bringing twenty additional Italian stonecutters into the same company, an accomplishment that further strengthened Italian representation in the construction industry.[31]

The ability of Italians to rely on kinship and previous skills in acquiring jobs modifies recent interpretations of Italian immigrant workers, which had argued that they gravitated mainly toward outdoor occupations because of their Old World familiarity with casual, outdoor employment and work rhythms that were of a seasonal nature. Historian Virginia Yans-McLaughlin, who found Italians predominating in building construction in Buffalo as they did in Pittsburgh, reveals that Italians had supplemented their agricultural em-

ployment by wages earned in fishing or construction in Italy. To claim
that they attempted to replicate their seasonal pattern in America,
however, is to mitigate the intense pressure they were under to use
any available resource, whether it be kin or skills, to secure occupational footholds in the competitive atmosphere of the city.[32] If studies
which suggest that Italians had definite rising expectations are valid,
moreover, it would be logical to expect them to pursue the higher occupations. In Pittsburgh, outdoor skilled laborers such as stone masons,
bricklayers, cement finishers, and slate and tile roofers earned between
30 and 40 cents an hour more than inside workers, such as Poles, in
the Pennsylvania Railroad shops or other factories and foundries.[33]

Thus far we have examined the occupational roles of adult males
among the three groups under consideration. Working-class adult
females in Pittsburgh often worked longer, under equally difficult
conditions, and perhaps harder than their husbands and sons. Their
work in Pittsburgh, however, was usually confined to the home and
will be examined in chapter 4. Their male counterparts, with the
slight exceptions recorded by the German-Poles, Italian tailors, and
those in the building trades, regardless of age, in 1900 dominated the
lowest two levels on the occupational strata. Black workers generally
moved into unskilled and semiskilled service and transportation industries while the immigrants went overwhelmingly into the metal industries. The great majority of all groups, however, began their work
careers in Pittsburgh in the lowest level occupations.

Simultaneous with the process of obtaining work was the problem
of securing a place to live. Both were immediate matters that could
not be deferred and were quite closely interrelated. Again, new industrial workers had to transcend their previous experiences and deal
with existing structures, including a shortage of suitable housing and
the necessity of living within some degree of proximity to the workplace and necessary services. Thus neighborhood development in
Pittsburgh, as in most American cities, resulted from a combination of
free choice, economic necessity, and social pressure and exclusion.
Each of the groups in this study arrived in Pittsburgh under somewhat
similar circumstances and faced several common conditions. They all
lacked money and were in search of a job. They all entered a rapidly
growing city, in which the number of well-paying occupations was
scarce. Finally, housing of all types, but particularly affordable housing
convenient to low-cost public transportation, was also scarce. Under
these common conditions, and barring other noneconomic concerns,
one might expect to find the three groups scattering in all directions

throughout the city, and to some extent they did. All three groups were located in nearly every ward in the city in 1900. Most, however, settled in a small number of already established settlements. Major clusters of Poles could be found in the Strip District, Polish Hill, and Lawrenceville sections, and on the Southside of the city. Significant numbers of both blacks and Italians lived in the Strip District, the lower hill, and East Liberty sections of the city. Black workers also resided in the upper hill, while Italians established the foundations of a community in the 8th ward, Bloomfield district, and in the McKees Rocks section, just west of the city (see the map in chapter 1). The explanation for these settlements lies in a complex set of interrelated social, economic, and historical forces.

The communication networks that brought migrants to Pittsburgh did not end at the city limits. Newcomers most often resided for a short time with those responsible for their migration to the city. They usually established their own residence in the same neighborhood. Thus, as the flow of immigrants to the "steel city" swelled, clusters began to develop around the area of initial settlement. Russian- and German-born Poles and a small number of southern-born blacks and Italians, for example, settled in the Strip District flood plain, along the Allegheny River, in the early 1860s and 1870s. Located along a major transportation route and housing both heavy industrial and commercial enterprises, the area became a prime attraction for blue-collar workers. These early settlers in turn attracted others in substantial numbers. By the end of the century major settlements of Russian- and German-born Poles clustered along the district's main arteries, Liberty and Penn avenues. The small proportion of Italians and blacks and the complete absence of Austrian Poles in the area demonstrated the importance and strength of the communication network on settlement patterns. Austrian Poles did not arrive in Pittsburgh in significant numbers until the 1890s. Without relatives or friends to attract them to the Strip District, they settled in other areas of the city. The small Italian and black clusters grew somewhat by the end of the century, but other important settlements throughout the city proved more attractive. With few of their friends and relatives to induce them to settle in the 2nd ward, they generally ignored the area.

The competition for available space and the cost of available housing also influenced the patterns of ethnic distribution across the landscape. Industrial and commercial firms, such as those located in the Strip, already controlled a large portion of Pittsburgh's most desirable land. Their growing need for space, moreover, inflated land and housing costs and prevented any further growth of the area as a residential neighborhood.

Pittsburgh natives and descendants of earlier inhabitants also dominated other valuable territories. Poles, blacks, and Italians, among the poorest and least desired immigrants, received the least desirable land — that with the highest density, that with the oldest and most deteriorated housing, or that located on the most formidable terrain. The settlement of large numbers of immigrants in these areas usually exacerbated these difficult conditions. As ethnic newcomers arrived, the land became even less desirable to others in the city. Sensational new articles headlined "Like to have a Darky Neighbor?" or "Italians Engage in Vicious Encounter" clearly contributed to the existing fears and prejudices in Pittsburgh.[34] A *Pittsburgh Leader* series on Pittsburgh's political wards described an Italian section as filled with "throngs of greasy, unkempt Italians standing around in front of crazy little grocery stores, jabbering or smoking, while slovenly women with filthy youngsters sit on steps or parade up and down in the street strewn with old vegetables, filthy water, and rubbish of all kinds."[35] Of the black neighborhood, Hayti [sic], the *Leader* was kinder, concluding that it contains mostly "good negroes . . . although the moral tone of the ward is not above reproach."[36]

Native-born inhabitants, obviously sharing the perceptions of the city's leading newspaper, rapidly abandoned their former neighborhoods to the incoming group. As late as 1887 more than 300 professional workers resided in the 5th ward, the Hill District area, including seventy-seven engineers, forty-three attorneys, thirty-two doctors, three bank presidents, and two judges. By 1900 the number had declined to less than fifty.[37] The decline of native-born residents at the same time from 60 to 10 percent of the 3rd ward's total population typified the ethnic succession.[38]

The importance of the journey-to-work on residential patterns has been demonstrated by several historians.[39] Blue-collar workers, lacking the time or money to use public transportation, walked to work for some time after the introduction of the street railway. In Pittsburgh a majority lived within two miles of their place of employment and continued to walk to work as late as 1917.[40] Thus, while several of the Polish, black, and Italian communities developed near important transportation lines, the location of work rather than the availability of public transportation influenced the location of these communities.

Equally as important as the location of work on residential patterns was the type of work in which one engaged. Nearly 60 percent of the

Poles sampled from the 1900 census lived within one mile of the ten steel firms located along the Allegheny River. An additional 31 percent settled in the Southside within a mile of the Jones and Laughlin and the Oliver Iron and Steel mills.[41] The need and desire of Pittsburgh's Poles to live as close as possible to work was clearly expressed by John B.: "No one wanted to spend time commuting after 12 or 13 hours in the shop. All you wanted to do was go home and collapse."[42]

Not all of the work performed by the newcomers to Pittsburgh, however, was concentrated in the steel industry. Italian workers, as noted earlier, held jobs in construction, street paving, laying gas pipe lines or railroad track, or as independent artisans and small merchants. Pittsburgh's blacks were employed in an even greater variety of unskilled and semiskilled occupations. The job sites of both groups consequently were more diffuse than those of the Polish workers. Nevertheless, both groups formed residential clusters, although the pattern and motivation for the location of the clusters differed.

Nearly two-thirds of the blacks sampled settled near the central city (wards 3 and 5), near their predecessors, and within easy access to work in all parts of the city. The casual and often temporary labor they performed required maximal mobility in the frequent search for work. Since many performed service jobs or worked as drivers, they chose residential sites near the center of the greatest population concentration to ease the selling of their services.

The heavy concentration of blacks in the city's Hill District, however, did not result in the creation of an isolated ghetto. Black clusters around Fulton, Crawford, Wylie, Clark, and Center streets were interspersed with sections of Russian Jews, Italians, Syrians, Hungarians, and a few Germans and Irish remaining from earlier days. The number of foreign-born whites exceeded black residents in the 3rd ward by more than 5,000. The *Pittsburgh Leader* proclaimed the section the most cosmopolitan in the city, noting "were a section of the great East Side of New York transplanted bodily into the populous district bounded by Franklin, Logan and Fulton Streets that territory could not be a more typical and vari-colored neighborhood."[43] By 1910 Russian Jews had built seven synagogues and converted four Christian churches into orthodox houses of worship. Greeks, Syrians, and Italians also created specialized business districts in the area. Italians who settled in Pittsburgh's central city were apparently motivated by the same factors that influenced black residents. Italian tailors, carpenters, shoemakers, and peddlers all benefited by their location near the center of population. By 1900 one-fifth of the Italian immigrants still lived in the Strip and Hill districts, justifying the press's characterization of the area along Webster and Washington streets as "Little Italy."

Occupational availability also influenced the location of Italian communities in Bloomfield and East Liberty, although less directly than either the Polish or the black community. Many of the activities associated with city building – laying streets, pipelines, railroad tracks – moved east beyond the central city limits. Italians originally commuted to these jobs. By 1900, however, they began to populate the former German section of Bloomfield. One six-block area south of Liberty Avenue was nearly equally divided between German and Italian residents by 1900. Twenty years later it housed Italians exclusively.[44] Other Italians (25 percent of the sample), many of them independent artisans or truck farmers, settled even further out of the city in the 11th and 12th wards, where land was abundant. They were followed in 1905 by a group of construction laborers employed by the city to build its new filtration plant. This East Liberty community eventually became the largest Italian settlement in the city.

That the location of available work directly influenced the placement of blue-collar communities across the cityscape is abundantly clear. Also obvious is that as particular ethnic groups performed certain work, they would locate near or with other groups performing similar work and away from those with different occupations. The density and homogeneity of each ethnic cluster and its durability, however, cannot be explained solely in terms of work. One historian recently argued that southern and eastern European groups in America were simply "doing what came naturally." Indeed, she argued that they would have created clusters without the economic and occupational considerations previously discussed. This need to cluster, she concluded, derived from "the social imperatives of their [premigration] cultural systems."[45] While accurate, this need to cluster is only part of the explanation.

Both the Italian and Polish groups lived in villages before their departure for America and all three groups used a network to carry them to Pittsburgh. They no doubt wished to re-create, to a degree, the premigration village. But they did more than replicate an Old World pattern. They transformed it, creating new institutions and relationships. The ethnic communities in Pittsburgh contained parts of the Old World village, but they were not mirror-images. The longevity of the ethnic community in the face of the incredible transiency of its residents and its increasing homogeneity over three decades suggest that its strength may lie in the special services it performed and the loyalties it fostered.

First and foremost, migrants to the city realized that adjustments would be required to survive in urban America. Most, in fact, had already made important adjustments in their lives before coming to Pittsburgh. Long absences from home and the transition from agriculture to industrial work and from rural to urban life all demanded important changes. Many also realized that proximity to members of their same group would facilitate an easier adjustment to an alien culture. Earlier arrivals, as we have observed, helped other Poles and Italians secure steady work. Blacks, while not as effective in job procurement, may have been helpful in suggesting where other blacks might find work. Kin and friends who preceded one might also provide advice in matters such as dealing with public officials, locating housing, or traveling about the city. Indeed, one required immediate assistance in all matters dealing with outsiders. Viewing the development of ethnic communities in this manner demonstrates the interaction between the individual, his premigration culture, and the urban society to which he migrated. "The cities," Stanley Lieberson argued in his earlier comparison of ethnic patterns in ten American cities, "were in existence with their patterns of housing and commercial establishments before each wave of immigrants arrived during the great era of foreign migration to our cities. Into this pattern or structure of the city came each group of immigrants and, whatever else they might do in the city, they had to adapt to its structure and order."[46] The development of ethnic clusters, Lieberson concluded, "may be viewed as a form of adaptation" to an already existing situation.[47]

The importance of the ethnic community in assisting newcomers explains its initial attractiveness and cannot be overemphasized. The longevity of ethnic communities in Pittsburgh and probably other American cities, however, is due to both the shared experiences of members of the group and the development of institutions and organizations that could provide long-term services.

By the turn of the century community development was under way in the Polish and Italian neighborhoods and in the black neighborhood (Hill District). Inevitably fraternal associations were created first, followed by the building of churches. Each fostered loyalties that provided the foundation for lasting communities. The ethnic church protected one's family and preserved one's culture in a foreign society. It preserved the language and educated children. It baptized, married, and buried church members. It also performed a myriad of social functions — from charitable fund raising to parish picnics at Kennywood Park, from musical concerts to discussions on discrimination

and housing. It provided valuable information to parishioners and
assisted young and old in the adjustment to the urban industrial environment.[48] The building of a church usually symbolized a group's
intention to settle in an area. The erection of a church and the estab-
lishment of fraternal groups were almost always the first organized
actions in the community, demonstrating their importance to the people. By the time any of the groups under investigation had a few
hundred inhabitants in the city, they had a church and often a fraternal association meetinghouse.[49]

In 1850 Pittsburgh contained approximately 2,500 black residents;
the Hill District probably had less than 1,000. Yet two black churches,
the AME (African Methodist Episcopal) Bethel on the corner of Wylie
and Elm and the AME Zion at 40 Arthur, already existed within a
dozen blocks of each other. The role of these early black churches
paralleled that played by the ethnic church several decades later.
Serving as a kind of settlement house and social club, they enabled
migrants to meet new friends, to seek employment, or to build a
following for one's profession.[50] During the next three decades, as the
number of Hill District blacks expanded to 8,300, a dozen new black
churches were erected in the area. By 1900 there were fourteen black
churches in the Hill District, a number that represents 50 percent of
the black churches in Pittsburgh. This profusion of churches reflected
the relative autonomy of the black church in America. It also likely
reflects a class hierarchy within the black community. The black
church in Pittsburgh was, as Kenneth Kusmer suggested for Cleveland,
"the most important indicator of status in the black community."[51] As
the black neighborhood developed, a social class system also developed. Several churches by 1900 were recognized as elite institutions
by both the black and white populations of the city. The Reverend
George Howard of the Ebenezer Baptist Church, for example, advised
on matters of civic importance and served as the black representative
on several citywide boards. Between 1896 and 1900 his parishioners
contributed $16,000 towards the upkeep of the church and $4,000 annually for the pastor's salary.[52] The Grace Methodist Memorial Presbyterian Church, an offshoot of an earlier integrated but predominantly
white church, and the AME church at Fulton and Clark also attracted
the older, more affluent residents of the city.

Black churches sponsored a variety of organizations and services, in
addition to attending to the religious needs of their patrons. The AME
Zion Church, for example, sponsored a youth organization for the
children of working women; meetings of the Epworth League were
held at the Warren Methodist Episcopalian Church; the AME Bethel

sponsored the Arnett Literary Society, and St. Benedict's provided a
school and raised funds for a variety of black charities.[53] Frequent
debates such as the one by the pastors of two black congregations,
"The Power of Electricity Versus Steam," supplied intellectual stimulation, while strawberry and ice cream festivals complete with instru-
mental performances provided a meeting place for young men and
women.[54]

Church leaders, mindful of their status in the community, also
attempted to provide an element of social control. Speaking from the
pulpit or through the press, black ministers denounced dancing,
drinking, and other forms of "sin" while calling for moderation,
promptness, and hard work. Racial discrimination would cease, one
black minister claimed, when blacks acquire "morals, mind, and man-
ners."[55] Following a series of racial disturbances in the South, the
Pittsburgh black ministry counseled its members that "the act of one
vicious Negro may entail speedy retribution on the entire race in this
vicinity. What are we going to do about it? It calls for calm and
considerate judgment for the end is not in sight. Mass meetings and
resolutions will not prevent it. . . . Avoid crowds and avoid street discussions."[56] Ministers were also quick to condemn prostitution, gam-
bling, and other vices as destructive elements in the community.

The black church in Pittsburgh permeated all facets of black life.
Religious services such as baptisms and weddings and the celebrations
that followed occurred there. Education, occupational and charitable
assistance, and social functions all took place in the church. It provided the lone all-black refuge in a white world. (Even in the black
neighborhoods whites outnumbered blacks.) An earlier study of the
migration patterns of Pittsburgh blacks demonstrated the close relationship between the church and the community. As blacks moved to
new areas, they "moved the old church or started a second new one
nearer to the area of second settlement."[57] The black church continued
to play an important role in the black community well into the twentieth century.

The Polish and Italian churches also facilitated the creation of communities by providing needed services and serving as a focal point
for their groups. The rapidity with which each group built impressive,
expensive structures, in spite of a weak economic position, attests to
the importance of the church in their lives. The churches and church
leaders, in turn, influenced the lives of most community residents.

The first Poles began arriving in Pittsburgh around 1870. During
the next five years they donated their services, time, and in some cases
money to erect a small chapel, St. Stanislaus, at 21st and Smallman

streets in the Strip District. Immediately after its completion they began to plan for a new, larger church to meet the needs of a rapidly growing Polish population. By 1891 this community of largely un- skilled blue-collar workers managed to replace the old structure with an impressive $100,000 Romanesque-style building. They erected a $41,000 school designed to house 900 students about the same time and built a parish house (twenty-three rooms) for $70,000 in 1900.

During the first decade of the twentieth century, Poles established settlements further east and on the Southside, and church construction again followed rapidly. Two wooden structures, St. Adalbert's (1890) and St. Josaphat's (1902), were erected to serve the Southside Polish community. The St. Josaphat parishioners built a new more elaborate structure just fourteen years later. Whatever sacrifices were required of the residents of each community, however, had just begun. Schools, social halls, and eventually new church buildings were erected in each community over the next decade and a half.[58]

Workers settling on Polish Hill took even less time to build a church than their Southside counterparts. In 1895 Polish families moved into the relatively unsettled 138-acre piece of land later known as Polish Hill. The sharp grade of the slope had deterred building, and less than a dozen homes existed on the hill. During the next decade they built or rented homes along Brereton, Phelan, and Paulowna streets. Homebuilding and the rigors of their work, however, could not deter them from the process of church-building. Within ten years of their arrival on the hill, they erected an imposing structure, the Immaculate Heart of Mary Church, on a choice fourteen-lot parcel in the area. The size of the church dwarfed the residential structures, symbolizing its importance to the community. A school, a lyceum, and a convent were added a few years later.

Polish priests were available for all three congregations, and they quickly became the dominant and unifying force in each community, presiding over every function from birth to burial. They solicited funds and worked to support church and school construction. They held supreme authority in the operation of the school and led processions through the community to inaugurate religious and secular festivals. The extent of their influence is revealed in the pictorial histories of the three congregations mentioned. In nearly every photograph, whether of the women's sodality, the dramatic circle, various charity groups, or a church social, the parish priest dominates the scene. While the Polish priest seems to have had less influence than did some black ministers throughout the city, their importance pervaded the Polish community.

The role of the Italian Catholic church in the Italian community in Pittsburgh paralleled that of the Polish Catholic church in its community. The Italians, who settled in areas formerly inhabited by Irish or German Catholics, shunned the already established churches in favor of their own. In Bloomfield Italian residents met in a former blacksmith shop rather than attend the German St. Joseph's, until they could complete their church in 1905. Italian Catholic churches were erected in East Liberty in 1897 and in the Hill District (ward 3) in spite of the presence of other Catholic churches in each area. The three congregations shared the city's only Italian priest, Salvadore Lagorio, rather than tolerate an "outsider." The increase in Italian Catholic priests from one in 1900 to eleven in 1906 reflects their importance to a growing Italian Catholic population. Elementary schools erected in all three congregations by 1911 employed Italian nuns and provided instruction in Italian.[59] Italian Catholic congregations provided most of the services supplied by the Polish Catholic church. They also held "Americanization" classes (mostly teaching English) and "industrialization," cooking, and sewing classes. They served, as one contemporary noted, "as a social center, a charity agency, an employment bureau, an Americanization center, a friendship center and a home."[60]

Religious institutions supplied the black, Polish, and Italian migrants in Pittsburgh with an impressive variety of social and economic services. Their roles were similar in many respects. The proliferation of black churches and the monolithic nature of the immigrant church in the respective communities, however, represent one important difference. A single church acted as the major unifying element in the immigrant community. It brought members together for worship — Italian males less so than others — for social activities and for education. Whether members engaged in physically constructing a building, in rehearsing for a play, or in preparing foods for a festival, the church became the focal point for the entire community. Men and women from a variety of villages now represented a single community and ethnic background. Their shared experiences both within the church and without were important elements in the creation of a community.

As blacks were scattered among occupations, they also belonged to a variety of religious congregations. Blacks in the Hill District, as noted earlier, could attend any one of fourteen established churches. Storefront ministries added to the alternatives. Church jurisdiction followed no geographic or neighborhood lines. Members frequently traversed the entire Hill District, passing several churches to attend the one of their choice. (One church, St. Benedict's, had jurisdiction over all black Catholics within the entire city of Pittsburgh.)[61] In no case did members represent a particular section of the city in either worship or other church-related activities. No single pastor spoke to or for the entire black population of any area. While certain black ministers carried influence in the city, their impact was less within their own neighborhood. Recognizing this dilution, the Protestant black ministry attempted to speak in unison on matters of importance such as housing conditions or discrimination. The incidences of such agreement, however, were too general in nature and too infrequent to provide much cement for the creation of a black community. Black areas in Pittsburgh, partly as a result of the multiplicity of religions, became an amalgamation of geographic areas rather than unified neighborhoods. The impact of this failure, as will be demonstrated, continued throughout the next generation.

Three other factors supplemented the work of religious institutions in the community-building process. The development of fraternal and social organizations, the publication of local newspapers, and the success of a small core of local businessmen — a business district — all contributed to community creation.

The Liberty Street Athletic Club, the Union Social Club, and the Imperial Hall all provided social services, and the latter two supplied death benefits to blacks in Pittsburgh. Other organizations, including the Loendi Club, the Goldenrod Social Club, the White Rose Club, the Aurora Reading Club, the Black Elks, Masons, Moose, and several dozen other clubs also attended to the social needs of blacks. An Afro-American Building and Loan Association and a cooperative supermarket sponsored by the same organization granted loans to prospective black homebuyers and supplied adequate food at reasonable costs.

Two black newspapers, the *Pittsburgh Courier* and the *Colored Home Journal*, regularly reported on events of national and local interest. They also carried advertisements of black merchants throughout the city. The *Pittsburgh Courier*, for example, regularly advertised the following black businesses between 1911 and 1913: five restaurants; three tailors; two each: funeral directors, insurance agents, and billiard rooms; an industrial school for girls; a chauffeur school for boys; a hotel; and "the largest colored grocery in Pittsburgh."[62] The *Courier* also occasionally gave advice to black businessmen. In 1911 the editors counseled,

> Are you attending strictly to business? Are you on the job early
> and late and giving your patrons full value for their money? If not,
> do so at once, as it is most essential and the road to success. Study

your business from A to Z and keep up-to-date. You have got to spend money to make it, and let the public know what you are doing and what you have got to offer by advertising it thoroughly: Keep in the limelight always, for if you don't the progressive man will get your trade. Do you make your places attractive, and have you cultivated those nice courtesies and practiced them upon your customers, which you find will win you friends and dollars? We have some barber shops now on the Hill as well as some other places of business that the Bureau of Health ought to put out of business. If you are not giving your customers their money's worth, get out of business. Don't complain about not getting the patronage and support of your people, if you are not giving full value and doing your part to deserve it.[63]

The *Pittsburgh Courier* at the same time noted the fragmentation of the black business community. Black businesses were scattered all over the Hill District, along the Allegheny River, in the Lawrenceville district, and in the city of Allegheny. They did not concentrate enough to form even a small identifiable business district. Recognizing the benefits of concerted action, the *Courier* frequently called for unity among black businessmen. At one point its editors suggested that

The colored business men of the Hill should come together about once a month and talk "shop," as such meetings ought to be helpful. You should be members of the UPTOWN BOARD OF TRADE. If helpful to the white merchant, why not you?

Do you buy everything you can from the Race's Enterprises? Where do you get your clothes made, your groceries and soft drinks, if you please? Who's your doctor, dentist and lawyer? It is very inconsistent for any church, institution or individual to patronize elsewhere.[64]

Social and beneficial organizations and the black press provided important services but they, like the black church, contributed to the fragmentation of black neighborhoods by serving either a tiny segment of the population or by attempting to serve the entire black population of Pittsburgh without regard to neighborhood. The offices of the Afro-American Building and Loan Association and its related food cooperative were not even located in the black residential areas. The *Pittsburgh Courier* at the same time became a national newspaper. Local blacks thus were forced to depend upon The *Pittsburgh Press*'s weekly "Afro-American Notes" column or the "Local News" section of the *Courier* for brief comments on local events of interest. The inability of Pittsburgh's black organizations to unite or represent a distinct geographic area and the absence of a totally indigenous newspaper weakened the potential for community development. The associations spoke for and to segments of the neighborhood. In addition, they usually served social and recreational purposes rather than providing needed community services. The *Courier* spoke to a national audience. Neither fostered the development of black communities in Pittsburgh during the early part of the century.[65]

Poles and Italians in Pittsburgh also had social and beneficial organizations, local newspapers, and a small number of successful businesses. Unlike the black experience, however, all of these forces related directly to the ethnic communities in the city, and all were tied to specific geographic areas. Each reinforced the role of the ethnic church in fostering the development of strong neighborhood units.

In 1890, for example, a group of Polish Catholic men from Polish Hill established the American Union Polish Brotherhood of St. Joseph, a fraternal and beneficial society for mutual aid and for the assistance of "widows and orphans of deceased members." In their charter they announced their intention to provide a sick benefit of $6 per week.[66] In 1892 some of the same men also signed the charter of the St. Franciscus Xavier Polish Roman Catholic Beneficial Society of the Thirteenth Ward (Polish Hill), the purpose of which was "fostering among its members a spirit of faithful performance of their civil duties as men and especially their duties as Catholic Christians." It also provided benefits to members.[67]

Polish beneficial associations and the Polish Alliance maintained semiautonomous locals in each Polish residential area of the city. The local communities elected their own officers, collected their own fees, and planned their own activities. Several communities maintained Polish Falcon meeting and social halls. On Polish Hill the Polish Lyceum and Polish Falcons occupied the abandoned buildings of the Western Medical College, and a Polish singing society occupied a building at Herron and Paulowna. These nationality groups frequently competed against other Falcon "nests" in sporting, music, and other events. More important, for neighborhood development, they always competed as geographic units, e.g., the Polish Hill Falcons versus the Southside Falcons, thus strengthening local bonds. Italian societies and organizations were frequently tied to local areas, too. The Ateleta Club and the Castel de Sangro as well as three other associations contained almost exclusively migrants from those Italian villages who lived in the Bloomfield area. The Societa Operia Italiania M.S. di East End also represented Italians living in a particular community. Most citywide Italian societies also contained local community chapters.[68]

Polish and Italian newspapers in Pittsburgh also served local interests. The *Gazeta Pittsburgska* informed Pittsburgh Poles of national and international news and frequently reported events in any area of the Polish homeland. The paper also devoted considerable space to items of local interest. Moreover, while the Polish press generally dealt with city news, it also reported regularly on notes of interest within the local community clusters.

Italians were served by five newspapers and two local Italian magazines. Two of the papers (*Unione* and *La Trinacria*) provided mainly national news, and one (*Vita*) attempted to convert Italians to the United Presbyterian Church. The others, edited by two successful Italian professional men, dealt almost exclusively with news of the Pittsburgh Italian communities. These papers, according to one student of the Italian community, were "an indirect Americanization school for the immigrant. . . . These papers have taught him English; have directed him where to settle; have informed him where he could find work; have championed his cause when prejudice arose against him."[69] The Polish and Italian presses in Pittsburgh did not necessarily grow out of the local communities, but they carefully and frequently spoke to their needs and interests, and, in doing so, they played an important role in community development.

The presence of a small business district serving the needs of those in the immediate area also played a significant part in the process of community development. Self-employed businessmen symbolized the success some immigrants sought. They had status and represented stability — symbolically, if not always in fact — in a rapidly changing world. Their enterprises, in addition, became meeting places for the entire community, a source of local gossip, and a center of ideas. Their willingness to extend credit often made them the only friendly fortress in difficult times. Buying "on tick" or "on the book" often became the means of survival for beleaguered workers.

Tiny business districts grew in the Polish sections of the city; those in the Italian section were more substantial. Both, however, were located within the confines of the neighborhood and served primarily local populations. More than a dozen Polish grocers operated businesses in the Polish Hill and Southside sections of Pittsburgh. Each section also contained at least one confectioner, a barber, a dry goods store, and an undertaker.[70] The Italian business districts were larger, offered more variety, and continued to grow each year. By 1910 one six-block area in Bloomfield contained six Italian grocers, a butcher, and two confectioners. The East Liberty area supported a dozen grocers, several restaurants, tailors, shoemakers, several doctors, and a variety of other merchants. It was, as one researcher claimed, "more distinctly an Italian colony than any other settlement in the city. It [was] a unit in itself."[71]

The attainment of work and the maintenance of one's family required the constant attention of working-class families in twentieth-century Pittsburgh. The ability to develop neighborhood life eased the burden somewhat and enabled various groups to cope with an alien society. At the same time many groups and individuals made adjustments within their own lives to meet the demands of urban-industrial life. Poles and Italians, for example, relied on kin to secure work. Blacks, denied this access to work, relied upon their own initiative and guile to find employment. These different methods produced different results. Poles worked in metal industries; Italians, in the metal and construction industries and small entrepreneurships; blacks concentrated in the services. All groups labored mainly at unskilled or semiskilled occupations.

Occupation interacted with ethnic background to help determine the place of residence. Immigrants in Pittsburgh performing similar work resided in immigrant or ethnic clusters that often eased the burdens of settlement and assisted families and individuals in adjusting to their new life. For Poles and Italians, the church, associations, schools, social groups, and business districts transformed these clusters into ethnic communities — communities that provided identity and a sense of belonging for entire groups. The development of these communities facilitated the sharing of difficult and joyous experiences and no doubt eased the pain associated with adaptation in America.

Early black migrants, on the other hand, were unable to create identifiable communities in Pittsburgh society. Neighborhood clusters remained small because of the scattered locations of places of employment for blacks and the presence of other migrants in their settlement areas. Black neighborhoods remained mixed within a patchwork of ethnic, racial, religious, and economic groups. The unified institutional infrastructure that aided in neighborhood creation for other groups failed to materialize for blacks. Churches were divided spiritually and socially. They represented large geographic areas rather than small identifiable neighborhoods. Indigenous schools did not exist. Other forces that might have fostered community development — associations, newspapers, and businessmen — served a citywide or even national population. They did not identify with the local neighborhood.

Blacks arriving in Pittsburgh at the turn of the century were frustrated in their job search and denied the comfort and security provided by the existence of community. Poles and Italians, on the other hand, while facing constant struggles for survival, could rely on both kin and community. These differences would have an impact.

NOTES

1. Charles S. Johnson, *The Negro in American Civilization* (New York, 1930), 16-17; Katherine Stone, "The Origin of Job Structures in the Steel Industry," *Radical America* (Nov.-Dec. 1973), 30-34.
2. Interviews with Stanley N., Sept. 22, 1976; Joseph B., May 30, 1976; John B., Mar. 3, 1976; Agnes G., June 25, 1974; Peter H., June 26, 1974; Ignacy M., July 2, 1974; Joseph D., Sept. 17, 1976; Edward R., Sept. 10, 1976; John S., Sept. 30, 1976; Charles W., Dec. 10, 1976; Francis P., Jan. 16, 1976; Martin T., Mar. 25, 1977, Pittsburgh Oral History Project (POHP).
3. Robert E. Foerster, *The Italian Emigration of Our Time* (Cambridge, Mass., 1919), 326-27; Rudolph J. Vecoli, "Italian-American Workers, 1880-1920: Padroné Slaves or Primitive Rebels," in S. M. Tomasi, ed., *Perspectives in Italian Immigration and Ethnicity* (New York, 1977), 38, 46. Vecoli questions the assumption by Philip S. Foner, *History of the Labor Movement in the United States*, 4 vols. (New York, 1964), 3:257, that Italians concentrated in construction because it was all they could get. The reliance on kinship rather than on padroné is also suggested by John W. Briggs, *An Italian Passage: Immigrants to Three American Cities, 1890-1930* (New Haven, Conn., 1977), 69. See also J. S. Mac-Donald and L. D. MacDonald, "Chain Migration, Ethnic Neighborhood Formation and Social Networks," *Milband Memorial Fund Quarterly*, 46 (Jan. 1964), 82-97, and "Urbanization, Ethnic Group and Social Segmentation," *Social Research*, 29 (1962), 433-48.
4. Paul U. Kellogg, ed., *Wage-Earning Pittsburgh*, The Pittsburgh Survey (New York, 1914), 39.
5. Interviews with Nicholas R., June 23, 1977; Frank A., May 18, 1977; Martin D., Mar. 15, 1977; Frank D., July 27, 1977; Dan C., Mar. 31, 1977; Lidwina P., May 26, 1977, POHP.
6. Interviews with Anthony B., Mar. 14, 1977; Amico L., July 28, 1977, POHP; *Statuto Della Societa Di Beneficenza Ateleta* (Pittsburgh, 1924) in Ateleta Beneficial Association Folder, Archives of Industrial Society, University of Pittsburgh.
7. Interviews with Vincent L., June 21, 1977; Lou G., May 11, 1977; Frank A., May 16, 1977; Lidwina P., May 26, 1977, POHP.
8. Helen A. Tucker, "The Negroes of Pittsburgh," *Charities and Commons*, 21 (Jan. 2, 1909), 602. Although blacks had not made large incursions into the steel industry, their average wages in 1910 exceeded those of Polish and Italian workers in the mills. See U.S. Senate, *Reports of the Immigration Commission, Immigrants in Industry, Part 2: Iron and Steel Manufacturing*, 61 Cong., 2nd sess., Serial no. 633, 2 vols. (Washington, D.C., 1911), 1: 290, 304. Blacks had made greater inroads into manufacturing in Pittsburgh than other northern cities, including Cleveland and New York. See Kenneth Kusmer, *A Ghetto Takes Shape: Black Cleveland, 1870-1930* (Urbana, Ill., 1976), 66-67. Thomas Sowell, *Race and Economics* (New York, 1975), 120, has called the period before 1910 a "promising" period for urban blacks because they established a

good many small businesses. See Charles H. Wesley, *Negro Labor in the United States, 1850-1925* (New York, 1965), 244-47, for a discussion of blacks' experience with iron manufacturing in the South. Abraham Epstein, *The Negro Migrant in Pittsburgh* (Pittsburgh, 1918), 30-34; Kellogg, ed., *Wage-Earning Pittsburgh*, 39-41.

9. Interviews with Leroy M., July 1974; Jasper M., July 12, 1976, POHP.
10. Interviews with Ben E., July 27, 1974; Olive W., July 23, 1976; Jean B., June 29, 1976; Gertrude D., Nov. 3, 1976; Anonymous, Sept. 2, 1976; Floyd T., May 11, 1976; Hezikiah M., Oct. 8, 1976, POHP.
11. Interviews with Harrison G., Aug. 23, 1974; Ben E., July 31, 1974; James N., June 28, 1976; Ernest F., Apr. 20, 1976, POHP.
12. Louise V. Kennedy, *The Negro Peasant Turns Cityward* (New York, 1930), 122. Of course, discrimination kept blacks out of some jobs. In one glass plant "white workers ran them out," and the company abandoned further attempts at hiring blacks. See Epstein, *The Negro Migrant in Pittsburgh*, 132. On the other hand, in 1910 hundreds of blacks found jobs as laborers, furnacemen, heaters, and pourers. Carnegie Steel employed about 1,500 blacks before 1916. See Kellogg, ed., *Wage-Earning Pittsburgh*, 112; Epstein, *The Negro Migrant in Pittsburgh*, 31. In nineteenth-century Philadelphia blacks complained about their inability to get skilled jobs for their sons, a suggestion that black kinship was being frustrated. See Theodore Hershberg, "Free Blacks in Antebellum Philadelphia: A Study of Ex-Slaves, Freeborn and Socioeconomic Decline," *Journal of Social History*, 5 (1972), 190-204.
13. Epstein, *The Negro Migrant in Pittsburgh*, 31. The Carnegie Steel plants employed 1,500 blacks in 1916; Jones and Laughlin employed 400.
14. U.S. Congress, *Cost of Living in American Towns*, 62nd Cong., 1st sess., Serial no. 6082, 4 vols. (Washington, D.C., 1911), 4: 338.
15. Ira Reid, "The Negro in the Major Industries and Building Trades of Pittsburgh" (M.A. thesis, University of Pittsburgh, 1925), 8.
16. Tucker, "The Negroes of Pittsburgh," 602.
17. Ibid.
18. Florette Henri, *Black Migration: Movement North, 1900-1920* (New York, 1975), 149.
19. Kennedy, *Negro Peasant*, 71-78.
20. Stephan Thernstrom, *The Other Bostonians: Poverty and Progress in the American Metropolis, 1880-1970* (Cambridge, Mass., 1973), 189-90; Allan H. Spear, *Black Chicago: The Making of a Negro Ghetto* (Chicago, 1967), 30.
21. Interview with Joe R., July 21, 1974, POHP.
22. John R. Commons, "Wage Earners of Pittsburgh," in Kellogg, ed., *Wage-Earning Pittsburgh*, 120.
23. Interview with Michael M., Apr. 10, 1978, POHP.
24. Salvatore Migliore, "Half-Century of Italian Immigration into Pittsburgh" (M.A. thesis, University of Pittsburgh, 1928), 23.
25. Commons, "Wage Earners," 122.
26. Reid, "The Negro in Major Industries," 35.
27. Thernstrom, *The Other Bostonians*, 189.
28. David Montgomery, "Immigrant Workers and Managerial Reform" in

Richard L. Ehrlich, ed., *Immigrants in Industrial America, 1850-1920* (Charlottesville, Va., 1977), 96-110.

29. Interviews with Martin D., Mar. 15, 1977; Domenica M., Mar. 18, 1977; Felix D., Mar. 17, 1977; Vincent L., June 21, 1977; Frank A., May 18, 1977, POHP; Migliore, "Half-Century of Italian Immigration," 28. This information casts serious doubts on Thomas Kessner's argument that the Italian peasant experience equipped them only for the periphery of the city economy as menial laborers. Kessner badly underestimates the extent of supplemental skills Italians held and certainly the effectiveness of kinship in obtaining jobs. See *The Golden Door: Italian and Jewish Immigrant Mobility in New York City, 1880-1915* (New York, 1977), 38-39.

30. Interviews with Michael M., July 16, 1977; Nicholas R., June 23, 1977; Ray L., Aug. 24, 1977; Martin T., Mar. 25, 1977, POHP.

31. Migliore, "Half-Century of Italian Immigration," 28-29; interview with Frank D., May 19, 1977, POHP.

32. Virginia Yans-McLaughlin, *Family and Community: Italian Immigrants in Buffalo, 1880-1930* (Ithaca, N.Y., 1977), 41. McLaughlin also underestimates the importance of ethnic stereotypes held by foremen in determining job patterns. She claims Poles predominated in Buffalo's foundry because of their previous industrial experience in Europe. However, she fails to give sufficient weight to her own evidence (p. 41) that Poles were preferred over Italians in Buffalo's mills. That a similar case existed in Pittsburgh has already been suggested. Also in Milwaukee, Italians were not highly prized as mill workers and were thought to be "itinerant, lazy, and quarrelsome." See Gerd Korman, *Industrialization, Immigrants, and Americanizers: The View from Milwaukee, 1866-1921* (Madison, Wis., 1967), 45. The heavier concentration of Poles than Italians in inside work is seen in U.S. Senate, *Reports of the Immigration Commission, XXVI: Immigrants in Cities*, 61 Cong. 2d Sess., Serial no. 633 (Washington, D.C., 1911), 652. Frank D. and several other Italians in the Bloomfield section left outdoor work as soon as they could for mill jobs because they disliked the "idleness" of cold weather months and wanted "continuous work." Interview with Frank D., May 19, 1977, POHP.

33. "Union Scale of Wages and Hours of Labor Collected the 15th of May Each Year, 1919-1924," *Pennsylvania Department of Labor Bulletin, 1924* (Harrisburg, 1924), 50-96. In 1921, for instance, stonemasons earned $1.25 per hours and bricklayers earned $1.30, but boilermakers in railroad shops — an occupation that employed many Poles — received only $0.75 per hour.

34. *Pittsburgh Leader*, May 27, 1900, p. 20; May 22, 1900, p. 1.

35. H. M. Phelps, "The Stormy Fifth," ibid., Nov. 5, 1905, pp. 7-8.

36. Ibid., Nov. 26, 1905, p. 7.

37. Alex Pittler, "The Hill District in Pittsburgh: A Study in Succession" (M.A. thesis, University of Pittsburgh, 1930), 20-24.

38. The *Pittsburgh Leader* in a series of weekly articles on Pittsburgh's political wards described the succession of ethnic groups throughout the central city. See Oct. 1905 and thereafter. "Many men of family," the *Leader* noted (Nov. 26, 1905), "have found it absolutely necessary to

move out lest their children be contaminated by vile association."
39. For an analysis of journey-to-work patterns in Pittsburgh, see Joel A. Tarr, *Transportation Innovations and Changing Spatial Patterns in Pittsburgh, 1850-1934* (Chicago, 1978).
40. Ibid., 21.
41. 1900 sample data (see chap. 2).
42. Interview with John B., Mar. 3, 1976, POHP.
43. H. M. Phelps, *Pittsburgh Leader,* Nov. 19, 1905.
44. U.S. Bureau of the Census, Manuscript Census of Pittsburgh, 1900. The six blocks include all of the area bounded by Liberty Avenue and Juniper, Edmond, and Pearl streets.
45. Caroline Golab, *Immigrant Destinations* (Philadelphia, 1977), 120. Golab argues that "peoples of Southern and Eastern Europe had a very different sense of society and personal identity from those of Northern and Western Europe." By implication she concludes that southern and eastern Europeans carried a cultural propensity to cluster. Others did not. This view, in our opinion, ignores the considerable Irish and German communities in most early nineteenth-century American cities.
46. Stanley Lieberson, *Ethnic Patterns in American Cities* (New York, 1963), 5.
47. Ibid.
48. Information on the variety of roles performed by churches in Pittsburgh was culled from several sources. Most useful were church histories supplied by the AME Bethel, Ebenezer Baptist, St. Josaphat's, Immaculate Heart of Mary, Immaculate Conception, and Our Lady Help of Christians. Church histories and church records of all churches mentioned are with the respective churches.
49. The Hill District estimate is based on 1870 data supplied by Jacqueline Wolfe, "The Changing Patterns of Residence of the Negro in Pittsburgh" (M.A. thesis, University of Pittsburgh, 1964). Wolfe indicates that only 1,352 Negroes lived in the Hill District in 1870.
50. Alonzo Moron, "Distribution of the Negro Population in Pittsburgh, 1910-1930" (M.A. thesis, University of Pittsburgh, 1933), 40.
51. The black congregations that were located in the Hill District in 1900 were: AME Bethel, Wylie and Elm (ward 3), the Reverend I. S. Lee; AME, Fulton and Clark (ward 3), the Reverend D. W. Shaw; AME Zion, 40 Arthur (ward 3), the Reverend George Johnson; Carron Baptist, 135 Carron (ward 3), the Reverend J. H. Thompson; Center Avenue Baptist, Center and Robert (ward 3), the Reverend J. H. Adams; Central Baptist, 55 Lawson (ward 5), the Reverend James Smith; Ebenezer Baptist, 2001 Wylie Avenue (ward 3), the Reverend George Howard; Mt. Zion Baptist, 2224 Bedford (ward 3), pastor unknown; Grace Memorial Presbyterian, Arthur and Center (ward 3), the Reverend M. B. Lanier; Hoods Chapel, 228 Wylie (ward 3), pastor unknown; St. Benedict's Roman Catholic, 13 Overhill (ward 3), Father Michael Ward; Plymouth, Fullerton (ward 3), pastor unknown; Warren ME, Center at Watt (ward 5), pastor unknown; Grace Chapel, Soho near Gazzam (ward 5), pastor unknown. Ibid. The Kusmer quotation is from his book, *A Ghetto Takes Shape,* 93.
52. "Notes for the Afro-American," *Pittsburgh Press,* Oct. 21, 1900.

53. See various issues of the *Pittsburgh Press*. "Notes for the Afro-American 1900" was occasionally listed as "Afro-American Notes."
54. "Notes for the Afro-American," ibid., June 17, 1900. Debates among clergy provided funds for the Antioch Baptist church.
55. "Afro-American Notes," ibid., June 17, 1900; Aug. 19, 1900.
56. *Pittsburgh Leader*, Nov. 25, 1900.
57. Moron, "Distribution of the Negro Population in Pittsburgh," 42.
58. The church histories of St. Stanislaus, St. Adalbert's, St. Josaphat's, and Immaculate Heart of Mary Church are the sources for this information.
59. Several Italian Protestant ministries, staffed by Italian ministers, experienced little success in converting Italians to the Presbyterian or Baptist denominations. Their "Americanization" night schools, however, succeeded in attracting several hundred immigrants at any one time between 1910 and 1920. For an account of the Italian Protestant movement in Pittsburgh, see Migliore, "Half-Century of Italian Immigration."
60. Ibid., 44.
61. Moron, "Distribution of the Negro Population in Pittsburgh," 44.
62. See advertisements of various issues of the *Pittsburgh Courier*, 1911-12.
63. Ibid., Oct. 11, 1911.
64. Ibid.
65. R. L. Hill, "A View of the Hill: A Study of Experiences and Attitudes in the Hill District of Pittsburgh, Pennsylvania, 1900-1973" (Ph.D. diss., University of Pittsburgh, 1973), 76.
66. Allegheny County, Pennsylvania, Recorder of Deeds, Charter Books, 16: 24-29, County Office Building, Pittsburgh.
67. Ibid., 18: 132.
68. Italian societies in Pittsburgh in 1900 included: Ateleta Club; Castel de Sangro; Societa di M.S. Beneficienza; Societa Fraterna Italiana di M.S.; Societa Garibaldi di M.S.; Societa Christoforo Colombo de Beneficienza; Per la Barsaglieri; Societa Umberto Lo di M.S. eB.; Militari in Concedo; Societa De Conte di Torina; and Societa Operia Italiana M.S. di East End.
69. Migliore, "Half-Century of Italian Immigration," 65.
70. *Pittsburgh and Allegheny Directory, 1904* (Pittsburgh, 1905).
71. Ella B. Myers, "Some Italian Groups in Pittsburgh" (M.A. thesis, Carnegie Institute of Technology, 1920), 10.

4

Family Dynamics

Undeniably the maintenance of occupations and residential bases was crucial to establishing a foothold in the city, even if all groups did not have access to the same factories and homes. But central to the entire migrating process was a kinship network that played an even more decisive role in adjustment by largely defining the respective trajectories newcomers took into the industrial structure. That family remained viable in the face of urban social and economic forces is no longer a surprise. An abundance of scholarship has already overturned the notion that industrialization was less than destructive to kinship associations. A recent study of black movement to Boston concluded that migration northward strengthened the family, and examinations of urban Italians and Poles have revealed active, vital family networks functioning over several generations.[1]

The somewhat triumphant view of the enduring family must not be taken too far, however. Families were not isolated from the pressures of the surrounding wage economy and urban structure. To emphasize familial durability at the expense of probing the interaction among family, economy, and social structure obscures historical complexity and the very pragmatic way in which specific families effected particular life strategies. That family systems persisted meant that they neither escaped difficulties nor functioned similarly in respective migrant and immigrant communities. Families were ultimately not a rigid, static entity, but an adaptable, malleable system.

Clearly, working-class families had problems. Beyond the shared concern of all kinship associations to make ends meet, difficulties and tensions in the migrant household were widespread, even if not debilitating. Blacks incurred high rates of tuberculosis. Immigrant steel workers, faced with constant extremes of heat and cold, contracted pneumonia continuously, and industrial accidents, especially before World War I, were widespread. Illness, injury, and pressures emanating from the workplace and the urban milieu manifested themselves repeatedly in domestic tensions. Consider the case of Guiseppe X.[2] Four years after his arrival from Italy he was working as a steelworker. His wife came to the American Service Institute to report that he was frequently beating not only her but also their daughter. One evening after the daughter returned home from a date, Guiseppe beat her so badly she could not go to work for a week, even though the girl had quit school in the ninth grade to help support the family. Eventually the father's brutality caused the daughter to leave home and his wife to acquire a "drinking problem."[3]

The prevalence of industrial accidents and the incapacitation of working fathers frequently presented challenges that were not always met successfully. Wladimir X., who emigrated from Russian Poland in 1913, became blind while mixing lime at the Jones and Laughlin steel plant. Confined to his home, Wladimir became "highly nervous" and convinced that he had lost the affection of his family. When his wife admitted to him that she saw other men, he exclaimed that he felt like an "outcast" in his own home.[4] The marriage of Stella X. began to dissolve after the death of a son in 1930. Stella blamed the boy's death on her husband, whom she claimed "had not paid sufficient attention" to the youth's needs and had fed him improperly while she was hospitalized at a regional mental clinic.[5]

These examples, while not characteristic of most black, Italian, and Polish families, demonstrate the extreme pressures placed upon family life. That more did not experience disorder and disintegration is truly surprising and, no doubt, additional unrecorded problems and tensions existed. Nevertheless, the overwhelming preponderance of evidence indicates that black, Italian, and Polish families functioned in positive, if different, ways in helping members adapt to the demands of industrial Pittsburgh.

Yet if families were neither victims nor simply residues from a premigration past, the question remains as to exactly how they did interact with the economic and social structure of Pittsburgh. It has already been suggested that they assisted blacks, Italians, and Poles tremendously in moving to the city. But divergent occupational and residential behavior was not the same for all groups. Logic would almost dictate that in the specific contact between group culture and industrial structure distinctions would emerge that would prove pivotal to subsequent adaptation. It may not be too much to say that in the nexus between familial networks and socioeconomic structure, the origins of disparate adjustment and ultimately urban inequality can be found.[6]

Especially noticeable in examining the internal attitudes of black families in Pittsburgh was a strong sense of individualism. The socialization process in black migrant families generally included lessons for children in securing their goals and, given the nature of class and racial subordination, young blacks emerged from their formative years with a realization that survival would ultimately depend upon their own personal resourcefulness.[7] Rather than emerging as adults fixed to the responsibilities of their families of origin, migrants and their children looked toward a future that they alone would shape. Sally S. recalled that her brother left the family farm in Mississippi for a Florida sawmill "when he was big enough to work on his own." After several years her brother left Florida for Washington, D.C. Roy M. "had the urge to leave home" at age sixteen. He reasoned that if he could work in the fields of Arkansas, he could surely work for his own wages. His move north, not uncharacteristically, was preceded by a period in an Arkansas sawmill. Before he was twenty, Grant W. had moved to Pittsburgh, obtained a job in a glass factory, worked at a steel foundry, and launched a semiprofessional baseball career. Several female respondents left home on their own at early ages either to attend school, perform domestic service, or hire out for "day work" in Pittsburgh. The father of William H. told his son on his twenty-first birthday, "You are your own man and you can go on your own." Ernest F. never even told his father when he left school to procure a job, although his father generally allowed him to make his own decisions.[8]

Often rising individual aspirations clashed with parental authority, which suggested a certain tension between parents' emotional ties and their pragmatic conclusion of what was needed for adult survival. The resulting strain pushed some young blacks in search of their own means of sustenance. Jasper A. left his family farm not only because he was sick and tired of farming but because his father worked him "pretty hard." Roy M. expressed similar displeasure with "strict parents who would not allow him to pursue his own interests." Characteristically, both the brother and father of Olive W. had run away from home at age fourteen to work in Florida sawmills. One Pittsburgh respondent had the feeling that his father was "too repressive" and showed insufficient "trust" in his son. Grant W. argued with a stepmother over keeping his own wages and left home twice before age seventeen to work on his own, although he felt "close" to his father.[9] A striking example of black individualism and self-reliance was Gertrude D., who, at age sixteen, lived alone in Nashville after her mother died. She acquired a job scrubbing laundry on her own and became completely self-supporting. After several years she married and accompanied her husband to Pittsburgh.[10]

Early employment among children in working-class families was certainly not unique. A recent study of Philadelphia concluded that most urban American families were able to operate within a margin of comfort only to the degree that they could count on a steady contribution from their laboring children of both sexes.[11] Such a pattern was not as evident among Pittsburgh's black migrant families. This is not to say that black children never contributed their wages to their parents. They sometimes did, although often for a specific purpose such as the education of a brother or sister. But as a subsequent analysis of immigrant families revealed, black progeny were considerably more likely to retain their own wages rather than relinquish them to parents. Grant W., for example, contributed part of his wages until he was sixteen so that his sister could finish high school. As soon as she graduated, he kept his earnings for himself. Floyd T. unloaded box cars as a teenager but discussed the matter of his wages with his parents and was allowed to "manage for himself." Jasper A. described his relationship with his parents as intimate, but he seldom sent money to them in the South. Ernest F. hauled bricks at age fifteen and used his earnings for himself. Queen E. kept her own wages at age fifteen when she went to Norfolk to do domestic work. A young worker, whose family moved from Virginia, did give some of his wages to his family but kept most for himself. James N. kept a similar portion of his early wages. Olive W. gave her parents occasional support but kept most of her wages for her own use. She did not recall her brothers or sisters turning anything over to her parents. Similarly, a survey of unmarried black migrants in Pittsburgh in 1918 found that less than 45 percent sent money to relatives.[12]

Recent studies have offered additional evidence that blacks were choosing an individual rather than a collective approach to survival — which is not to imply an absence of emotional attachments or kinship assistance among blacks. Numerous instances exist in Pittsburgh and elsewhere of blacks caring for orphaned relatives and other kin. The role of kinship in the migration process itself has already been described. But out of a deep concern for their children, black parents were nurturing attitudes of self-sufficiency because they were unable to offer material resources or social connections to assist their children's survival in adult life. Historian Crandall Shifflett in a study of rural black families in 1880 in Virginia found additional evidence that corroborates the data from Pittsburgh. In contrast to white families, Shifflett found Virginia black families reduced the number of non-working consumers in their household during the early years of marriage so that there would be fewer mouths to feed. As families progressed to middle years and children became old enough to work, Shifflett discovered the ratio of consumers (nonworkers) to workers gradually diminishing. Middle-aged black parents had fewer nonworking relatives to feed.[13] One reasonable explanation for Shifflett's declining consumer population in middle-aged black families was the departure of young black workers to pursue their own individual quests.

If black migrants frequently resorted to individual resourcefulness in launching a career and leaving the family of origin, Poles stood in stark contrast. In hard times a family could survive by drawing upon the wage-earning potential of older children or by allowing those children to care for themselves, thus reducing the number of household consumers. If the latter alternative was chosen, greater reliance would be placed on the wage-earning potential of the mother. While reliance on working women and self-supporting children characterized black migrant families, Poles kept married women at home and developed a highly authoritarian parent-child relationship, which was designed to temper the individualistic inclinations of youth for the sake of family interests. Polish immigration itself was usually part of a family plan to survive or to purchase additional land rather than an individual act.[14]

Unlike black youth who tended to retain their own wages, young Polish workers contributed all of their earnings to their parents. Socialization in Polish families functioned in a manner that insured both the inevitability of child labor and the relinquishing of earnings for family use at least until marriage. Before 1930 young Poles learned their lessons well. Ray C. expressed his reason for remaining in Lawrenceville as a young man. "I felt down deep I had an obligation to take care of my mother." Joseph D. never had to be told to assist his family. "I always thought dad had hard luck so I would stick with [my parents] until the other kids got old enough to work," he explained. The tendency of young Poles to consider family obligations was stated clearly by Edward R.: "We looked forward to the time when we got to the legal age. When we got to that point we quit school and got a job because we knew the parents needed money. . . . That's just the way we were raised."[15]

Carrying out the dictates of their upbringing, Polish youth nearly always gave their earnings to their mother, the usual manager of Polish family finances.[16] Stanley N. "hustled newspapers" at mill gates and gave his profit of $3 per week to his mother. Joseph B. and his brothers sold enough newspapers on Polish Hill to nearly equal their father's weekly salary of $12.50. After the father of John K. had his leg crushed at Carnegie Steel, John began working in a grocery store and giving his wages to his mother. At age sixteen Peter L. helped his parents by working in a butcher shop. Hundreds of young Poles were employed by glass manufacturers on the Southside by the age of fourteen, including many who worked at night, in order to assist their families.[17]

Young Polish girls were also expected to assist parents until marriage. In fact, it was not uncommon for Polish children to live in the same house with their parents for many years after marriage, a pattern rarely found among blacks. On the Southside, Polish girls packed and inspected nuts and bolts at Oliver Iron and Steel. Stephanie W. recalled that all her sisters worked either at H. J. Heinz or the Southside Hospital and contributed their wages to their mother. Stephanie at age sixteen worked in a store that needed a "Polish girl" for its Polish clientele. Josephine B. left school after the eighth grade and did "day work" for wealthy families. She relinquished all her earnings, as did her brother who worked in a nearby coal mine. Joseph D. recalled that all of his sisters left school at age thirteen and worked in a cigar factory.[18]

While black and Polish families differed in their attitudes toward children, Italians revealed a third pattern in their attempts to enter the structure of the industrialized city. Generally the Italian family in America and Italy has been described as a closely knit institution emphasizing familial over individual interests. Some observers of the Italian peasant family assumed that the constraints of familial solidarity were so well established that any form of individual aims or rights was impossible. From interviews conducted in New York City in the 1940s, Leonard Covello concluded that these newcomers were ill prepared to compete in an individualistic society such as urban America.

Recent historical scholarship has challenged Covello's framework and argued that rather than being dysfunctional in urban society, the Italian-American family proved readily adaptable to new surroundings. A study of Buffalo demonstrated how Italian kinship expanded its functions in America by strengthening social ties with friends and neighbors as well as relatives. These expanded ties were seen as a basis for the formation of particular occupational and housing arrangements. Traditional practices such as restrictions on women's work outside of the home and the direction of children's careers, of course, persisted in both Buffalo and Pittsburgh, and Italian survival continued to rest on mutual dependence. Indeed, the point is no longer whether the Italian family survived immigration or whether it was dysfunctional, but specifically how did it operate in various circumstances.[19]

Consider Italian patterns of child socialization. Working-class families approached survival in collective terms and frequently counted on children to leave school at an early age and contribute to the family economy either directly, by relinquishing wages, or indirectly, by becoming self-supporting. Such behavior would appear to be a simple continuation of the peasant ties in the family with authoritarian parents carefully directing children into the work place and exerting restraints on the individualistic inclinations of their offspring. Two recent historians of Italian-Americans, Josef Barton and John W. Briggs, have modified this view and have stressed that Italians displayed rising expectations for themselves as individuals in coming to America. Briggs uncovered a wealth of information suggesting a growing desire for education and social improvement for their children on the part of Italian parents in Italy by 1900. He reported that in Abruzzi, the home of many Pittsburgh Italians, letters from relatives in America urged parents to make whatever sacrifice was necessary to send brothers and sisters to school. Briggs thought that emigration heightened the lower-class interest in schooling and that where children left school early, it was due to poverty or a strained parent-child relationship.[20]

An examination of Pittsburgh Italians leaves a clear impression that newcomers from southern Italy functioned somewhat differently. For example, the total commitment to schooling as a means of advancement that Briggs and others have posited goes too far in characterizing Italian immigrant behavior. The traditional preeminence of parental influence and familial goals over individualistic ones continued to prevail in Italian Pittsburgh. Children left school early not only in "poor families" but in nearly all households before 1940. At the same time, however, parents manifested a concern for children's well-being and future. Parents labored persistently to assist their progeny in acquiring skills and jobs that would serve both the interests of the individual and the family. Their goals were modest; their commitment to formal schooling noticeably less than blacks. But in their unique way they employed traditional practices in new circumstances to adapt to the industrial city.[21]

Michael M. recalled that his parents stressed "hard work and a feeling that nothing was given to you." While expressing an early interest in becoming a physician, Michael was forced to leave school early because he was the oldest child. Already at age eleven he was employed on a part-time basis at a creamery, catching milk cans as they moved down a conveyor. At age sixteen he became a butter-maker by observing the techniques of fellow workers. By this time his brothers were helping his father at the family produce business. While neither Michael nor any of his brothers finished high school, they all turned their earnings over to their mother until marriage. Michael explained that he was reluctant about leaving school after only the fourth grade, but his parents wanted him to join his father "huckster-ing" with a pushcart. He entered the creamery, however, because he preferred not to knock on people's doors. Mary I. recalled that her parents removed her from school at age fourteen to assist at home. Martin D. insisted that "if you finished the eighth grade in Bloomfield you were lucky." His parents asked all of his brothers and sisters to leave school early to "help out." When Martin wanted to play sports instead, his father told him not to "waste his muscle but go to work instead." At age fifteen Martin, therefore, worked as a barber's helper and then as a day laborer for a contractor. Felix D. recalled vividly one day that at the age of twelve his mother slapped him over the head and urged him to "quit playing and go to work" in order to "stay out of trouble" and help with family expenses. Felix readily agreed since he had been ridiculed in school several times and had come to dislike it. He became a janitor and later worked in a tire repair center. His brother, who was also dissatisfied with school, became a sign painter. When Felix's father died several years later, his mother never had to work outside the home because she was supported by her four children.[22]

While most Italian parents expected support from their children, instances did exist where parents encouraged children to finish high school. A few second-generation Italians completed the twelfth year of schooling, but most did not. Like Poles, the desire to leave school early and assist their family was as likely to emerge from the child as it was from the parent. Indeed, parents who wanted their sons or daughters to remain in the classroom often found them unwilling. When her father died, Lidwina P. wanted desperately to quit high school and work. She remained in school only at the insistence of her mother, but she also secured a part-time job cleaning for a Jewish family and turned her earnings over to her mother. Lidwina's desire to help was strengthened considerably by a belief that her foreign-born mother would be unable to manage her own economic affairs in America. Other Italians resisted parental attempts to keep them in school and started working to assist their parents as soon as possible. Umberto B. found employment as a shoeshine boy and was able to turn over nearly $15 a week to his father. Amico L. discounted his mother's argument that he remain in school. Revealing the accumulated weight of peer pressure that resulted from the decisions of thousands of young Italians, Amico noted that because most of his friends took jobs "wherever they could get them," he became a "roofer's helper." Ray L. entered a spring factory at age fifteen. He reasoned, "I wanted to go to work in the worst way because my parents found it difficult paying the rent and the loan on my father's barber shop." Lou G. reiterated the attitude. He explained that young Italians would seldom think of leaving home and going out to live on their own. Rather, they would work to relinquish earnings to their parents. Lou emphasized that "you never left your mother and father. I wanted to help my father for what he had done for me." Martin T., who like most young Italians remained at home until marriage, discussed his decision to leave school at length: "As I was growing up after my father left us, I was really eager to have an income, to help my mother. . . . I turned most of [my earnings] over to my mother. That's what I was working for. . . . I was raised with the idea that my mother was my mother and my family, and they kept me. When I wasn't earning she would give me whatever she could. I was family. She was my mother."[23]

While Italians relied on kin wherever they could, they also urged their children to acquire a trade or skill in an attempt to insure that their working-class pursuits would provide somewhat steadier remuneration and employment. Sons were admonished to do more than simply assist their parents. They were directed to improve themselves as individuals by finding jobs at places other than factories and mills, something Poles seemed reluctant to do. When he was thirteen, the parents of Lou G. indicated to him he should learn a craft and placed him in a shoemaker's shop, much as was done in Italy. Lou explained his father's decision by saying that his father insisted a trade would be necessary if he was to find a good job. Frank D. never entered high school because his parents felt it would be preferable for him to learn a "good trade." At age twelve his father took him to a tailor he knew and obtained an apprenticeship for Frank.[24] The father and brother of Ray L. learned barbering in Pittsburgh from Ray's uncle and grandfather. Ray's father sent him to barbering school as well, but Ray disliked the profession and entered a mill. Ray elaborated on the decision:

"My parents were most in favor of learning a trade such as barber, blacksmith, or shoemaker. If a person got a trade, they felt you would never starve. Most of the Italians who came, even as young people, had a trade. If you got an education, there was still a possibility that you would still have to know someone before getting a job."[25]

Certainly a sense of responsibility toward the well-being of the entire family prompted both parents and children in Italian immigrant families to enter the work place as soon as possible. While this emphasis on familial goals appeared to be a simple transmission of premigration values, the press of industrial capitalism with its subsistence wages, unpredictable employment cycles, and continual threat of worker incapacitation did little to generate alternative modes of familial behavior. Italian and Polish family cohesiveness, unlike that of blacks, was supported significantly by the fact that both groups could rely on kinship ties in gaining employment. The Italian occupational pattern even diverged from Poles, however, because of their widespread experience with supplemental skills. Immigrants from Italy not only directed the placement of their sons in the occupational spectrum but also secured for them opportunities to learn familiar trades and skills that would assist them as they toiled in Pittsburgh. If blacks were denied opportunities and Poles seized those that were closest at hand, Italians implemented and eroded tradition at the same time by transcending familial obligations and nurturing an attitude of self-improvement. Of all three groups, tradition and circumstance were mingling most effectively for Italians as they attached themselves to the urban-economic structure.

Worthy of mention is that alternative sources of income besides boarders and children seemed of little use in Pittsburgh. The employment of married females was rather limited. The sample data from the 1900 manuscript census revealed that only among northern-born blacks did the percentage of employed females exceed 10 percent. Blacks also had the highest rate of female-headed households among the sample groups, although in no case did women head more than 18 percent of black households.[26]

Women were an integral part of the family as a producing unit. Yet during the late nineteenth and early twentieth century in Pittsburgh they seldom worked for wages and were generally excluded from the manufacturing operations. Working women, mostly unmarried, labored primarily as domestics, and a few found work as seamstresses, milliners, or laundresses. More than half of all late nineteenth-century white, unmarried women in Pittsburgh held domestic occupations. Domestic service was also the single most important occupation of unmarried black women. Of those who worked, 90 percent engaged in domestic work.[27]

Twentieth-century Pittsburgh women also found work mainly in the home or in the needle trades. Nearly one-half of all working women held jobs as domestics, 20 percent as saleswomen, and 14 percent in textiles. Opportunities in manufacturing, however, increased during the first decade of the century. In her investigations for the Pittsburgh Survey, Elizabeth Butler found women coremakers at seven Pittsburgh foundries, mica splitters and coil winders at Westinghouse Electric, hingemakers at a Northside plant, and more than 500 women employees at three screw-and-bolt firms. Most of the 2,000 females in manufacturing, identified by Butler, received wages on a piece-rate basis, earning between $3 and $7 per week. Male workers performing the same operations received approximately double that amount.[28]

Female migrants to Pittsburgh among the Poles, blacks, and Italians generally reflected the citywide distribution of women workers, although a smaller proportion — 5 to 15 percent of each group — worked outside the home. Nearly all female wage earners in the Pittsburgh sample held domestic jobs or worked in laundering. The prejudices black males faced in securing work no doubt proved an even greater bar to black women. Butler, for example, failed to note even a single instance of black females in Pittsburgh manufacturing.

Italian women, too, failed to secure work in the trades, although for different reasons. Only 5 percent of the Pittsburgh sample of Italian women held jobs outside the home. Italian women, Butler suggested, were

> an unimportant factor in the industrial life in the city . . . the ties of tradition that keep the girl to her house and early marriage are still too strong for more than a very few to break. . . . The garment industry here is of a different sort from that which had flourished and given employment to its thousands of outworkers in New York City. Such outwork as there is dates to a time before the Italian women were here in numbers, or had grouped themselves into particular districts and it fell naturally into the hands of the Irish and Germans.[29]

Because support from children was so widespread, few Italian women found it necessary to work outside the home after marriage. It is true that restrictions existed against working women in Italian culture, but these could be compromised somewhat, as Virginia Yans-McLaughlin found among Italian women working in canneries near Buffalo. In Pittsburgh, however, these cultural restrictions were easier to maintain because work for women was scarce. By 1920, in fact, only 6 percent of all women over age fifteen found employment in Pittsburgh, while about 10 percent were able to work in Boston, Chicago, New York, and Cleveland. A decade later Pittsburgh still ranked below these cities.[30]

A recent study of working-class women in Pittsburgh before 1900 concluded that because occupational opportunities for women were comparatively limited, females were prevented from broadening their power within the family, and thus the traditional role segregation of men and women was reinforced.[31] Interviews with Italian families in the city, however, suggested that while opportunities were truly limited, young Italian females aspired to early marriages and departures from outside employment. Because their adolescent years, like those of young men, were devoted to supporting their families of origin, immigrant daughters married as soon as possible not only because it was a cultural norm but because nuptiality supposedly offered an escape from work routines and family burdens. The new burdens marriage itself might entail were not always thoroughly perceived. Thus women married earlier than men, who remained tied to the parental household longer. Their widespread direction over household budgets, moreover, indicated that women were not without power.

Lidwina P. was representative of the young Italian woman's decision to marry. As a girl, she wanted only to marry and have children, a goal that her mother shared for her and a sister. After supporting her mother until she was twenty-two years old, Lidwina married. She remained in Bloomfield, however, to offer care for her mother. As a young girl, Albina B. felt she should marry and "help your husband." She did so by keeping boarders and working in a shoe store during her married life.[32]

Indications that marriage offered an opportunity for Italian women to transfer their obligations from one family to another surfaced in the interviews. Many young Italian girls emigrated to America almost exclusively to marry a man whom they knew hardly at all. In Bloomfield the father of Martin D., because he was literate, wrote letters to the old country on behalf of other Italians in an attempt to arrange marriages. Consequently a greater age disparity existed between Italian husbands and wives, as young Italian girls came to start families with older established immigrants. Whatever aspirations they may have had in entering American marriages, however, family obligations continued to supersede individual inclinations. In fact, such age differences may have accounted for the ability of Italian males to command support and assistance from their wives. Thus, Domenica M., thirteen years younger than her husband, came from Abruzzi in 1913 and remained at home while her husband worked for the Carnegie Steel Company. "My husband don't believe a woman should have to go to work," she explained. Domenica did handle family finances, however. Similarly, the mothers of Felix M. and Martin T. came from Italy to marry, and they remained at home caring for boarders. Other young girls followed older men to America and established families of their own. An eleven-year difference existed between the parents of Lidwina P. The mother of Mary I. married when she was fifteen and her husband was twenty-five. The father of Dan C. returned from Pittsburgh to Abruzzi only once, to marry a girl eight years younger whom he had come to know only through correspondence.[33]

Polish women were also unlikely to seek employment outside the home, although some did work in industries. Butler noted Polish women working on the Southside at an enameling factory, a screw-and-bolt works, and at Jones and Laughlin's core works. Others worked at a Northside hinge factory and at the H. J. Heinz cannery. While few industrial workers labored under even tolerable conditions, Polish females were offered only the worst jobs. In the screw-and-bolt works, for example: "One can see lanes of women, all of them Polish of the peasant class, whose strong arms . . . work . . . at a threader in fish oil . . . most of the girls stand at their work. . . . Noise and filth are accepted as in the nature of things. Ten and a half hours a day the girls work, and one or two nights overtime until nine o'clock. For these hours the girls are paid seventy-five cents a day."[34] "The place of the Polish woman . . . is the lowest industrially among the women workers of Pittsburgh," Butler concluded.[35]

Racial and ethnic prejudices, the nature of industrial work, cultural traditions, and low wages all combined to keep Pittsburgh's black, Italian, and Polish women mainly in the home. Nevertheless, more black women did tend to seek employment than those who were foreign-born. By 1930 nearly one-third of black females were employed; only 16 percent of immigrant women were. Other investigations have reinforced the views that black women were forced to leave the household more than immigrant females and that there was a decline in black fertility ratios as blacks became more urbanized between 1880 and 1920. Historian Elizabeth Pleck has argued that black married women worked more than Italian women because of cultural norms that kept Italian women at home rearing children.[36] Reasons for declines in fertility are not entirely known, although some scholars have linked the decline to the greater participation of black women in the labor force. If the Pittsburgh experience is any indication, however, and black children were pursuing individual rather than family goals, then black mothers would not only have to share a greater burden in supplementing family income but would be disinclined to make investments in children who offered uncertain economic benefits.[37]

Yet additional income was often required if families were to survive. Margaret Byington revealed that 72 percent of all immigrant workers in the Pittsburgh area earned less than $12.00 per week. She calculated that a minimum of $13.22 per week would supply only the barest of necessities: three rooms without sanitary conveniences for a family of five; 24¢ per person per day for food; $5 for clothing, fuel, insurance, and other necessities.[38] Even occasional unemployment, in a time when most laborers faced unemployment an average of two months per year, would destroy such a meager budget.

Faced with mounting economic pressures and little possibility of outside employment, many working-class women opened their homes to outsiders — usually unmarried men. To the women fell the responsibility of cooking, cleaning, washing, mending, and generally caring for the family plus a number of unrelated boarders. The income produced by taking in boarders often meant the difference between deprivation and starvation. Comfort was not among the realm of possibilities for these early migrant families. Table 5 demonstrates the extent to which the sample households in this study relied upon unrelated boarders.

Table 5. Unrelated Boarders in Sample Households in Pittsburgh in 1900

Ethnic/Minority Group	Number of Households Sampled	Number of Households with Boarder(s) (%)	Average Number of Boarders
Northern-born black	125	24 (19)	4.5
Southern-born black	586	176 (30)	3.3
Russian Pole	215	99 (46)	3.4
Austrian Pole	33	11 (33)	5.4
German Pole	206	25 (12)	1.2
Italian	183	70 (38)	4.4

NOTE. The source is U.S. Bureau of the Census, Manuscript Census for Pittsburgh, 1900. A 20 percent sample of black, Italian, and Polish families was derived for this study and comprised the sample data.

The burden of caring for boarders fell unevenly upon the women in the Pittsburgh sample. Both northern-born black and German-Polish women escaped the tasks associated with taking in outsiders. Few homes in either group contained boarders. Most northern-born black families and the German Poles had been in Pittsburgh for a considerable time. They were also older than the other families in the sample. Their children were grown, and the need for boarders had dissipated somewhat. Nearly one-third or more of the remaining Poles, Italians, and southern-born black families took in an average of three to five boarders. In return for lodging, food, and a number of personal services, a single boarder paid $3 to $4 per month plus the cost of food. The average family taking in boarders, among the Pittsburgh sample, then added approximately $12 to $16 to its monthly income. The system benefited single men also, by providing room and board at approximately $11 per month and permiting them to save a substantial amount of money. Earning money and returning home or sending for one's family on $9.90 per week became a realistic possibility under such a system. Subsistence, even savings, for the boarding family was also possible.

A glimpse at the average number of employed individuals in a household at successive stages of family development further explains the ability of families to survive under the most meager of circumstances. To provide this analysis we have organized migrant families into four groups: newlyweds, young families, midstage families, and mature families. The characteristics of each are explained in Table 6.

Table 6. Mean Number of Workers per Household by Ethnicity
and Family Stage in Pittsburgh in 1900

Ethnic/Minority Group	Number of Households	Newlyweds	Young Families	Midstage Families	Mature Families
Northern-born black	125	5.3	2.8	5.2	5.4
Southern-born black	586	4.7	2.7	4.6	5.1
Russian Pole	215	5.1	2.4	3.9	3.8
Austrian Pole	33	5.0	2.7	3.3	0.0
German Pole	206	3.6	2.3	4.2	4.1
Italian	183	4.7	2.5	4.1	5.8

NOTE. The source of the data is the 20 percent sample of black, Italian, and Polish families derived for this study. The family stages are defined as follows: newlyweds are newly married couples without children; young families consist of a wife less than 45 years old with children, but no child is either working or married; midstage is a couple in which the wife is of any age, but in which children are employed or married; mature families consist of a wife over 45 years old, and all children have left home.

Significantly, newlywed families built a foundation by maximizing income before the arrival of children. All groups reduced the number of workers in the household between the newlywed and young-family stage, however, as the arrival of young children in all households put greater demands upon the primary wage earner. As children became old enough to gain employment at midstage, blacks, especially in northern-born families, continued to employ more individuals per household than other groups. Undoubtedly lower wages necessitated such a pattern. But not to be discounted is the evidence that children in Polish and Italian homes were relinquishing most of their wages, a practice that would reduce the need to acquire more workers per household. That Poles continued to maintain the lowest levels of workers per household even when children left the home in the mature stage is a further suggestion that parents may still have been receiving assistance from children who lived in households of their own. Also striking is that in the mature stage Italians had the highest average number of workers per household. If Italian youth were more upwardly mobile and some likely to build careers of their own, they may have been less likely to remain in their parental households, a reaction that would have forced parents to depend more heavily on boarders. It is suggestive that at the mature stage Italian households did contain more boarders per household than any other sample group.

The mean number of unrelated boarders per households further elucidates these familial patterns (Table 7). Between the young family and midstage, when children reached an employable age, only in black households did the average number of unrelated boarders in-

Table 7. Mean Number of Unrelated Boarders
per Household Containing Boarders,
by Ethnicity and Family Stage, in Pittsburgh in 1900

Ethnic/Minority Group	Number of Households	Newlyweds	Young Families	Midstage
Northern-born black	24	2.8	1.2	1.7
Southern-born black	176	2.9	3.1	6.4
Russian Pole	99	2.8	3.6	3.5
Austrian Pole	11	0	2.3	0
German Pole	25	0	1.3	1.0
Italian	70	2.9	4.9	`4.2

NOTE. The source of the data is the 20 percent sample of black, Italian, and Polish families derived for this study. See Table 6 for the definitions of the family stages. While several percentages for the boarders may be high, it should be remembered that samples were drawn from a period of heavy emigration and migration. It might seem strange that the mean number of unrelated boarders per household occasionally exceeded the mean number of workers, as with Russian Poles, for example, at the newlywed stage. However, the mean number of workers was computed for all sample households, while the figure for un-related boarders was computed only for households with boarders in them. Thus, averages for unrelated boarders were high and often decreased when computing a total household sample that included many residences wih no boarders and only one worker.

crease. Polish households displayed an opposite trend as boarders became superfluous when children began to contribute earnings. Again, however, Italians proved to rely on unrelated boarders. No doubt the Italian levels resulted partly from strong migration networks, which caused Italian households to care for newcomers from the homeland. But similar networks existed in Polish and black communities. If Italians were pushing more rapidly into business pursuits, however, they may have brought more workers into their households who were potential labor for their entrepreneurial ventures. Household arrangements influenced their path of economic entry as much as cultural residues from a premigration past.

A further understanding of family strategies can be gained by looking at household structures at various stages in the development of the nuclear, core group within a household (Table 8). Where data are sufficient, similar trends appear again between Italians and blacks. From the newlywed through the midstage levels, both southern-born blacks and Italians drifted steadily from the nuclear levels of their early years of marriage. In other words, they resorted to bringing

Table 8. Household Structure by Family Stage and Ethnic Group
in Pittsburgh in 1900

Family Stage	Ethnic/Minority Group				
	Northern-Born Black	Southern-Born Black	Russian Pole	German Pole	Italian
Nuclear					
Newlyweds	72.7	81.6	64.3	80	71.4
Young family	76.9	63.4	72.6	80.4	66.2
Midstage	68.8	52.2	90.2	93.2	50
Mature family	85.7	71.4	77.8	100	50
Extended					
Newlyweds	18.2	3.0	7.1	20	25.6
Young family	15.4	13.4	10.3	9.8	5.6
Midstage	31.3	17.4	0	0	0
Mature family	0	21.4	22.2	0	0
Augmented					
Newlyweds	9.1	15.4	28.6	0	3
Young family	7.7	23.3	17.1	9.8	28.2
Midstage	0	30.4	9.8	6.8	50
Mature family	14.3	7.1	0	0	50

NOTE. The source of the data is the 20 percent sample of black, Italian, and Polish families derived for this study. See Table 6 for the definitions of the family stages. The sample of Austrian Poles was too small to yield reliable results, and this group was not analyzed for this table.

boarders or relatives into their homes as their children became old enough to work. Russian Polish and German Polish families, on the other hand, grew progressively more nuclear during the same stages, a strong indication that children rather than outsiders were relied on for sustenance.

It is also helpful to learn something about who lived in various households at specific stages. Indeed, at the crucial midstage, when children became employable, only blacks had significant percentages of extended households. Apparently they brought in other relatives. It is possible, of course, that immigrants were unable to do so, since many of their relatives remained abroad. But blacks also exceeded Poles in attracting unrelated boarders into the home at the midstage, and Italians were most likely of all to attract boarders into the home at the stage when children became eligible to work and marry. At the period of family life when children could contribute to family income, Poles were almost always living in nuclear families, while about one-half of southern-born blacks and Italians decided to house boarders and relatives, although we can assume probably not for the same reasons.

If Poles were more likely to exclude relatives and boarders as families matured, they were ironically quite willing to open households at the newlywed stage. Russian Poles were the least likely of all sample groups to live in nuclear households when they were first married, with most of the outsiders being unrelated boarders, a hint of how these families established themselves. Southern-born blacks displayed the greatest tendency to live alone as newlyweds, no doubt a reflection of their young ages at marriage and an extension of the independent spirit they revealed in adolescence. This inclination, however, withered considerably as families struggled to maintain themselves. At the late stages of family life most groups lived largely in nuclear family arrangements, with the exception of Italians who continued to rely on boarders. At the mature stage about one-fifth of both southern-born black and Russian Polish homes were likely to contain relatives in addition to the basic core group. While all immigrant groups had reduced the number of relatives in their household from the young-family to midfamily stages, only blacks took in more. In old age, however, while the available data are limited, differing familial strategies began to merge into remarkably similar patterns.

While all the reasons for black family strategies at the crucial midstage are not evident, a glimpse of the occupational status of household heads at various stages in family development does offer additional clues (Table 9). Most household heads were working people,

Table 9. Occupational Status of Heads of Households by Family Stage
in Pittsburgh in 1900

	Occupational Status				
Ethnic/Minority Group	Unskilled	Semiskilled	Skilled	Low White Collar	High White Collar
Young Family					
Northern-born black	30.8	50.0	11.5	7.7	0
Southern-born black	48.0	34.5	12.3	1.2	3.5
Russian Pole	62.0	9.9	19.7	6.3	1.4
German Pole	78.6	3.3	9.8	8.3	0
Italian	65.7	7.1	24.3	2.9	0
Midstage					
Northern-born black	56.3	31.2	12.4	0	0
Southern-born black	51.1	26.7	13.3	4.4	2.2
Russian Pole	37.5	17.5	32.5	10.0	2.5
German Pole	81.8	4.5	4.5	6.8	0
Italian	68.4	5.3	21.1	5.3	0

NOTE. All data are percentages. The source of the data is the 20 percent sample of black, Italian, and Polish families derived for this study. See Table 6 for a definition of the family stages. The sample of Austrian Poles was too small to yield reliable results, and this group was not analyzed in this table.

and their status was generally below the skilled level, regardless of their ethnic or racial background. Differences existed within the manual class, and most workers remained in either unskilled or semiskilled categories throughout their lifetimes. While Table 9 represents the occupational distribution of workers in 1900, it is still clear that young black families held better jobs than did those at midstage. The proportion of black household heads in unskilled jobs increased slightly between the young-family and middle stages, whereas the percentages declined in the semiskilled categories from 34.5 percent to 26.7 percent for southern-born blacks and from 50.0 to 31.3 percent for blacks born in the North. At a time when black children were ready to enter the marketplace, their parents were losing rather than strengthening previous occupational strongholds and were increasingly unable to transfer jobs and skills. German Poles experienced a contrary pattern, with slight improvement in semiskilled and skilled levels; Russian Poles encountered marked increases in these job categories, which enhanced their ability to attract kin into their places of work. The better showing by Russian Poles could be attributed to their predominance in numbers over German Poles, which allowed them to seize more skilled openings for themselves and their friends and kin. Inexplicably, midstage Italian heads held fewer skilled positions, although more white-collar jobs, than did young family heads. This difference, however, may have reflected the recent arrival of both groups into the city rather than a decline in status over time. It should also be remembered that the total amount of skilled tasks was declining in Pittsburgh and that, except for the Russian Poles, most groups were unable to expand their representation in this area measurably. Young Italians, as demonstrated earlier, received intensive direction into specific skills and trades. That nearly one-third of the young Italian heads held skilled jobs reflected their parents' urging to acquire a skill as well as the assistance in job procurement provided to young Italian workers and does not pay heed to their ability to hold on to such employment.

Based on these findings in Pittsburgh, it is difficult to cling to sweeping generalizations about working-class families and their behavior in the industrial city. That all newcomers struggled to establish some sense of order and predictability in their domestic life is evident, but this did not mean that similar economic plateaus caused all workers and their families to act in concert. Racial barriers and restricted opportunities caused black families to stress self-sufficiency among their children, to rely on working women, and to attract boarders in middle life stages when children initiated employment to maintain their households. Poles, consolidating their clusters in industrial workplaces, tightly controlled their progeny, used their income in lieu of boarders and working wives, and gradually excluded outsiders from their homes over the course of their lives. Curiously enough, Italians opted for a different tact altogether. Emphasizing both child support and individual improvement, they slowly injected themselves into skilled tasks and, later, small businesses. This pattern generally eliminated the need to send females outside the home into the workplace. They also continued to attract boarders into their homes as employees in their entrepreneurial pursuits — and sometimes because children, who had been taught to achieve as individuals, drifted away from their familial moorings and refused to remain in parental households, contributing to their support.

NOTES

1. See Herbert Gutman, *The Black Family in Slavery and Freedom, 1750-1925* (New York, 1976), passim; Elizabeth Pleck, *Black Migration and Poverty, Boston, 1865-1900* (New York, 1979), 202-3; Pleck, "Two Worlds in One: Work and Family," *Journal of Social History*, 10 (Winter 1976), 178-95; Tamara Hareven and Randolph Langenbach, *Amoskeag:*

Life and Work in an American Factory City (New York, 1979), passim; Virginia Yans-McLaughlin, *Family and Community: Italian Immigrants in Buffalo, 1880-1930* (Ithaca, N.Y., 1977), passim; Paul Wrobel, *Our Way: Family, Parish, and Neighborhood in a Polish-American Community* (Notre Dame, Ind., 1979), passim; John Bodnar, "Immigration and Modernization: Slavic Peasants in Industrial America," *Journal of Social History*, 10 (Fall 1976), 44-71; Bodnar, "Immigration, Kinship, and the Rise of Working-Class Realism," ibid., 14 (Fall 1980), 45-65.

2. Cases are drawn from the American Service Institute Papers (AIS), file 4, case 5754, Archives of Industrial Society, University of Pittsburgh. The last initial of each name has been changed to "X" to insure anonymity.

3. Ibid.; see also case 5694.

4. Ibid; case 5694.

5. Ibid.; case 5524.

6. See Louise A. Tilly, "The Family Wage Economy of a French Textile City: Roubaix, 1872-1906," *Journal of Family History*, 4 (Winter 1979), 381-93, for insightful remarks on the impact of a wage economy on family structure.

7. See Eugene D. Genovese, *Roll Jordan Roll: The World the Slaves Made* (New York, 1974), 504-5. Genovese found a similar strong individualism in slave families and argued that the relatively "happy" childhood of slave children resulted in "independent, spirited adults."

8. Interviews with Sally S., June 18, 1978; Roy M., July 9, 1974; William H., June 17, 1978; Ernest F., Apr. 20, 1976; Anonymous, Sept. 2, 1976; Grant W., July 12, 1976, Pittsburgh Oral History Project (POHP).

9. Interviews with Jasper A., July 12, 1976; Roy N., July 9, 1974; Olive W., July 23, 1976; Grant W., July 12, 1976, POHP. Interview with Walter W., Feb. 14, 1973, provided by Clarence R. Turner, University of Pittsburgh. Kenneth Soddy, *Men in Middle Life* (London, 1967), 293, stated that during periods of rapid social change children achieve an increasing degree of independence. This movement toward independence may emanate from parents as well as children.

10. Interview with Gertrude D., Nov. 3, 1976, POHP.

11. John Model, Frank Furstenberg, and Theodore Hershberg, "Social Change and Transition to Adulthood in Historical Perspective," *Journal of Family History*, 1 (Autumn 1976), 29.

12. Interviews with Grant W., July 12, 1976; Floyd T., May 11, 1976; Jasper A., July 12, 1976; Ernest F., Apr. 20, 1976; Queen E., Oct. 8, 1976; Anonymous, July 11, 1974; James N., June 28, 1976; Olive W., July 23, 1976, POHP. Abraham Epstein, *The Negro Migrant in Pittsburgh* (Pittsburgh, 1918), 24.

13. Crandall Shifflett, "The Household Composition of Rural Black Families: Louisa County, Virginia, 1880," *Journal of Interdisciplinary History*, 6 (Autumn 1975), 244-45. The black elderly were less likely to live with their children in America in 1900 than other groups. See Daniel Scott Smith, "Life Course, Norms, and the Family System of Older Americans," *Journal of Family History*, 4 (Fall 1979), 297.

14. See Victor Greene, *The Slavic Community on Strike* (Notre Dame, Ind., 1968), 24-25. William I. Thomas and Florian Zaniecki, *The Polish*

Peasant in Europe and America, 5 vols. (New York, 1920), 4: 11-22, noted the widespread conflict between parental authority and the individual needs of children. That parents were increasingly unable to pass on land (or anything else) to children may have caused some tension. Industrial conditions in urban America may have led to a restoration of family unity among Poles.

15. Interviews with Joseph D., Sept. 17, 1976; John K., Sept. 13, 1976; Ray C., July 1, 1976; Edward R., Sept. 10, 1976, POHP.

16. Polish women, unlike black women, seldom worked after marriage unless their husbands were killed or incapacitated. In addition to managing finances, they usually paid all bills and insurance. See interview with Francis P., Jan. 16, 1976, POHP.

17. Interviews with Stanley N., Sept. 22, 1976; Joseph B., May 13 and 20, 1976; John K., Sept. 13, 1976; Peter L., Sept. 17, 1976, POHP. Elizabeth Voltz, "The Child Labor Question," clipping in Civic Club of Allegheny County Records, 1846-1849, Box 3, Archives of Industrial Society. Occasionally, a son would rebel and run away from home; see interview with Bernard C., June 20, 1974, POHP.

18. The employment of young girls at Oliver Iron and Steel was detailed in the *Pittsburgh Leader,* Apr. 5, 1912, 1, 16. Interviews with John B., Mar. 3, 1976; Stephanie W., Mar. 21, 1976; Josephine B., Mar. 3, 1976; Francis P., Jan. 16, 1976; Stanley E., Sept. 9, 1976; Joseph D., Sept. 17, 1976; Peter L., Sept. 17, 1976, POHP. Similar employment of young girls for family reasons in the early industrial revolution is discussed in Louise Tilly, Joan Scott, and Miriam Cohen, "Women's Work and European Fertility Patterns," *Journal of Interdisciplinary History,* 6 (Winter 1976), 447-76.

19. Leonard Covello, *The Social Background of the Italo-American School Child: A Study of the Southern Italian Family Mores and Their Effect on the School Situation in Italy and America* (Leiden, 1967), 87, 149-50. Covello went on to argue that Italian family solidarity was similar to that found among Polish peasants. A similar interpretation of Polish families emphasizing authoritarian child-raising patterns is found in Caroline Golab, *Immigrant Destinations* (Philadelphia, 1977), 30; Yans-McLaughlin, *Family and Community,* 62-64.

20. Josef Barton, *Peasants and Strangers: Italians, Rumanians, and Slovaks in an American City* (Cambridge, Mass., 1975), 117ff.; John W. Briggs, *An Italian Passage: Immigrants to Three American Cities, 1890-1930* (New Haven, Conn., 1977), 55-56, 238. Cf. Carolyn Sutcher, "School Attendance in Nineteenth-Century Pittsburgh: Wealth, Ethnicity, and Occupational Mobility of School Age Children, 1855-1865" (Ph.D. diss., University of Pittsburgh, 1977), who stressed class over ethnicity as a factor in low school attendance.

21. Briggs, *An Italian Passage,* passim; Timothy L. Smith, "Immigrant Social Aspirations and American Education," *American Quarterly,* 21 (Fall 1969), 522-25.

22. Interviews with Michael M., July 16, 1977; Mary I., May 13, 1977; Martin D., Mar. 15, 1977; Domenica M., Mar. 18, 1977; Felix D., Mar. 17, 1977, POHP. Other Italian youth expressed displeasure with school because teachers mispronounced and changed names. See interview

with Martin D., Mar. 15, 1977, POHP.

23. Interviews with Lidwina P., May 26, 1977; Umberto B., Mar. 14, 1977; Amico L., July 28, 1977; Vincent L., June 21, 1977; Ray L., Aug. 8, 1977; Lou G., May 11, 1977; Martin T., Mar. 25, 1977, POHP. Covello in surveying Italians in the early 1940s in New York City found that while 56.1 percent of Italian students thought all their wages should be given to their parents, only 24.7 percent of black students felt that way. Blacks (53.1 percent) preferred to give one-half to mother and keep the balance. *Social Background of the Italo-American School Child*, 377.

24. Interviews with Lou G., May 11, 1977; Frank D., July 27, 1977, POHP.

25. Interview with Ray L., Aug. 24, 1977, POHP.

26. Data from the U.S. Bureau of the Census, Manuscript Census for Pittsburgh, 1900, revealed the following percentages of female-headed households: northern-born blacks, 16 percent; southern-born blacks, 17.9 percent; Russian Poles, 0.4 percent; German Poles, 2.0 percent; and Italians, 3 percent. While the percentage of women working outside the home increased substantially among all groups by 1900, it was more firmly established among black than white women. See Kenneth Kusmer, *A Ghetto Takes Shape: Black Cleveland, 1840-1930* (Urbana, Ill., 1976), 88. Corinne Azen Krause did find Italian women in Pittsburgh more likely to remain at home than Slavic or Jewish women. See "Urbanization without Breakdown: Italian, Jewish, and Slavic Immigrant Women in Pittsburgh, 1900-1915," *Journal of Urban History*, 4 (May 1978), 276-97. This view of Italians is reaffirmed in Elizabeth B. Butler, *Women and the Trades, Pittsburgh, 1907-1908* (New York, 1911), 21. A national study of 55,224 women in 1913 confirmed a low rate of employment for Italian females but showed Polish patterns to be even lower for women over age twenty-five. Black women did have higher rates for women over eighteen but had a rate lower than Poles and Italians before that age, a result, perhaps, of their tendency to remain longer in school. See U.S. Congress, *Report on Conditions of Women and Child Wage Earners in the United States*, 61st Cong., 2nd sess. Soc. Doc. 645, Serial no. 5702, 19 vols. (Washington, D.C., 1913).

27. Susan Kleinberg, "Technology's Stepdaughters: The Impact of Industrialization upon Working Class Women, Pittsburgh, 1865-1890" (Ph.D. diss., University of Pittsburgh, 1973), 181-82.

28. Elizabeth Beardsley Butler, "Pittsburgh Women in the Metal Trades"; "The Working Women of Pittsburgh"; and "The Industrial Environment of Pittsburgh's Working Women," *Charities and Commons*, 21 (Oct.-Apr. 1908-9), 40-42, 574, 1118.

29. Butler, "The Working Women of Pittsburgh," ibid., 570-71.

30. U.S. Bureau of the Census, *Fifteenth Census of the United States, 1930, IV: Occupations* (Washington, D.C., 1933), 81. Briggs, *An Italian Passage*, 116, found only 13 percent of Italian women working outside the home by 1925 and only 30 percent in 1893.

31. Susan Kleinberg, "Technology and Women's Work: The Lives of Working Class Women in Pittsburgh, 1870-1900," *Labor History*, 17 (Winter 1976), 71. Ethnic culture as a determinant of women's employment is stressed in Thomas Kessner and Betty Boyd Caroli, "New Immigrant

Women at Work: Italians and Jews in New York City, 1880-1905," *Journal of Ethnic Studies*, 5 (Winter 1978), 24-28.

32. Interviews in Pittsburgh with Lidwina P., May 26, 1977; Albina B., Mar. 19, 1977; Mary I., May 13, 1977, POHP.

33. Interviews with Martin D., Mar. 15, 1977; Domenica M., Mar. 18, 1977; Felix D., Mar. 17, 1977; Martin T., Mar. 25, 1977; Lidwina P., May 6, 1977; Don C., Mar. 31, 1977; Mary I., May 13, 1977, POHP. See also Carla Bianco, *The Two Rosetos* (Bloomington, Ind., 1974), 116-17, for a discussion of arranged marriages.

34. Butler, "Pittsburgh Women in the Metal Trades," 42.

35. Butler, "The Working Women of Pittsburgh," 579-80. A recent survey of women in the city reinforced the conclusion that Italian immigrant women were considerably more likely to remain at home than Slavic women. See Corinne Azen Krause, *Grandmothers, Mothers, and Daughters: An Oral History of Ethnicity, Mental Health, and Continuity of Three Generations of Jewish, Italian, and Slavic-American Women* (New York, 1978), 80ff.

36. Elizabeth Pleck, "A Mother's Wage: A Comparison of Income-Earning among Urban Blacks and Italian Married Women, 1896-1911," *Signs*, 1 (Winter 1977), 49-63. Pleck found, too, that black daughters were more likely to retain their own paychecks than Italian daughters. See also Kusmer, *Black Cleveland*, 88-89; *Industrial Databook for the Pittsburgh District* (Pittsburgh, 1936), 15.

37. Stanley L. Engerman, "Black Fertility and Family Structure in the United States, 1880-1940," *Journal of Family History*, 2 (Summer 1977), 117-38; Robert Higgs, *Competition and Coercion: Blacks in the American Economy* (Cambridge, 1974), 18-19; Herman Lantz and Lewellyn Hendrix, "Nineteenth Century: A Reexamination of the Past," *Journal of Family History*, 3 (Fall 1978), 251-61.

38. See Margaret Byington, *Homestead: The Households of a Mill Town*, The Pittsburgh Survey, ed. Paul U. Kellogg (New York, 1910), 104.

5

Persistence and Occupational Mobility: The First Generation

Work dominated the lives of Pittsburgh's immigrant and black families during the first third of the century. Whether they toiled before the open-hearth door, installed pipeline for the Equitable Gas Company, or drove one of the city's numerous freight wagons, their lives centered on work. Family patterns, neighborhood life, and position within the community all depended upon the ability or inability to secure steady employment. Most migrants, as has been shown, did manage to acquire manual work upon their arrival in the "steel city." Their ability to improve upon these initial occupations affected families and neighborhoods still further. A better job reduced the economic pressure on families; it often afforded the security of home ownership. Children could be permitted, even encouraged, to remain in school rather than put to work to assist the family. Crowding within the family might become less pervasive. Improved health, better sanitation, and other environmental conditions also accompanied the climb up the occupational ladder. In short, occupational achievement often provided the key to improving the quality of life for an entire family.

The continued interest by historians in the process of occupational mobility reflects its importance in the lives of the workers themselves. The focus of this concern, however, has shifted somewhat since 1964.[1] The earliest research concentrated on examining the "myth of mobility" in American society. These works usually identified modest but divergent rates of mobility, based on ethnicity or family position, frequently concluding that in most American cities enough mobility occurred to perpetuate the hope of occupational success. Longitudinal studies also speculated about whether the American social order was becoming more or less rigid.

The more recent analyses sought to uncover causal factors contributing to the differing rates of mobility among various groups. In some cases these explanations revolve around the interaction among the social and economic conditions of urban society and the effects of industrialization on individual or aggregate success.[2] Gordon Kirk demonstrated, for example, that industrialization hindered the occupational opportunities of migrants to Holland, Michigan, as access to farm labor and farm ownership declined.[3] Kenneth Kusmer noted that union and management prejudices and a surplus of immigrant labor contributed to the occupational decline of Cleveland's black population.[4] Thomas Kessner described the strong link among mobility, technology, and urbanization. "In an increasingly urban and technological society," such as New York City, Kessner observed, "the effect of parental status receded in importance. Relatively independent factors like education, entrepreneurial skill and craftsmanship took precedence. . . . In this type of swirling atmosphere the immigrant could hope to achieve success for himself and his children."[5]

These recent studies have moved far from the limited dimensions of work of an earlier period. Nearly all consider a multiplicity of factors contributing to the success or failure of individuals and/or groups. Josef Barton and Caroline Golab stress the importance of premigration backgrounds and values on occupational success.[6] Others demonstrate the significance of economic and social forces in the migrant's adopted city. What remains unexamined, however, are the interplay among premigration backgrounds, the expectations of the migrants themselves, and the structural forces that they encountered in the city.

This analysis attempts to rectify this deficiency by comparing the outward signs of success or failure (occupational achievement or the accumulation of property) with the goals and aspirations of each group against the backdrop of a highly industrialized, urbanized society. Previous chapters have demonstrated how Pittsburgh's industrial structure and extant community values interacted with premigrant cultures to produce divergent patterns of adjustment. These variables continued to operate throughout the early decades of the twentieth century. Each group's ability to adjust to the industrial environment, for example, depended, in part, on the occupational alternatives available to it. The aspirations of the workers, in turn, influenced their perception of those alternatives as well as their own measurements of occupational success. Workers with limited occupational goals achieved satisfaction more easily and seldom sought alternative work careers. Workers interviewed for this study frequently assessed their lives as "successful" when, in fact, they had achieved little or no occupational progress. Their perceptions of success concomitantly influenced future occupational behavior.

This study employs the conventional measurements of occupational mobility (movement from one occupational level to another) to determine an individual or group's relative ranking over time and to permit comparisons with other groups in other cities. It attempts to measure success, however, in terms of the goals and objectives of those people being studied. In this manner we may determine not only their success in American society but also their satisfaction as measured by the groups themselves. Information about differing goals and aspirations also helps to explain the dissimilar patterns of behavior and adjustment among various ethnic groups in Pittsburgh. The crucial questions are: (1) What were the aspirations of the various groups? (2) What factors explain these goals? (3) How successful or unsuccessful were the groups in achieving their goals? (4) What were the limits on their achievement? (5) How did their success or lack of success influence subsequent behavior?

The wide variation in migrant expectations, discussed in chapter 2, demonstrates that an evaluation of success based upon occupational advancement or even the accumulation of property is incomplete. Polish workers in Pittsburgh sought either enough money to return home and purchase land or a measure of economic security and stability in the "steel city." Some Italians also desired to return home. Those who remained expected to acquire skilled occupations or to own their businesses. Black migrants, who had already experienced slight upward mobility before coming to Pittsburgh, sought skilled employment, private businesses, or even professional positions.

That Poles would achieve greater satisfaction and face less frustration in reaching their goals seems obvious. Nevertheless, it is in the light of these aspirations that occupational achievement must be measured. The goals of individuals motivated certain behaviors and influenced the ways in which they adapted to the city. Their success in achieving their own objectives also strongly influenced their outlook toward urban life and, in particular, the neighborhood in which they resided. Thus, throughout the remainder of this chapter the occupational achievement of the three groups will be compared with respect to each other, with respect to the occupational structure of the entire city, and, most important, in the light of the occupational goals of the specific group.

It is particularly important to know both the existing occupational structure at a given point and the changes in that structure over time within the entire city. The distribution of all workers within the city at one point in time provides a valuable baseline from which to evaluate the position of a particular group. If, for example, the occupational structure of a city were evenly distributed among five categories, ranked from high to low, one might expect to find 20 percent of any group in the top category, 20 percent in the second, and so on. The extent to which a particular group deviated from the norm provides important evidence regarding that group's social and economic standing within the city.

Changes within the city's occupational structure over time are also important because they influence the occupational distribution and advancement of the group in question. For example, a shift in the San Francisco economy in the 1870s from commerce to manufacturing had a deleterious effect on the status of that city's persisting merchant population. The change, at the same time, provided new opportunities for blue-collar workers. More than one-third of the city's leading manufacturers had at one time held blue-collar jobs.[7] The development of the locomotive and machine-tool industry in Paterson, New Jersey, presented similar opportunities to that city's skilled blue-collar workers. Riding the crest of industrialization, most of Paterson's successful manufacturers employed their technological skills to catapult from craftsman to owner within a few decades.[8] New York City's occupational structure, in contrast, expanded at all levels, providing a wide range of opportunities. The relatively even growth, however, did not provide greater opportunities in one occupational category than in another. The occupational advancement of Jews and Italians in New York, according to Kessner, was therefore due to factors other than a change in the city's occupational structure.[9]

An upward shift in a city's occupational structure, of course, does not guarantee a corresponding improvement in a group's occupational standing. It merely illustrates that better jobs do exist, usually in greater numbers. Other outside factors usually decide how those jobs will be distributed. White-collar jobs in Cleveland, for example, increased from 22 to 28 percent of the city's total work force between 1890 and 1930. The proportion of unskilled laborers fell during the same period by 7 percent. Black workers nearly matched the citywide increase in white-collar work, but those performing unskilled work also increased during the period from 25 to 41 percent.[10] This increase, resulting from a variety of factors, provides a clear illustration of the declining status of blacks in the city of Cleveland.

The shift in Pittsburgh's labor force away from unskilled and skilled work and toward semiskilled and white-collar work began during the late nineteenth century. This trend, similar to the direction taken in Cleveland, continued throughout the first third of the twentieth century. As illustrated in Table 10 the absolute number of unskilled jobs increased by 44 percent between 1900 and 1910, then declined during the next two decades. In contrast, the proportion of day laborers, as a percentage of the total work force, fell steadily during the same period, from 32 to 22 percent. A variety of factors, particularly the continued installation of labor-saving devices in Pittsburgh's factories, contributed to this decline. Blacks and immigrants coming to Pittsburgh without skills would find increasing competition for work at the lowest level of the occupational scale.

Table 10. Vertical Occupational Distribution of the Total Male Population in Pittsburgh, 1900-30

Skill Level	Decade						
	1900	1910		1920		1930	
High white collar							
No. (% change)	2,575	10,504	(308.0)	11,067	(5.3)	13,891	(25.5)
% of work force	2.4	5.4		5.8		6.7	
Professional							
No. (% change)	4,429	6,825	(54.0)	8,822	(29.3)	12,276	(39.1)
% of work force	4.1	3.8		4.6		5.9	
Low white collar							
No. (% change)	19,344	35,571	(83.8)	40,710	(14.5)	45,354	(11.4)
% of work force	17.9	19.6		21.2		21.7	
Skilled							
No. (% change)	20,969	30,316	(46.9)	31,678	(2.8)	30,030	(-6.2)
% of work force	19.4	16.9		16.5		14.4	
Semiskilled							
No. (% change)	22,002	39,429	(79.5)	41,573	(5.4)	50,114	(20.4)
% of work force	20.4	21.7		21.7		24.0	
Unskilled							
No. (% change)	34,728	50,154	(44.4)	48,256	(-3.8)	45,840	(-5.0)
% of work force	32.2	27.6		25.2		22.0	

NOTE. The data are compiled from the following: U.S. Bureau of the Census volumes on population: *1900 Census*, Vol. 2, Part 2 (1902), pp. 582-84; *1910 Census, Vol. 4, Occupation Statistics*, pp. 180-93; *1920 Census, Vol. 4, Occupations*, pp. 1197-1200; and *1930 Census, Vol. 4, Occupations*, pp. 1416, 1418. The totals do not add up to 100 percent because of the elimination of certain small miscellaneous categories, e.g., those in agricultural and extractive industries.

The proportion of skilled workers also decreased slightly during the 1900-30 period. The number of skilled jobs increased by 47 percent between 1900 and 1910, then remained relatively constant during the next twenty years. This stability within the skilled classification, in effect, reduced opportunities for craftsmen working at lower level occupations. Even in an expanding economy, one might expect relatively little mobility out of the skilled classification. Workers could hardly be expected to abandon occupations requiring years of training even for the attractions, imagined or real, of white-collar work. Excepting the Paterson and San Francisco examples previously mentioned, skilled workers in nearly every American city studied thus far were the least mobile, both geographically and occupationally, of any blue-collar group.[11] Normally only death or old age removed them from their artisan occupations. The stability within the skilled group meant that opportunities for others occurred mostly through new openings, rather than through replacing former skilled workers who had moved on to higher level positions. In Pittsburgh there was little net change in the number of skilled positions between 1910 and 1930, while the combined Polish, black, and Italian population increased by 50,000. Few could count on achieving skilled work regardless of their prior training.

The dramatic increase in semiskilled and white-collar work, particularly during the first decade of the century, demonstrated the growing opportunities in each of these areas. Semiskilled operatives in the mills and in the services and white-collar workers, particularly retail dealers (8,277), sales persons (6,310), and clerical workers (17,042), were much in demand in the "steel city."[12] Regular advertisements in the Pittsburgh newspapers heralded the availability of these positions.[13] Opportunity both for obtaining an initial occupation and for advancement was presumably greater in semiskilled and white-collar work. Both classifications expanded throughout the first third of the century.

In spite of the abundance of white-collar work, few immigrants or blacks, as noted earlier, were able to secure these jobs upon their arrival into the city. The changes in the structure of the work force suggest, however, the growing availability of work at both the semiskilled and white-collar levels. Given the aspiration to do so, newcomers willing to work hard and acquire the necessary skills might reasonably expect advancement into those positions, provided they remained in the city long enough. Considering the goals and premigration experiences of each group and the changing work structure in Pittsburgh, one might hypothesize the following: blacks possessing high aspirations and a willingness to shift from job to job would move into an expanding white-collar work world; Italians with blue-collar skills would find it increasingly difficult to exercise those skills in a declining skilled labor market, while the expansion of small proprietorships would present ample opportunities to satisfy Italian entrepreneurial goals; Poles seeking occupational security would encounter increased competition for their jobs at the unskilled level. Many would be forced to acquire some skill, even within the mill, or face unemployment. The extent to which these predictions occurred, or failed to occur, illustrates the complex relationships among premigration cultures, mobility aspirations, the occupational structure of the city, the existing social structure, and the ability of migrant peoples to adapt. This chapter examines the impact of these relationships on the mobility patterns of first-generation blacks, Poles, and Italians in Pittsburgh.

The earliest and the most significant way that newcomers coped with the harsh Pittsburgh environment was to abandon it. Recent mobility studies have demonstrated that between 40 and 60 percent of all workers left most nineteenth-century cities in a single decade. This information and the hypothesis that southeastern Europeans and recent black migrants might prove even more volatile led us to double the size of our sample from 10 to 20 percent of each group's population. Moreover, to increase the number of possible observations per worker, we conducted traces at intervals of less than the customary ten years. In spite of these precautions, the rate of outward migration, when one considers the total sample population, proved surprisingly high. Only 24.2 percent of the 6,059 individuals from the entire 1900 sample remained in the city for as long as five years. It must be remembered, however, that 56 percent of those labeled as family heads were single males, mostly young and not burdened with children. They could be very mobile and those intending to return to their former residences likely did so within a short time. Indeed, it seems reasonable to suggest that workers no longer in the city by 1905 may have left as early as 1901 or 1902.

More than 57 percent of those remaining in 1905 were still in the city by 1910, and approximately two-thirds of that group remained into the 1930s. This declining trend in outward migration suggests that as families adjusted to the environment, Pittsburgh became a more attractive place to live, probably in terms of providing work or housing opportunities during the period. It also suggests, however, that migration may be a function of a stage in the life cycle. As workers grew older and took on family obligations, they became more settled, less likely to pick up and leave a city to escape adverse conditions. The association between the tendency to move and the duration of stay may result from various social and psychological processes. Strong social relationships, for example, may contribute to an individual's continued persistence. Successful adjustment to the environment may lead others to remain rather than face, once again, the challenges of migration. In still other cases, as one researcher noted, "The longer an individual has been in a given state, the less oriented toward defining and evaluating opportunities and the less skilled in exploiting them he might become."[14] For immigrant workers already familiar with the problems of adjustment, several of these processes may be operating simultaneously.

The results of the analysis of persistence by ethnicity support the previous findings and also reveal marked differences in the staying power of various groups. To control for the effects of age and to eliminate sex-related biases created by the use of city directories, we have removed nonworking individuals under age sixteen and all females from this analysis. The ethnic characteristics of the sample of adult males who persisted in Pittsburgh for at least five years during the 1900-30 period are presented in Table 11.

The crucial interval in Table 11, which measures the persistence rates of each ethnic sample, is the 1900-5 period. Clearly, blacks were more likely to stay in Pittsburgh than Poles or Italians. If oral data are any indication, blacks were originally more intent on remaining in the city. For them, it represented more of a final destination. Northern- and southern-born blacks, for instance, persisted at nearly identical rates throughout the 1900-10 period. Immigrants, especially Austrian and Russian Poles and Italians, were more inclined to depart — perhaps to return home — and were predictably more transient, even though they were able to assist kin in obtaining industrial work. Among migrants who remained in the city for a decade or more, persistence rates became less divergent.

Approximately one-third of the northern-born black workers present in Pittsburgh in 1900 were there five years later. While this record of persistence is not dramatically high, it does fall within the ranges recorded by blue-collar workers in most nineteenth-century American cities. Moreover, it exceeds the rates of the recent Pittsburgh immigrants included in the study sample. The persisting northern-born black workers continued to remain in the city beyond the first recorded observation. Over half of the remaining 1905 group remained until 1910, and 56 percent of those workers persisted through 1915. This most likely reflects their age and length of stay in the community rather than any of the other independent variables. Many of the 254 northern-

Table 11. Percentage of Persisting Working Adult Males
for Indicated Intervals between 1900 and 1930, by Ethnic Group

Ethnic/Minority Group	1900 (n)	Percentage of Persistence				
		1905	1910	1915	1920	1930
Northern-born blacks	254	35.5	57.4	56.0	46.4	38.5
Southern-born blacks	1,157	34.0	57.4	64.5	59.2	41.4
German Poles	268	27.1	44.1	70.5	83.3	75.0
Russian Poles	544	15.0	48.1	62.5	72.0	38.8
Austrian Poles[1]	99	7.1	...	...	...	...
Italians	507	14.1	35.0	70.3	78.9	66.6

NOTE. The data are compiled from the U.S. Bureau of the Census, Manuscript Census for Pittsburgh, 1900, and the Pittsburgh City Directories of 1905, 1910, 1915, 1920, and 1930. The table displays the percentage of working adult males present in one time period who persisted until the next period. Thus, 35.5 percent of the 254 northern-born blacks present in 1900 were still in Pittsburgh in 1905; 57.4 percent of the 1905 persisters remained through 1910. Observers of nineteenth-century population movements frequently generate census samples for subsequent decades to determine differences in mobility rates over time. Census data are not available beyond 1900, and subsequent sampling is impossible at this time. The high incidence of single males among the 1900 sample groups obviously contributed to the lack of persistence discussed here. A trace of 1910 or 1920 residents would likely produce significantly greater stability. In addition, the 1900 Pittsburgh city directory underenumerated each group as follows: northern-born blacks, 7 percent; southern-born blacks, 11 percent; German Poles, 11 percent; Russian Poles, 13 percent; Austrian Poles, 15 percent; and Italians, 9 percent. Subsequent directories likely erred in equal proportions. Thus, the persistence rate of each group recorded here probably underestimates the actual persistence of these groups and should be adjusted upward accordingly. The proportion of black persisters should be adjusted upward by perhaps as much as 12 percent. This proportion represents the black adult workers in the original sample who were untraceable because of their common names. The 1905 directory, for example, contained nineteen John Blacks, thirty-six Tom Browns, and 142 William Smiths. Even the presence of a middle initial—seldom supplied in the 1900 census—frequently failed to assist the tracing process; there were sixteen William H. Smiths, for example.

[1]The small number of Austrian Poles made calculations beyond 1905 not feasible.

born black adult workers were born in Pennsylvania. A large portion of these men may have been born in Pittsburgh, although the 1900 census does not provide this information. By 1910 over half of the workers in this sample were over forty years of age. Barring any drastic economic setbacks, one could not expect these life-long residents to leave the city in great numbers. In addition, only one-third of this group held unskilled jobs in 1900. They received somewhat better pay and worked under more tolerable conditions than their foreign-born counterparts who labored in Pittsburgh's steel mills. Thus, the long residence pattern of this group, their ages, and their occupational experience in the community clearly contributed to their continued longevity.

Most southern-born blacks, conversely, arrived in Pittsburgh after 1890, had a history of geographic mobility, and expressed strong occupational aspirations. One might expect this group to continue its pattern of migration if aspirations were not fulfilled, and nearly two-thirds did leave Pittsburgh after a few years. Interviews with southern blacks in Pittsburgh illustrate the frustration and general hostility they felt. Local newspaper articles about blacks were illustrated with grossly disfigured caricatures. Long-term black residents of the city seemed unfriendly or unconcerned with the plight of their southern-born counterparts, and black neighborhoods provided little assistance in the adjustment process. These negative conditions, as well as long employment lines and hostile employers, no doubt sent many blacks out of the city in a hurry. Yet the persistence rate (1900-5) recorded by this group matched that of northern-born blacks.[15] This is especially striking, since those born in the South were more likely to be in unskilled jobs than their northern-born brothers. Despite their somewhat lower economic status, they persisted as much as the northern-born. For many, this stability may reflect their perception of the limited occupational opportunities elsewhere. Disillusioned in Pittsburgh, they were unwilling or unable to undertake another move to yet another unrewarding city. For others, their stability demonstrated their adjustment to industrial conditions. Recruited to the city by kin and friends, they decided to remain, attempting to build worthwhile lives within the Pittsburgh environment. That the proportion of those who remained increased at each successive interval until 1920 attests to their ability to do so.

Immigrants left the city at even higher rates than did the city's black workers. Only one group—the German Poles—recorded persistence rates exceeding 25 percent during the initial five-year interval. This evidence seems to support the notion that many southern and eastern European migrants were indeed "birds-of-passage," intent on earning and saving money in the United States and returning home after a short stay. The number of such "birds-of-passage" for any particular group is unknown, and the available data are often conflicting. They do, however, provide useful clues. One source, for example, estimates that between one-half and three-fourths of all Russian Poles returned to their native land during the first decade of the twentieth century. Less than 20 percent of the Poles persisted in some Philadelphia neighborhoods between 1905 and 1910, and Theodore Saloutos estimated that only the Italians, among all groups, exceeded the Poles in repatriates between 1908 and 1931.[16] The Dillingham Commission Report on Immigration in 1911 estimated that approximately one-half of all migrants eventually returned to Italy. Italian government records set the rate of annual return for the 1907-11 period at 150,000 individuals, or 65 percent of the annual migration to America. A more recent study estimated that 2.4 million Italian immigrants arrived in the United States between 1900 and 1910 while 1.2 million returned to their homeland. During the depression of 1907-8, the number of repatriates exceeded the migration to the United States by 46 percent.[17] These data, based on government records of passengers arriving in Italian ports in third-class accommodations, probably understated the number of repatriates somewhat. It does seem clear, however, that approximately three of every five Italian migrants to America eventually returned to Italy.

The extent of repatriation by both Poles and Italians, and perhaps southern-born blacks, is somewhat troublesome since our interviews were obviously conducted among the persisters. Fortunately, data do exist to enable us to compare, at least for Italians, the characteristics of all immigrants with those who repatriated and with those who persisted. While the data are not totally comparable, some rough approximations are possible. It appears that Italians entering the United States were roughly similar to those leaving in occupation, marital status, and region of Italy from which they migrated. Nearly 86 percent of those migrating to America gave their occupation as laborer while 84 percent of the returnees between 1908 and 1914 also held unskilled positions. Approximately two-thirds of each group were unmarried, and exactly 88 percent came from and returned to the seven regions in the *mezzogiorno*. Repatriates were, however, slightly older and more likely to be male than those entering the United States.[18] The age differences, of course, represent the length of their stay in the country. Repatriating workers remained in America an average of five years and, as a group, had aged by a roughly similar amount of years.

A detailed comparison of repatriates with persisters is not possible because of the incompatability of the data. Again, however, some rough estimates are possible. As one might expect, persisting Italians from the Pittsburgh sample held somewhat higher level occupations (23 percent skilled compared with 15 percent among repatriates) and were more likely to be married (66 percent and 52 percent, respectively) than the national sample of repatriates. Both groups emanated from southern Italy and were comparable in average age and male/female ratio.[19]

Thus, if the Italians provide any clues, those who migrated to the United States and those who returned home differed only slightly. Each year, of the new migrants who arrived to replace those who returned home, the names and faces differed, but the characteristics were remarkably similar. More important for this and other studies that have studied only persisters, repatriates did differ from those who remained in occupation and marital status, but the differences are not striking. Thus, while this analysis focuses primarily on those who remained in Pittsburgh, we have not lost much by our inability to trace those who left. In most important variables the elusive outmigrant mirrored his or her more stable counterpart.

The proportion of successful repatriates, of course, cannot be determined. Many must have returned home frustrated in their goals and disillusioned by their experience. Working conditions and an unpredictable economy no doubt sent many home in defeat. In a single month, following the panic of 1907-8, 15,000 "foreigners departed the city," and the *New York Times* reported that traffic in that port city was "noticeably heavy from the Pittsburgh district and the territory adjacent."[20]

Thousands, of course, did return to Europe with savings that enabled them to improve their lives. The Pittsburgh Survey reported that several banks in Pittsburgh operated foreign exchange departments, serviced by foreign-speaking tellers. The Survey noted that one bank frequently sent money "home to the old country." The postal savings system in Pittsburgh held savings for forty-seven Italians, averaging $141 each.[21] In Abruzzi so many men returned to buy additional land that a usury industry emerged because they had excess money to loan. Income from abroad eventually became a major factor in the Italian economy, and after 1901 official government policy encouraged both emigration and repatriation. Luigi Rossi, a member of the Italian Council on Emigration, concluded in 1910 that most emigrants returned to Italy richer than when they had left: "One can say, almost with certainty, that compared to the great number of those who gain evident benefits from their expatriation, the number is negligible of workers who spend a certain number of years abroad without having any positive result. Repatriates from abroad frequently return with between 1,000 and 5,000 *lire*. Sometimes the amount is as high as 10,000 *lire*. The savings are generally proportional to the length of stay abroad."[22]

A number of earlier studies have suggested a relationship between an individual's failure to persist in a community and the lack of occupational mobility or property ownership. Measured in conventional terms these relationships seem firm. However, considering the reported goals of many immigrants — to earn money and return home — and the evidence presented above, the conclusion must be modified somewhat. Measured in their own terms many of these workers had succeeded. In fact, it was precisely their success in earning and saving money that enabled them to leave the city. Unfortunately, it is not possible to determine what proportion of immigrant — or black — repatriates succeeded in their short stay in Pittsburgh. What does seem clear, however, is that any relationship between outward migration from the city and economic success or failure is speculative at best.

In addition to economics, other factors also influenced the decision to remain in the city. Skill level, for example, made a significant difference. No matter which ethnic group one belonged to, the higher the occupation the greater was the likelihood of remaining in the city. Homeowners were twice as likely to persist as renters. An analysis of several other variables — family structure, marital status, or position within the family — provided little predictive power on whether an individual would persist or leave the city. In most cases persisters closely resembled leavers.

Household conditions do provide, however, some indication of why certain groups — black and German Polish workers — remained in the city in greater numbers than did others (Table 12).

Southern-born black workers, as discussed earlier, remained in Pittsburgh at a rate nearly identical to that of the northern-born blacks. The short distance from their Virginia homelands apparently presented little geographical barrier, and those who migrated alone were quickly joined by their families. Both northern- and southern-born blacks exhibited similar household patterns in Pittsburgh at the turn of the century. Their occupations, their ages, and their position within the household provide the most likely clues to the similar persistence rates recorded by each group. One-half of the blacks in Pittsburgh were identified as household heads. Most had wives, children, and family obligations. Nearly one-fourth had children under the age of fifteen. For them, the act of moving represented a decision to uproot family, often for the second or third time. A decision to move affected not only themselves but others. The logistics of moving an entire family deterred some from such a decision. Many black household heads were also in their early forties by 1905, perhaps beyond the optimal age of migration. They also held a disproportionately large share of the semiskilled work among the sample groups. The possibilities for continued occupational success induced many to remain in the city. They hoped to achieve higher levels eventually,

Table 12. Analysis of Households of Sample of Working Adults in Pittsburgh in 1900, by Ethnic/Minority Group

Areas of Analysis	Northern-Born Blacks (n=254)	Southern-Born Blacks (n=1,157)	German Poles (n=268)	Russian Poles (n=544)	Austrian Poles (n=99)	Italians (n=507)
Family structure						
Nuclear	47.6	32.9	76.8	29.0	23.2	24.2
Extended	17.3	11.8	9.7	6.9	4.0	8.1
Augmented	35.0	55.0	13.4	63.9	72.7	67.6
Marital status (%)						
Single	44.4	41.9	20.4	46.4	62.6	46.4
Married	47.1	47.6	75.9	52.4	36.4	52.4
Relationship to head of house (%)						
Household heads	53.8	50.6	88.0	39.3	33.6	37.3
Related boarders	9.5	8.5	5.6	6.0	5.1	6.7
Unrelated boarders	36.6	40.8	6.4	54.5	61.3	56.0
Mean age (yrs)						
Heads	38.6	37.7	38.7	36.0	31.6	37.5
Boarders	25.9	30.1	33.4	28.1	27.7	30.8
Family stage (%)						
Newlywed	5.1	4.8	6.3	5.1	7.0	3.7
Young family	23.6	23.0	35.8	22.0	16.1	15.6
Midstage	4.7	3.9	15.2	3.6	2.0	3.9
Mature	1.5	0.8	1.1	0.9	0	0.5
Female headed	4.7	5.0	1.4	0	0	0.7
No spouse	39.3	50.6	21.2	57.9	55.0	60.3
Unknown	20.8	11.7	18.6	10.2	18.1	14.9

NOTE. The data are compiled from the U.S. Bureau of the Census, Manuscript Census for Pittsburgh, 1900.

but the semiskilled occupations provided a sound and acceptable base from which to launch a career.

German-born Poles came to Pittsburgh earlier than the other migrant groups, were older by 1900, and more than three-fourths were married. Almost four of every five lived in nuclear family units, and more than half had children. They recorded higher persistence rates than any of the foreign-born migrants and nearly as high as that of Pittsburgh's black workers. This evidence seems to confirm the hypothesis that migrants who moved in family units were more likely than unrelated individuals to remain in the city and that migration was related to age and family responsibility. Migrating in kinship units reduced the incidence of further mobility. The Prussian Poles, who migrated to

Pittsburgh attempting to prevent a further erosion of their economic status in German-held areas, sought occupational security. Once a job was acquired, they tended to remain in Pittsburgh. The initial occupation, moreover, tends to support this assessment. Nearly four of every five Polish immigrants from German territory held unskilled occupations in 1900. As suggested earlier, recent studies of ethnic mobility have concluded that workers leaving American cities were generally unskilled or downwardly mobile. These workers supposedly moved from city to city in search of better jobs and economic success. The German Polish experience, however, illustrates that workers with limited aspirations could find stability in low-skill, low-paying occupations. Many of those who did leave Pittsburgh likely moved to another industrial city and acquired a job similar to the one they left. The increased rates of persistence found at each subsequent observation in Table 11, moreover, suggested that as these workers grew older they were more likely to persist in the community despite their low economic status. For them, moving represented a high cost in terms of convenience and lost social ties. The decisions to pull up stakes and settle again in new territory proved simply too difficult for many older, more settled workers.

Russian Poles and Italian-born migrants in Pittsburgh left the city at very similar rates. Members of these groups arrived in Pittsburgh later than the German Poles, were generally younger, and were more likely to be single, unrelated boarders, unencumbered with children. Less than one-fifth of either group remained for as long as five years. Polish workers born in Galicia were the most recent arrivals to the city. They recorded remarkably low persistence rates during the first five years of this century. Nearly 95 percent left Pittsburgh within a few years of their arrival. This should not prove too surprising, since Poles from Galicia arrived in Pittsburgh later, were younger in age, and had fewer family ties than any other group of immigrants. (Only 18 percent had children, and nearly two-thirds had no relatives at all in Pittsburgh.) Many, moreover, reported a desire to earn enough money to return to their homeland to purchase a small farm. Whether they succeeded or not cannot be determined. What is clear is that this young group of workers hardly remained in the city long enough to establish any lasting ties.

The differences in persistence rates demonstrate that adaptation to the urban milieu was a complex process that depended on several important factors. It mattered what the intention of migrants was, the period in their lives at which they migrated, and possibly the type of work they were able to acquire. The clearest pattern — the increased stability found at each subsequent observation — suggests that as a worker's stage in life cycle changed he tended to become more sedentary regardless of his ethnic or occupational background. The high initial rates of geographic mobility found in Pittsburgh and other American cities may be largely due to a relatively young population structure and other variables normally associated with young age. Table 13 displays the rates of persistence by age of members of the sample group to examine this possibility.

Table 13. Persistence by Age of Males and Family Heads in Pittsburgh, 1900-30

Age in 1900	1900 (*n*)	Percentage Remaining after 1900				
		1905	1910	1915	1920	1930
Under 15	1,393	16.5	69.5	76.8	69.1	67.0
16-19	254	25.6	46.5	78.7	73.1	63.2
19-29	1,188	23.7	56.5	76.1	75.2	58.2
30-39	1,053	24.3	54.4	65.2	63.0	48.3
40-49	536	30.4	51.5	57.1	50.0	33.0
50-59	194	25.8	56.0	39.2	36.0	0
60 +	80	16.2	46.1	0	0	0

NOTE.   The numbers are derived from the sample data for 1900 compiled for this study.

The persistence data when age controls are provided reveal only a small relationship between age and residential stability. With the curious exception of the group between sixteen and nineteen in 1905, each successive age group between twenty and fifty recorded slightly higher persistence rates than the one before. The difference, however, with the exception of those under sixteen and those over sixty proved statistically insignificant. The very young, of course, had no control over their residential movement while the lack of persistence in the group sixty years old and over is likely the result of death. Persistence rates for each successive observation support the previous conclusion that length of stay in the community had a marked effect on the continued tendency to remain. Persistence rates for all age groups increased at each interval of observation. Less than 25 percent of the 1900 sample persisted in Pittsburgh through 1905. The proportion remaining doubled during the next five years, to 54.5 percent. The rate of persistence for all age groups continued to increase substantially at each interval until 1930.

Thus, when all variables are considered, stage in the life cycle provided the strongest influence on the patterns of persistence. Length of residency and stage in the life cycle, in fact, probably represented similar pressures to remain in the city. Ethnic background and aspirations were also crucial, especially for the first decade of urban living. Widely varying, but in all cases high rates of transiency occurred among the six groups during their early years in Pittsburgh. Once a decision was made to stay beyond five years, however, future persistence became more a function of age and stage in the life cycle than ethnicity.

The preceding analysis of persistence provides a glimpse at what must have been the most common of all experiences in early twentieth-century Pittsburgh: that of the migrant or transient laborer. It is not possible to account for the tens of thousands of blacks and foreign-born who spent six months or a year or two laboring in the "steel city" between 1890 and World War I. Their contribution to the industrial development of the city was no doubt important but unfortunately remains anonymous.

A significant number — although a minority in all cases — did remain to work and establish residences and eventually communities. Their goals differed, but oral interviews suggest that most of those who remained originally intended to establish permanent residence in the city. (Based on the proportion who repatriated, leaving was relatively simple and inexpensive. Few individuals, regardless of their low wages, were forced to remain in the city because of economic considerations.) In spite of the long hours, low pay, debilitating work conditions, and often overt discrimination, these families remained to build new lives in Pittsburgh. Each group and individuals within each group established their own measuring devices and finishing lines in attempting to achieve satisfaction in their lives. The larger Pittsburgh society measured the achievements of newcomers in greater, perhaps unattainable, milestones. A series of turn-of-the-century articles in both the *Pittsburgh Press* and the *Pittsburgh Leader* clearly identified the Pittsburgh business community's definition of success. In an article discussing "The Young Man's Chances," the *Press* remarked

> We heard a good deal during the recent elections . . . that owing to the conditions of modern competition, it was impossible for the young man of today to emulate the notable figures of the past who had risen from poverty and obscurity to wealth and prominence. . . .
> The American people believe today, as they have always done, that there is a chance for everybody in this great country to become what he wishes to become . . . if he possesses the requisite courage, pluck and perseverence.
> Nowhere is this belief more strongly developed than right here

in Pittsburgh. Nowhere have so many men risen to better positions than in the great industrial section, of which Pittsburgh is the center.[23]

The *Pittsburgh Leader* in an article entitled "Is the Present the Young Man's Era?" interviewed a number of prominent Pittsburgh business leaders all of whom testified that the early twentieth century was indeed "the best age . . . for a young man to rise in business and professional life."[24] Their messages differed somewhat, but each made it clear that his definition of success consisted of high achievement in the business or professional world. The *Leader* identified a prominent undertaker as the example whom newcomers should emulate: "Forty years ago he came to Pittsburgh with only a few dollars in his purse and set up in the undertaking business. His path was of exceedingly uphill character. Starting by renting a little backroom, Mr. Sampson persevered until today he is reputed worth a large fortune."[25]

Pittsburgh newspapers never tired of elevating Andrew Carnegie as an example — or quoting the pronouncements of the great Iron Master on the "Blessings of Poverty" — that young men, particularly immigrants, should set for themselves. That, as one historian recently demonstrated, only five of the city's 360 iron barons in nineteenth- and early twentieth-century Pittsburgh could claim a true rags-to-riches experience made little difference to the city's news or business leaders.[26]

Blacks, Poles, and Italians who came to Pittsburgh, however, carried with them much more limited aspirations. Even the black migrants, who held the highest aspirations of the three groups, did not hope to emulate the Carnegie experience or achieve the great wealth discussed by Pittsburgh businessmen or the press. Worker satisfaction did not depend upon spectacular achievement but upon modest gains and a measure of economic security. For migrants to Pittsburgh, Carnegie's experience was an inescapable fact. He was not, however, their model.

Previous experiences, various orientations to urban life, and cultural differences all combined to mold the expectations of migrants to Pittsburgh. Blacks arrived with rising expectations and hope for some occupational advancement. Italians had higher level skills than Poles or blacks but were highly transient because they migrated as individuals who expected to return. Those who remained sought skilled work that would use their prior training. Austrian and Russian Polish migration resembled the Italian, consisting mainly of single men. Many expected to return to the homeland while those remaining sought steady jobs that would provide economic security. German Poles migrated in family units and were less likely to leave Pittsburgh than other Poles. They shared, however, the limited expectations of the other Polish groups.

The harsh industrial environment took its tool on the dreams of all of these workers. High infant mortality, industrial accidents and deaths, recurring economic setbacks, and a constant struggle to create decent living conditions were common to the lives of workers in early twentieth-century Pittsburgh. The analysis of the career patterns of the divergent groups in this study over a span of thirty years illustrates how well they met this struggle and how well their aspirations fared when faced with these realities.[27] Table 14 presents a general overview of the occupational movement or stability experienced by the black, Polish, and Italian workers of 1900 at subsequent intervals through 1920.[28] The initial occupational distribution of each group appeared in Table 4.

The occupational goals reported by black workers moving to Pittsburgh suggested that they would move from job to job in search of improved occupational positions. The proliferation of newspaper advertisements for white-collar workers alerted them to the expansion of higher level occupational opportunities, and they were likely to become quickly disenchanted with jobs offering little opportunity for advancement. Their career patterns as presented in Table 14 reflect this search for improvement. Both northern- and southern-born black workers began their careers in Pittsburgh at the unskilled-semiskilled levels. They left these initial levels at an increasing rate throughout the two decades. By 1910, only one-half of each group remained in its original skill level classification, and one decade later the proportion had dwindled still further. More significant, the proportion moving into higher level positions increased at nearly every five-year interval. Better than one in five obtained improved occupational status by 1905 and one-third did so by 1910. Northern-born blacks continued to improve their position in 1915 and 1920, with nearly two-thirds of those persisting in the city enjoying some occupational advancement. Blacks from the South, at the same time, slipped slightly in 1915, but the acute labor shortages during World War I enabled many to recoup their gains, and then some. By 1920, 41 percent held better jobs than their original ones. Thus, while blacks were unable to rely upon the assistance of kin or friends to secure work, their aggressive job procurement techniques and unwillingness to settle for menial work did lead to better jobs for many.

Unfortunately for the city's black workers, their occupational movement also included considerable downward mobility. Between 15 and

Table 14.　Occupational Mobility of Adult Workers in the 1900 Population Sample in Pittsburgh, 1900-20

Ethnic/Minority Group	1900 n	1905				1910				1915				1920			
		% Same	% Up	% Down	I¹	% Same	% Up	% Down	I	% Same	% Up	% Down	I	% Same	% Up	% Down	I
Northern-born blacks	264	49.4	22.0	28.6	-0.133	43.1	36.4	20.5	0.368	19.4	61.3	19.4	2.16	07.7	61.5	30.8	3.990
Southern-born blacks	1,134	60.9	24.3	14.9	0.154	50.5	32.7	16.8	0.315	31.9	15.0	53.0	0.318	41.2	41.2	17.6	0.570
Russian Poles	560	76.9	21.7	01.3	0.265	72.2	25.0	02.8	0.307	39.1	52.2	08.6	1.113	50.0	50.0	…	1.000
Austrian Poles²	99	57.2	42.8	—	—	—	—	—	—	—	—	—	—	—	—	—	—
German Poles	289	79.5	14.1	06.4	0.097	69.5	21.2	09.0	0.174	64.3	21.4	14.3	0.110	56.5	26.1	17.4	0.154
Italians	507	77.6	19.4	02.9	0.205	61.5	30.7	07.7	0.375	41.2	52.9	05.9	1.140	50.0	28.6	21.4	0.144

SOURCE. U.S. Bureau of the Census, Manuscript Census for Pittsburgh, 1900; Pittsburgh City Directories, 1905, 1910, 1915, 1920, 1930, 1940, 1950, and 1960. Traces were conducted through 1960, but the number of individuals remaining after 1920 rendered the presentation of such data meaningless. The table displays the proportion of workers from each group who remained at the same skill level between 1900 and 1905, the proportion who acquired higher level occupations by 1905 than they held in 1900, and the proportion who moved downward since 1900. The 1910, 1915, and 1920 columns measure similar moves, with the 1900 occupation as the initial measuring point.

¹The net mobility index (I) was computed by subtracting the percentage of the downwardly mobile workers from the percentage of upwardly mobile workers and dividing the difference by the percentage who persisted in the same occupational class. It should be remembered that those who persisted in the community beyond the first observation point (1905-6) generally remained for a considerable period of time. This and all subsequent tables in this chapter measure the stable members of the Polish, black, and Italian populations. One should not conclude, as has been frequently suggested, that those remaining constitute the more successful elements of the sample population (e.g., they were successful, thus they stayed; or their staying contributed to their success). We are attempting to measure *satisfaction* against the goals held by the migrant groups. Thus, many of those who failed to persist, as suggested earlier, were likely to achieve those goals.

²Austrian Poles were dropped from this table because of their small number.

30 percent lost occupational standing some time during the 1900-20 period. The tenuous, often seasonal nature of their work, competition from other incoming migrants, and at times overt racial hostility frequently led to periods of unemployment followed by lower level occupations. Even blacks who apparently lived and worked in the city for long periods of time frequently suffered these declines in occupational levels. Northern-born blacks, many of them born and raised in Pittsburgh, were even more susceptible to occupational slippage than those born in the South. As a group, of course, they held better jobs in 1900 and were more subject to downward mobility. A striking example of the fragile nature of their hold on skilled occupations occurred in 1908. Following a rejection of their bid to join the union, twenty-five black "hoisting engineers" (all northern-born) secured work building a new "downtown skyscraper." They agreed to work for wages substantially under union scale. Within three months the union admitted all twenty-five and demanded union wages for its new members. The contracting firm, losing the initial economic advantage, promptly replaced all black skilled workers with white union labor. The union accepted this change without appeal.[29]

The negative experience of the black hoisting engineers with labor unions was not unique. Prior to 1920 blacks were systematically excluded from the city's labor organizations. They were, according to one union official, "too timid, listen to their bosses, and also have a kind of distrust of white labor unions." That same official admitted that "while he himself would have no difficulty working with colored people, the rank and file of his union would not work on the same floor with a colored waiter."[30] Only the hod carriers union, in addition to the hoisting engineers, admitted blacks before World War I. Clearly black workers could expect no help in maintaining their jobs from organized labor in Pittsburgh.

The decline of black businesses catering to a white clientele also accounted for the downward mobility of some blacks. The proportion of black barbers, restaurant owners, grocers, and merchants in the Pittsburgh population and among our sample declined during the 1900-20 period. Only four of twenty-one black businesses that regularly advertised in the 1913 editions of the *Pittsburgh Courier* were in operation seven years later. Six restaurants, three clothing establishments, two billiard parlors, two cigar stores, and a grocery all closed during this period. All of these businesses, as one researcher noted, were individual proprietorships subject to closing with the death or migration of the owner.[31] Growing racial antagonisms and the initial movement of whites from the city's black neighborhoods contributed to the precarious nature of black-owned businesses. White business-men, it should be noted, captured a growing share of the black-patronized businesses in the city's Hill District. By 1930, less than 4 percent of the city's gainfully employed black workers owned their own businesses; 17 percent of the white population owned theirs.[32]

The decline of black skilled workers and entrepreneurs was not unique to Pittsburgh among northern cities. Blacks in Cleveland, New Haven, New York, and Philadelphia all experienced similar occupational declines during the 1900-20 period.[33] In each of these cities, like Pittsburgh, the number and proportion of proprietors expanded during the decade while blacks were losing hold of this traditional vehicle of upward mobility. By 1920 the black businessman was a rarity in the urban northeast.

Polish and Italian workers experienced much greater job stability especially during the first decade of the century than did blacks (Table 14). This might be expected since Poles were seeking occupational stability and whatever economic security it brought. Once a job was secured, regardless of its level, it was not readily abandoned, and nearly 80 percent of the German and Russian Poles remained at their initial jobs for at least five years. Most, of course, were unskilled. Nearly one-fourth of the Italian sample, on the other hand, managed to secure skilled work upon their arrival in the city. Contrary to the general decline in demand for skilled labor, the kind of skills they possessed remained in short supply throughout the entire twenty-year period. Construction of residential and commercial buildings, road construction, and the installation of utilities all continued to proceed at a rapid pace. Wages of skilled workers were also considerably higher than those of either the unskilled or the semiskilled groups; conditions were better and hours were shorter. Thus, in spite of their high aspirations, it is unlikely that they would give up their skilled occupations unless a definite opportunity for advancement presented itself.

During the second decade of the century, however, nearly half of the men in each group did manage to shift occupational classifications. This movement, similar to that experienced by the blacks, was both up and down the occupational ladder. By 1920 one-half of the Russian Poles and one-fourth of the German Poles and Italians managed to find better jobs in Pittsburgh. For the latter two groups, however, this upward movement was tempered by a decline of 17 and 21 percent of each group, respectively. Thus, the amount of net upward movement for each group was relatively small.

None of the groups was occupationally stagnant during the period. None was locked into a particular job or classification. They all moved both up and down the job scale, with blacks exhibiting the most volatile experiences. To control for the effects of this bifurcation and to enable us to compare the occupational changes of the various groups, we have created a rough index of net occupational movement (Table 14). An index number of 0 indicates no net movement; positive numbers show net upward movement; negative numbers indicate a net downward movement. One can hypothesize, of course, a situation where one-third of a group moves up, one-third moves down, and one-third remains the same, thus providing an index number of 0 for a highly mobile group. We wish to show, however, the net direction for a particular group, thus enabling us to make comparisons of the direction of movement. In addition, the magnitude of the index numbers is not weighted to the distance of the occupational movement, e.g., unskilled to professional. This presents little problem, since, as will be seen shortly, few workers from any group moved more than one step from their point of origin. The net mobility index, then, illustrates the difference among the movement of various groups away from absolute stability. It should be considered along with the percentages presented earlier.

The data displayed in the occupational mobility index suggest that while blacks as individuals moved both up and down the occupational scale in great volume, their general direction as a group was nearly always up. More significant, the upward movement of the northern-born blacks always exceeded that of any other group. Southern-born blacks, in spite of considerable occupation slippage, also experienced a gradual increase in the group's net upward movement during each time period. This is particularly revealing since both groups of black workers began their careers at slightly higher level occupations than did the immigrants. Hence, they had positions from which to slip. European-born workers also experienced a gradual net upward movement during the period. Russian Poles, who experienced almost no downward mobility, moved upward more than any group other than the northern-born blacks. Much of this movement, however, is due to the low starting position of the Russian Poles — 90 percent of this group began as unskilled laborers. The reported limited aspirations of this group and their impressive movement suggest, however, that many achieved their personal goals.

German Poles and Italians experienced much more limited net mobility, although the reasons differ. German Poles were the most stable of any group in absolute terms. Most continued to labor in the steel industry throughout their lives. Whatever upward movement did take place occurred within the context of the mill. The shift

toward semiskilled work within the mill did provide some limited opportunity for upward mobility. Semiskilled work, however, was not
significantly different from unskilled work, and slightly higher wages
and greater job security were the only tangible rewards. The sparse
net upward movement of Italians, on the other hand, may be due to
several factors. As suggested earlier, Italian artisans likely clung to
their skilled positions. Those who did attempt other work could always
return to masonry or carpentry, for example, in the event the new
experience failed. In addition, one could enter many ethnic-related
businesses — street vending, peddling, huckstering — with almost no
accumulated capital. The majority of cases of upward and downward
mobility among Italians resulted from ventures into and out of private
entrepreneurships and almost always within the context of the ethnic
neighborhood. Salvatore Migliore's early study of Italian migrants, for
example, found twenty-six Italian fruit stores, nineteen grocers, twenty
shoemakers, six meat markets, seven barberships, and eight tailors
conducting business in the Italian section of East Liberty during the
1920s. Many, he noted, remained in business for a year or two only
to be replaced by another "energetic Italian."[34]

The preceding discussion and data provide a glimpse of the direction and the amount of mobility among the various groups under
consideration. We know that all groups moved upward as groups but
that many individuals moved either up or down. Table 14 obscures
several important elements of mobility, which we may now examine.
We need to know the starting points of each group and the extent to
which they were mobile. That is, how far did they go in achieving the
aspirations identified earlier?

Previous mobility studies have emphasized that occupational success depended not only upon ethnocultural background but also upon
the level of entry into the labor force. As we have seen earlier, the
workers included in this study emanated from widely differing backgrounds and entered the labor force with differing dreams and aspirations. Neither background nor goals, however, exercised much influence on their initial skill level in the Pittsburgh labor force. Between
75 and 94 percent of each group began work in Pittsburgh at the lowest
two skill levels in 1900. The difference in these two skill levels, nevertheless, presents a methodological problem. It is almost tautological,
for example, that unskilled laborers will experience more upward
mobility than will other groups. They have nowhere to go but up.
Conversely, semiskilled workers may move up, but they are also able
to move down. Any meaningful comparison, therefore, must control
for the effect of initial occupation on mobility. Because these two

levels were so similar in Pittsburgh in terms of wages, working hours, level of skill required, and the type of life-style they provided, we have combined them in Table 15 to compare the extent of upward mobility into skilled and white-collar work among the various groups. (Fewer than half a dozen blue-collar workers from the entire sample ever moved into the high white-collar group. We have, therefore, merged both white-collar classes.) Thus, three broad categories — unskilled/semiskilled; skilled; white collar — permit a reliable measurement of Polish, black, and Italian mobility in Pittsburgh.

The most significant information contained in this table is that Poles and southern-born blacks had an equally difficult time escaping the lowest occupational levels. As late as 1920, one-half the Russian Poles and nearly three-fourths of the German Poles and southern blacks had failed to move from the bottom of the occupational classes. What appeared earlier to be considerable occupational movement for the Russian Poles and southern-born blacks was in part shifting about — up and down — among unskilled and semiskilled jobs. Northern-born blacks and Italians, conversely, moved out of the lower skill levels with increasing frequency each decade.[35]

Most groups moving upward rose to skilled positions rather than into the white-collar classification. Indicative that many had skills upon their arrival, Italians moved most quickly into the skilled positions. By 1905, in addition to the 25 percent who held skilled jobs in 1900, nearly 20 percent moved from the unskilled/semiskilled group to become artisans. The proportion doubled by 1910. Both their prior training and the kin network that they employed to secure the first job aided the upward mobility of Italians. In addition, some occupational categories fostered upward mobility. Unskilled or semiskilled Italians in the construction trades, for example, could acquire the skills of a craftsman on the job. Unlike the puddler and the roller in the iron mill, their skills did not become obsolete during the era of industrialization. On the contrary, if newspaper ads are any indication, the demand for skilled construction workers increased almost annually from 1890 through 1920. As new skilled positions opened or old ones became vacant, Italians were able to assist their kin in making the move from laborer to artisans. Some worked their way up through the ranks, but most Italians interviewed acknowledged the assistance of the word of a relative or friend at the proper time to the job foreman or superintendent in securing a better job. Only a small proportion of Italians ever moved into white-collar work during the 1900-20 period. Even if we include the 120 Italians from the sample who held skilled jobs in 1900, this proportion does not change. Italians aspired to hold

Table 15. Occupational Mobility in Pittsburgh for Adult Males Whose Initial Position Was Classified as Unskilled/Semiskilled, 1900-20

Ethnic/Minority Group	1900 (n)	% of Total[1]	% to Skilled				% to White Collar				% Same			
			1905	1910	1915	1920	1905	1910	1915	1920	1905	1910	1915	1920
Northern-born blacks	216	82	7.6	11.1	29.6	...	10.8	19.4	25.9	...	81.5	69.4	44.4	...
Southern-born blacks	992	87	8.4	11.2	8.7	11.8	6.2	10.6	14.3	15.8	85.3	78.2	77.7	72.4
Russian Poles	504	90	14.3	7.7	25.0	23.1	6.3	3.8	12.5	23.1	79.4	88.5	62.5	53.8
Austrian Poles[2]	93	94	14.3	—	—	—	14.3	—	—	—	71.4	—	—	—
German Poles	250	87	4.5	14.3	8.3	15.8	4.5	3.6	4.3	10.5	90.9	82.1	87.5	73.7
Italians	385	75	17.9	38.5	44.4	46	2.6	7.7	11.1	15	79.5	53.8	44.4	39

NOTE. The data were compiled from the U.S. Bureau of the Census, Manuscript Census for Pittsburgh, 1900, and Pittsburgh City Directories for 1905, 1910, 1915, and 1920. Three dots = not available.

[1]Indicates proportion of each group holding unskilled or semiskilled jobs in 1900.

[2]The Austrian Poles were excluded in this table for the years after 1905 because of their small number.

skilled positions; some desired small entrepreneurships. The skills they possessed, acquired after long years of training, continued to be in demand in Pittsburgh. Talented artisans gained both a measure of material comfort and a sense of pride. They were afforded a margin of prestige in the city but especially within their own neighborhood. Their mobility into, but not out of, the skilled worker classification demonstrates the interaction of their own Old World background and the structure of the city.

The experience of German and Russian Poles also demonstrates this interaction. Their desire for occupational security and the continued demand for factory workers coincided to create a stable Polish work force that would remain in the mill for at least a generation. Unlike construction work, which fostered upward mobility, jobs in the steel mill tended to retard mobility. For most workers, factory work was, in effect, a dead end, although it did provide the desired job stability.[36] Thus, Poles who arrived from the Old World with limited aspirations were funneled via the kin network into jobs that provided economic security but little opportunity for upward mobility. Initial occupations in the metal industries often became, for those who remained in the city, life-long careers. Even those few who did move into skilled and white-collar positions did so within the context of industry. More than one-half of the upward mobility enjoyed by the two Polish groups came via skilled and foremen positions within the factory.

Black workers, however, would not be content with either factory or skilled blue-collar work. Prior work experiences had led them to expect continued upward movement. Private entrepreneurships and professional careers remained high on their list of goals. Southern-born blacks, however, were to remain frustrated in both areas. Only 15 percent of the 992 individuals from this sample ever achieved white-collar work. Most of these became petty proprietors or clerical workers. Not a single one achieved professional status. Southern blacks were generally as successful as German Poles and not far behind the level achieved by Russian Poles. Yet the expectations created by small amounts of earlier success led to disenchantment and frustration. Leroy M., for example, began work as a water boy at the Jones and Laughlin plant. Over the years he moved steadily upward from water boy to cinder-snapper, apprentice-helper, furnaceman, brakeman, and finally a crane operator. In spite of his success he related, "It was pretty mean; it was pretty rough. . . . I quit the J & L because there was no room for advancement. . . . Now I'm as far up as I can go."[37]

Another black, interviewed in 1925, also revealed both hope and frustration in his poignant statement. "I've worked here 19 years. There are just two things to remember. One is that you're a Negro. Another, if you can do a thing show them — you'll get your chance. The foreman said, when I asked for that job that 'niggers were hired to do the rough work.' All the best jobs were for the white men. Plenty of hard work here but there is no chance to get anywhere. Colored men work at the same jobs from year to year while white men and foreigners are promoted in 2 or 3 months after coming here."[38]

Northern-born and in many cases Pittsburgh-born blacks, in contrast, achieved the highest rates of upward mobility, particularly into the white-collar level. Their higher rate of success no doubt reflected their familiarity with the city and the occupational opportunities it presented. By 1915 one-fourth of those who began at the bottom had achieved a white-collar position, although only two, one clergyman and one dentist, ever achieved professional status. The extent of their mobility was primarily into petty proprietorships and reflects the volatile nature of the black work force noted earlier. It was precisely this group that frequently moved from semiskilled work to petty proprietorships, then fell backward.

Thus far we have examined the average mobility of workers over several short intervals. This analysis provides a general picture of workers who arrived in Pittsburgh at the turn of the century. We are now in a position to examine the career experiences of each specific group.

Again, matrices were developed for all six groups of workers for five occupational levels in each of six time periods. However, since we are interested primarily in the comparative experiences of workers who remained in Pittsburgh for some period of time, we simplified matters as before. Table 16 summarizes the career patterns of approximately 1,000 workers who remained in Pittsburgh for several time periods between 1900 and 1930. The table compares the occupation in 1900 of each individual worker with his last known occupation in Pittsburgh and provides an index of net occupational mobility for comparative purposes. Since the vast majority of all workers in each of the sample groups began work in the unskilled/semiskilled classifications and most mobile workers moved only a single step, we lose little by measuring career mobility in terms of upward and down-ward movement.

The data on career mobility indicate that northern- and southern-born blacks experienced a considerable amount of occupational movement during their careers in Pittsburgh. Nearly one-third of each

Table 16. Career Mobility for Selected Ethnic Groups in Pittsburgh:
A Comparison between the First and Last Occupation, 1900 and 1930

Ethnic/Minority Group	1900 (*n*)	1930 Up	Down	Same	Net Mobility Index[1]
Northern-born blacks	130	33.0	22.3	44.6	0.240
Southern-born blacks	400	30.3	17.2	52.5	0.250
Russian Poles	97	26.8	14.1	59.1	0.220
German Poles	103	20.4	7.8	71.8	0.175
Italians	79	21.5	6.3	72.1	0.210

NOTE. The data are compiled from the U.S. Bureau of the Census, Manuscript Census for Pittsburgh, 1900, and the Pittsburgh City Directories of 1905, 1910, 1915, 1920, and 1930. Austrian Poles were not included in this table because of their small number.
[1]See n. 1 to Table 14 for a definition.

group experienced some upward mobility between 1900 and 1930. The data from which this table is drawn also reveal that half of the northern-born black unskilled workers and 40 percent of the southern-born unskilled blacks moved to better occupational positions. Black semiskilled workers, at the same time, generally moved both up and down the occupational ladder in equal proportions. Nearly one-third of both northern- and southern-born black workers fell to the unskilled level, while one-third of the northern-born blacks and one-quarter of those born in the South moved up. Most, however, moved within the blue-collar division. Only 25 percent of those born in the North and 15 percent migrating from the South were ever able to cross the occupational gap between blue and white collar. This proportion, perhaps impressive in itself and particularly so when compared with the gains of immigrants in Pittsburgh and in other American cities, failed to satisfy the city's black population. They came to Pittsburgh with some urban and a variety of industrial and semi-industrial experiences. They had no language obstacles to overcome, and the cultural differences were minimal when compared to those of the foreign-born worker. That they enjoyed greater success than the foreign-born provided little satisfaction, although this finding raises questions about the frequently quoted hypotheses that suggest that immigrant mobility came simply at the expense of blacks who took their place at the bottom of the occupational ladder.[39] Immigrant groups were able to rely on kin in securing their initial urban jobs. Partly because of discrimination, blacks were able to use kin less often than Poles or Italians. But this fact may have caused Poles, for instance, to move routinely into limited opportunity blue-collar jobs without considering many alternatives. In 1900 young German Poles and Italians in their twenties were more likely to already possess a skilled or white-collar job than southern-born blacks, yet subsequent occupational movement was much more modest. Blacks, of course, continually sought alternative opportunities and logically took more risks. It should not be surprising, therefore, to discover that they made greater gains as well as suffered more losses. Blacks coming to Pittsburgh after 1917 would experience much greater difficulty (see chapter 8). First-generation Poles and to some degree Italians, on the other hand, simply persisted on the job.

Length of residence in Pittsburgh clearly exercised only a marginal effect on the occupational experiences of the city's black workers. Those born in the city held better jobs than did recent migrants, but their net career mobility was nearly identical. Both groups experienced occupational discrimination in securing and keeping jobs, and — as the interviews revealed — both groups felt equally frustrated at not achieving their career goals. The downward mobility among both groups of black workers is substantial and should not be surprising for blacks willing to risk job security for a chance at upward mobility. Between 17 and 22 percent fell to lower level occupations during their working careers. A great majority of this slippage is due to the large proportion of blacks who initially held semiskilled work and to the precarious nature of that work. More than 40 percent of the northern-born blacks and one-fourth of those born in the South reported their occupations in 1900 as, for example, waiter, porter, or domestic. As suggested earlier, many of these occupations were improvements over unskilled factory jobs only in the general work environment. The positions required little skill and offered little financial reward or occupational security. The bulk of the downward mobility among black workers came from this original semiskilled group. Few upwardly mobile workers, however, ever returned to their old positions or fell to an occupation below where they had started.

European immigrants to the "steel city" presented a somewhat different picture. Slightly more than one-fifth of the Italians and two Polish groups acquired better jobs during their lives in Pittsburgh, but the overall results differed substantially. A number of Italians who began their careers as unskilled laborers moved into skilled positions. Others retained their initial craft occupations while a small minority moved into white-collar—usually ethnic-related—proprietorships. Italians hardly ever experienced any downward career movement. Thus, by the mid-1920s the typical Italian immigrant, from the sample group, worked at a skilled occupation often related to the construction industry or owned a small shop. In contrast to black workers, more than half of the persisting Italians achieved their reported occupational goals.

Russian and German Poles enjoyed as much upward mobility as did Pittsburgh's Italian workers and relatively little downward movement. Approximately four-fifths of each group, of course, began work at the bottom of the occupational scale. Hardly any moved into white-collar positions, and only a small number achieved even skilled work during their lifetimes, most mobility being confined to going from the un-skilled to semiskilled classification. In sum, the Poles who moved quickly into the low-level metal trades remained in those positions throughout their entire lives. Combining all the evidence — both quan-titative and qualitative — two interrelated forces contributed to their lack of mobility. Mill work provided immediate, although miniscule, economic rewards but little opportunity for occupational advance-ment. The limited expectations of Poles, at the same time, may have made them content with their initial occupations. Oral interviews reveal few examples of Poles seeking alternative occupations during the early decades of the century. Few Poles lusted after the historian's brand of success through occupational achievement. They perceived their success in much more limited terms — a steady income, a pleasant neighborhood, respect of peers. Edward M., a Pole, confirmed the importance of caring for self and family. When questioned about achieving success, he replied, "Yes, I think I did. I never been on welfare, never collected one unemployment check. . . . I never, never collected a dime unemployment or never got a dime from anybody, you know. So I feel good about it. I feel I've progressed."[40] Joseph K., a life-long steel laborer, measured his success another way. "Oh, I think I did myself [succeeded]. I don't know what anybody else thinks about it. I didn't get into trouble. I worked pretty good. I was fortunate. I was healthy. I was never sick or anything. I worked steady, that was the main thing, you know. As far as I think myself, I did."[41]

These last few pages have provided information about the occupa-tional mobility of five groups of workers. Variables such as age, length of residence in the community, or stage in the life cycle were found to have no statistical effect on upward occupational mobility.[42] Pre-migration backgrounds, occupational aspirations, ethnicity or race, and the economic structure of the city all exercised greater influence on a worker's experience in Pittsburgh. It is not possible to determine which of those factors exercised the strongest impact on a group or individual. A comparison of the experiences of these same groups in other Amer-ican cities may provide clues to the impact of the urban-industrial structure on occupational mobility, however.

We may reasonably assume that premigration backgrounds and aspirations of a given group of workers remained relatively constant, regardless of the city to which they migrated. And sufficient studies now exist to enable us to hold time constant, too. Given similar aspirations and the same time period, we may hypothesize that the intergroup experiences of Polish, black, and Italian migrants during the first three decades of the century would differ to the extent that the various cities differed. Similarities, conversely, would result from common backgrounds and from similarities in the urban-industrial structure in each city.

The data were gathered by a number of researchers employing a variety of methodologies. Sufficient similarities, however, do permit a comparison of the experiences of Pittsburgh's black and Italian populations with those in four other northern cities and of the Poles in Philadelphia. These cities all differed in size, age, stage of industrial development, and occupational structure. Steelton, Pennsylvania, was both the smallest and most industrialized of all cities examined to date. Nearly 90 percent of the town's male labor force received its wages from the Pennsylvania Steel Company. Philadelphia, Boston, and New York, large, old, and highly diversified cities, represented the other end of the industrial spectrum.[43] To be sure, all three of these eastern seaboard metropolises had industrialized, but none depended on heavy industry to the extent present in Steelton, Pittsburgh, or even Cleveland.[44] It is not possible to present a detailed discussion of the industrial environment in these cities. The analyses presented here, however, can provide an approximation of interurban differences and similarities. The results are suggestive and important if we are to grasp the complexities of the adjustment process.

An examination of the occupational distributions of Poles, blacks, and Italians in six cities for which data are available reveal that all three groups were overrepresented in the manual classes in all cities. Poles and blacks, not surprisingly, occupied the bottom two rungs of the blue-collar ladder. A substantial number of Italians (approximately one-fifth) performed skilled work in four of the five cities and between 12 and 20 percent engaged in white-collar work in all cities except Pittsburgh. Table 17 presents detailed information on the occupations of the three groups between 1900 and 1915.

From these data it appears that Boston, New York, and Cleveland provided greater initial opportunities for blacks and Italians than did either Pittsburgh or Steelton. At least 20 percent of the black workers and one-third of the Italians held skilled or white-collar jobs in the early 1900s in those cities. Comparable data do not exist for the Poles,

Table 17. Percentage Distribution by Occupation of Migrants in Six American Cities

Ethnic/Minority Group, Level of Work	Pittsburgh	Steelton	Philadelphia	Boston	New York	Cleveland
Blacks						
White collar	2.4	2.0	NA	7.8	NA	6.9
Skilled	12.2	5.0	NA	13.2	NA	11.1
Low manual	84.6	93.0	NA	79.0	NA	62.8
Italians						
White collar	1.9	16.0	NA	12.0	20.1	14.4
Skilled	22.7	0	NA	23.0	21.8	20.5
Low manual	75.9	84.0	NA	65.0	58.2	65.1
Poles						
White collar	3.2	NA	12.0	NA	NA	NA
Skilled	6.6	NA	24.0	NA	NA	NA
Low manual	90.1	NA	60.0	NA	NA	NA

NOTE. The data for this table are compiled from the following sources: Pittsburgh—sample data from the U.S. Bureau of the Census, Manuscript Census for Pittsburgh, 1900; Steelton—Bodnar, *Immigration and Industrialization*; Philadelphia—Golab, *Immigrant Destinations*, 102 (1915 data); Boston—Thernstrom, *The Other Bostonians*, 52; New York—Kessner, *The Golden Door*, 52; Cleveland—Kusmer, *A Ghetto Takes Shape*, 74, and Barton, *Peasants and Strangers*, 95. NA = not available.

but Golab suggests that they were somewhat better off in Philadelphia, where one-fourth held skilled and semiskilled jobs and 12 percent wore white collars in 1915.[45] Greater diversity in commerce and manufacturing in each of these cities probably provided expanded occupational opportunities even to these recent arrivals. In Cleveland, for example, one-third of the Italians began their careers as grocers, fish merchants, clerks, and shopkeepers.[46] New York presented opportunities for Italian shoemakers, tailors, masons, and a variety of shopkeepers. A small proportion of blacks managed to acquire white-collar positions in Cleveland and Boston.[47] Pittsburgh and Steelton, on the other hand, each dominated by heavy industry, provided limited alternative work opportunities. Eastern European migrants, guided by kin, moved quickly into the work most available to them — factory laborer. Italians secured a variety of laboring and skilled positions, while blacks who could not enter the mill received the remaining semiskilled and unskilled positions.[48]

We are not suggesting that other factors did not contribute to these differences. The available data, however, do hint that the "industrial mix" of the community influenced, to a degree, the opportunities available to nineteenth- and twentieth-century immigrants. One must also conclude that the initial work experiences of specific groups of migrants to all five cities were more alike than different. Italians were a bit better off than blacks who, in turn, began their careers slightly above the Poles. All three groups, of course, were near the bottom of the industrial-urban structure.

Occupational mobility patterns also reveal interesting intercity differences. Few of Philadelphia's major industries, for example, employed large numbers of unskilled workers; thus the city never attracted Poles, who came to America without skills. Those who disembarked at the Philadelphia port usually moved quickly to other more industrialized cities. Poles who did remain often possessed or acquired industrial skills and eventually jobs to match their talents. Golab provides little data on the occupational movements of Philadelphia's Poles but concludes that many Poles "found Philadelphia very attractive, speaking some English, familiar with the ways of American industrial organization and, most important possessing skills acquired while in the mines or mills, they had excellent prospects of finding appropriate employment in Philadelphia."[49] For Poles the interaction of immigrant expectations and the industrial structure of the city operated differently in Philadelphia than in Pittsburgh, for Pittsburgh attracted Poles with limited skills and expectations to match. Perhaps predictably, it provided work that fulfilled those limited expectations. Philadelphia attracted Poles who possessed greater skills (and perhaps greater aspirations) and enabled many to use their talents. A kin-communication network operated in both cities to inform migrants of prospective job opportunities. They apparently acted selectively to match their own skills, or lack thereof, with the most appropriate city. In this respect Polish immigrants controlled their own destinies to a greater extent than has been formerly understood.

Italians also operated selectively in their choice of city as the existence of village–chain migration patterns suggest. In their case, however, the selection may have been cultural as well as economic. The strong relationship Barton observed in Cleveland between village chains and persistence also existed in Pittsburgh.[50] The types of skills Italians brought to America, or could acquire through kin assistance, were in demand in most American communities. The process of city building required masons, carpenters, and bricklayers as well as railroad and public works laborers. In each city examined to date, Italians were more successful than their Polish or black counterparts in transforming these demands into satisfactory blue-collar or even lower level white-collar work. Italian occupational success in New York and Cleveland paralleled the upward movement of their brethren in Pittsburgh. In both New York City and Cleveland 40 percent of the unskilled Italians improved their positions; one-third of the semiskilled attained skilled or white-collar jobs, and more than 15 percent of the skilled workers moved into white-collar positions.[51] These figures, of course, exclude the countless number of successful and unsuccessful migrants who returned to their Italian villages. Thus it appears that the early aspirations expressed by many Italians entering American cities at the turn of the century were fulfilled. The second generation, as we shall see, made even more impressive gains.

The rates recorded by black migrants during the first three decades are more erratic and are always related to racial discrimination and their exclusion from specific industrial occupations. In Pittsburgh, as noted, blacks moved up and down the occupational scale, although their net direction was upward. Blacks in Steelton, too, moved upward, but all moves in this small manufacturing city were confined to moves from unskilled to semiskilled work.[52] After two decades blacks in both cities remained clustered at the lower two occupational levels. Blacks in Cleveland, conversely, had made some shortlived inroads into skilled work late in the nineteenth century. Beginning in 1900, they began a dramatic decline in occupational status. Shifts in the city's occupational structure, exclusion from labor unions, and the decline of black businesses all led to a deterioration of the position of black workers.[53] By 1910 they, like their counterparts in Pittsburgh and Steelton, performed much of the "forest city's" unskilled/semiskilled labor. Finally, in Boston, black workers remained almost static, trapped in the same two low-skill, low-paying positions. According to Stephan Thernstrom, "There was virtually no improvement in the occupational position of black men in Boston between the late nineteenth century and the beginning of World War II. In 1890, 56 percent of the black males were unskilled day laborers, servants, waiters, janitors or porters. Three decades later the fraction was 54 percent. . . . As of 1890, a mere 8 percent of Boston's blacks held white collar jobs; half a century later the figure was only 11 percent."[54] While Thernstrom provides no specific mobility data for this generation of Boston's blacks, we may reasonably infer only limited upward movement, if at all, for any cohort within this forty-year period. They again remained at the bottom of the city's occupational ladder.

These brief comparisons of mobility in a few northern American cities clearly suggest the influence of intraurban differences — migrants enjoyed greater opportunities in more diversified cities — but they also point to the presence of two widespread trends. Italian migration occurred at a most fortuitous time, coinciding with the era of city building. No matter which city they entered — as long as it was in the process of building its physical infrastructure — their aspirations and skills often matched the critical needs of the city. The match resulted in the slow, and difficult to be sure, upward climb into skilled or modest white-collar positions.

Black aspirations faced another growing urban trend — racial discrimination. Regardless of the cause — whether deep-seated fears, competition for jobs and neighborhoods, or simply ignorance — blacks in all cities studied thus far were excluded from industrial work, labor unions, certain skilled occupations, and white-collar work. No matter where they started, by 1920 they were overwhelmingly overrepresented in semiskilled/unskilled work, a situation exacerbated by the great migration beginning in 1915-16.

All three groups arrived in Pittsburgh at approximately the same time under somewhat similar circumstances. Their backgrounds and aspirations differed, and the city treated each group differently. By the beginning of the Depression, they were on remarkably different occupational paths.

Attaining a better job was not the only factor in creating a better life for self and family. Homeownership often provided a measure of security and independence in the migrants' lives. The hardships of unemployment could be muted somewhat if one owned a home. Boarders could be added or evicted, depending on economic circumstances. Perhaps, most important, owning a home could provide a sense of pride in a world where work often denied one feelings of worth. But a home could not be obtained easily, especially when wages were minimal and work was unpredictable. Obviously the more erratic one's work was, the more difficult it would be to purchase a home. But some of Pittsburgh's newcomers found ways. Others, especially the blacks, as Chapter 6 shows, did without.

NOTES

1. Stephan Thernstrom's pathbreaking analysis of Newburyport, Massachusetts, first appeared in 1965. *Poverty and Progress: Social Mobility in a Nineteenth-Century American City* (Cambridge, Mass., 1965).
2. See, for example, Peter Decker, *Fortunes and Failures: White-Collar Mobility in Nineteenth-Century San Francisco* (Cambridge, Mass., 1978); Thomas Kessner, *The Golden Door: Italian and Jewish Immigrant Mobility in New York City, 1880-1915* (New York, 1977); Gordon W. Kirk, Jr., *The Promise of American Life: Social Mobility in a Nineteenth-Century Immigrant Community, Holland, Michigan, 1847-1894* (Philadelphia, 1978); Caroline Golab, *Immigrant Destinations* (Philadelphia, 1977).
3. Kirk, *Promise of American Life.*

4. Kenneth Kusmer, *A Ghetto Takes Shape: Black Cleveland, 1870-1930* (Urbana, Ill., 1976), 67-70.

5. Kessner, *The Golden Door,* 123.

6. Josef Barton, *Peasants and Strangers: Italians, Rumanians and Slovaks in an American City* (Cambridge, Mass., 1975); Golab, *Immigrant Destinations.*

7. Decker, *Fortunes and Failures,* 186.

8. Herbert Gutman, "The Reality of the Rags-to-Riches 'Myth': The Case of the Paterson, New Jersey, Locomotive, Iron and Machinery Manufacturers, 1830-1880," in Stephan Thernstrom and Richard Sennett, ed., *Nineteenth-Century Cities: Essays in the New Urban History* (New Haven, Conn., 1969), 121-22.

9. Kessner, *The Golden Door,* 66-67.

10. Kusmer, *A Ghetto Takes Shape,* 66ff.

11. Gutman, "Rags-to-Riches 'Myth,'" 121. The Paterson workers studied by Gutman appear to be an exception to this pattern.

12. U.S. Bureau of the Census, *Thirteenth Census of the United States, 1910, Vol. 4: Occupational Statistics: Pittsburgh* (Washington, D.C., 1913), 180ff.

13. *Pittsburgh Leader* and *Pittsburgh Press* "Help Wanted Ads," as well as other sections of both papers, of the first and third weeks of every month for 1900 were analyzed. Advertisements for white-collar clerical workers were more common than for semiskilled operatives, most of whom secured their jobs by applying directly to the company employment office.

14. Ralph Ginsberg, "Semi-Markov Processes and Mobility," *Journal of Mathematical Sociology,* 1 (1971), 233. Ginsberg labels this process the "theory of cumulative inertia."

15. R. L. Hill, "A View of the Hill: A Study of Experiences and Attitudes in the Hill District of Pittsburgh, Pennsylvania, 1900-1973" (Ph.D. diss., University of Pittsburgh, 1973); Peter Gottlieb, "Migration and Jobs: The New Black Workers in Pittsburgh, 1916-1930," *Western Pennsylvania Historical Magazine,* 61 (Jan. 1978), 13. These figures are somewhat deflated, since a number of black workers had common surnames and could not be traced. Of the original 1,423 black adults, 171 were untraceable for this reason.

16. Golab, *Immigrant Destinations,* 99. Golab, in fact, characterizes these people as migrant workers. Theodore Saloutos, *They Remember America* (Berkeley, Calif., 1956), 30.

17. U.S. Senate, *Reports of the Immigration Commission,* 61 Cong., 2nd sess., Senate Document no. 633 (Washington, D.C., 1911), III; Kessner, *The Golden Door.* Italian government data were from *Statistica della emigrazione* and reported, ibid., 28.

18. Betty Boyd Caroli, *Italian Repatriation from the United States, 1900-1914* (New York, 1973), 38, 41.

19. Data cited above were compiled from the various tables, ibid., 15ff., and the 1900 sample data from the manuscript census of Pittsburgh.

20. *New York Times,* Nov. 22, 1907, 1. Quoted in Peter Shergold, "Wage Rates in Pittsburgh during the Depression," *Journal of American Studies,* 9 (1975), 185.

21. Peter Roberts, "Immigrant Wage Earners" in Paul Kellogg, ed., *Wage*

Earning Pittsburgh, The Pittsburgh Survey (New York, 1914), 53.

22. Commissariato Generale dell' Emigrazione, *Bollettino dell' Emigrazione,* no. 18 (1910), 45.

23. "The Young Man's Chances," *Pittsburgh Press,* Nov. 16, 1900.

24. "The Best Age for Young Men," *Pittsburgh Leader,* July 21, 1900, 28.

25. Ibid.

26. John Ingham, *The Iron Barons: A Social Analysis of an American Urban Elite, 1874-1965* (Westport, Conn., 1978), 32. The five iron barons Ingham identified as "Carnegie types" were Carnegie himself, his brother Tom, H. W. Borntrager, William ("Captain Billy") R. Jones, and Henry Phipps. The latter three were all officers in the Carnegie steel empire.

27. The customary way of comparing the occupational mobility rates of various groups over time is to provide a set of matrices for each group that detail the various occupational moves from one level to another. This method provides the greatest detail about the mobility of both groups and individual clusters. The analysis of six groups of workers over six time periods, however, requires the presentation of thirty separate five-by-five matrices, each showing the initial skills position of a group and movement or stability at a subsequent date. Even detail of this magnitude does not provide a totally accurate picture of the changing status of each group. Nineteenth-century census takers customarily missed between 10 and 23 percent of the population. City directories were equally unreliable. In addition, most members of the sample left the city, and some died, before the subsequent trace. Comparisons of the traceable individuals then provide only a rough approximation of the mobility patterns of the groups in question. Since we are interested in trends and in drawing comparisons of the migrants, we lose little by sparing the reader the tedium of several dozen tables.

28. Matrices for all observations are available in the archives of the Pennsylvania Historical and Museum Commission, Harrisburg.

29. Ira Reid, "The Negro in the Major Industries and Building Trades of Pittsburgh" (M.A. thesis, University of Pittsburgh, 1925), 36.

30. Abraham Epstein, *The Negro Migrant in Pittsburgh* (Pittsburgh, 1918), 36.

31. Hill, "A View of the Hill," 68ff.; *Pittsburgh Courier,* 1913, 1920.

32. Howard D. Gould, "An Analysis of the Occupational Opportunities for Negroes in Allegheny County" (M.A. thesis, University of Pittsburgh, 1934), 18.

33. See Kusmer, *A Ghetto Takes Shape,* 66ff.

34. Salvatore A. Migliore, "Half a Century of Italian Immigration into Pittsburgh and Allegheny County" (M.A. thesis, University of Pittsburgh, 1928), 33.

35. Members of a lower skill level, it must be recalled, left the community more frequently than those at the upper levels. In part, therefore, the reduced percentages in the 1915 and 1920 "Same" columns are due to attrition. However, since we are attempting to compare, and since all groups were subject to similar pressures to leave the community, the differences among the "Stable" percentages remain important.

36. Grace Anderson noted a similar relationship between an occupational

category and upward mobility in twentieth-century Toronto. She identified construction and demolition occupations as "stepping stones." Service jobs such as hospital orderly and janitor, conversely, acted as "occupational traps" since they seldom led to other related jobs at higher skill levels. Individuals were forced to change occupational categories if they expected to achieve any upward mobility. Mill work in Pittsburgh also acted as an "occupational trap." See *Networks of Contact: The Portuguese and Toronto* (Waterloo, Ontario, 1974), 97.

37. Interview with Leroy M., July 14, 1974, Pittsburgh Oral History Project (POHP).
38. Reid, "The Negro in the Major Industries," 31.
39. See Stephan Thernstrom, *The Other Bostonians: Poverty and Progress in the American Metropolis, 1880-1970* (Cambridge, Mass., 1973), 167-78; Oscar Handlin, *Boston's Immigrants: A Study in Acculturation* (Cambridge, Mass., 1959), 70; Nathan Glazer and Daniel P. Moynihan, *Beyond the Melting Pot* (Cambridge, Mass., 1959).
40. Interview with Edward M., Sept. 30, 1976, POHP.
41. Interview with Joseph K., Sept. 13, 1976, POHP.
42. Multiple regression analyses were conducted on occupational mobility with use of initial occupation, age, length of stay, and stage in the life cycle as independent variables. The resulting coefficients demonstrated that only initial skill level influenced the likelihood of occupational mobility, and in all cases the values were negative – that is, begining a career at any point above the unskilled level lessened the likelihood of increasing the occupational level. The size of the coefficients also revealed that semiskilled workers were more likely to move up than skilled workers. These results were predictable and shed no new light on the problem. Because none of the other variables in the regression was found to have a significant effect at the 0.05 level, they have not been included here. Mobility regressions are available with the other data from this project at the archives of the Pennsylvania Historical and Museum Commission.
43. John Bodnar, *Immigration and Industrialization: Ethnicity in an American Mill Town, 1870-1940* (Pittsburgh, 1977); Golab, *Immigrant Destinations;* Thernstrom, *The Other Bostonians;* Kessner, *The Golden Door.*
44. Kusmer, *A Ghetto Takes Shape;* Barton, *Peasants and Strangers.*
45. Golab, *Immigrant Destinations.*
46. Barton, *Peasants and Strangers,* 95.
47. Kessner, *The Golden Door,* 55; Boston's large manufacturers, like those in Pittsburgh, systematically excluded blacks. See Thernstrom, *The Other Bostonians,* 193.
48. Kusmer, *A Ghetto Takes Shape,* 67.
49. Golab, *Immigrant Destinations,* 106.
50. Barton, *Peasants and Strangers,* 55.
51. Ibid., 96; Kessner, *The Golden Door,* 114-15.
52. Bodnar, *Immigration and Industrialization,* 73.
53. Kusmer, *A Ghetto Takes Shape,* 67ff.
54. Thernstrom, *The Other Bostonians,* 194.

6

Homeownership

In the early twentieth century the purchase of a home was the most common form of wealth accumulation achieved by persisting unskilled workers and newcomers to the city. Homeowning was not a value that would-be Americanizers and middle-class reformers needed to impose upon immigrant newcomers. It was a primary goal for families who decided to remain in America permanently. The Polish and Italian immigrants came from traditional agricultural areas where status derived from landowning. "Without land," wrote sociologists William Thomas and Florian Znaniecki in their exhaustive study of Polish migration, "the family can still keep its internal solidarity, but it cannot act as a unit with regard to the rest of the community. It ceases to count as a social power."[1]

The intensity with which the European immigrants shared this priority was apparent not only from contemporary accounts but also from the oral history interviews. Joe B., whose father migrated from Russian Poland in 1900, recalled that "the moment my folks accumulated enough money to put down on a house they decided to look for property. We bought it for $3,000. It still was a lot of money but they were able to float a loan through the . . . building and loan. . . . And then their time was devoted to paying off the mortgage. Really it was the prime thing on their mind, the paying off the mortgage, and they did."[2] Margaret Byington, in her study of the industrial town of Homestead, wrote of the "heroic efforts to buy the house" among steel workers and their families. The value was so pervasive that she entitled her section on the east European workers "The Slav as Homesteader."[3]

The priority placed on homeowning among black migrants, in contrast, was less apparent than it was among the immigrants. Since blacks were systematically denied the opportunity to acquire property during and after slavery, ownership as a particular form of status or prestige may have had less significance for blacks than for eastern and southern European groups fighting to hold onto land that became so important for them in the latter part of the nineteenth century. The oral history interviews indicate that blacks came to Pittsburgh with a general desire to improve their status and to pursue some career. Rarely was homeownership even mentioned as a specific goal.[4]

Studies of social mobility on a wide range of communities and ethnic groups have placed considerable emphasis on the role of homeownership. The wealth it represents has been viewed as a major form of success.[5] This is particularly valid if we define achievement in terms of the newcomers' aspirations and priorities. For the Poles and Italians, at least, homeowning and the creation of stable neighborhoods were clearly high priorities. Moreover, homeowning had several distinct advantages over renting. In addition to providing a sense of status, it gave the owners greater control over their environment, provided a form of enforced savings with a resultant equity, and had the potential of providing a source of income.[6]

Ownership increased the family's control over its immediate environment because there was no landlord to criticize the behavior of family members or to evict the family if there were too many children. If relatives arrived from the home village, the owner, in fact, could evict another family to make room for his kinfolk. The other family, or families, with whom the owner shared his dwelling helped to meet the mortgage payments. When the house mortgage was paid off, the tenant could be retained as a source of income. A paid-up home with a renting family could provide a considerable measure of security for old age in a day before pensions. It was common for owners in the Polish and Italian neighborhoods to erect second homes at the rear of their lots after the first house was paid off, thus providing an additional source of income. The rear house could also be used to provide a start for married children. Edward M., whose parents migrated from Poland, recalled that they evicted tenants from a rear dwelling and fixed it up for him when he married.[7]

At the turn of the century most families in Pittsburgh and other large cities rented their homes. The cost of homes and the short repayment period of most mortgages precluded the majority of families from owning. A story in the *Pittsburgh Leader* revealed the dilemma of many. A young wife spent several days chasing about the city in hope of finding a suitable house to rent in her price range. Then she saw a notice in the paper: "Why pay rent?"

> You hadn't thought of a Utopia where rents are not paid. "Why not own your own home?" the interrogatory printer asks. "Put it on easy payments." An elysian dream opens before you and your brain begins to reel in the ecstasy of contemplating the delights of owning your own home. You break pellmell for the "Why pay rent?" man. He explains the great possibilities of easy payments. His reasoning is very alluring, but you haven't the bank account to draw on for a first payment of 50 per cent, and you don't feel like tying yourself down for 20 years without it.[8]

In 1900, according to the U.S. Census Bureau, 26.3 percent of all householders in Pittsburgh owned their homes. Among foreign-born whites the figure was 30.2 percent; the percentage for native whites was 23.6. Only 8.4 percent of black household heads owned in that year.[9] It would appear that the foreign-born, in general, had a greater propensity to buy.

These rates of homeownership tabulated by the Census Bureau are somewhat misleading. What the agency considered a household would today be called a dwelling unit: essentially a self-contained premises.[10] However, a careful inspection of the census rolls reveals that there were numerous families, particularly small ones, that boarded with another family and were not counted as a separate household in the census. This practice was more widespread among some groups than others, but, if each of these families was considered separately, the percentage of homeowners would show considerable variation. Table 18 shows the percentages of homeowners as reported in the census returns and as tabulated from our sample for each ethnic group. The percentages of ownership by household are comparable, but the percentages by total families give a more complete picture of the condition of these newcomers. Subsequent analysis of the 1900 sample data will be based on the total number of families.

It is hardly surprising that only a small proportion of blacks and eastern European immigrants were homeowners in 1900, since most were quite recent arrivals from impoverished rural areas. Although these homeowners were atypical of all newcomers in 1900, they had already achieved a form of mobility that many of their fellow migrants were hoping for and would achieve in subsequent decades. Who these early owners were, therefore, and the mechanisms that enabled them to purchase homes are valuable in understanding the adjustment of these groups to the city.

In 1900 German Polish families had significantly higher rates of

Table 18. Percentage of Households and Families Owning Homes
in Pittsburgh in 1900, by Place of Birth

Ethnic/Minority Group	Percentage of All Households Owning in 1900		Percentage of All Families Owning in 1900, from Sample
	From Census Returns[1]	From Sample	
All households	25.9	. . .	. . .
All native-born whites	23.6	. . .	. . .
All blacks	8.4	. . .	. . .
Northern-born blacks	. . .	11.0	5.4
Southern-born blacks	. . .	6.5	3.2
All foreign-born whites	30.2	. . .	. . .
All Poles	13.1	. . .	. . .
German Poles	. . .	24.7	17.6
Russian Poles	. . .	2.9	1.1
Austrian Poles	. . .	6.7	2.1
All Italians	8.1	9.6	3.2

NOTE. The data are compiled from the U.S. Bureau of Census, *Twelfth Census. Population,* 736-37 (Table 111), 751-53 (Table 115), and the sample data derived from the Manuscript Census for Pittsburgh, 1900. Three dots = data not applicable or not available. Pittsburgh and Allegheny City are treated as one unit.
[1]The percentages for Poles and Italians from the census returns are based on the birthplace of parents.

homeownership than any other group. Northern-born blacks had the second highest levels of homeowning, substantially higher than that of southern blacks but far below that of the German Poles. One cannot immediately conclude, however, that the German Poles placed a greater priority on owning than the other groups. In addition to cultural values, there were several interrelated factors that determined the rate of homeowning.

A family's housing needs fluctuated with its stage in the life cycle. Young, single adults rarely established their own households; they were customarily boarders or lodgers. Young married couples required less space than those in their thirties and forties. Childless couples themselves were often boarders. Those couples in the middle years of adulthood with a number of children had the highest incidence of ownership. They had the most children at home, and they also had had time to accumulate a down payment. Older couples again required less space; if they owned, they usually took in boarders. (See Table 8 for the relationship between stage in life cycle and presence of boarders in the home.)

By comparing homeowning by stage in the life cycle and occupation, we can more clearly determine the role of cultural values or preferences in owning. The correlation of ownership and life cycle stage reveals that older, midstage families (those with married or working children) showed a greater propensity to own—twice the rate of all families for all groups combined (Table 19). At each stage, however, the German

Table 19. Percentage of Family Heads Owning Homes by Life Cycle Stage for Each Ethnic Group in Pittsburgh, 1900

	Blacks		Poles			
Family Stage	Northern-Born	Southern-Born	Russian	German	Italians	All Groups
Newlyweds	7.7	1.7	0	0	0	2.0
Young families	6.9	5.0	3.0	21.6	5.4	7.6
Midstage	11.5	11.9	0	26.0	17.9	15.0
Female-headed	11.1	4.3	. . .	20.0	16.7	6.1

NOTE. The data are compiled from the sample data of the 1900 Manuscript Census. This table is not a single cross-tabulation, but a composite of several tables. The first cell reads: 7.7 percent of northern-born black newlywed families owned their homes in 1900. There were too few mature families or Austrian Polish families to include in this analysis. Three dots = not available. See Table 6 for definitions of each family stage.

Poles still stand out with the highest rates of ownership. In addition, the correlation between occupation and ethnicity demonstrates that cultural variation does not disappear when occupation is held constant. Although the number of white-collar family heads was small, they had substantially higher rates of ownership across all categories. Most of these white-collar workers were, in fact, petty proprietors and shopkeepers—grocers, bakers, butchers, barbers—whose business and residence were at the same location. Almost half of all German Polish white-collar family heads owned their homes. Italians also showed a high level of ownership in this group, but German Poles were the only group to demonstrate a substantial rate of ownership among skilled workers as well (Table 20).

German Poles, on the average, migrated to the United States earlier than the other Polish groups or than the Italians. The average year of migration for each of the foreign-born family heads was: German Poles, 1886; Russian Poles, 1889; Austrian Poles, 1891; Italians, 1889. When we compare rates of ownership by year of arrival in the United States for the foreign-born, some of the differences between German Poles, Russian Poles, and Italians disappear. Table 21 shows the percentage of homeowners by year of arrival for these groups. Among the small number who came before 1880 (many of whom were also petty proprietors by 1900), a substantial portion of each ethnic group were owners. In

Table 20. Percentage of Family Heads Owning Homes by Occupation for
Ethnic/Minority Group in Pittsburgh in 1900

Occupational Level	Blacks		Poles		Italians	All Groups
	Northern-Born	Southern-Born	Russian	German		
Unskilled	5.4	2.4	1.3	14.5	1.9	3.6
Semiskilled	2.0	2.6	10.7	0	5.6	3.3
Skilled	6.3	1.8	3.5	21.4	5.7	5.6
White collar	16.7	19.4	5.6	46.2	50.0	15.1

NOTE. There were too few Austrian Polish families to include in this analysis.
The data are compiled from the sample data of the 1900 Manuscript Census.

Table 21. Percentage of Family Heads Owning Homes in 1900
in Pittsburgh for Foreign-Born Groups by Time of Arrival

Year of Arrival	Russian Poles	German Poles	Italians
Before 1880	22.2	15.4	26.7
1880-89	6.9	24.0	8.3
1890-94	0.5	6.6	1.9
1895-1900	0	0	0

NOTE. There were too few Austrian Polish Families to include in this analysis.
The data are compiled from the sample data derived from the 1900 Manuscript
Census.

fact, both Russian Poles and Italians had higher percentages of owners
than did German Poles. However, among the larger group that arrived
in the 1880s, German Poles did show a substantially higher percentage
of owners, and even a few of the migrants who came in the early 1890s
managed to buy a home by 1900. The higher rate of ownership among
German Poles was partly a function of their longer tenure in the country. As a group, they were also less likely to repatriate than Russian
Poles or Italians, which may have provided a greater incentive to save
for a down payment and to invest in a home.

One might expect to find similar rates of ownership between German
Poles and northern-born blacks, many of whom were natives of Pittsburgh, since both groups had presumably been in the city ten to
twenty years. Although northern blacks had higher rates of owning than
southern blacks, their overall ownership rate, whether we use households or families as a base, was substantially lower than that of German
Poles or that of all foreign-born whites. The lower rate of black ownership resulted from a combination of job discrimination, greater independence of the children who might otherwise have contributed to
savings, and perhaps more interest in career than property acquisition.

In the first thirty years of the twentieth century homeowning among Pittsburgh households increased substantially as it did in all large cities. By 1930, 40.2 percent of the city's households owned their homes, but this average disguised considerable variation by ethnic groups.[11] The 1930 census reported the following ownership rates for the Pittsburgh populations: all foreign-born whites, 52.2 percent; Italians, 50.1 percent; Poles, 49.2 percent; all native whites, 38.1 percent; blacks, 17.0 percent. Italians and Poles clearly made remarkable strides in those years; their ownership rates were almost equal to that of all the foreign-born. Blacks, while doubling their rate of ownership since 1900, still lagged far behind. In 1900 the black rate of ownership was one-third of the rate for all households and a little over one-quarter of that for all foreign-born whites. By 1930 the black ownership rate was 40 percent of the rate for all households and one-third of that for all foreign-born. The gap had narrowed, but not by much.

Persisting sample members were traced through the county property assessment records to determine their rates of ownership to 1930 (Table 22). The number of persisters was small, but the data do show rates

Table 22. Percentage of Persisters among 1900 Sample Families Owning Homes, 1910-30

Sample Families	1910	1915	1920	1930
All persisters	13.6	13.1	20.1	23.4
German Poles	26.2	21.2	36.6	20.0
Russian Poles	17.6	18.2	23.2	30.4
Italians	17.6	10.3	13.0	33.3
Northern-born blacks	8.3	3.5	11.3	18.4
Southern-born blacks	10.8	12.3	16.0	21.2
No. owning	64	54	54	36
Mean age of all owners	43.7	44.3	46.2	48.9

NOTE. The data are compiled from the sample data of the 1900 Manuscript Census, and Allegheny County, Pa., Assessment Rolls, 1910, 1915, 1920, and 1930, Court House, Pittsburgh.

comparable to the published returns. The rates in most cases are lower than published returns because the sample data show the rate for all adult males at each time period. German Poles continued to lead the other groups in the percentage of family heads who owned homes until 1930, when Italians displaced them. By 1930, however, many of the early-arriving German Poles were passing away. More important, the range of variation among the percentage of owners in that year was not that wide.

Black families who persisted for thirty years also showed substantial gains in ownership. By 1930 southern blacks had a higher rate of ownership than German Poles, which suggests that blacks who were native to the city and early-arriving southern blacks who chose to remain were able to make some significant gains in terms of home-ownership, despite their uneven and erratic pattern of occupational mobility. This is the clearest indication that blacks who arrived at the same time as the immigrants and remained in the city were able to achieve some level of success.

Although a minority of adult males owned homes throughout the period, the clear upward trend in ownership among the persisters indicates the vital importance of this form of social mobility to the overall adjustment of the new migrants. Owning a home was increasingly possible for most of the persisters, and growing numbers of them were taking that option. The process by which they were able to do this, how long it took them to save for a down payment, how much they had to save, how great their indebtedness was, and where they turned for mortgages reveal a great deal about their economic and social adjustment to an urban-industrial environment. To examine the ownership process we have focused on several small areas of the city where large numbers of the subject groups resided: Polish Hill, Bloomfield, East Liberty, the Hill District, and Homewood.[12]

The area known as Polish Hill lies at the far northeast end of Herron Hill, overlooking the Strip District and Lawrenceville. Although the gradually sloping western and southern sides of Herron Hill filled with homes in the 1860s and 1870s, the far steeper northern slope remained undeveloped. During the 1880s and early 1890s, the expansion of industry along the Strip District provided a growing number of jobs for unskilled labor. The isolation of the steep hillside was precisely what made it desirable for the men who took those jobs: the land was relatively inexpensive. The early arrivals focused their economic and social activities on the Strip District and Lawrenceville. As late as 1898 no trolley line penetrated the Polish Hill area; the nearest service to the central business district was another 100 feet up the hill.

The early residents of the area were German Polish immigrants, primarily unskilled labor, with a few German and Irish immigrants and blacks mixed in. In the 1890s the Poles established a parish on Brereton Avenue, Immaculate Heart of Mary Roman Catholic Church, and built a frame structure with a school behind it. In 1905 a new impressive stone and brick church building was under construction, and its steeples still dominate the Polish Hill horizon. The size of the structure and the relatively early date of its erection attest not only to the commitment and esteem of the people for their religious institutions, but also to the large sums that they were able to raise to support the construction of the building and the school.[13]

The Polish Falcons and the St. Joseph and the St. Franciscus Xavery beneficial societies, mentioned earlier, were only three of many such organizations founded in the first generation of settlement. Among those institutions were several building and loan associations, and it was to those organizations that the homeowners in Polish Hill turned for their mortgages. The earliest building and loan associations in the area were founded by Germans in the Lawrenceville district. But in December 1887 seventeen men, most of whom were Polish, subscribed to the initial shares of Pulaski Building and Loan. The original officers were Charles Zulawski, Jacob Phillips, Victor Malka, and Stanislaus Michalski. Within a year another group founded the T. Kosciusko Building and Loan.[14]

The building and loans financed the vast majority of purchases in Polish Hill through the 1920s. These associations often had no permanent place of business but met, usually monthly, in a store or fraternal hall. The officers were local businessmen in the community. The customary procedure was for the borrower to subscribe to a certain number of shares equivalent to the amount of the loan. When the shares were paid in full, the mortgage was cancelled. Regular depositors could also buy shares to save for a down payment or another purpose. Dividends were paid, usually semiannually, on the amount of shares fully paid. Since commercial banks could not provide long-term mortgage money, the building and loans became quite popular, particularly in the northeastern states in the late nineteenth century. In 1893 there were 1,350,000 shareholders and 402,000 borrowers nationally.

The most common plan in the 1890s was to pay $1 or $1.25 per share per month, with each share worth usually $100; the payment was $10 or $12.50 per month per $1,000 borrowed. Interest was deducted from this payment, and the dividend was credited on the number of shares fully paid. The effective rate of interest was between 6 and 7 percent. The repayment schedule was kept as low as possible, but members were encouraged to pay larger sums and to pay off the loans as soon as they could.[15]

A fairly typical building and loan of the period was Smokey City Building and Loan Number Two, which operated in the Lawrenceville and Polish Hill area. The board members were primarily shopkeepers, small building contractors, and real estate and insurance agents. They were mainly German, but they lent extensively to the growing Polish community. Each share in Smokey City was equivalent to $100. A borrower had to put down 25 percent of his purchase price and pay 75¢ on each share every two weeks, of which 50¢ went toward principal and 25¢ to interest. This came to $195 per year per $1,000. The loan, if payments were made on schedule, matured in between six-

and-a-half and six-and-three-quarter years at an interest rate of between 6.7 and 7.6 percent. However, since borrowers also received a semiannual dividend on their paid-up shares, the true interest rate was slightly lower. At Smokey City there was also a penalty of 10¢ a share for late payments.

The application procedures for a loan were considerably less formal than they are now. Although the property was appraised and the title searched, credit references and a man's occupation were less important. As the long-time secretary of the association said, "A man's character meant more than anything." Reputation and reliability were most important. Smokey City did not even inquire into the amount of a man's annual income. Further, the association often carried mortgagors for six months or longer if they were unemployed or ill, a not uncommon practice among the building and loans of the period.[16]

By the 1920s building and loans nationally, on the average, charged $12.98 per $1,000 per month with a usual repayment period of ten years, which came to 6.98 percent interest per annum. The average down payment was 36 percent. Most building and loans in Pittsburgh and elsewhere lent only for construction on an unencumbered lot. They did not lend for initial purchase of a vacant lot, nor did they give second mortgages except when a second house was built on the property.[17]

An examination of the financial arrangements of the homeowners can reveal much about their assets and how much money newcomers were able to save over a given period of time. There are no records of building and loan associations available for this period, but some insights can be gained from the deed and mortgage records. Before the 1920s deeds usually indicated the purchase price of each property. Mortgages showed the amount of the debt, the terms, and the date of satisfaction. No source can be considered completely accurate, but the deed and mortgage books were kept meticulously. An individual could buy a lot without recording it in the court house, but he ran the risk of losing his property at a later date. Homeowners could have borrowed privately from friends and relatives for a purchase, but unless recorded, it would not be officially considered a mortgage. The deeds of Allegheny County are indexed by property location only for the period since the 1930s. Every title in the study areas was traced backwards from the 1930s to the 1890s or 1880s. The name of each Polish or Italian owner was then checked in the mortgage indices. It is possible that some error was introduced at this stage: because of inaccurate spelling of names, mortgages on record may have been missed in the index search. However, the names were indexed by the Key Letter method, similar to the soundex system used for the 1900 census.[18]

Where owners could be located in the 1900 census, additional demographic information supplemented the data from the deeds and mortgages. The soundex index to the 1900 census was also used in an attempt to locate some post-1900 owners who might have been living elsewhere in Pittsburgh, or in Pennsylvania, at the time of the census. The names of owners were also checked in the city directory to determine their occupation at the time of purchase. For Poles and Italians, names were used to identify ethnicity where the owners could not be found in the census. Although titles were also traced in the black neighborhoods, positive identification by race was much more difficult. The 1900 census and the county voter registration cards, which began in the mid-1930s, were the principal sources of identification. These sources yielded only a very small number of known black owners, and the results are only suggestive of their financial situation. Because buyers purchased and sold lots over a thirty-year period, during which time there was considerable price inflation, cash values have been converted to constant, 1913 dollars. Where both current and constant values are provided, the constant, 1913 value is in parentheses; where only one amount is given, it is the constant dollar value.[19]

The Polish Hill data proved to be the most valuable because the Poles moved heavily into the area when it was first developed and because a large number of them were already owners at the time of the 1900 census. To analyze the Polish purchases we must divide the owners into two main categories: those who bought lots and those who purchased complete dwellings. Each of these groups will be further subdivided according to the financial terms of their purchase. For those buyers of undeveloped lots we will discuss separately: (1) those who purchased without a mortgage, (2) those who required a mortgage to buy their lot, and (3) those who took a mortgage at the time of purchase and immediately built a dwelling.

Most of the lots in Polish Hill passed from the subdividers to the future homeowners in a short period between 1888 and 1893 when Pittsburgh, like most other large cities, experienced a substantial building and real estate boom. The lots were fairly typical for Pittsburgh at that time, measuring 25 feet across and 120 feet deep or 3,000 square feet. In almost all cases the buyers purchased a single lot and built a home on it either right away or a few years later. Most of the builders moved into their homes; a few were nonresident investors. There was only one case of a contractor buying multiple lots. (This case is not included in the analysis.) It is possible, of course, that some owners also had property elsewhere in the neighborhood or the city. It was not feasible to check all of the holdings of all of these owners. The average purchase price of all of the lots was $546 in current prices, $644 in constant 1913 dollars. The average year of purchase was 1891.

All of the original transactions in the sample area were analyzed, but Poles accounted for only 55 percent of the initial purchases. The other buyers were primarily English, German, and Irish immigrants. The occupational distribution of Poles and non-Poles, together with the average purchase price of each group, is provided in Table 23. Poles

Table 23. Purchase Price of Unimproved Lots
in Polish Hill District of Pittsburgh, by Ethnic Group and Occupation

| Ethnic Group, Occupation (n) | Mean Purchase Price | | Percentage of Known Cases in Occupation |
	Current Dollars	Constant Dollars	
Poles (48)	$515.83	$642.28	
Unskilled (21)	398.29	518.27	58.3
Skilled (8)	823.90	948.50	22.2
White collar (8)	621.88	781.65	19.4
Non-Poles (38)	569.47	737.44	
Unskilled and semiskilled (16)	546.88	708.54	61.5
Skilled (4)	634.58	712.98	15.4
White collar (6)	508.33	666.78	23.1

NOTE. The occupation is indicated only for known cases, which explains the discrepancy in the number and percentage totals. The data are compiled from the county deed and mortgage books, the 1900 Manuscript Census, and the city directories.

paid less on the average for their lots, primarily because they tended to buy on the side streets while the non-Poles more often bought along Brereton Avenue, which emerged as the principal commercial street of the neighborhood.

Out of eighty-six initial buyers, thirty-one purchased lots without a mortgage. They paid an average of $570 ($687) for their properties. Seven of these buyers resold their lots without making any improvements. They held onto the property for an average of thirteen years and made an average profit of $209. In two cases they held their properties from 1889 to 1913 while the market value, in constant dollars, rose from $320.50 to $600. Little detailed information was available on these owners.

A group of eleven buyers subsequently built on their lots without ever taking out a mortgage. They may have borrowed privately from family or friends, but there were no recorded mortgages on their properties. Most of these owners were German or English, but one, at least, was an immigrant Polish laborer who migrated to America in 1884, bought a lot in 1889 for $400 ($512), and sold the house and lot in 1905 for $2,355 ($2,707). Most of these homes were not intended for speculation; they were built and occupied by the owners and held for ten to twenty years. Fourteen buyers who could afford to purchase their lots for cash later took out a mortgage in order to build. These families paid an average of $652 ($798) for their lots. They were primarily Poles who built homes for themselves and owned their properties for an average of 24.5 years.

Who were these early buyers who did not even require a mortgage to purchase their lots, and how did they manage to save $500 to $600 in the late 1880s and early 1890s? The background of many is obscure, but those who stayed in the neighborhood until the census of 1900 or were listed in the city directories provide a valuable profile of the entire group (Table 24). Both Polish and non-Polish buyers were in

Table 24. Profile of Buyers of Undeveloped Lots Who Did Not
Take a Mortgage at Time of Purchase

Ethnic Group	Mean Purchase Price		Mean Age	Mean Years in United States	Mean Amount of Later Mortgage (constant dollars)
	Current Dollars	Constant Dollars			
Poles	$672	$865	34.5	10.6	$2,207
Non-Poles	575	739	36.1	12.5	1,775

NOTE. The data on purchase prices include information from all of the cases. Name identification was used for ethnicity when no other information was available. The age and the years in the United States were provided only for owners located in the 1900 census: fourteen Poles and nine non-Poles. The sources for the data were the deed and mortgage books, the 1900 census, and city directories.

their mid-thirties at the time of their initial purchase. This coincides with the evidence from the 1900 sample of the concentration of owners in that stage of the life cycle. All of the owners except one were foreign-born, and they had been in the United States an average of ten to twelve years at the time of purchase. Most of the Polish owners had migrated in the early 1880s while a few had come in the early 1870s. The non-Polish buyers exhibited a similar pattern, several having migrated in the 1860s and early 1870s as children, while the others came in the early 1880s. The length of tenure of the foreign-born had no bearing on the amount of money the owners paid for their property or the size of subsequent mortgages they may have taken out. The occupations of these early buyers who did not take mortgages reveal that they were not typical of the overall distribution of the foreign-born, particularly of the Polish migrants. Out of seventeen Polish buyers in this group whose occupation at the time of purchase could be ascertained, seven were laborers and ten were skilled artisans or petty proprietors, including several grocers. Among the non-Poles, six out of eleven were laborers, two were craftsmen, two were shopkeepers, and one was a policeman. These men were born in England, Germany, and Ireland. One was an American born of Irish parents; he was also the youngest buyer, having just turned twenty-one and been married when he purchased a lot in 1889. Out of twelve Poles who were located in the 1900 census, eleven were from the German territories, and the other was a Russian Pole. These data on occupation and origin are not a random sample of all cases, but do coincide with the analysis of the 1900 sample.

This general profile is what might be expected of a group of immigrants who were able to buy home lots in the late 1880s without a mortgage. Men who had been in the country as little as five to ten years and could invest $400 to $600 in a house lot either brought some assets with them or were remarkably successful in their business or trade. The experiences of a larger group of initial buyers who required a mortgage to purchase their properties reveal even more about the finances and savings of the immigrants (Table 25). Initial buyers who

Table 25. Profile of Buyers of Undeveloped Lots
in the Polish Hill District Who Had a Mortgage at the Time of Purchase

| | Mortgage | |
Profile	Less than Purchase Price	Greater than Purchase Price
Number	12	17
Mean age at purchase[1]	33.2	33.3
Mean no. of years in United States at purchase[1]	15.1	7.1
Mean purchase price[2]	$728	$569
Mean amount down[2]	$208	. . .
Mean percentage down	27.7	. . .

NOTE. The data are compiled from the deed and mortgage books and the 1900 manuscript census.

[1]Only for cases located in the manuscript census for 1900.
[2]In constant 1913 dollars. If the mortgage was less than the purchase price, the buyer required a mortgage to purchase the lot. The down payment was assumed to be the difference between the purchase price and the amount of the mortgage. If the mortgage exceeded the purchase price, the buyer built a home at the time of purchase. Since the cost of the home was not known, the amount of the down payment could not be calculated.

took a mortgage at the time of purchase can also be separated into two categories: those who required a mortgage to buy the lot and only built later, and those who bought their lot and proceeded to build immediately.

Twenty-five initial buyers required a mortgage to finance the purchase of their lots. The average price of these lots was $613 ($728), more than for those who purchased without a mortgage. The average down payment on these mortgages was $197 ($208). On the average the down payment was 28 percent of the purchase price, but in several cases the down payment was only 10 percent, representing as little as $50 or $75 ($64-$96). The mortgages were privately placed because building and loan associations would not lend on undeveloped land. Most often the subdividers took up the mortgages. The terms called for repayment within three to five years with interest at 5 to 6 percent per annum paid semiannually. The Polish buyers in this group were considerably younger than either the non-Polish buyers or the Polish buyers who purchased without a mortgage. The mean age of the Polish buyers in this group was 30.8 years, and the mean year of migration was 1883.5; the mean age of the non-Polish buyers was 35.7, and the mean year of migration was 1870.5.

Most of these buyers paid off their small mortgages within five years. Ten owners subsequently sold the lots without making any improvements, while the others took larger mortgages and built homes. It is not possible to determine the down payments on these later mortgages because we do not know the cost of the homes that were erected; most likely the owners used the paid-up value of the lot as their equity for the new mortgage. These later mortgages averaged slightly over $2,100. As with the buyers who did not require a mortgage, these owners were not entirely representative of the Polish migration. Of six owners who remained in 1900, two were unskilled laborers, two were mechanics, and two were proprietors.

A third group of initial buyers was able to commence building at the time of purchase. Their mortgages were greater than the price of the lots, so we cannot calculate the amount or percentage of their down payment because we do not know the cost of the homes. The purchase price of the lots averaged $459 ($569), which was less than that of the other groups of initial buyers and which may partially explain why they were able to build right away. It is probable that these buyers purchased their lot outright and used it for a partial or full down payment for their loans, which averaged 69 percent of the combined value of lot and first mortgage.

The Polish buyers in this group evidenced characteristics similar to those who took a mortgage to buy their lots. For thirteen cases in which the owners could be located in the 1900 census, the mean age of the Polish buyers was 34.6 years, and the mean year of migration was 1884.8. On average, these men were in the country just over six years before they made their purchase. The few non-Polish buyers in the group, on the average, were three years younger and migrated four years earlier. The Polish buyers bought less expensive lots and took larger mortgages than did the non-Polish buyers. In fourteen cases for which the occupation of the Polish buyers could be ascertained, eleven were laborers, one was a carpenter, and two were proprietors. The larger number of laborers may reflect the lower price of the lots. All but three were German Poles. Among five non-Polish buyers in this group, only one was a laborer; the others were a teamster, an electrician, a grocer, and an insurance agent. They were from England, Ireland, and Germany; one was born in Virginia of Irish parents. Most of these owners paid off their mortgages at the time of sale, so it is not possible to calculate how much equity they had in their home, but an examination of some individual cases in which the mortgage was paid off before sale provides additional insight into the time required to save a specified sum.

Frank Szurzewski was born in German Poland in 1851. He married Johanna in 1876 and they had a son, Peter, in 1878. In 1880 they migrated to America; they had another son the following year. By 1900 Johanna had borne eleven children, but three had died. In 1889 Frank bought a lot at 338 Harmar Street in Polish Hill for $325 ($417). He took out a mortgage with the T. Kosciusko Building and Loan for $500 ($641), which he paid off in 1899. In 1900 Frank worked in a foundry as a laborer, Peter worked in a cork factory, and the second son was a finisher in a steel mill. In 1902 Frank took another mortgage—probably to enlarge the house—for $1,200 ($1,428), and he paid it off in four years. In 1935 Frank sold the house to his youngest son, Charles, who was born in 1896; Charles still resided there in 1978. In 1900 Frank rented out part of his dwelling to another family, and the income he received was undoubtedly essential in paying off his mortgages so quickly.

Frank Paczkowski was born in Russian Poland in 1858, but his parents were from the German sector, and he may have migrated back there, since in 1880 he married a German Pole, Antonina Gratkowski. The couple may have had children in the early 1880s, but only four of their eight children were living in 1900. In 1883 Frank migrated to the United States, leaving his wife behind. He apparently had no particular skill or trade. In 1886 he either returned to Poland to bring over his family or sent for them. In October 1891, after eight years in

America, Frank purchased a lot at 3116 Brereton Avenue for $700 ($921). In January 1892 he took a mortgage with T. Kosciusko Building and Loan for $1,500 ($1,948) and paid it off in eighteen months. In November 1894 he took another mortgage for $1,000 ($1,370), which he satisfied in 1899. In the interim he took yet another $1,500 ($2,027) loan. Since building and loans did not customarily make second mortgages, the new mortgage was undoubtedly to build a second house at the rear of the lot. A complete record of the mortgages of Frank Paczkowski at 3116 Brereton Avenue follows: (1) $1,500 ($1,948), January 1892–June 1893; (2) $1,000 ($1,370), November 1895–July 1899; (3) $1,500 ($2,027), February 1896–July 1900; (4) $600 ($750), September 1900–July 1903; and (5) $1,100 ($1,250), July 1903–March 1904. The last two mortgages were essentially an extension of the debt from the third mortgage.

In 1900 Paczkowski had four children living at home, plus his mother-in-law, a sixty-one-year-old widow, who migrated in 1890. In addition, there were four other families living in the two houses at that location. All the family heads were laborers at the steel mills and were either German or Russian Poles. One of the renters was Wladislaw Gratkowski, probably a younger brother or cousin of Antonina Gratkowski Paczkowski.

Frank Paczkowski died in 1917, and Antonina in 1925. Her children sold the property in 1926 for $6,300 ($3,581) to another Polish family who owned it for the next 43 years. Thus, a first-generation unskilled laborer who arrived in 1883 was able, with an initial investment that represented half to three-fourths of his annual income, to build a substantial equity for his family.

Although many initial buyers held onto their lots for a generation and sometimes passed the property to their children, numerous lots changed hands in the early decades of the new century. Between 1890 and 1920 there were 156 buyers of improved properties in Polish Hill. In 85 percent of these transactions the buyers were Polish; the neighborhood was becoming increasingly homogeneous. The few non-Polish buyers were, as before, from Germany, Ireland, and England. There was a single black purchaser in the neighborhood. These buyers of improved lots paid an average price, in 1913 dollars, of $3,049.

In seventeen cases the buyers were able to purchase their homes without a mortgage. These owners may have sold another property to make the new purchase. In any event, this small but remarkable group was able to pay an average price of $2,832. None of these buyers could be located in the 1900 census, and few were found in city directories. Four laborers in this group, who bought homes between 1909 and

1918, were able to pay an average price of $1,855. They may have taken private loans from their family, but no mortgages were located for them.

The vast majority of the buyers required a mortgage to finance their purchase. The characteristics of these buyers revealed few differences from those who purchased unimproved lots and then built their own homes (Table 26). The later buyers were more recent arrivals in the

Table 26. Profile of Buyers of Improved Lots, Polish Hill, 1890-1920

Profile Characteristics	Mean Purchase Price[1]	N	Mean Down Payment[1]	Mean Percentage Down	N	Mean Age at Purchase	Mean Years in United States at Purchase	N
All cases	$3,049	146	$1,292	34.1	107	36.9	11.9	36
All Polish buyers	3,154	126	1,277	34.1	93	37.2	12.2	25
Unskilled and semiskilled	2,569	47	1,103	40.5	37	39.6	13.3	20
Skilled and white collar	2,816	18	1,430	40.9	10	27.6	8.2	5
Occupation unknown or not given	3,706	61	1,368	38.0	46	. . .	. . .	
All non-Polish buyers	2,381	20	1,510	39.7	14	35.6	17.3	5

NOTE. The data are compiled from the deed and mortgage books, 1900 Manuscript Census, and city directories. Three dots = data not available.
[1]In constant 1913 dollars.

country, and, because they were buying homes instead of lots, they had to save larger down payments. The average year of migration for the later buyers was 1886; the average year of migration for all buyers of unimproved lots was 1880.

Despite their later arrival in the country, these buyers tended to be about the same age and to have been in the country the same length of time when they purchased their homes as had the buyers of unimproved lots. On the average, the later Polish buyers were here 12.2 years when they bought and during that time managed to accumulate an average down payment of $1,277. For the cases where occupation could be identified, a majority of the family heads were unskilled laborers. Not surprisingly, the unskilled bought less expensive homes and made smaller cash down payments than did the skilled and white-collar group.

The Michalski family was typical of many of the homeowners in Polish Hill at the turn of the century. Adam Michalski was born in Prussian Poland in 1853. He married Antonia in 1875, and they migrated to America in 1881. In their first twenty-five years of marriage the couple had five children, but only two were living in 1900. Their son John was born in 1885 and Walter in 1887. Adam Michalski worked as a laborer in the steel mill. In 1891, after a decade in the country and at the age of thirty-eight, he purchased a home at 3115 Brereton Avenue for $2,500 ($3,289) by putting down $700 ($921) and borrowing the balance. A year later he had paid $900 ($1,169) on this debt. In 1896, five years after purchase, he satisfied the $1,800 mortgage in full—a rate of savings of $380 a year! In December 1897 he took a new mortgage for $500 ($667) and the following summer returned for another $1,200 ($1,600). These latter two loans were most likely to start a second house at the rear of his property. In July 1904 he paid off both of those debts. In 1910 he took another mortgage for $1,500 ($1,563), which he repaid in 1912.

The 1900 census listed four families at Michalski's two houses. The other family heads were, respectively: a newly arrived German machinist, age thirty-one; a Russian Polish car inspector for the railroads who migrated in 1893; and a German Polish laborer who came in 1888. These other families were helping Michalski to make his mortgage payments.

Michalski died in 1917 and his wife the following year, at which time their real estate was valued at $6,000 ($3,509). In 1919 son Walter sold his share to brother John, and in 1923 John sold the entire property back to Walter for $2,500 ($1,464) down and a $4,000 ($2,392) mortgage. In 1978 Walter Michalski still owned 3115 Brereton, although he no longer lived there.

The most striking aspect of the financial arrangements of the Polish buyers was the large sum of money that they were able to accumulate within ten to fifteen years of their arrival in America. Some buyers, notably the artisans and shopkeepers, may have brought assets from Europe. But unskilled laborers, less likely to have arrived with any significant savings, were also putting down $500 to $1,100 within a decade or so of migration. During those years unskilled laborers earned, at best, $12 to $15 per week. In 1913, U.S. Steel paid 20¢ per hour for common labor, or $12 for a sixty-hour week and $14.40 for a seventy-two-hour week. City garbage collectors earned between $2 and $2.25 per day for a six-day week.[20] It must be reiterated that the early buyers were not typical of the 1900 Polish population as a whole. They were older and more established, key factors in enabling them to accumulate their down payments. They were also most likely the lucky ones, who had avoided industrial accidents, disease, or despair. There were other men who saved considerable sums of money, but who chose instead to take their nest egg and return to family in Europe. The importance of the financial picture drawn here is that it demonstrates what was possible.

The level of savings achieved by early Italian homeowners and the amounts and percentages of their down payments were similar to those of the early Polish buyers. Because the Italian influx into Pittsburgh lagged behind the Polish migration by a few years, there was one difference in how these two groups established themselves in certain neighborhoods. The areas in which Italians predominated were first built up in the same decades as Polish Hill, from the mid-1880s through the 1890s; however, Italians did not move into those areas until after 1900. Consequently, almost all of the Italian buyers purchased existing homes rather than lots. But their rates of saving and the amounts they saved were similar to those of Polish immigrants who bought homes in the same years.

The Bloomfield section of Pittsburgh has long been identified with the city's Italian community. It is located less than a mile from Polish Hill, although a ravine 200-feet deep separates the two neighborhoods and they developed differently. Liberty Avenue, the main business artery of Bloomfield, begins near the Point in the central business district, runs through the middle of the Strip District to Lawrenceville, and then turns east into Bloomfield. As early as the 1880s cable cars ran on Liberty Avenue from downtown to Bloomfield, and the area began to fill with two- and two-and-one-half story frame homes. Most of the early buyers were German and Irish blue-collar workers, who formed the bulk of the city's work force in those years. A substantial proportion of them were skilled artisans. There were few large industrial firms in the immediate area, but a number of smaller shops were located in Bloomfield and Lawrenceville, and the cars passed through the heavily industrial Strip District on their way downtown.

A mile east of Bloomfield is the neighborhood of East Liberty. Although the area was about three miles from the central business district, it also had good cable car service in the 1880s and trolley service in the 1890s. In addition, the Pennsylvania Railroad stopped there, and the ride downtown only took twenty-eight minutes. East Liberty was a streetcar suburb of the 1880s and 1890s, with a middle and lower class population living in two- and three-story frame homes at a slightly lower density than Bloomfield. Both neighborhoods had a predominantly German and Irish population, with large numbers of American-born residents and a smattering of other West European groups.[21]

The Homewood section, located six miles from downtown near the city limits, was at one time a separate village along the line of the Pennsylvania Railroad. By the turn of the century railroad and trolley services were stimulating development as the built-up area of the city reached out to it. Homewood never became a major Italian neighborhood as did Bloomfield and East Liberty, but it did house a number of Italian families in the early twentieth century. The same immediate vicinity also contained a cluster of black families, and blacks later came to dominate the neighborhood. In 1900 Homewood was only partially developed. The housing stock consisted primarily of small detached frame houses with a few two-story row homes mixed in.[22]

Because the neighborhoods examined here were partially built up by 1900, there were only six instances of Italians purchasing undeveloped building lots. The six buyers paid an average price of $727, similar to the amount paid by Polish buyers. They put down an average of $223 of the purchase price for their lots. Only four of the six could be located in any other sources; three men were laborers, and the other had a butcher shop.

Between 1899 and 1924, eighty-eight Italian families purchased homes in the Bloomfield, East Liberty, and Homewood study areas. Since there were no appreciable differences among the characteristics of the buyers in the three areas, they have been grouped together for this analysis. The average year of purchase for these buyers was 1912. The families paid, on average, $2,585 for their homes, with a down payment of $1,118. The average purchase price was several hundred dollars less than that for homes on Polish Hill. The reason for this, in part, may be the absence of a commercial street in the Italian study areas comparable to Brereton Avenue, where prices tended to be somewhat higher. Further, most of the homes in Polish Hill were brick, whereas many of those in the Italian section were frame. The amount of the down payments made by the Italians was similar to that of the Poles, suggesting at least some members of both groups were able to save at comparable rates (Table 27).

The demographic and occupational characteristics of the Italian home buyers were similar to that of the Poles discussed above. They tended to be in the child-rearing years of the life cycle and to have been in the country more than a decade when they purchased their homes. Although most of the buyers were laborers, a disproportionately large percentage were artisans or shopkeepers.

Since the Italian buyers purchased homes after 1900, few could be located in the census rolls. The names of all buyers before 1910 were searched in the soundex index of the 1900 census, but only seven of thirty names could be located anywhere in Pennsylvania in 1900. Only for those few cases can we determine age and years in the country at time of purchase. On average, those household heads were 38.5 years

Table 27. Profile of Italian Buyers of Improved Lots
in Bloomfield and East Liberty, 1899-1924

Occupation	Mean Year of Purchase	Mean Purchase Price[1]	Mean Down Payment[1]	Mean Percentage Down	N
All cases	1912.8	$2,585	$1,118	43.2	88
Unskilled and semiskilled[2]	1911.5	2,128	860	40.5	30
Skilled and white collar[2]	1912.6	2,908	1,488	51.2	21

NOTE. The data are compiled from deed and mortgage books, the 1900 Manuscript Census, and city directories.

[1]In constant 1913 dollars.

[2]Only for cases in which the occupation at purchase could be located.

old when they bought a home and had been in the country for sixteen years; four were laborers, and three were stonecutters or masons. Their homes cost an average of $2,534, for which they put down an average of $1,005. Although this is a very small number of cases from which to draw firm conclusions, their ages and years in the country were very similar to those of the larger group of Poles who were located in the census rolls. Further, their purchase price and down payments were similar to those of all Italian buyers.

If we turn to the occupational listings in the city directories, we can gain greater insight into the characteristics of the Italian buyers. Fifty-eight percent of the home buyers could be positively identified or had an occupational listing in the directories, and 60 percent of them were laborers. The remainder were skilled artisans, particularly stonecutters, masons, and tailors, or small proprietors. The laborers bought less expensive homes and made smaller cash down payments than the artisans and shopkeepers. The average down payment of the laborers was $860 compared to one of $1,488 for the craftsmen and proprietors. It was a remarkable indicator of the tenacity of their desire to save and to own.

The experience of Francisco Cammuso and his children highlight not only the financial dimension of ownership, but also the family dynamics as well. Cammuso was born in Italy in 1842; in 1872 he married Felice, nine years his junior. The couple had four children, and all migrated to America in 1885. A decade later Cammuso was able to purchase a small home at 27 Carver Street in East Liberty for $1,900 ($2,603) by making a $500 ($685) down payment. Four years later he paid off the $1,400 mortgage in full. During those years Cammuso worked as a laborer. In 1900 the family shared their small home with four boarders.

By 1904 Cammuso's daughter, Mary, had married one of the boarders,

Michael Mincini, an Italian stonecutter. In that year the couple purchased 31 Carver Street, two doors away, for $2,200 ($2,529) with a $1,600 ($1,839) mortgage. Francisco died in 1910, but his widow continued to live at 27 Carver until her death thirteen years later. Furthermore, she was able to remain in close contact with her children. Her daughter Rose and her husband bought 28 Carver Street in 1910, and son Angelo purchased 29 Carver Street in 1916.

It was not unusual in this period for Polish and Italian family groups to remain in close proximity, although it was not always possible to identify the relationship as well as in this particular case. We do not know whether the parents came with any assets or whether they loaned their children money for their down payments. Nonetheless, in 1920 four members of the Cammuso family were property owners on Carver Street in East Liberty.

In 1900 Pittsburgh's blacks were more scattered than either its Italians or Poles. There were, however, several clusters that by World War I had emerged as predominantly black neighborhoods. The analysis of black ownership is based on a detailed examination of three small areas located in the lower Hill District (ward 3), the upper Hill District (ward 5), and the Homewood section (ward 13). All titles in these areas were traced back to 1900, but positive identification of black owners was extremely difficult.[23]

The lower hill adjoins and is within convenient walking distance of the central business district. Red brick row houses and two-family doubles were built in the 1860s and 1870s when horse cars began to ascend the steep slopes. Most of the early homes lacked central heat or indoor plumbing. Many of the private residences never had central heat, and flush toilets were often added in the basement or sometimes even the porch or the yard. In 1900 the area housed a polyglot mixture of blacks and recent European immigrants, particularly Jews and Italians.[24] By the 1920s, the housing stock was decayed and in disrepair. A description of housing conditions on one block of the study area reported: "The houses on Crawford Street are almost all old brick dwellings, which years ago were first class homes. Age and neglect have told upon them, inside walls and ceilings need replastering, roofs are in poor condition, stairs are rickety, windows and doors warped so that air vents are left around them. Front yards are entirely lacking and rear yards are small and usually very dirty. All these buildings have flush toilets, but a large number of them are outside, particularly so on the west side of the street."[25] The investigator further noted that eight of the toilets were not working at the time. Electricity was more common than hot water or bathtubs.

The original lot dimensions for the lower hill were similar to lots in other parts of the city of the same age. Most lots were 24 to 30 feet wide and 100 to 120 feet deep; there were alleys behind most of the streets. As the city grew, population in the lower hill became extremely dense. Rear houses facing the alleys appeared on almost all of the lots; there was virtually no open space.

In the mid-1950s the lower hill study area was completely razed for the Civic Arena. When the assessors for the Redevelopment Authority canvassed the neighborhood, they found the homes to be extremely deteriorated. Apartment houses often lacked fire escapes, hot water, or central heat. Foundations were crumbling; windows were broken. The notation of 59 Logan Street read: "Tenants live under miserable conditions, but always all occupied." The building was labeled a "fire trap."[26]

The homes farther up the hill in ward 5 were somewhat newer and, at least in 1900, in better condition. The upper hill contained several small pockets of blacks who were mixed among an immigrant and working-class population. The portion of the upper hill chosen for this analysis was north of Bedford Avenue and was built shortly after World War I. It consisted of two-story brick row homes and some larger single-frame dwellings. The area was never very carefully laid out; there were a number of private alleys and odd-shaped lots. The row homes were on lots averaging 1,280-1,300 square feet (16 x 80); the larger homes on lots of 3,600 to 4,000 square feet. The area contained a mixed black and Jewish population from the outset; by the 1940s it was quite substantially black. In 1938 the city's first public housing project, Bedford Dwellings, was erected across a playground just to the east of this neighborhood. A black church and cemetery and a number of old frame homes were razed for the project. In 1951 the study area was also razed to make room for an addition to the earlier project. At that time the appraisers for the housing authority found many homes with central heat and indoor plumbing. The brick row houses were valued at $4,500-5,000 ($1,854-2,060).[27]

The Homewood section, discussed earlier, was a strikingly different neighborhood. Located along the eastern city limits, it was a low-density, middle-class residential neighborhood. The lots were 25 feet wide by 100 feet deep, but few rear houses were ever built there. A black enclave in Homewood dated from the late nineteenth century. In 1900 the Homewood AME Zion Church, a frame structure at Tioga and Dunfermline streets, was the focal point of the local black community.[28]

The financial burdens and hardships involved in homeownership of immigrant families were compounded for the blacks. Not only did blacks earn little pay, but their jobs were less steady, and they suffered from a pervasive discrimination that affected not only their work opportunities but their housing as well. To be sure, Poles and Italians also endured discrimination. A long-time real estate agent in Lawrenceville recalled that the Germans had tried to resist the Polish invasion of the neighborhood and were angry at neighbors who sold their homes to Polish families.[29] Nonetheless, the discrimination against blacks was more deeply rooted and enduring than it was against the immigrants. In the newspaper story quoted earlier, the young wife searching in vain for a suitable house to rent rejected one offering in Homewood, partly because she noticed that there was "a settlement of very respectable colored folks close by."[30]

Because of the small number of black homeowners who could be positively identified, there are not enough cases to warrant any statistical tabulations. A few representative cases drawn from each of the study areas will serve to indicate the characteristics and finances of black owners.

The blacks living in Homewood at the turn of the century were primarily small businessmen or skilled workers. They came to Pittsburgh in the 1880s or even earlier. Isaac Watson was typical of the early black buyers. He was born in Kentucky in 1848. In 1890 he married Carrie, a Virginian born in 1864, and they purchased 7322 Tioga Street for $1,000 ($1,282) with a $750 ($961) mortgage. Watson gave his occupation variously as a waiter or butler. In 1894 he borrowed $3,700 ($4,805) to build a second house. In 1900 he lived in one of the homes with his wife, six children, and four boarders. In 1911 he paid off his debt. During those years he was also a trustee of the AME Zion Church of Homewood. He died in 1937.

John T. Writt was born in Virginia in 1848; his wife, Susan, was born in Pennsylvania the same year. The couple married in 1873 and had six children, but two died before 1900. In 1883 Writt purchased 7225 Susquehanna Street in Homewood for $1,900 ($2,346) with only a $200 ($247) down payment. In the 1880s Writt was listed in the city directory as a janitor, but in the mid-1890s he entered the catering business and advertised his downtown location in the city directory.

Other black family heads who purchased in the Homewood study area around the turn of the century included a cook, a musician, a coachman, and two laborers. The value of their homes and their financial arrangements were similar to that of immigrant buyers in those occupational groups.

Samuel H. Golden was the only black homeowner living in the lower hill study area in 1900. Golden cannot be considered typical of Pittsburgh blacks, but his experiences, pieced together from census rolls, wills, deeds, mortgages, and the city directory, are revealing of what was possible. Golden was born in Baltimore in 1815 and first appeared in the Pittsburgh city directory in 1860, where he was listed as a porter. In 1866 he purchased a brick row house at 140 Fulton (Fullerton) Street for $2,000 ($1,942), taking a mortgage of $1,200 ($1,165) from the seller. How he accumulated an $800 down payment is not known. He paid off the mortgage in 1868. The census of 1870 showed him living there with his wife, Margaret, then forty years old, who had been born in Tennessee, and his seven children. During the next decade Margaret died and Golden remarried; in 1880 he lived with his new wife, Henrietta, a forty-year-old housewife born in Kentucky, and his oldest son, a barber. In 1893 he purchased another house at the corner of Kirkpatrick and Rose in the upper Hill District for $1,550 ($2,067) with a $550 ($733) mortgage that he paid off in three years. Sometime during those years he also built two small houses at the rear of his Fulton Street property facing the alley. No mortgages were recorded in connection with those buildings. He also purchased a house in Washington, Pennsylvania.

In 1900 Golden was still living at Fulton Street; Henrietta had died, but he lived with his eldest son, also a widower, and his son's children. Golden died in 1904 at the age of eighty-nine, leaving four houses valued at a total of $25,000 ($28,736). Throughout all his years in Pittsburgh he was listed as only a porter, driver, or laborer, and he signed his will with an "X."

Although blacks formed an increasing proportion of the population in the lower hill area after 1900, they did not buy homes in large numbers until the 1940s. The homes they bought were already substantially depreciated in both condition and value, but they did provide an opportunity to own. Pearl Smith, a Texas-born seamstress, purchased 132 Fullerton Street in 1945 for $2,850 ($1,580). William Johnson, who was born in Virginia in 1891, bought 1403 Hazel in 1945 for $2,500 ($1,386). Andrew Harris was born in Arkansas in 1895. He migrated to Pittsburgh in 1937 from Saginaw, Michigan. The following year he was living in a rented room at 6 Townsend Street and gave his occupation as a mechanic. A decade later he purchased the property for $2,100 ($913) with a $1,000 ($434) mortgage that he paid off in 1949. These owners, and others like them, were the people forced to sell to the Urban Redevelopment Authority in the mid-1950s to make way for the building of the Pittsburgh Civic Arena.

The upper hill study area was not developed until immediately after World War I. Some of the properties were sold directly to blacks who built their own homes. It was one of the few areas of the city in which blacks had the opportunity to occupy new houses. The experiences of James Coleman and Walker Pratt are representative of the early black buyers in the area.

In 1923 James and Lucy Bell Coleman purchased a lot at 845 Perry Street for $325 ($191). Coleman worked as a laborer, and his assets must have been limited because he required a mortgage to buy the lot. In 1925 he paid off this debt and took two new mortgages for $2,000 ($1,142) each to build a two-story brick veneer house. Coleman completely paid off these loans in 1944. In 1951 he sold his property to the Housing Authority for $7,000 ($2,668).

Walker Pratt, a Georgia-born laborer, purchased a lot at 819 Whitesides Road in 1925 for $1,050 ($595). In 1926 he borrowed $7,500 ($4,264) to build a two-and-one-half story brick duplex. The depression must have hit Walker Pratt hard. In 1934 he refinanced his debt with the Home Owners Loan Corporation. At the time he owed $6,699 ($4,962). His terms were 5 percent interest with fifteen years to repay at $52.97 per month. In May of 1937 the corporation foreclosed on Pratt.

The census reports and the sample data make it clear that homeowning in 1900 was available to only a small minority of Pittsburgh's Poles, Italians, and blacks. The early owners were primarily in their late thirties when they bought; the immigrants had been in the country about twelve to fifteen years at the time of purchase. Among those families that persisted in the city for thirty years, all three groups evidenced similar rates of ownership. Large numbers of blacks continued to migrate to the city after the European immigration had passed its peak. That fact, together with discrimination in jobs and housing, accounts for the lower aggregate rate of black ownership. Furthermore, when blacks finally did begin to purchase homes in substantial number, redevelopment and housing projects sometimes destroyed their neighborhoods.

In 1900, and in the subsequent two decades, the black and immigrant home buyers were disproportionately skilled workers or petty proprietors. It is not surprising to discover that those groups were most likely to purchase at an early date. What is more striking is that unskilled laborers were able to put down $1,000 or more on a house after ten or fifteen years in the city.

In the early twentieth century, a six-room row house or small single home with heat and indoor plumbing rented for $25 per month and up. An older four-room house lacking those amenities rented for $15 to $18 per month, depending on location. Monthly payments on a typical mortgage with a building and loan were about $33 per month for a

$2,000 loan. Insurance and taxes added another $4 to $8 per month. Thus, a laborer earning $15 per week who might have been able to afford a four-room house, perhaps with some amenities if he had working children, committed himself and his family to much larger payments, crowding, and lack of privacy in order to achieve his ambition of being a Pittsburgh homeowner.[31]

The experiences of the Dobrejcak family in Thomas Bell's novel about mill town life in the Pittsburgh region illustrate perhaps best the importance of homeownership in the lives of the region's blue-collar workers. Throughout his life Mike Dobrejcak and later his offspring, Dobie, struggled to maintain decent living conditions. Dobie, like his father, spent most of his adult life laboring in the Edgar Thomson works of U.S. Steel. His success in securing a decent home elicited a strong pride:

> Dobie went on to his own gate and on to the kitchen in the back. His house was set into the hill . . . and was reached by a long skinny flight of wooden steps. Thus overshadowed, it looked smaller than it was. But it had gas and electricity and a bathroom . . . and from its front porch one got as fine a view as one could want: Braddock and North Braddock spread out before one, the river, the hills, and on summer evenings the lights of Kennywood Park winked through the smoke above the blast furnace.[32]

The romantic view of a bathroom or even the blackening sky above the blast furnace from a front porch illustrates the role of housing and neighborhood in the life of the migrant family. To many who shared living quarters with strangers throughout much of their lives, a private home must have proved highly satisfying. Certainly a house was tangible proof that the long struggle to get to Pittsburgh, acquire a job, and render mutual assistance had not been in vain. However, many had to find satisfaction elsewhere as ownership escaped their reach. The struggle, moreover, would become more difficult as Pittsburgh's economy began to slow, gradually after World War I and then precipitously during the 1930s.

NOTES

1. William I. Thomas and Florian Znaniecki, *The Polish Peasant in Europe and America*, 5 vols. (New York, 1920), I: 162. See also Josef Barton, *Peasants and Strangers: Italians, Rumanians and Slovaks in an American City* (Cambridge, Mass., 1975), 101, 119; Caroline Golab, *Immigrant Destinations* (Philadelphia, 1977), 69-70, 153; Thomas Kessner, *The Golden Door: Italian and Jewish Mobility in New York City, 1880-1915* (New York, 1977), 151; Virginia Yans-McLaughlin, *Family*

and Community: Italian Immigrants in Buffalo, 1880-1930 (Ithaca, N.Y., 1977), 35-36; Edith Abbott, *The Tenements of Chicago* (New York, 1970), 380; Victor Greene, *The Slavic Community on Strike* (Notre Dame, Ind., 1968), 56; Robert Woods and Albert Kennedy, *The Zone of Emergence*, ed. Sam Bass Warner (Cambridge, Mass., 1969), 35, 39.

2. Interview with Joe B., May 13, 1976, Pittsburgh Oral History Project (POHP).
3. Margaret Byington, *Homestead: The Households of a Mill Town*, The Pittsburgh Survey, ed. Paul U. Kellogg (New York, 1910), 36-57. See also chs. 4 and 10.
4. Interview with Hezekiah M., Oct. 8, 1976, POHP.
5. Howard Gitelman, *Workingmen of Waltham* (Baltimore, 1974), 64, 90, 98; Kessner, *The Golden Door*, 135; Golab, *Immigrant Destinations*, 77; Barton, *Peasants and Strangers*, 101; Stephan Thernstrom, *Poverty and Progress: Social Mobility in a Nineteenth-Century American City* (Cambridge, Mass., 1965), 162.
6. For another point of view, see Daniel D. Luria, "Wealth, Capital and Power: The Social Meaning of Home Ownership," *Journal of Interdisciplinary History*, 7 (Autumn 1976), 262-82.
7. Interview with Ed M., Sept. 30, 1976; see also interviews with Joe B., May 13, 1976; John K., Sept. 13, 1976; Stanley N., Sept. 22, 1976, POHP. Abbott, *Tenements of Chicago*, 382.
8. "Woes of a Woman House Hunter," *Pittsburgh Leader*, Feb. 18, 1900.
9. U.S. Bureau of the Census, *Twelfth Census, 1900. Population* (Washington, D.C., 1902), 709-10. Figures are for Pittsburgh and Allegheny City combined.
10. Ibid., clvi.
11. U.S. Bureau of the Census, *Fifteenth Census, 1930. Population* (Washington, D.C., 1933), 57; *Special Report on Foreign-Born White Families by Country of Birth of Head* (Washington, D.C., 1933), 135.
12. The Polish Hill neighborhood has the following boundaries: from the the corner of Thirtieth and Wiggins, south on Thirtieth to the lot line between Paulowna and Bigelow Boulevard, east to Herron Avenue, north to Hancock, north on Hancock to Dobson, west on Dobson to the rear of the lots on the east side of Harmar Street, north to the Pennsylvania Railroad line, west to Wiggins, south to Thirtieth. A second Polish neighborhood for which titles but not mortgages were traced will be referred to in later discussions as the Southside. This study area is bounded by Josephine Street, Barry Street, the lot line between Mission and Holt streets, Caesar Way, Sterling Street, Scott Way, and the lot line between Leticoe and Josephine, including lots on both sides of Eleanor Street.
13. On location and employment in the area see Sanborn Map Co., *Insurance Maps of Pittsburgh* (New York, 1905), vol. 1; (New York, 1928), vol. 2. The Library of Congress map division has an uncorrected set of the 1905 edition. The Archives of Industrial Society, University of Pittsburgh, has the 1905 edition corrected to 1923 and the 1928 edition corrected to 1938. R. L. Polk, *Map of Cities of Pittsburgh and Allegheny* (n.p., 1898).

14. Allegheny County, Pennsylvania, Recorder of Deeds, Charter Books, 12: 43; 13: 201, County Office Building, Pittsburgh. The other major Polish building and loans were Kordecki (chartered in 1901), Charter Book, 27: 502, and Polish (chartered in 1909), Charter Book, 45: 155.

15. Alan Teck, *Mutual Savings Banks and Savings and Loan Associations* (New York, 1968), 19-28, 41; Morton Bodfish and A. D. Theobald, *Savings and Loan Principles* (New York, 1938), 2-12, 40-46; U.S. Commissioner of Labor, *Ninth Annual Report, 1893, Building and Loan Associations* (Washington, D.C., 1894), 327-37, 387-88; see also 222-27, 394, 398, 403-4, 470-72. For the terms of a specific mortgage, see Allegheny County, Pennsylvania, Recorder of Deeds, Mortgage Book, 1131: 615, County Office Building, Pittsburgh.

16. Interview of William Pow by R. Simon, July 1978. Interview notes are in possession of R.S.

17. The President's Conference on Home Building and Home Ownership, *Home Finance and Taxation*, 12 vols. (Washington, D.C., 1932), 2: ix, xi, 67; on the unique Philadelphia plan, see William Loucks, *The Philadelphia Plan of Home Financing*, Studies in Land Economics and Research, Monograph no. 2, Institute for Research in Land Economics and Public Utilities (Chicago, 1929), 1, 56.

18. Allegheny County, Pennsylvania, Recorder of Deeds, Deed Books, Mortgage Books, Block and Lot Card File, County Office Building, Pittsburgh, hereafter referred to as Deed and Mortgage Books. The names of owners for specific times can be obtained from the real estate atlases, but the deeds provided the purchase price and full name of all owners, essential information for checking mortgages. All case histories cited in this chapter were reconstructed from an analysis of the deeds, wills, mortgage transactions, and census data of all individuals named. G. M. Hopkins, *Plat-Books of the City of Pittsburgh* (Philadelphia, 1900, 1901, 1904, 1911).

19. National Archives and Records Center, Washington, D.C., Soundex Index to the 1900 Census of Population, microfilm; Allegheny County Voter Registration Card File, Archives of Industrial Society, University of Pittsburgh. The constant dollar figures are based on U.S. Department of Commerce, *Historical Statistics of the United States* (Washington, D.C., 1960), 127 (Series E 157 and 159). The values for years after 1926 use the consumer price index, compiled by the Department of Labor, converted to a 1913 base.

20. Paul U. Kellogg, ed., *Wage-Earning Pittsburgh,* The Pittsburgh Survey (New York, 1914), 119n, 120, 122; John A. Fitch, *The Steel Workers*, The Pittsburgh Survey, ed. Paul U. Kellogg (New York, 1910), 151, and ch. 12 passim. Byington, *Homestead*, chs. 3, 4, 9, 10, 11, appendices I-IV.

21. The Bloomfield study area is bounded by Essex Way, Lima Street, the rear lot line of the east side of Edmond Street, the ravine behind Juniper, Short, and Lorigan streets, and the lot line between Pearl and Sapphire streets. The East Liberty area is bounded by Larimer, Mayflower, Indiana Way, Linn Way, Kennesaw, and St. Andrews and Meadow streets. Sanborn Map Co., *Insurance Maps of Pittsburgh* (New York, 1905), vols. 1-4; Polk, *Map of Cities of Pittsburgh and*

Allegheny, 1898; Joel Tarr, *Transportation Innovations and Changing Spatial Patterns in Pittsburgh, 1850-1934* (Chicago, 1978), 47-49

22. The Homewood study area is bounded by Finance, Homewood, Tioga, and Dunfermline. Sanborn Map Co., *Insurance Maps of Pittsburgh,* vol. 4. Polk, *Map of Cities of Pittsburgh and Allegheny, 1898;* Tarr, *Transportation Innovations,* 47-49.

23. Blacks were identified by the 1900 census or by voter registration cards. These cards only go back to the mid-1930s, but they indicate age, birthplace, color, address, and in some cases occupation and year of arrival in the county. They are arranged in alphabetical order and located in the Archives of Industrial Society.

24. The lower hill study area is bounded by Logan, Wylie, Crawford, and Clark. It is now the site of the Civic Arena. Ira Reid, *Social Conditions of the Negro in the Hill District of Pittsburgh* (Pittsburgh, 1930), 25-39 and passim. On the development of the site, see Roy Lubove, *Twentieth Century Pittsburgh: Government, Business, and Environmental Change* (New York, 1969), 130-32.

25. Reid, *Social Conditions of the Negro,* 34.

26. Wiley Hall, "Negro Housing in the Hill District of Pittsburgh" (M.A. thesis, University of Pittsburgh, 1929), 17-30; Files of Parcels Civic Arena site, Urban Redevelopment Authority, Pittsburgh.

27. Files of Parcels for Bedford Dwellings Addition West, PA 1-8W, and Property Line Map, Bedford Dwellings Addition, Housing Authority of the City of Pittsburgh; Robert K. Brown, *Public Housing in Action: The Record of Pittsburgh* (Pittsburgh, 1959), 15-18. The upper hill study area is bounded by Bedford Avenue and Kirkpatrick, Ridgeway, and Erin streets.

28. Sanborn Map Co., *Insurance Maps of Pittsburgh,* vol. 4. Allegheny Co., Recorder of Deeds, Block and Lot maps; the city directory listing of churches in Pittsburgh indicated which were black congregations.

29. Interview with William Pow by R. Simon, July 1978; notes are in the possession of R.S.

30. "Woes of a Woman House Hunter," *Pittsburgh Leader,* Feb. 18, 1900.

31. J. T. Holdsworth, *Report of the Economic Survey of Pittsburgh* (Pittsburgh, 1912), chs. 2, 4.

32. Thomas Bell, *Out of this Furnace* (Pittsburgh, 1976), 300. In the Afterword to the 1976 reissue of this 1941 novel, David P. Demarest establishes its autobiographical substance.

A Southside Polish immigrant household around 1900.

An Italian road crew, 1908.

Sherrer's Saloon in Pittsburgh's Southside around 1900.

Pittsburgh's Hill District in 1900.

Black migrants having arrived in Pittsburgh in 1900.

Concrete mixers at work in Pittsburgh's upper Hill District around 1939.

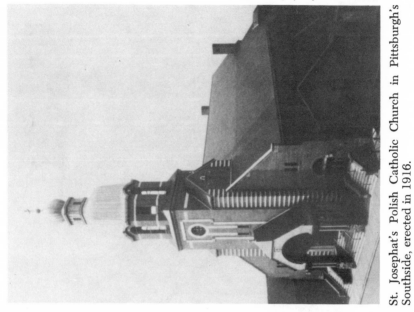

St. Josephat's Polish Catholic Church in Pittsburgh's Southside, erected in 1916.

Ebenezer Baptist Church in Pittsburgh's Hill District, erected in 1874. The stone facing was applied in 1930.

Macedonia Baptist Church in Pittsburgh's upper Hill District, 1938.

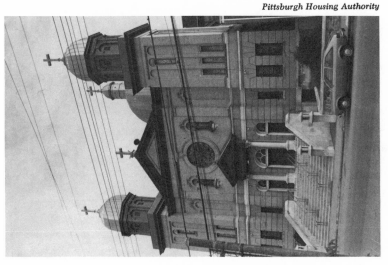

Our Lady, Help of Christians Church in Pittsburgh's East Liberty district, erected in 1897.

Photograph by Michael Weber

Brereton Avenue in Pittsburgh's Polish Hill district.

Photograph by Michael Weber

27-33 Carver Street in Pittsburgh's East Liberty district.

Whitesides Road in Pittsburgh's upper Hill District in 1951, shortly before the area was demolished for urban renewal.

Bedford Avenue in Pittsburgh's upper Hill District in 1951, shortly before the area was demolished for urban renewal.

An unidentified alley in Pittsburgh's lower Hill District in 1951.

A view of part of Pittsburgh's Southside.

Juniper Street in Pittsburgh's Bloomfield district in 1950.

Mayflower Street in Pittsburgh's East Liberty district.

Mission Street in Pittsburgh's Southside.

7

New Generations: Demographic Change and Neighborhood Development

Stagnation and obsolescence characterized the economy and industrial structure of Pittsburgh after World War I. Factors that contributed to the city's early competitive advantage—the dominance of heavy industry, the concentration of the labor force into large plants, and the abundance of coking coal—also contributed to its lack of growth early in the twentieth century. The development of by-product coke ovens ended the district's near monopoly on that valuable product. It also stimulated the development of iron and steel plants throughout the country, as access to markets, rather than proximity to coking coal, became a major profit factor. Capital, formerly invested in the Pittsburgh district, was diverted to metal production in Chicago, Gary, and Birmingham and into other more profitable non-Pittsburgh industries.

An erratic Pittsburgh economy at the same time produced periods of boom and bust. Pittsburgh firms worked overtime during both world wars producing the needed heavy industrial products. During the 1916-19 period, for example, total business activity exceeded normal ranges by as much as 25 percent. Production during World War II rose by an even greater percentage.[1] Unemployment during each of these periods fell to near zero, and new workers were recruited to meet increased demands. Deep recessions followed each boom period: unemployment reached an estimated 12 percent in 1923 and 10 percent in 1953.[2] The Depression of the 1930s hit the city particularly hard, as industrial production fell 59 percent from the 1929 average. A careful analysis by Philip Klein revealed that "substantially more than half the

manufacturing wage earners received materially less than $1,500" in
1930. A Brookings Institution study for the same year concluded that
"a family income of $2,000 may ... be regarded as sufficient to supply
only basic necessities." Conditions continued to deteriorate during the
next three years, and nearly 31 percent of the city's white work force
and 48 percent of the black workers were without jobs in 1933.[3] Unemployment for the entire country was 24.9 percent.

Unstable business cycles may mean only temporary employment dislocations. If the net effect had been a sustained rate of growth, only
those workers not capable of being absorbed into expanding industries
would have suffered long-term hardships. The long-range trends in
Pittsburgh, however, illustrate the general decline of industrial production and employment. Manufacturing expansion and production increases in Pittsburgh nearly ceased after World War I, growing by only
1 percent per year. Iron and steel production in 1929 was only slightly
higher than in 1916. Coal and coke production declined each year after
1909, with the exception of the war years.[4] Other industries including
electrical products, glass making, meat packing, and the services expanded during the same period but failed to compensate for the decline
of heavy industry in the city. Economist Glen McLaughlin estimated
that industrial employment in Pittsburgh declined by 9 percent during
the 1920s. In 1929 he noted that between "5 to 10 percent of the
workers were entirely without jobs. Moreover, those who had jobs suffered an appreciable loss of working time ... being idle in various
months from 4 to 16 percent of the time."[5] Unemployment and underemployment in the city's declining basic industries no doubt exceeded
those rates.

The small shift in the industrial structure of the city from iron and
steel production toward the manufacture of other goods or to the services only partly offset the accompanying employment losses. That the
production of electrical goods or printed matter expanded meant little
to the displaced iron or steel worker. Many older laborers faced permanent displacement or frequent underemployment. Newcomers and
second-generation migrants seeking work in heavy industry would find
job procurement increasingly difficult, necessitating continued reliance
on the kin and friendship networks formed earlier.

Population trends in Pittsburgh, not surprisingly, reflected the bleak
postwar economic picture. The total population grew by more than one-
third during each decade between the Civil War and the end of the
century. After 1920, however, the rate of growth declined sharply and
eventually reached a no growth or negative growth position. Excluding

all areas annexed to the city after 1920, the population grew by less than 5 percent during any subsequent decade interval.

Pittsburgh's foreign-born population declined during each decade interval after 1920 (Table 28). Native-born white Americans, conversely,

Table 28. Population Distribution in Pittsburgh, 1920-60

Category	1920	1930	1940	1950	1960
Total	588,343	669,817	671,659	676,806	604,332
Native white	429,995	505,245	524,630	528,842	458,387
Black	37,725	54,983	62,216	86,453	100,692
Total of foreign born	120,266	109,072	84,903	64,983	45,253
Polish	15,537	15,251	10,848	7,840	4,471
Italian	15,371	18,154	16,241	13,466	9,793
English	7,374	6,293	4,211	3,136	5,556
German	16,028	14,409	9,805	5,898	5,233
Irish	13,889	11,246	7,301	4,816	3,742

NOTE. The data are compiled from the U.S. Bureau of the Census, population censuses from 1920, 1930, 1940, 1950, and 1960.

continued to increase in number, accounting for the bulk of the city's white population growth. The expansion of the native-born cohort suggests that in the absence of any significant in-migration, natural increase accounted for much of Pittsburgh's limited population growth. Many of these new residents were undoubtedly children of immigrants. By 1930, more than one-third of the city's population came from this group while the proportion of foreign-born slipped to 16 percent. Only St. Louis and Cincinnati among fifteen northern cities experienced a greater decline, although the immigrant population fell in all fifteen cities except Detroit.[6] Italian and Polish migration to Pittsburgh fell dramatically with the coming of World War I. By 1930, however, these two groups outnumbered all other foreign-born groups in the city.[7]

Several factors contributing to the decline of foreign immigration to Pittsburgh illustrate the importance of local, national, and even international events on the lives of immigrant workers. The stagnant labor conditions in Pittsburgh directly influenced the would-be migrants' decision. If immigrants to Pittsburgh supplied relatives and friends with information about late nineteenth-century job opportunities in the "steel city," they also supplied warnings when opportunities declined. Increasing numbers of unsuccessful repatriates provided clear evidence of the difficulties encountered in Pittsburgh. Potential migrants supplied with increasingly negative information about the city and work opportunities likely chose another city as their destination or decided to remain at home. The restrictive legislation of the 1920s generally closed the door to further migration from southern and eastern Europe. The long and often bitter agitation for such legislation need not be discussed here, although it serves as a vivid reminder of strong nativist attitudes in the United States. The war and the legislation that followed, however, marked the conclusion of the so-called new immigration. It also signified a turning point in the history of ethnic groups in American cities. The free flow of individuals back and forth across the Atlantic Ocean ceased by 1924. American-born children of immigrants began to replace their parents in Pittsburgh's ethnic communities by 1930.

Second-generation immigrants and the black population both increased in number during the early 1920s, accounting for nearly all of the city's population growth after 1910. The causes of their growth, however, differ. Enough immigrants remained in Pittsburgh and established homes to add to the overall population of the city. Pittsburgh's immigrant populations had given way to a second generation. A considerable number of children of early black migrants also made permanent homes in the city. The 1910-20 migration, in addition, replenished the supply, replacing those who left and adding another 47 percent to the total black population in the city. By 1920 the city's black population contained two groups: children of the pre-1900 migrants and new first-generation migrants.

The Great Migration of 1916-19 brought between 500,000 and 1,000,000 black workers from the South to northern industrial cities. In Detroit, Cleveland, Buffalo, and Chicago the black populations more than doubled between 1910 and 1920. Black populations in eight other cities increased by more than 50 percent. Pittsburgh also felt the impact of the migration but to a lesser extent; black residents increased from approximately 25,000 to 38,000 in that decade. The number of inmigrants must be adjusted upward substantially, however, since nearly two-thirds of the 1910 black residents left the city before the 1920 census. In addition, many blacks who lived in Pittsburgh during the decade were most likely not present in either census year. In his survey of 505 black workers in 1917, Abraham Epstein found that only 7 percent had resided in Pittsburgh more than one year. This survey likely overstates the case, since Epstein's interviews ignored self-employed blacks or those working in small companies, many of whom were the most stable of all black residents. Epstein estimated that approximately 9,750 black migrants moved into Pittsburgh between 1916 and 1919. Our analysis of black persistence, however, suggests that as many as one-half of the 25,623 black residents in 1910 had moved by 1915. Thus nearly 25,000 black migrants would have had to move into the city during the era of the Great Migration to bring the total to 38,000 in 1920.[8]

Blacks continued to migrate to Pittsburgh during the 1920s, swelling their number to 55,000, 8 percent of the city's total population by 1929. A portion of this increase was due to natural growth, but the larger part by far was due to in-migration. A comparison of the 1920 and 1930 populations, allowing for death, suggests a net population gain of approximately 14,000 new black residents during the 1920s.[9] Thus, considering the 25,000 new migrants between 1910 and 1920 and another 14,000 in the 1920s, it is clear that while the Poles and Italians in Pittsburgh were moving toward their second generation in the city, nearly two-thirds of the black residents in 1930 were relative newcomers. The children of immigrants were in a position to build upon a generation of struggles and achievements of their parents. For the majority of blacks, job procurement, community development, and even establishing households would have to begin again, but without the assistance of the social networks that continued to aid second-generation immigrant groups.

Our earlier data on southern-born blacks demonstrated that they proceeded to Pittsburgh, via a chain migration, through a series of better jobs and increasingly urban communities. Friends and relatives informed them of opportunities along the way. The great majority, in addition, came from Virginia. They were motivated almost exclusively by the search for improved occupational and economic status.

Blacks came to Pittsburgh after 1915 for the same reasons, but the circumstances surrounding their arrival differed greatly. The kin-friendship communication network, which earlier had induced black workers to Pittsburgh, continued to operate through the 1920s, but other networks developed to inform southern-born blacks about potential work opportunities in the industrial north.

The *Chicago Defender* added its voice by publishing in its national edition letters from successful migrants and by carrying help-wanted ads from northern manufacturing firms. The desire for work clearly attracted an ever increasing number of southern-born blacks to northern cities to live and work. Nearly every black interviewed for this study reported that work opportunities were paramount in the decision to leave the South. Almost two-thirds of the 505 migrants interviewed by Epstein reported coming to Pittsburgh in search of higher wages and economic opportunities, although more than one-half also added that they sought better treatment. "If I were half as well treated [at] home as here," one worker explained, "I would rather stay [in the South], as I had my family there and had a better home and better health."[10]

Shortages of labor in the industrial North brought on by the sudden decline of the immigrant labor pool and increasingly hostile actions toward blacks in the South also stimulated the black exodus. Labor agents roamed the South in search of willing workers for northern factories. A special train, for example, carried 191 black migrants from Bessemer, Alabama, to Pittsburgh in early 1917.[11] The Carnegie Division of U.S. Steel, Jones and Laughlin, and Westinghouse Electric all employed labor agents to recruit black workers to Pittsburgh. Jasper A. was recruited from Jacksonville, Florida, in 1916 to work on the Pennsylvania Railroad in Pittsburgh. "The Pennsylvania Railroad was short of help," he related, "and they was recruiting people from all over the country.... And there was one [recruiter] come to Jacksonville and I got with him to come here. It was about ten or twelve carloads of us come in at a time. But I had [moving North] in mind well before that. Before I come, there was several [recruit trains] had come up here from Jacksonville. But this man would still keep coming down to Florida getting people to work for the Pennsylvania Railroad."[12] Nearly one-fifth of the blacks interviewed by Epstein reported coming to Pittsburgh at the expense of the railroads or other industrial concerns. This proportion is likely an underestimation of the number recruited by labor agents. Many of those recruited were single men who remained in Pittsburgh a very short time and were probably missed by Epstein's survey.

The differences in the recruitment methods of Pittsburgh's early black population and those who arrived after 1916 influenced the age, marital status, and place of origin of the migrating population. The new migrants were younger, more likely to be unmarried, and more probably from the deep South than those who arrived two decades earlier. Table 29 compares 1,559 black adults from the 1900 sample universe with 567 black migrants who arrived in Pittsburgh after 1915.

The early chain migration to Pittsburgh clearly operated best in nearby states. Three-fourths of the in-migrants came from Virginia, Maryland, and the nation's capital. Many leapfrogged from city to city, working along the way. They had both urban and industrial experiences prior to their arrival in Pittsburgh. Most—74 percent—were also married, although approximately one-third of those arrived in Pittsburgh without their families. As expected of individuals migrating in search of work, most were young men—four of every ten were under the age of thirty, and another one-third were in their thirties.

By 1917 the communication network that brought earlier blacks to Pittsburgh, buttressed by the work of company labor agents, penetrated further into the deep South. Georgia, Florida, Mississippi, and

Table 29. Black Migration to Pittsburgh, 1900 and 1916

Descriptive Category	1900	1916
Origin		
Md., D.C.	11.0	2.9
Va.	66.0	5.8
N.C., S.C.	5.2	9.3
Ga., Fla.	2.6	16.2
La., Ala., Miss.	2.4	34.7
Ky., Tenn.	5.2	6.2
W.Va.	4.3	2.6
Other	3.3	10.4
Unknown	...	10.9
Marital status		
Single	23.0	40.0
Married	74.0	60.0
Other	2.0	...
Age		
Under 30	41.0	52.0
Thirties	31.0	27.0
Forties	16.8	14.0
Fifties	6.9	6.0
60 and over	2.0	1.0
N	1,559	567

NOTE. Data are given as percentages. The data for 1900 were compiled from the sample data generated from the U.S. Bureau of the Census, manuscript census for Pittsburgh, 1900. The data for 1916 were taken from Abraham Epstein, *The Negro Migrant in Pittsburgh*, 10, 18, 25. The age groupings are not totally compatible. The age groups in column 1 (1900) were 30-39, 40-49, etc. Epstein's groups were aged 30-40, 40-50, etc.

particularly Alabama supplied half of the new migrants to Pittsburgh. Almost one-third of those interviewed by Epstein came from Alabama. Virginia, formerly the prime source of black migrants, supplied only 6 percent of Epstein's sample. The new group was also younger and less likely to be married than those who preceded them.

These demographic features and the characteristics surrounding the new black migration suggest a number of important implications regarding the adjustment of blacks to life in Pittsburgh. Nearly one-half, Florette Henri estimated, came from rural backgrounds and at least one-third of Epstein's sample came directly from agricultural work.[13] The pre-1915 black migrant tempered the potential cultural shock inherent in the shift from a preindustrial to an industrial society by a series of urban-industrial experiences before his arrival in Pittsburgh. Many later arrivals moved in a single step—often in the course of a few days—

from the rural South with a low density of people to the crowded urban surroundings of Pittsburgh's Hill District. The required adjustments were clearly as great as those demanded of the nineteenth-century Polish or Italian immigrant. The young ages, the single marital state, and even the short duration of the migration process suggest that many would find the adjustment too difficult and return home or move elsewhere. Complaints by northern employers suggest that many migrants did quickly abandon unsatisfactory work conditions. One Pittsburgh firm reported losing 700 of approximately 1,000 imported black workers in less than a year.[14]

But the degree to which later black arrivals were unprepared for urban life has been somewhat overstated. As subsequent evidence will show, most of these newcomers did hold nonagricultural jobs prior to coming to Pittsburgh. The majority (60 percent) arrived with their families or sent for them within a short period of time. They expressed a desire to seek better employment, to provide educational opportunities for their children, and to keep their families intact. An estimated 80 percent of the migrants who were married sent weekly contributions home, illustrating their commitment to family life.[15] The initiative and courage they exhibited in their migration to the North would be tested many times in industrial Pittsburgh. Declining job opportunities, continued discrimination, and shifting spatial patterns would remain pervasive obstacles to black adjustment.

The steady outward migration of Pittsburgh's native-born white population altered the city's spatial patterns and contributed to the increased homogeneity of the inner city neighborhoods. The *Pittsburgh Leader* advertised no less than eight new blue-collar residential communities outside the city limits. Several offered a year's free transportation to induce settlement. Others pointed toward clean air or recreational space for children.[16] The development of industrial towns along the Ohio and Monongahela rivers—Aliquippa, Ambridge, Rankin, Clairton, Duquesne, and Glassport—and the relocation of the Westinghouse plant from East Liberty to the Turtle Creek Valley all lured workers from the city.

The completion of the street railway network and the opening of new highways at the same time fostered the development of white-collar communities both within the city limits and in rural suburbia. By the beginning of World War I the street railway system carried an estimated 67,000 riders per day over its 583 miles of track. Most of these riders traveled from a residential neighborhood to the central business district and, as Joel Tarr has shown, were white-collar workers.[17] The opening of several key highways during the 1920s also accelerated the separation of work and residence for white-collar Pittsburghers. The construction of Bigelow Boulevard in 1916 and the Boulevard of the Allies in 1924 provided direct access to the eastern residential areas in Oakland and Squirrel Hill. Tunnel construction in 1926 and the subsequent opening of the Liberty Bridge in 1928 spurred the development of half a dozen suburban communities in the south hills. Between 1920 and 1933, the number of miles of improved roads in the district more than doubled from 511 to 1,300 and provided access to suburban living in all directions from the city center.

The city's population, not surprisingly, shifted outward as the interstices between the existing trolley lines were filled. The central business district, the Strip District along the Allegheny River, and the North- and Southsides of the city all lost population. Even the Hill District (wards 3 and 5), which absorbed thousands of black residents between 1916 and 1925, lost more than 10 percent of its population in the 1920s. Every area near the city limits, conversely, gained between 9 and 92 percent in population.[18]

The availability of trolley service and automobile transportation provided residential alternatives to those who could afford these modes of transportation. Automobile ownership in 1934 was highest in the most affluent neighborhoods. The 14th ward (Squirrel Hill), for example, had the highest percentage of homes in the $10,000 and over class and the highest automobile ownership rate in the county.[19] The impact of this relationship between wealth and availability of transportation alternatives contributed in Pittsburgh, as in most American cities, to the creation of increasingly homogeneous neighborhoods. The poor remained nearest the central city; the more affluent built homes at the city limits or in the suburbs.

The growth of suburbia and exurbia proceeded so rapidly in Pittsburgh that by 1930 only Los Angeles of all American cities had a greater proportion of its population living in the county area immediately adjacent to the city. By the beginning of the Depression 124 separate governmental units existed in Allegheny County, more than any other metropolitan area in the nation, and half of the county's residents lived outside the city of Pittsburgh.[20]

This is not to say, however, that a wholesale flight to the suburbs occurred during the 1920s and 1930s. A 1939 study demonstrated that almost 70 percent of those moving from wards 1 through 4 in 1936 moved within one-half mile of their original residence; 40 percent moved within the same census tract. The vast majority—83 percent—moved to homes in the same rent range as those from which they left. The same study found a strong relationship between movement within the city and economic, racial, and ethnic characteristics.[21] Rental cost, housing conditions, the presence of racial or ethnic groups, and transportation facilities, the study concluded, all contributed to family movement in Pittsburgh during the 1920s and 1930s.

Inner city neighborhoods, at the same time, continued to attract new residents to replace those who left. Population densities shifted erratically during the 1910s and 1920s but remained substantially higher in the inner city than in the outlying neighborhoods. Considering the land area between the Monongahela and Allegheny rivers, one may construct two semicircles delineating the older (pre-1900) and the newer (post-1920) sections of the city. Population density in zone one, containing the first six wards in the city, fell slightly between 1900 and 1930, from 52 to 42 persons per acre, but still remained the highest of any area in the city. Several census tracts within zone one contained more than 100 persons per acre, and nearly one-third contained more than the 1900 average. Density in the outlying zone—tracts 7A through 15E—doubled between 1900 and 1930, increasing to 26 persons per acre, but the zone still provided much greater living space than the inner city.

More than one-third of the tracts in zone two contained less than twenty persons per acre. Only the Italian sections in Bloomfield and East Liberty exceeded the average density found in zone one.[22] A third zone, the Southside, with its large eastern European concentration, fell between zone one and two in density, but several tracts—almost exclusively Polish—resembled those in zone one with more than sixty persons per acre.[23]

Intra- and intercity movements did not result in a substantial change in the pattern of population density throughout the city, but they did contribute to the increased concentration of ethnic and racial groups in certain areas. As higher income residents vacated inner city neighborhoods, they were replaced by low income southern and eastern Europeans and recently arrived blacks. Whether the homes were first vacated, creating an inviting void for incoming migrants or whether their incursion into an area pushed the original residents out cannot be determined. What is certain is that between 1900 and 1930, while racial and ethnic clusters continued to exist throughout the city (see 1930 distribution maps in Appendix B), certain neighborhoods became larger in number and increasingly homogeneous.

Pittsburgh's Italian, Polish, and black populations all followed this pattern. Italians, for example, were overrepresented in fourteen areas in 1910, including the central business district, lower hill, Strip District, Bloomfield, East Liberty, Larimer, Hazelwood, and Homewood areas. By 1930 land use changes, from residential to commercial, contributed to their evacuation from the central business and Strip districts. Increased racial tensions in the Hill District in the 1920s and 1930s, moreover, foreshadowed the Italian departure from this area within the next decade. Several new but small areas of Italian concentration—the Bluff, Beechview, and ward 31—increased the number of Italian clusters to fifteen in 1930. The great majority of the city's Italians and their children, however, crowded into three Italian districts, the lower hill, Bloomfield, and the East Liberty–Larimer Avenue area. These three districts contained over one-half of the city's Italian stock, and nearly 15,000 people resided in the latter two neighborhoods. Crowding was even more evident in certain census tracts within these areas. In the 8B section of Bloomfield one contemporary observed, "Not a foot was spared . . . for yard or porch. Row after row of porchless buildings stand flush with a narrow street."[24] Population densities in all three areas exceeded the city-wide average by more than twenty-seven persons per acre, and the density in the lower hill Italian section exceeded 115 persons per acre.

As the number of Italians and their children increased, of course, the proportion of non-Italians in each neighborhood decreased. A more detailed analysis of two Italian neighborhoods appears in chapter 8, but both demographic and physical evidence confirm that portions of Bloomfield and East Liberty retained their early Italian village atmosphere. Nearly 70 percent of the family heads in census tract 8B (Bloomfield) and 77 percent in tracts 12C, D, and E (East Liberty) were Italian. Both areas by 1920 contained Italian churches, social clubs, and business districts. One observer noted that the East Liberty–Larimer Avenue area "contained Italian doctors, interpreters . . . two schools (for Italians), a convent and a monastery. . . . In possessing both a large business district and a still larger residence district, the neighborhood is more distinctly an Italian colony than any other settlement in the city."[25]

Polish migrants, like their Italian counterparts, also maintained the patterns of residence established at the turn of the century. The increasingly commercial Strip District continued to lose population while both the Polish Hill–Lawrenceville section and the Southside attracted new Polish residents. By 1930 both sections became synonymous with "Polonia" in the Pittsburgh district. More than three-fourths of the residents in Polish Hill and in certain Southside tracts were of Polish extraction. The proportion reached 100 percent on some streets. Population density in both neighborhoods exceeded the city-wide average but was not as extensive as in either Italian community. Polish Hill contained forty persons per acre, and between forty and sixty-five persons per acre resided in selected Southside tracts. Nevertheless, multiple family living and boarding-in was as characteristic of the Polish experience in 1930 as of the Italian.

If concentration in small areas was a common element in the lives of Italians and Poles in 1930, it was even more so in certain sections of the black community, although blacks remained widely distributed throughout the city. Blacks lived in all but twenty-two of the city's 189 census tracts in 1930. The main areas of concentration, the Hill District and Homewood-Brushton, contained 45 percent and 16 percent of the city's black population, respectively. These neighborhoods housed 12 percent of the city's white inhabitants. Indexes of concentration (commonly known as dissimilarity indexes) have not been developed for 1930 for most American cities, and so comparisons are difficult. Some suggestive data, however, do exist. Seventy percent of the 1930 Chicago black population lived in an area containing only 4 percent of the white population. In Cleveland, St. Louis, Buffalo, Milwaukee, and New York City, more than 80 percent of the black populations lived in areas containing less than 10 percent of the white populations.[26]

Neighborhood and ward-level data conceal the intense concentration of blacks in certain smaller sections of the city. While blacks everywhere mixed with the white population, particularly with Italians and Jews, six census tracts, all located in wards 3 and 5 were more than 50 percent black, and more than 80 percent of the residents in two tracts were black (the maximum black concentration in 1910 was 40 percent in one Hill District tract), and several streets within these tracts were more than 95 percent black. Density within these sections of the Hill District also increased as blacks continued to migrate to the city during the 1920s.[27] By 1930 three contiguous tracts in ward 3 contained over 110 persons per acre, making it by far the most densely settled section of the city. The more sparsely settled black neighborhood in Homewood-Brushton contained slightly over fifty persons per acre, double the city-wide average.

The heavy population densities coupled with the low incomes of the residents, the overall age of the neighborhood, multiple-family dwellings, and rapid population changes gave the Hill District all of the conditions described by Ernest W. Burgess as characteristic of zones of transition. Ira Reid, director of research for the National Urban League, conducting an extensive examination of social conditions in the Hill District in 1930, was careful to avoid the hyperbole of the social critics of the day. He nevertheless echoed the conclusions of four earlier studies, deploring the unsanitary, indecent, and inadequate conditions.[28]

Perhaps most revealing, Reid introduced his study on the Hill District environment with the following quote from Scott Nearing's *Black America*: "Or climb the hill above the Union station in Pittsburgh. The streets are ill-kept, dirty. The houses are dilapidated. Some of them even abandoned. Many of them are built of wood. Throngs of unemployed Negro workers stand gossiping at the principal corners. The whole community speaks of poverty, neglect and physical hardship."[29] A series of studies on the Hill District, both published and unpublished, appeared frequently from 1930 through 1960. They differed in tone and emphasis—education, mortality, crime, health conditions—but all described the same dreary conditions so aptly chronicled by Nearing. An intensive social survey by Philip Klein found one-third of the homes in the Hill District either unfit for living or in need of major repairs.[30] Elsie Witchen reported on the crowded conditions. "Frequently six or more persons shared a bedroom; occasionally they shared the same bed. In fact, almost one-half of all persons seen shared their rooms with two or more people."[31] And the Pittsburgh Housing Association in 1935 supplied the following description of the structural conditions of one black Hill District neighborhood: "A parapet wall of 29 Townsend Street is leaning dangerously over onto 31 Townsend; a tall chimney at 33 Townsend slopes about 15 degrees from the vertical and another chimney at 27 Townsend appears ready to topple over. The front wall of 1410 Clark Street is also cracked and slightly bulged.... In view of the bad sanitary structural conditions, all of the houses should be placarded as unfit for habitation and occupancy prohibited."[32]

Not all blacks experienced the degrading conditions present in the Hill District. Middle-income blacks began moving into the Homewood-Brushton (ward 13) section of the city just after the Civil War. The population was sufficient by 1871 to warrant the founding of the area's first AME church. By 1930, 16 percent of the population (1,057 persons) in census tract 13C were black. A field survey conducted in the early 1930s indicated that the area contained both working-class black families and the more affluent "negroes who were able to live at some distance from their work in the city." The survey somewhat condescendingly concluded that "in most cases the ... negro families were respectable, working people desirous of making their home and neighborhoods as attractive as possible and consequently, the physical appearance of the area showed few signs of deterioration."[33] This area would receive the greatest number of new black residents during the next thirty years.

Several other small areas of black concentration existed in Pittsburgh in 1930. The Beltzhoover section in ward 18 and a small area in the city's Northside held substantial black clusters. Both neighborhoods existed as early as 1910 and contained mainly second-generation blacks.[34] In each neighborhood, as in the Hill District and Homewood-Brushton, the white population declined more rapidly than the numbers of blacks increased between 1910 and 1930. Both areas also suffered from inadequate housing and a high density of population. The combination of blighted dwellings, crowded conditions, proximity to noxious industries, and racial attitudes contributed to the migration of whites from all four areas. Pittsburgh's black neighborhoods in 1930, as illustrated earlier, were not as segregated as those in other northern cities, but they were moving in that direction.

The development of only one new black neighborhood after World War I illustrates the tendency of blacks of the new migration to settle near those who preceded them. The Hazelwood-Glenwood section attracted more than 1,100 black residents between 1917 and 1930. Most of those employed worked at the Jones and Laughlin and Carnegie mills, the Baltimore and Ohio Railroad, and the Southern Carwheel Company. A survey of the area in 1933 revealed that most residents had migrated from the deep South after 1916 and that jobs provided the main attraction. Although three black churches had opened, the district contained little else. There was not, as one resident described, "a lawyer, nor a doctor, nor a dentist, nor nothing, not even a garageman among our own people."[35]

Most neighborhoods were not as devoid of services as the Hazelwood-Glenwood area, but all, lacking both the stable population and the community-focused institutions, remained fragmented during the second third of the century. Residential instability increased rather than declined after 1915 as hundreds of blacks moved into and out of the city almost daily. A study completed in 1935 estimated that 85 percent of Pittsburgh's black population migrated to the city after 1917. More than 40 percent had lived in the city less than ten years. "No wonder they are disorganized," the study concluded, "there is an insufficient number of people who are adjusted to the environment and at the same time mature enough to serve as its leaders."[36] Longer term black residents, particularly those from the lower Hill District, frequently moved within the city to escape deteriorating physical and social conditions. Those who could afford to do so moved to the outskirts of the city. Others migrated to the less densely settled sections of the Hill District or the Northside of the city. Inadequate housing conditions and low ownership rates also contributed to residential instability. One field survey found a direct relationship between residential persistence and the number of rooms occupied per family. Predictably, families with four or more rooms in 1928 experienced substantially less residential mobility than those living in three or less rooms.[37]

In the face of almost insurmountable problems it is not surprising that black organizations had little effect in their own neighborhoods. Some organizations inadvertently contributed to neighborhood fragmentation. Others exhibited considerable community concern but were too weak, financially and politically, to overcome increasingly adverse conditions.

Black churches proliferated in the black neighborhoods but, like those studied by Allan Spear in Chicago, continued to represent spiritual rather than local social interests. The number of organized black churches (excluding storefront ministries) increased from twenty-seven in 1910 to fifty-six in 1930.[38] In addition, five of the original churches closed during the interim, and half of those remaining moved to new locations. Three left their original neighborhoods. The Hill District (wards 3 and 5) alone contained forty-five black churches and eighteen classified as "store fronts."[39] Three claimed 1,000 or more members but only four churches, investigated in 1930 by Reid, sponsored any community, social, or welfare-type activities. The most active of the four, the Ebenezer Baptist Church, sponsored a travelers' organization to assist incoming blacks and later a Home Finder's League.[40] Of the nine largest Hill District churches, two sponsored youth athletic teams, two maintained orchestras, and four sponsored youth clubs. Two churches provided the services of a community social worker, but lack of financial support forced one church to discontinue this service.[41] "The church program," reported Reid, "is basically one of evangelism." Black churches, Reid recommended, must "consider [adopting] a unified social program in their neighborhoods."[42]

Available evidence on church activities from 1930 through 1960 is spotty and represents only a small portion of the black community. The data do suggest, however, that such a unified program was not forthcoming. By 1960 the number of black religious organizations in the city again doubled, while the black population grew by 82 percent. Church activities continued to focus upon religious rather than social concerns.[43]

School enrollment statistics reflect the increasing segregation within the black neighborhood. The number of elementary schools containing a majority of black students increased from two to seven during the 1920s. Three became more than 90 percent black. That the schools contributed little toward developing a community cohesion, however, seems self-evident. The City of Pittsburgh School Board, an all-white body whose members were appointed after 1911, exercised sole control over all school activities. That only two of thirteen Hill District elementary schools could pass the school board's own "educational efficiency rating" reflected that body's lack of concern over black education. None of the schools offered after-school social activities, and only a few maintained a parents-teachers organization.[44] All teachers were white, as the Pittsburgh school district continued to exclude black teachers from its professional staff.[45]

In 1930 Reid reported the existence of two types of black social organizations: (1) those whose roots reach down into the masses of the black population, and (2) those having no roots.[46] The former organizations, excluding churches, included fraternal lodges, several local black clubs, and the neighborhood women's clubs. These organizations, he concluded, have shown little interest in the social issues of the black community. The women's clubs "have done more in a community way than any other group ... not only are they making efforts to remedy untoward conditions, but they are endeavoring to stimulate forces to bring improved conditions about."[47] However, these women's organizations, the director lamented, were too few and lacked the power to have a significant impact on social conditions. As for the Urban League itself, Reid, recognizing the lack of neighborhood focus, recommended that the league "continue, but to a greater degree and more definite purpose, its neighborhood organization.... the organization's work is for the whole of Pittsburgh, it might find a more central location in the mid-hill."[48]

The rootless social organizations included numerous "good time" men's clubs among the black community. The *Pittsburgh Courier*, for example, noted more than 250 such clubs on its social pages during 1928. Clubs such as the "Frogs," the "Big Eight Social Club," the "Goldenrod Social Club," the "Honey Boys," and even the black "Elks" and "Moose" no doubt provided an important leisure-time outlet for blacks in the "steel city." It appears, however, that they possessed little civic or neighborhood consciousness. One black researcher explained the lack of solidarity among social organizations: "I have heard enough through extensive interviews, reading and living experiences not to suggest, but state emphatically that ... these groups could have formed the link of brotherhood to preserve the dignity of us all.... There was no particular unity between the religious institutions who preach comradeship every day. Now why would you expect it of us in business and social affairs?"[49] Whether they possessed roots or not, black neighborhood organizations proved unable to cope with the constant turnover of residents. They provided only limited assistance to the thousands of new migrants attempting to adjust to life in Pittsburgh.

Ethnic neighborhoods, in contrast, received few newcomers after 1930. Yet during the next three decades the neighborhood Catholic churches and schools, fraternal associations, local business establishments, newspapers, and other organizations flourished, providing assistance, comfort, and leisure activities to two generations of residents. These institutions were products of a community whose real stability evolved from the intergenerational access to steady work and acceptable living accommodations. Without the fundamental foundation achieved by the first generation, the ethnic neighborhoods of the 1930s and 1940s would have been in disarray. The institutions did not cause community stability, but they provided a base of support.

Church activities, for example, were and remained a significant force in the Polish and Italian community. During what William Galush has called "the golden age of Polonia," the focus of the Polish Catholic church continued to be the neighborhood parish. "This was a new world equivalent of an *okolica* [rural district orientation], with the center here being the new parish created with so much effort."[50] Parish priests continued to officiate at every important family event—religious and secular—from birth to death. Indicative of the continuing importance of the church, membership increased almost annually at the major Polish churches on Polish Hill, in Lawrenceville, and on the Southside. The Italian neighborhood congregations experienced similar increases. Perhaps more revealing, financial contributions remained steady during the Depression and increased substantially thereafter.[51] The Immaculate Heart of Mary Church on Polish Hill and Our Lady, Help of Christians in East Liberty both distributed food and clothing during the Depression. They sponsored scrap and paper drives during the war. Community social activities as well as religious services continued to be regular functions of all four neighborhood ethnic churches during the era. The mother in one Italian family perhaps best illustrated the hold the ethnic church exercised on its parishioners when she was urged by a social worker to move to a better neighborhood that had an American Catholic church. Protesting that she preferred her present neighborhood with its Italian Catholic church and priests, she explained: "I want my own religion for the children."[52]

Schools affiliated with each of the neighborhood churches supplemented the community-based activities in the respective areas. Local scouting groups, holy-name societies, ladies sodalities, and innumerable athletic teams helped to maintain community identity. Interneighborhood competition was often fierce, and the local team received wide support by the adult members of the community.[53]

Fraternal associations also retained their importance in community life, although their function changed somewhat. Originally formed as beneficial societies, social brotherhood and political action became important by the mid-1930s. Members, of course, continued to pay for and receive sickness and death benefits, but other functions became paramount. Buildings to house "nests" of Polish Falcons, local colonies of the Polish National Alliance, Sons and Daughters of Italy, or provincial organizations such as the Ateleta club sprang up in every ethnic community. Several, including the Southside Polish Falcons, contained gymnasiums and small libraries. Nearly all had social-gathering places, including gaming tables and, after prohibition, drinking facilities.[54]

Several Polish associations formed a Central Council of Polish Organizations in 1935 to provide interaction among the groups and to represent their common interests. Initial goals of the council included the following:

    I. Education: this division undertakes to supply information, literature and other cultural resources to Poles on request. It hopes to interest the school board [of Pittsburgh] in permitting Polish to be offered as a second language.
    II. Nationality Interests: will encourage observation of Polish national holidays. . . .
    III. Citizenship: to give information and aid to Polish people desiring to prepare for American citizenship.
    IV. Social Service: there is much concern as to the alleged amount of juvenile delinquency among children of Polish background. The council has a special worker for boys brought before the court.[55]

The expansion of the functions of the Italian and Polish fraternal associations enabled them to play a continuing role in the lives of first- and second-generation residents. By the 1930s many organizations offered recreation and educational facilities and economic assistance and fostered other ethnic concerns; they also provided an additional link between generations and among members of the community.

By 1930 Poles, Italians, and blacks were scattered all over the city. Italians could be found in 91 percent of the city's census tracts, while blacks and Poles resided in three-fourths of the tracts. The density of each group, however, had increased substantially in former areas of concentration. The great majority of the city's Italians lived in two neighborhoods—Bloomfield and East Liberty; Poles resided primarily in the Strip District, in Polish Hill, and on the Southside. Blacks clustered in more neighborhoods than either immigrant group but dominated several areas of the Hill District and small portions in Homewood-Brushton and the Northside. Between one-third and nine-tenths of the residents of these neighborhoods were black. Environmental conditions in immigrant and black neighborhoods varied somewhat, but none of the areas could be described as affluent. All exhibited overcrowding, structural deficiencies, and a lack of sanitary facilities. A fundamental difference, however, existed between the immigrant communities and the black neighborhoods.[56] The Polish Hill, Bloomfield, East Liberty, and South-side immigrant areas were all becoming second-generation neighborhoods by 1930. They would provide continuing kin and friend contacts during the Depression and war years ahead. The black neighborhoods experienced an almost complete turnover during the era of the Great Migration. A second wave of in-migration in the 1940s contributed to the churning characteristic of the black population. The three groups that began their existence in the city under relatively similar conditions were now dramatically different. Poles and Italians had developed stable communities to assist them in their adjustment to the conditions of the urban-industrial environment. Black neighborhoods, on the other hand, were in a constant state of flux, losing white immigrants and native-born families while gaining large numbers of recently migrated blacks. Many were young single males from the deep South, who were also often without skills and illiterate.

The role of social institutions and organizations in ameliorating living conditions represented a second major difference between the ethnic and black neighborhood. Polish and Italian neighborhood organizations, now nearly thirty years old, buttressed the familial and work ties around which the immigrant children organized their lives. Pittsburgh's early black population, in contrast, denied the opportunity to secure steady work, moved from job to job and neighborhood to neighborhood. Unable to build a stable community in either physical or social terms, they were inundated by each subsequent wave of arrivals from the South. The pattern initiated earlier would continue throughout the second third of the century. Polish and Italian neighborhoods remained relatively stable; black residential areas changed constantly. These contrasting conditions, as chapter 8 demonstrates, exercised a marked impact on the ability of each group to adjust to life in Pittsburgh during the subsequent thirty years. They reinforced the growing conclusion that in the initial confrontation of new arrivals with the industrial-economic structure of Pittsburgh, patterns of networks emerged that would shape the immigrant and black experience over several generations.

NOTES

1. Philip Klein, *A Social Study of Pittsburgh* (New York, 1938), 138. Data compiled by the Bureau of Business Research, University of Pittsburgh.
2. Ibid., 145.
3. Ibid., 150, 279.
4. "Growth of Population and of Manufacturing Employment in the Pittsburgh Industrial Area in Comparison with Growth in Other Industrial Areas," *Pittsburgh Business Review*, 5 (May 1935), 27-28.
5. Glen McLaughlin and Ralph Watkins, "The Problem of Industrial Growth in a Mature Economy," *American Economic Review*, 29 (Mar. 1939), 2, 11.
6. Caroline Golab, *Immigrant Destinations* (Philadelphia, 1977), 16.
7. U.S. Department of Labor, *Annual Report of the Commissioner General of Immigration* (Washington, D.C., 1926), 180-86.
8. Abraham Epstein, *The Negro Migrant in Pittsburgh* (Pittsburgh, 1918), 7.
9. This in- and out-migration affected other cities in a similar manner. Thus, the estimates that perhaps as many as one million blacks participated in the migration seem reasonable. See Florette Henri, *Black Migration: Movement North, 1900-1920* (New York, 1975), 49ff., for a detailed discussion of migration estimates.
10. Epstein, *Negro Migrant*, 27.
11. U.S. Department of Labor, *Negro Migration in 1916-1917* (Washington, D.C., 1919), 64.
12. Interview with Jasper A., Apr. 12, 1976, Pittsburgh Oral History Project (POHP).
13. Epstein, *Negro Migrant*, 26; Henri, *Black Migration*, 52.
14. Epstein, *Negro Migrant*, 21.
15. Ibid., 24.
16. See advertisements, *Pittsburgh Leader*, Apr. 2, May 2, and June 2, 1900; *Pittsburgh Press*, Apr. 22, 1900.
17. Tarr has demonstrated that industrial workers in the Pittsburgh district were largely unaffected by the development of trolley service. He estimated that as late as 1917 a majority of Pittsburgh's industrial workers walked to work. "In the more outlying mill areas as high as 80 to 90 percent of the workforce walked to work." See his *Transportation Innovations and Changing Spatial Patterns in Pittsburgh, 1850-1934* (Chicago, 1978), 21.
18. Respective losses and gains of key areas were: Strip District, -38.6 percent; central business district, -17 percent; Hill District, -10 percent; Southside, -6.9 percent; Homewood, +9.6 percent; East Liberty, +11 percent; Beechview, +52.5 percent; and Squirrel Hill, +91.9 percent. The areas that gained population were all located in the outer sections of the city.
19. Tarr, *Transportation Innovations*, 27.
20. Klein, *Social Study of Pittsburgh*, 46.
21. Peter Alapas, "Mobility of Families in Selected Areas of Pittsburgh" (M. A. thesis, University of Pittsburgh, 1939), 60, 70.

22. For 1900 data see Tarr, *Transportation Innovations*, Appendix B; 1930 data from U.S. Bureau of the Census, "Areas and Population Densities of Census Tracts: 1930," Pittsburgh, Pennsylvania, table 21. The zones identified here are not totally compatible with those discussed by Tarr. His data examine density in the city's wards prior to the reorganization of 1907. The data do, however, provide a rough approximation of the changing population densities in the respective zones.

23. Data from U.S. Bureau of the Census, "Areas and Population Densities of Census Tracts: 1930," Pittsburgh, Pennsylvania, table 21.

24. Ella Burns Myers, "Some Italian Groups in Pittsburgh" (M.A. thesis, Carnegie Institute of Technology, 1920), 14.

25. Ibid.

26. A. G. Moran and F. F. Stephan, "The Negro Population and Negro Families in Pittsburgh and Allegheny County," *Social Research Bulletin*, Bureau of Social Research, Federation of Social Agencies, 1 (Apr. 20, 1933), 4.

27. Moran and Stephan estimated that 14,000 more blacks moved into Pittsburgh than left or died during the decade of the 1920s. Ibid., 2.

28. Ira Reid, *Social Conditions of the Negro in the Hill District of Pittsburgh* (Pittsburgh, 1930), 31. See this book, too, for a bibliography of other studies devoted specifically to the conditions in the Hill District.

29. Scott Nearing, *Black America* (n.p., 1929), quoted in Reid, *Social Conditions of the Negro*, 27.

30. Klein, *Social Study of Pittsburgh*, 273.

31. Elsie Witchen, "Tuberculosis and the Negro in Pittsburgh," Tuberculosis League of Pittsburgh, 1934, located in the Archives of the Industrial Society, University of Pittsburgh.

32. Pittsburgh Housing Association report, unpublished, 1935, in files of the Pittsburgh Housing Authority.

33. Delmer C. Seawright, "The Effect of City Growth on the Homewood-Brushton District" (M.A. thesis, University of Pittsburgh, 1932).

34. The Beltzhoover Section (Tract 18D) grew from 498 blacks in 1910 to 1,320 in 1930. Slightly over 900 blacks lived in Tract 25B on the Northside in 1930.

35. Alonzo Moran, "Distribution of the Negro Population in Pittsburgh, 1910-1930" (M.A. thesis, University of Pittsburgh, 1933), 34.

36. John Rathmell, "Status of Pittsburgh Negroes in Regard to Origin, Length of Residence, and Economic Aspects of their Life" (M.A. thesis, University of Pittsburgh, 1935), 27.

37. Wiley A. Hall, "Negro Housing and Rents in the Hill District of Pittsburgh" (M.A. thesis, University of Pittsburgh, 1929), 23.

38. Cleveland, New York, and Chicago all experienced explosions in the number of black churches, particularly the storefront pentecostal version. Nearly two-thirds of New York's black churches, James Weldon Johnson argued a half century ago, "could be closed and there would be left a sufficient number to supply the religious needs of the community." James Weldon Johnson, *Black Manhattan* (New York, 1930), 163. Churches in both Chicago and New York, like those in Pittsburgh, generally refrained from offering social welfare services. Those that did attempt to provide such services, such as Chicago's Olivet Baptist Church, incurred heavy debts and were often forced to cur-

tail welfare activities. See Kenneth Kusmer, *A Ghetto Takes Shape: Black Cleveland, 1870-1930* (Urbana, Ill., 1976), 207; Allan H. Spear, *Black Chicago: The Making of a Ghetto, 1890-1920* (Chicago, 1967), 175-79.

39. Moron, "Distribution of Negro Population," and 43-46, distribution map, 47. See also the *Pittsburgh City Directory* (Pittsburgh, 1930).
40. "Testimonial to the Reverend Junis Austin," Ebenezer Baptist Church, Pittsburgh, 1936, p. 8.
41. Reid, *Social Conditions of the Negro*, 99.
42. Ibid.
43. Church History, Bethel AME Church (Pittsburgh: mimeographed, n.p., n.d.); Eighty-fifth anniversary issue, the Ebenezer Baptist Church (1960); Trinity AME church, church bulletins (Pittsburgh, Pa., 1960-61).
44. Reid, *Social Conditions of the Negro*, 82-87.
45. Ibid.
46. Ibid., 95.
47. Ibid.
48. Ibid., 17. Not all members of the Urban League agreed with Reid's concern for neighborhood or his interpretation of the role of the League in community development. See ibid., 19n.
49. R. L. Hill, "A View of the Hill: A Study of Experiences and Attitudes in the Hill District of Pittsburgh, Pennsylvania, 1900-1973" (Ph.D. diss., University of Pittsburgh, 1973), 116.
50. William J. Galush, "Faith in Fatherland," in Randall Miller and Thomas Marzik, eds., *Immigrants and Religion in Urban America* (Philadelphia, 1977), 89.
51. Membership Rolls and Annual Financial Reports, 1926-1945, the Immaculate Heart of Mary Roman Catholic Church, Polish Hill; Our Lady, Help of Christians Roman Catholic Church, East Liberty; St. Josaphat's Roman Catholic Church, Southside. The data from all churches are incomplete and fragmentary but do substantiate the conclusion that membership and participation increased during the 1930s.
52. Church bulletins, Immaculate Heart of Mary, Polish Hill; Our Lady, Help of Christians, 1942, 1943. Quoted in Klein, *Social Study of Pittsburgh*, 251.
53. Ibid. See also church history, St. Josaphat's Church, Southside.
54. Interview with Mrs. K., Southside, by Donald Fastuca, Nov. 9, 1978; transcript of interview is in the possession of M.W.
55. Klein, *Social Study of Pittsburgh*, 267.
56. These neighborhoods, Spear argued, could not even be compared with the city's ethnic communities. Unlike their European-born counterparts, blacks did not cluster voluntarily to share common cultural traits. Blacks in Chicago "lived in the ghetto because discrimination gave them no choice; they were bound together less by a common set of cultural values than by a common set of grievances." See Spear, *Black Chicago*, 210. Discrimination in Pittsburgh also played a major role in the residential choice of the city's black population. Discrimination, however, was not the sole cause. Other factors such as the location of occupational opportunities, the settlement of earlier black migrants, and the availability of inexpensive housing no doubt also influenced their choice of neighborhood.

8

Seven Neighborhoods: Stability and Change, 1930-60

The Depression of the 1930s, World War II, and the events of the postwar 1950s all influenced life in the black, Polish, and Italian neighborhoods. Unemployment during the Depression halted the occupational progress of some groups; discrimination by employers and union leaders limited job opportunities for others. Urban redevelopment destroyed one neighborhood and changed several others. Educational opportunities provided by the G. I. bill, the widespread use of the automobile, and the growth of suburbia all tested the strength and vitality of the ethnic neighborhood. The importance of residential location, nevertheless, persisted for all three groups throughout most of the second third of the century. Community institutions, discussed in chapter 7, continued to influence the development of neighborhood life in Pittsburgh. The neighborhoods, in turn, contributed to each group's ability to develop organizations to ease the adjustment to the urban-industrial environment. Neighborhood life, however, did not depend solely upon the presence of formal institutions. Family and friend relationships, occupational patterns, and racial discrimination affected a group's ability or willingness to sustain its historic neighborhood. These variables and their impact on community life help to explain the widely divergent paths traveled by each group during two generations of existence in Pittsburgh.

Our previous examination of spatial patterns in Pittsburgh revealed numerous areas of major ethnic and racial concentration within the city. The longitudinal analysis, in addition, identified several neighborhoods of historic importance to Poles, blacks, or Italians. Seven loca-

tions exhibited both historical and numerical significance and thus
permitted an examination of the continuing role of neighborhoods in
the lives of the migrant groups.[1] Detailed samples, each extending approximately six blocks square and including every household on all facing streets, were generated from these seven neighborhoods. The Italian areas included a portion of census tract 8B in Bloomfield and part
of 12D in the East Liberty–Larimer Avenue area. Polish neighborhoods
selected included parts of tract 6B in Polish Hill and 16B on the Southside. Three, rather than two, black neighborhoods were selected because we wanted to compare change in both the inner city as well as
in the outlying neighborhoods.[2] Black neighborhoods that were selected included parts of tract 3C in the lower Hill District, 5A in the
upper Hill District, and 13C in the Homewood-Brushton area. Data
were then generated on every adult within every household for the
1930 period (a more detailed description of this sample may be found
in Appendix A). Analyses were conducted at subsequent ten-year intervals through 1960. First, all residents in 1930 were traced at each
decade interval to determine the residential, occupational, and homeownership patterns of this generation of Poles, Italians, and blacks.
Individuals who moved from their 1930 residence were followed as
long as they remained in the Pittsburgh area. Where it was possible to.
do so, blacks who participated in the post-1916 migrations were identified to determine differences in their careers from other 1930 blacks.
An examination of the residents in each household within the seven
neighborhoods in 1930, 1940, 1950, and 1960 provided a second level
of analysis, enabling us to determine the extent and nature of change
within the neighborhood. Thus, every adult living in any house in the
selected neighborhoods in either 1930, 1940, 1950, or 1960 was recorded. Because it proved so difficult to identify particular individuals
as definitely black, this examination was omitted for blacks. However,
since all three black neighborhoods by 1940 contained such high concentrations of blacks within the respective tracts and blocks, we were
able to substitute census-tract and block-level data. Since we were most
interested in examining changing patterns within the neighborhoods,
we lost little by this substitution. (The census reported nearly all
important block and tract data by race, but not always by ethnicity;
thus, this method was not possible for Poles and Italians.) Our information on the location of the ethnic neighborhoods, supplemented by
census and church records and oral interviews, permitted us to identify Poles and Italians by their distinctive family names. Voter registration records, supplemented by church records, enabled us to identify
definitely a number of black residents. Individuals whom we could not

identify as definitely black were excluded from the sample.

All seven neighborhoods became increasingly homogeneous during the 1920s. This, of course, comes as no surprise as segregation permeated most northern American cities by 1930. Studies in more than a dozen cities all point to the existence of highly segregated ethnic and racial neighborhoods. Italians and Russian Jews in New York, Poles in Chicago and Philadelphia, and blacks in Philadelphia, St. Louis, Chicago, and New York all had concentrated in distinct neighborhoods by 1930. A comparative analysis by Stanley Lieberson concludes that by 1920 blacks in a number of northern cities had become the most segregated group of residents.[3] Lieberson's data, however, are misleading on two counts. First, Lieberson relied upon U.S. census tract–level data as his basic unit of analysis. Tract-level data, however, often conceal small pockets of intense segregation. Second, his data ignore second-generation ethnics who already constituted an important part of the ethnic village population. An examination of seven selected Pittsburgh neighborhoods, for example, revealed that segregation remained more characteristic of the Polish and Italian neighborhoods in 1930 than of the black. Both Hill District neighborhoods and even the small section of Homewood-Brushton included in this study were more than 50 percent black. Yet each neighborhood contained a substantial number of Italians, Russian Jews, Greeks, and other foreign-born workers. One Pittsburgh Urban League member viewed this relative integration as a clear disadvantage. "The absence of a solidly Negro community in Pittsburgh," he suggested, "reduces very materially the power of the Negro population to compel retail dealers to employ Negro clerks in Negro residential districts and to secure Negro political representation as in some Northern cities."[4]

The Polish and Italian neighborhoods, in contrast, were more totally segregated. Three of every four families in the Polish Hill District and 80 percent in the Southside neighborhood were first- or second-generation Poles. The two longest streets in each neighborhood were more than four-fifths Polish, and the proportion exceeded 90 percent on several streets in each district. Several generations of blood relatives occupied many of the homes. Frank K. told of eight related families all living in the six-block Polish Hill area.[5] On the Southside, one respondent recalled, "Nearly every family on Mission, Josephine, Leticoe, and Koscuisko streets were Polish. The Wieczorkowskis owned the pharmacy and the Sorocyznskis and the Krismalskis ran grocery stores." During the Depression she noted that the men played horseshoes or pitched pennies on the street. "Neighbors could really trust neighbors then."[6]

The city's two major Italian neighborhoods, which originated around the turn of the century, grew larger and more concentrated each decade. The German population, which once dominated Bloomfield, gave way by 1930 to immigrants from Italy and their children. While some German residents continued to dwell along the fringes of the identified neighborhood—Juniper and Edmund streets—Italians now constituted 70 percent of the population. Here, too, kin chains seemed to prevail. While it is not certain that all of them were blood relatives, thirty-four Donatelli families, sixteen Sciullos, and twenty-two Sciullos lived in this six-block area. The East Liberty area, situated on relatively open land and lacking any physical barriers to in-migration, attracted the largest number of Italians, nearly 9,000 by 1930. It also began to attract a small number of black residents. Nearly one-fifth of the sample neighborhood's residents were black, while 70 percent were Italian. This also is not surprising, since the integration of Pittsburgh's Italian and black populations occurred as early as 1890 in the Strip District, in the lower hill, and in certain northern sections of the city. By 1930, every Italian neighborhood except Bloomfield contained black residents, and every black neighborhood contained Italians.

Social survey after social survey, beginning with the famous Pittsburgh Survey of 1907, decried the crowded living conditions in the Pittsburgh Hill District. Newspaper articles talked of "teeming" populations. Most studies suggested that the high population density contributed to a number of social ills. One study in 1924 went to great lengths to establish a link between morality and the presence of boarders in the home.[7] Others quite properly suggested a relationship among factors such as population density, the lack of sanitary facilities, and the incidence of disease. Crowded conditions nearly always existed throughout the Hill District area. Consisting of only 234 acres, the 3rd ward, the smallest in the city, held a gross density of nearly 100 persons per acre. Within their own neighborhoods and building structures, however, Poles and Italians experienced greater crowding than did blacks in 1930.

An average of 2.5 families resided in each residential structure in the Polish neighborhood in 1930 (Table 30). Two streets, Paulowna and Brereton, contained nearly three families per structure. Most living units consisted of two rooms running lengthwise, one room in front of the other. The front room served as a kitchen and sitting room; the rear, often partitioned, served as a multiple-person bedroom.[8] Families frequently shared their home with boarders. Many homes also contained at least one adult relative. Residential conditions on the South-

Table 30. Household Profiles in Seven Selected Neighborhoods of Pittsburgh in 1930

Category of Comparison	Black			Polish		Italian	
	Lower Hill	Upper Hill	Homewood-Brushton	Polish Hill	South-side	Bloom-field	East Liberty
Percentage of population	56.1	64.2	57.0	75.2	79.7	69.9	62.4
Density/ families per structure	1.31	1.10	1.19	2.50	1.84	1.40	1.50
Sex of working individuals (%)							
Male	74.5	86.0	81.5	90.0	93.0	93.0	91.0
Female	25.5	14.0	18.5	10.0	7.0	7.0	9.0
Occupation of heads (%)							
Unskilled	54.0	50.5	49.0	61.0	65.2	66.0	48.1
Semi-skilled	13.0	26.0	15.5	7.3	6.1	5.0	10.0
Skilled	11.0	7.0	10.0	11.4	7.5	16.3	23.2
Low white collar	4.5	3.0	4.5	8.0	8.2	5.6	10.6
High white collar	0	0	4.0	1.3	1.0	0	1.1
Unem-ployed	17.5	13.5	16.5	11.0	12.0	7.1	7.0
Marital status (%)							
Single	6.0	4.0	17.5	19	21	9	14
Married	79.0	93.5	74.0	71	71	82	79
Other	15.0	2.5	8.5	10	8	9	7
Homeowners (%)							
Own	0.5	13.2	12.5	21.0	39.0	45.0	31.0
Rent	99.5	86.8	87.5	79.0	61.0	55.0	69.0
Value of homes	$6,813	$5,000	$8,182	$4,098	$4,098	$4,676	$6,059
N	113	66	88	315	182	129	144

NOTE. The data on blacks are compiled from voter registration cards, 1930-53, located in the Archives of the Industrial Society, University of Pittsburgh; the *Pittsburgh City Directory*, 1930; and membership rolls of the following churches: Ebenezer Baptist Church, 1928; Bethel AME Church, 1932; Trinity AME, 1930; and the Homewood AME Zion, 1930. The data on Poles and Italians were compiled from street lists and occupation lists contained in the *Pittsburgh City Directory*, 1930.

side were similar but less crowded than on Polish Hill. Nevertheless, the
most common household contained a married couple, their young children, and one married son or daughter with spouse and infant child
and occasionally an unrelated boarder.[9]

Many Italian households also contained two generations of the same
family. Boarding, however, had ceased to be a common function of
the Italian household in Pittsburgh by 1930. Less than 5 percent of the
households examined in both Italian neighborhoods held unrelated
boarders in 1930.[10] Black families lived almost totally in single-family
dwellings. Some accepted unrelated boarders, but few housed married
children.

The incidence of multiple-family living in the Polish and, to some
extent, Italian households and its absence in black residences continue
the pattern of adjustment suggested earlier in this book. Both Poles and
Italians depended upon their children to assist in the income-producing
activities of the family. A report by the assistant superintendent of
schools in the Bloomfield district indicated that Italian parents continued to urge their male offspring to forsake school for work as soon
as possible. She lamented, "Education is still conceived by most parents
as completion of the 8th grade . . . the bleakness of their own educational experience makes that inevitable. Moreover, the economic pressure which presses so hard upon the parents . . . stifles interest in prolonged schooling . . . where the father works in the railroad yards or
the mills he averages ten hours a day. He wants help with his load, and
ever so slight an increase in the family income seems more imperative
than an increase in the family's knowledge."[11] In return for work, the
family provided food and shelter. In addition to passing on a trade or
an occupation to young sons, immigrant parents could now also provide
access to housing. Interviewees suggested that a majority of immigrant
children lived in the same home as their parents, often dividing the
dwelling unit into two or more apartments. Some like Stanley E. moved
into a second home that his parents had purchased some years before.
Such assistance was invaluable, especially because few immigrant children could afford housing outside the city or in more affluent urban
neighborhoods. In some cases, where available land permitted, an adult
offspring and his or her family moved into a home constructed on the
rear portion of the family lot. The Polish Hill, Bloomfield, and East Liberty neighborhoods all contain numerous examples of multiple residences
built on single lots. In fact, this tendency to divide households proved
so widespread that many realtors would not sell to Polish or Italian
families in more affluent neighborhoods by the 1950s for fear of disrupting higher priced single-family areas.[12]

Blacks continued to rely upon their own initiative to secure work during the 1930s and 1940s. Families and friends, according to those interviewed, were unable to provide much assistance during the Depression, and the acute labor shortages during the war years made such assistance unnecessary. Later, as work again became scarce and black unemployment rose, families remained unable to provide work contacts. As black children became old enough to work, they, like the generation before them, quickly struck out on their own in search of work. Abraham Epstein reported only nineteen (11 percent) of 162 black families with working children residing at home in 1918. By 1930 the percentage declined to less than 5 percent in the three sample neighborhoods.[13] Thus, despite intense crowding in the black neighborhoods, few households contained more than a single related family, while approximately one-fifth housed an unrelated boarder or two. Boarders obviously contributed to the upkeep of the black home as offspring created their own economically independent families.

The sex distribution and marital status of workers in 1930 also continued a pattern begun earlier in Pittsburgh. Daughters of neither Poles nor Italians held steady jobs outside the home while black females often worked for wages. If, as suggested above, female children of immigrants left school at age fourteen, they most likely remained in the parental home until marriage, assisting with the required domestic tasks. Some Pittsburgh immigrant women, one recent study has discovered, moved "in and out of the labor market dependent upon life stage, family need, marital status and whether there were small children at home." Italian women in the study cited were less likely to work outside the home than either Jewish or Slavic women.[14] Young black girls, in contrast, followed in the footsteps of their elder sisters or mothers, securing work as domestics, laundresses, or maids.[15] The small proportion of single workers in the black household suggests that these women, like their male counterparts, left home shortly after assuming work responsibilities.

Thus it appears that the typical black household in the Hill District in 1930 consisted of a recent migrant from the deep South, his wife and young children, and perhaps an unrelated boarder or two. A substantial minority of the black homes were also headed by females. The more affluent blacks in the Homewood-Brushton section differed from this norm, but only slightly. They were more likely second-generation residents and contained a larger proportion of unmarried working children. Polish households, in contrast, most likely contained two families— often from different generations; many also housed working unmarried males as well as unmarried females who assisted in household tasks.

Italian households resembled those of the Polish, except that they were somewhat more nuclear than extended. Both groups continued to discourage education beyond the eighth grade and expected children to contribute to the upkeep of the household.

The strong intrafamilial dependence among Polish and Italian groups and the location of their work induced many second-generation migrants to settle within the community of their youth. Young blacks, unable to rely on their parents for either job or housing assistance, retained the geographic independence exhibited by an earlier generation. The journey-to-work continued to influence the residential choices of all three groups of blue-collar workers but became a secondary concern after 1930. Family and kinship ties and the social and economic services provided by one's community, together with a perceived sense of belonging, exercised an increasingly powerful force on a choice of residence. For blacks, however, an equally pervasive force—racial discrimination—limited their residential options and overburdened the neighborhoods available to them.

The incidence of racial discrimination is difficult to grasp. Much of it is subtle and remains within the private worlds of those involved. Pittsburgh, like other northern cities, had no legal codes designed to isolate a particular group or to deny them equal opportunity. Blacks interviewed for this study, however, could all provide specific, concrete illustrations of discrimination. Some lost jobs due to race. Others, failing to rent an apartment or purchase a home in a specific location, were certain that the color of their skin became the major barrier. One black recalled being denied the right to walk on Herron Avenue during the 1930s. Others remembered being excluded from public facilities, particularly swimming pools in Schenley and Highland parks.[16] Labor unions systematically excluded black workers as recently as the 1960s. A 1940 survey conducted by the Pittsburgh Urban League revealed that only five of fifty-three labor unions in Pittsburgh had black members. Fifteen unions admitted to constitutional restrictions or "gentlemen's agreements" to exclude blacks. The remaining thirty-three responded that they had no black members at present "because none have applied for membership."[17] A black construction coalition nearly thirty years later led a demonstration protesting the refusal of unions to admit black workers.[18] As labor unions became more powerful in Pittsburgh, exclusion from union membership also meant exclusion from eligibility for a variety of occupations.

Often attitudes of racial separation filtered down to Pittsburgh's working classes from local institutions that ministered to their needs. Settlement houses throughout the city were beginning to divide their

activities and programs, such as athletics and dance classes, by the
1930s. The Brashear Association, which operated four different settlement houses, established Carver House in 1937 as a facility to be used
solely by blacks. Residents in the variety of other houses slowly came
to accept this institutionalized racism. Blacks from the other settlements gradually withdrew to Carver House, even if it meant traveling
a greater distance. The Kingsley House excluded blacks entirely, and
the Irene Kaufmann settlement, while providing services to blacks,
severely restricted their use of its facilities. Examples of white ethnic
hostility toward blacks occurred even before such actions by social
agencies. Russpolit field was established, for instance, by Russians,
Poles, and Italians who wished to exclude blacks from their play-
grounds. But certainly such racial attitudes were reinforced by institutional decisions.[19]

The increasing incidence of civil rights violations provides further
evidence of a deteriorating racial situation. Few civil rights cases
reached the Allegheny County courtrooms prior to 1935. This is not
surprising, given the courts' conservative interpretation of the state's
civil rights act of 1887. On September 1, 1935, the state general assembly amended the law, granting to all persons "within the jurisdiction of
the Commonwealth full and equal accommodations, advantages, facilities and privileges of places of public accommodation, resort or
amusement." Hardly a year went by thereafter when several civil
rights cases did not reach the courts. That only one of twenty-seven
cases tried between 1938 and 1949 resulted in findings for the prosecu-
tion no doubt served as a reminder to the city's black residents of their
weak position in the courts as well as in the community.[20]

Reported incidents of violence also increased after the 1930s, attest-
ing to the deteriorating racial atmosphere. Prior to 1927 most accounts of racial hostility reported in the press were isolated incidents
involving a few individuals. Early newspaper accounts revealed frequent clashes among Italians and blacks, but these were almost always
unrelated occurrences.[21] The degree of peaceful interaction that existed
between immigrants and blacks prior to the 1930s has been underestimated. Italians and blacks had integrated since the arrival of Italians
in the 1880s. The Strip, Hill District, Lawrenceville, East Liberty, and
Homewood-Brushton areas all contained substantial numbers of both
groups. Interaction, moreover, went beyond the location of one's home.
Joseph B. recalled a number of black businessmen operating in Lawrenceville. Black neighbors "helped out" the mother of John B. when
she was sick. One black recalled eating in Slavic homes and inviting
white neighbors into his home. John K. always played with black chil-

dren while growing up in Lawrenceville. A black mother recalled white children playing in her home and white friends helping her obtain a loan to build a porch on her home for her invalid husband. Another black female described the 1920s by stating, "We lived in black and white neighborhoods and ate at one another's tables and that is just the situation it was."[22]

By the 1930s, however, black-Italian relationships had deteriorated. The incidence of violence in integrated areas increased markedly. The continuing status of blacks as migrants, while immigrant families became more stable—in a sense, natives—may have increased tensions. More significant, members of the two groups began to undertake action to avoid each other. Delmer Seawright, in a 1932 study of Homewood-Brushton, reported that both blacks and Italians sold homes to avoid residential contact. "As a result," he observed, "certain streets became in the course of a few years, almost solidly Italian or Negro."[23] The East Liberty–Larimer area underwent a similar transition during the 1950s and 1960s.

Increased racial hostility within Pittsburgh naturally limited the choice of neighborhoods open to blacks. Coming at a time of major black in-migrations, existing neighborhoods absorbed thousands of new residents. Their sorely taxed institutions were clearly incapable of meeting the increased demands for services. Many counterparts were unable to wrest any assistance from their neighborhood and moved on. Residential persistence and migration between 1930 and 1960 reflected either the existence or the absence of community in a particular neighborhood (Table 31). It also influenced further community development.

The widely divergent persistence rates and migration patterns illustrated in Table 31 represent a major departure from the blue-collar migration patterns of the late nineteenth and early twentieth centuries. Historians have suggested that sometime early in the twentieth century blue-collar workers became more sedentary; Pittsburgh seems to verify that hypothesis. Less than one-third of any group from the seven 1930 neighborhoods left Pittsburgh during the 1930s. The high persistence of black workers is particularly impressive, since the previous fifteen years were highly volatile as hundreds floated in and out of the city almost daily. The initially high persistence rates, however, appear primarily due to the lack of opportunity elsewhere during the Depression, as black outward migration increased during the 1940s.

Geographic migration is a highly complex process and involves a variety of motivations and competing attractions emanating both from one's current residence and a potential future site. The potential place

Table 31. Residential Persistence as Determined from
a Sample of Second-Generation Poles, Italians, and Blacks
in Seven Neighborhoods of Pittsburgh, 1930-60

	1930-40[1]			1940-50			1950-60		
	Black	Italian	Pole	Black	Italian	Pole	Black	Italian	Pole
Same house	17.7	40.5	35.7	4.5	33.7	28.3	2.2	22.3	20.1
Died and house maintained by family	5.1	9.4	9.4	5.7	24.5	20.3	9.7	27.6	23.6
Same tract	16.2	12.4	16.1	6.3	17.1	17.0	8.6	19.6	13.1
Same ward	16.6	3.3	4.8	13.2	6.1	6.1	6.5	6.3	7.0
Other ethnic neighborhood	7.0	0.4	1.4	11.5	0.6	1.0	17.4	0.8	0.5
Other area in Pittsburgh	6.6	2.9	4.2	10.9	11.0	11.6	11.9	13.3	13.5
Left, died, or otherwise unaccounted for	30.3	31.0	28.3	41.3	6.7	15.4	42.3	9.8	22.1
N	270	274	498	174	163	310	92	112	199

NOTE. All data are percentages and are compiled from the sample of second-generation residents studied for this book. The decades 1940-50 and 1950-60 are adjusted to exclude those who failed to persist from 1930. Thus the data for 1940-50 include all individuals from 1930 still in Pittsburgh in 1940; the data for 1950-60 then present *that* group's persistence to 1960. N = the number of each group and is also only the number persisting. See Table 30 for the names of the seven neighborhoods.

[1]In 1930 7.7 percent of blacks, 37.2 percent of Italians, and 28.1 percent of the Poles owned houses.

of residence must offer enough advantages, real or perceived, to induce one to leave. Pittsburgh, during the Depression years, offered little, particularly in employment terms, to hold its blue-collar population. The possibilities of finding work in other cities, however, most likely appeared equally as grim, and this perception of workers regarding the shortage of employment opportunities in other locations no doubt contributed to their high persistence rates in Pittsburgh during the 1930s.

Community and family ties also induced many to remain in the city. Nearly every individual interviewed for this study spoke of "pulling together" during the Depression. The brother-in-law of one black worker offered him lodging and part-time employment in his print shop when he lost his job in 1935. Two married children of Mrs. Helen C., one of the first black residents in the Italian section of East Liberty, moved in with her temporarily during the Depression. The father of Raymond C., a self-employed Pole, went bankrupt in 1931. Several male members of the family contributed their entire monthly paychecks, earned from part-time jobs, to maintain the family. Familial obligations clearly contributed to Ray's residential stability. "Never gave [moving] a thought because I figured that was my obligation [to assist my parents]—things were tough . . . and I figured that I was old enough to help, I wanted to help. . . . [My parents] had helped me and I was going to return it." John K., a Southside Pole, echoed the experience of Raymond C. Three members of his family including himself dropped out of school to accept part-time work to contribute to the upkeep of the family. "Everybody had to go to work," he asserted. "We didn't make much, but we made something. One thing, we never went on welfare. In them days people were too proud to go on welfare."[24]

Ethnic identity also proved important. An Italian taxicab company dispatcher hired only Bloomfield Italians as drivers during the Depression. At one point the residents of Cedarville Street in Bloomfield held community dinners for all the families on the street, and nearly all those interviewed for this study could recall numerous instances of mutual aid among neighbors.[25]

Many families also opened their homes to boarders to supplement the family income. Boarders in Bloomfield paid between $3 and $5 per month for room, meals, and laundry service.[26] Evidence on the incidence of taking in boarders during the Depression by the various groups does not exist. However, the density of families per structure reached its peak in every one of the seven sample neighborhoods between 1930 and 1940, and density declined each decade thereafter.

Persistence of Poles and Italians within the city increased during each decade after 1930. In fact, since the rate of outward migration in Table 31 includes those who died, it is evident that almost none of the Polish or Italian families from the 1930 neighborhoods left the city after 1940. (It is likely, of course, that individual family members may have left Pittsburgh.) Many had resided in the same neighborhood for twenty, thirty, or more years, and attractions from other locations were not strong enough to induce them to leave Pittsburgh.

Persistence of black families from the 1930 sample declined during the 1940s and again in the 1950s. Weak community ties, occupational difficulties (discussed earlier), and increasing racial antagonism all made opportunities look better elsewhere. Whether those who left met greater success in their new locations cannot be determined. What is clear is that nearly four of every ten blacks left Pittsburgh, including some who had resided in the city for a full decade. Another 40 percent left after two decades. Thus, their rate of leaving, except for the Depression decade, was not unlike that of first-generation Poles or Italians.

Data on intraurban residential mobility reveal the strength of neighborhood associations and home ownership for both second-generation Poles and Italians. Nearly 50 percent of each group—combining household heads and those who inherited and resided in the family dwelling—remained in the same house each decade from 1930 through 1960. Those who did move, moreover, did not go very far. The typical mover went down the street a few houses or around the block. Nearly half of those who moved within the metropolitan area during each decade stayed in the same census-tract neighborhood. The next largest group left the tract but stayed within the ward. The pull of the ethnic neighborhood and the services it provided obviously remained strong. Even the so-called attractions of the suburbs and the threat of a black incursion that supposedly caused many to flee the city in the 1950s failed to lure the second-generation immigrant from his neighborhood. Most remained in the neighborhood, often within the same house, until both spouses had died. Most revealing was that 20 percent of the household heads on Brereton Street (in Polish Hill) in 1960 were widows. Homes in most families subsequently passed on to offspring. In fact, the proportion of household heads remaining in their parents' homes exceeded those moving to the suburbs by nearly 50 percent in each decade.

Most families, of course, contained three, four, or more children in 1930. Several families with several children often lived in each home in the ethnic neighborhood during the decade. Homes were sometimes constructed on the rear of tiny lots to accommodate additional families. Rooms and apartments were added to existing homes, often at odd angles. Densities within the neighborhoods had reached the saturation point. As the children grew and eventually started families of their own, it became obvious that they could not remain within the confines of the ethnic village. A desire for additional living space and shifting values, which placed greater importance on single-family accommodations, contributed to the attractiveness of Pittsburgh's suburban development. It was primarily this third generation, however, not the stable second generation, that participated in the so-called flight to the suburbs. A careful analysis of housing density in the 1930s would have led one to predict a coming population spread. Ethnic villages simply could not absorb many more families. Many third-generation families would be forced to move elsewhere. The available demographic data and the oral interviews suggest that while the outward migration was perhaps inevitable, it was undertaken with mixed feelings and usually to a developing area as close as possible to the urban homestead.[27]

A member of the original 1930 family continued to reside in the family dwelling in 28 percent of the Italian cases and 24 percent of the Polish cases through 1960. On some streets, such as Edmond and Cedarville in Bloomfield and Eleanor and Leticoe on the Southside, 40 percent of the homes were owned by sons and daughters of the original 1930 residents. Interviews indicate that many suburban-dwelling Poles and Italians retained familial and emotional ties with the ethnic community. Ethnic churches, particularly during the holiday seasons, are crowded with former residents. Many of those interviewed continue to shop occasionally in their old neighborhood. The Ateleta Club in Bloomfield and the Southside and Polish Hill Falcons clubs still contain dues-paying members who no longer reside in the neighborhood of their youth.[28]

Second-generation Poles and Italians, like their parents before them, made adjustments and created institutional associations to ease their lives in industrial Pittsburgh. These adjustments and associations, in turn, contributed to their remarkable residential stability. Black residents who remained in Pittsburgh, in contrast, moved more often and with greater regularity than did members of either ethnic group. The Depression years were clearly their most stable, with nearly one-fourth of the families remaining at the same address during the decade. The percentage fell to around 10 percent during the 1940s and 1950s. Most of those moving during the Depression, however, followed the same pattern of short moves established by the Poles and Italians. Nearly one-third remained in the same census tract or in the same ward. This is not too surprising, even in the absence of strong community ties, for several reasons. Black families in Pittsburgh were primarily renters and were often unemployed or underemployed during the Depression. The majority of homes in the Hill District and even in the Homewood-Brushton area rented in the $18 to $25 per month range.[29] Only a few areas in the city provided cheaper housing but these, including Polish Hill and the Southside, were dominated by second-generation immigrants and were apparently not open to blacks. Thus, few alternatives were available to residents of the black neighborhoods. Average rental, in addition, declined during the decade in the two Hill District neighborhoods to $20 per unit, making them economically more attractive to an impoverished population. Most of those few who did leave a particular ward moved within the Hill District neighborhoods.[30]

Movement out of the specified neighborhoods increased as the economic status of black families improved. During the 1940s they moved in all directions throughout the city, with nearly equal proportions moving out of the neighborhood but staying in the same ward, moving to another black neighborhood, or moving to other parts of Pittsburgh. The movement is even more pronounced when we isolate the three neighborhoods. Residents of Homewood-Brushton, one-fifth of whom owned their own homes by 1940, were much more stable. Forty-two percent remained in the neighborhood, and only 2 percent moved from Homewood-Brushton to either of the Hill District neighborhoods. Nearly all of the Hill District residents, conversely, who moved from one black neighborhood to another moved to Homewood-Brushton. The migration of families from the Hill District to Homewood-Brushton was given impetus, no doubt, by health and social conditions in the hill area. A Bureau of Social Research study (Table 32) found the lower Hill first among fifty-three neighborhood areas in incidence of homicide, deaths by pneumonia, and infant mortality. The area recorded the second highest rate of deaths by tuberculosis and other forms of communicable disease.[31]

It seems apparent that the lack of neighborhood identity and community-supplied services as well as overcrowded and deteriorating rental units and health conditions contributed to the lack of residential stability among Pittsburgh's blacks. Intraurban migration, at the same time, robbed the black neighborhoods of the stable core of residents needed to create a strong community. Conditions changed dramatically in all three black locations during the 1950s. One neighborhood (census tract 3C) disappeared, and the other two became almost totally segregated by race.

The events leading to the elimination of the lower Hill District neighborhood—a casuality of the "Pittsburgh renaissance" urban renewal project—have been amply reported by Roy Lubove and need not be detailed here. That 1,551 families were replaced by Edgar Kaufmann's contribution to the renaissance, a retractable domed arena and high-rent apartments, housing 594 families, attests to the lack of political power of the residents of the lower hill. "Glistening in isolated splendor amid expressways and parking lots," Lubove described the arena as "something of a civic incubus ... For the Negro community it has been a highly visible symbol of old-style renewal, indifferent to the housing needs and preferences of low-income families."[32]

The elimination of several census tracts in the lower hill intensified segregation in the Hill District and continued the shift of the city's black population toward the Homewood-Brushton section. By 1960 the remaining sections of the 3rd and 5th ward neighborhoods were more than 90 percent black. The most dramatic change, however, occurred in the East End (Homewood-Brushton), the recipient of most blacks leaving the lower hill. Homewood-Brushton shifted from 23 to

Table 32. Social Characteristics of Seven Neighborhoods of Pittsburgh, 1930-40

Characteristics	All of Pittsburgh (No.)	Lower Hill (No.)	(Rank)	Upper Hill (No.)	(Rank)	Polish Hill (No.)	(Rank)	Bloomfield (No.)	(Rank)	East Liberty (No.)	(Rank)	Homewood-Brushton (No.)	(Rank)	Southside (No.)	(Rank)
Deaths, 1930-39	78,123	4,015	4	3,726	6	770	27	2,084	10	921	40	3,518	35	1,634	41
Birth/death, 1930	23,532	-627	50	523	37	606	6	-24	15	697	15	1,953	2	1,554	3
Divorce, 1930	4,374	155	13	158	17	16	51	102	18	34	44	201	22	27	52
Families receiving aid, 1935	50,419	4,667	1	4,142	4	516	24	813	35	232	31	1,079	21	969	30
Old-age assistance, 1935	2,772	98	21	128	13	20	40	54	30	47	17	167	18	39	47
Aid to dependent children, 1935	950	43	10	64	1	16	5	15	40	12	30	60	16	33	13
Works Progress Administration projects, 1940	10,902	1,085	2	743	7	90	23	164	31	131	22	352	29	207	28
Child welfare, 1938	6,017	408	5	489	4	90	10	99	25	76	23	231	24	111	27

	Total														
		No.	Rank	No.	Rank	No.	Rank	No.	Rank	No.	Rank	No.	Rank	No.	Rank
Housing															
Less than 5 years, persistence	73,585	3,046	1	3,720	3	769	25	1,346	30	816	41	3,711	19	1,195	53
Lack income earner, 1934	33,167	2,165	1	1,764	8	535	6	855	11	407	26	1,717	21	690	30
Overcrowded, 1934[1]	38,233	1,648	18	1,980	13	884	9	622	33	492	26	1,580	30	1,802	3
Not in school (age 5-19), 1940	31,934	995	25	1,071	38	478	7	524	49	548	51	1,639	34	1,185	8
Death, 1930-39															
Murder	461	84	1	44	4	4	22	6	29	8	13	27	14	5	40
Suicide	799	30	17	23	34	5	48	12	43	8	40	34	35	14	42
By disease, general[2]	3,456	235	2	206	5	35	23	71	25	219	21	151	32	90	20
By tuberculosis	4,373	501	2	414	4	46	16	73	25	47	26	200	20	72	29
By pneumonia	9,740	781	1	578	35	102	15	201	17	109	29	382	34	152	44
Of Infants	5,597	287	1	273	11	106	6	92	42	75	39	290	27	189	17
Persons per acre	25.0	96.4		43.6		32.7		N.A.		8.3		35.3		18.6	

NOTE. These data are compiled from the National Youth Administration, *Social Facts*, Bureau of Social Research, Federation of Social Agencies of Pittsburgh and Allegheny County, Pennsylvania, vols. I, II, III, V (1941). The city was divided into fifty-three study units; the rank is the placement among these fifty-three units. N.A. = not available.

[1]Overcrowding is defined as units with more than one person per room.

[2]The category, "Disease, general" excludes the three subentries: by tuberculosis, by pneumonia, and of infants.

71 percent black in a single decade. The growth of the black population in the East End was not confined to the former black neighborhood (census tract 13C) but expanded to include nine contiguous
tracts in the 12th and 13th wards. Blacks became a majority in each
of these tracts. The white population in this area declined by 51 percent during the decade, as whites abandoned the area almost as fast as
blacks entered. Italians from both the Homewood-Brushton area and
from East Liberty moved just across the city lines into the contiguous
township of Penn Hills.

Scattergrams developed by another researcher substantiate these
findings. Between 1930 and 1960, but particularly between 1950 and
1960, black residents gathered increasingly in tracts that already contained substantial black populations.[33] Thus, while some blacks continued to reside in all of the city's tracts, the level of segregation increased markedly. The number of tracts more than 50 percent black
rose from six in 1930 to twenty-three in 1960. The decline in white
population in these same areas coupled with a corresponding influx
of blacks account for Pittsburgh's move from the twelfth most segregated northeastern city in 1940 and 1950 to sixth place in 1960.[34]

Three of the seven neighborhoods analyzed in this study underwent dramatic changes between 1950 and 1960. The lower hill, of
course, disappeared. The East Liberty–Larimer area changed from
an Italian to an integrated neighborhood and Homewood-Brushton became heavily black. Neighborhood change, however, was not limited
to racial distribution or to these three communities. All seven areas
changed between 1930 and 1960. Neighborhood profiles (Table 33)
demonstrate these transformations.

The available demographic data, when combined with oral interviews and on-site field investigations, reveal the complexities of community change. They also suggest that Pittsburgh's black and ethnic
communities moved in different directions between 1930 and 1960.

Young people dominated all seven neighborhoods during the 1930s
and 1940s. Typically young families between thirty and forty years
of age, with small children, lived in each community. By 1940,
second-generation Poles and Italians almost totally replaced their
foreign-born parents in the ethnic communities. While a few immigrants of retirement age remained, usually living with a son or daughter, their numbers were small. Large educational structures, containing ten, twelve, or more classrooms, illustrated the numerical importance of children in all four ethnic neighborhoods. The proliferation
of family church outings and youth socials provide further evidence of
the young age and family orientation of community members. Only

the age of the buildings—90 percent in all four neighborhoods were built before 1910—contrasted sharply to the youthful appearance of the Polish Hill, East Liberty, Southside, and Bloomfield communities in 1940.[35]

Structures in the three black neighborhoods were somewhat younger —most were built between 1900 and 1920—but those in the Hill District had seen much wear and at least one-third, according to two separate surveys, needed substantial repairs.[36] Like the ethnic communities, the age or the condition of the residential structures in the black neighbor-

Table 33. Profiles of Seven Neighborhoods of Pittsburgh: 1940, 1950, and 1960

Profile Characteristics	Lower Hill	Upper Hill	Homewood-Brushton	Polish Hill	South-side	Bloom-field	East Liberty
			1940				
% of population							
Black, Polish, Italian	70.7	90.0	17.2	71.4[1]	77.4[1]	62.5[1]	62.3[1]
Persons per household							
(city average, 3.38)	2.50	4.16	3.21	3.48	3.85	3.81	3.92
Age distribution (%)							
60 +	05.6	06.6	06.9	06.8	07.6	08.2	07.4
40-59	32.6	23.9	23.5	18.6	19.8	21.1	20.6
20-39	37.0	34.3	32.5	37.8	32.8	34.0	34.7
Under 20	24.7	35.6	37.1	36.7	39.7	36.6	37.3
Occupational distribution							
High white collar	01.7	03.6	05.1	01.1	01.2	01.4	00.6
Low white collar	08.9	10.6	14.3	08.1	05.8	06.6	12.1
Skilled	03.4	10.2	13.9	12.9	06.4	15.7	22.9
Semiskilled	32.9	33.6	37.6	05.1	06.4	03.3	12.9
Unskilled	09.6	17.9	10.3	58.1	69.6	62.3	37.9
Unemployed	43.2	23.8	18.6	14.6	10.5	10.7	13.6
Marital status							
Married	NA	NA	NA	75.3	78.4	83.5	76.5
Single	NA	NA	NA	11.1	09.9	05.8	08.8
Other	NA	NA	NA	13.7	10.5	10.7	14.7
Housing							
Homeowner	02.9	09.7	12.5	23.6	46.9	46.3	44.3
Renter	97.1	90.3	87.5	75.6	52.9	53.7	55.3
Average rent per month (city average, $29.21)	18.78	23.83	27.44	11.65	15.22	20.11	23.48

[1]Includes first- and second-generation ethnics.

Profile Characteristics	Lower Hill	Upper Hill	Homewood-Brushton	Polish Hill	South-side	Bloom-field	East Liberty
			1950				
% of population							
Black, Polish, Italian	84.3	96.6	23.2	60.7	62.7	62.9	59.4
Persons per household							
(city average, 3.1)	2.6	3.4	3.2	3.1	3.0	3.4	3.5
Age distribution (%)							
60 +	09.5	18.0	29.3	09.6	09.7	12.7	10.6
40-59	31.4	23.9	43.2	21.2	20.9	22.8	24.3
20-39	30.2	24.0	17.7	37.0	35.9	32.7	31.8
Under 20	27.6	33.9	18.6	32.0	33.7	31.7	33.0
Occupational Distribution							
High white collar	01.2	00.8	03.3	00.5	00.7	0	00.8
Low white collar	03.6	08.7	08.2	09.3	06.5	07.6	16.1
Skilled	03.2	04.8	07.3	17.6	13.0	12.7	30.6
Semiskilled	42.4	59.1	49.6	11.0	07.9	09.3	10.5
Unskilled	26.2	18.4	19.8	44.0	54.0	50.8	25.0
Unemployed	23.1	07.9	11.5	17.6	18.0	19.5	16.9
Marital status							
Married	55.7	72.1	63.5	80.2	74.8	75.6	80.6
Single	26.7	16.4	23.5	05.1	08.6	06.7	03.2
Other	17.5	11.4	13.0	14.7	16.5	16.8	16.1
Housing							
Homeowner	04.6	12.2	38.4	34.4	61.9	50.8	55.6
Renter	95.4	87.8	61.6	65.1	37.4	48.3	44.4
Average rent per month (city average, $35.83)	26.76	35.14	35.28	14.99	NA	25.11	30.42
			1960				
% of population							
Black, Polish, Italian	. . .	97.9	70.6	56.0	64.0	59.1	56.1
Persons per household							
(city average, 2.7)	. . .	3.8	3.0	2.9	3.0	3.2	3.0
Age distribution (%)							
60 +	. . .	14.1	08.6	14.0	12.6	15.7	16.6
40-59	. . .	30.9	20.1	27.0	23.5	24.2	23.5
20-39	. . .	26.6	29.3	24.9	25.0	24.2	26.0
Under 20	. . .	28.3	41.8	33.8	38.7	35.5	33.7
Occupational distribution							
High white collar	. . .	10.2	03.9	01.0	00.8	00.7	. . .
Low white collar	. . .	14.6	09.6	06.3	11.6	11.5	21.5

Profile Characteristics	Lower Hill	Upper Hill	Homewood-Brushton	Polish Hill	South-side	Bloom-field	East Liberty
Skilled	...	06.9	08.8	20.3	12.4	15.8	24.7
Semiskilled	...	50.1	55.8	09.7	09.1	10.1	10.8
Unskilled	...	08.1	11.4	31.9	37.2	32.4	23.7
Unemployed	...	09.7	10.1	07.8	07.4	06.4	06.3
Retired	...	NA	NA	23.1	21.5	23.2	13.1
Marital status							
Married	...	60.4	62.7	78.2	73.6	73.7	84.9
Single	...	19.3	20.0	02.4	07.4	06.6	02.2
Other	...	20.2	17.1	19.4	19.0	19.7	12.9
Housing							
Homeowner	...	10.7	35.0	58.3	61.0	60.9	74.2
Renter	...	89.3	65.0	41.7	39.0	39.0	25.8
Average rent per month (city average, $57.00)	...	54.00	77.00	30.00	40.00	45.00	54.00

NOTE. The black neighborhoods were the lower and upper Hill District; the Polish areas were Polish Hill and Southside; the Italian sections were Bloomfield and East Liberty. Lower hill, however, no longer existed as a residential area in 1960. Except for occupations, the data on black neighborhoods are from the U.S. census tract statistics for Pittsburgh and the U.S. census characeristics for housing, 1940, 1950, and 1960. The data on occupations come from tract statistics and the data generated for the second-generation sample. Data on the Polish and Italian neighborhoods, except for age distribution and ownership status, are from the data generated for the second-generation sample. Data on age distribution and ownership status come from the U.S. census tract and block statistics cited previously. NA = not available.

hood provided little indication of the ages of residents within them. Most were also young. Between one-fourth and one-third were under twenty, and another third were between twenty and thirty-nine years of age. A greater proportion of the adult population, particularly in the lower hill, were single men, reflecting that area's role as the recipient of recent migrants to the city. This fact no doubt contributed to the instability of the area and to its reputation as a center of vice and crime in Pittsburgh.

Occupational distributions within each neighborhood followed the patterns established by each group at least a generation earlier. Blacks continued to labor at semiskilled service occupations and domestic work. Very few managed to attain skilled work, although a considerable number performed skilled tasks during World War I and again during the 1919 steel strike.[37] Whatever occupational gains black workers made during these periods, they apparently lost by 1940. Others lost their jobs. Northern blacks suffered particularly severe job losses during the Depression, and those settling in Pittsburgh were worse off than most. Forty-three percent of the lower hill blacks and

23 percent from the upper hill had no jobs as late as 1940. The areas ranked first and fourth among fifty-three neighborhoods in families receiving public assistance in 1935.[38] Homewood-Brushton blacks, always more affluent than those residing in the inner city, reported 19 percent unemployment—a full four points higher than unemployment in any ethnic area.

Neither the Polish nor Italian neighborhoods had escaped the Depression, but unemployment had dropped substantially by 1940 and was lower than the citywide average in both Bloomfield and the Southside. Young workers in Polish Hill like their parents before them worked at one of the metal plants near the 6th ward; those on the Southside performed unskilled tasks at the Jones and Laughlin or U.S. Steel works. Some workers, of course, held better jobs, but few held high white-collar or professional occupations in either community. The typical resident of either Polish Hill or the Southside neighborhood, in addition to being young, also held a blue-collar job in a local mill or factory.

Blue-collar work, frequently in construction, also characterized the Bloomfield and East Liberty Italian districts, although some differences did exist. Bloomfield residents worked as laborers for the Equitable Gas Company, the Pennsylvania Railroad, or the City of Pittsburgh. Nearly two-thirds were unskilled. The small Bloomfield commercial district afforded a few opportunities for ventures into private businesses, and the community supported some small entrepreneurs. Nearly 16 percent, in addition, inherited the skilled occupations of their parents. Italians in East Liberty were somewhat more affluent than their counterparts from Bloomfield. A greater proportion held skilled jobs, and more than twice as many wore white collars to work. Most of these owned small businesses in the area's Italian business district.

All three groups reported aspiring to own their own homes, and the second-generation Poles and particularly the Italians succeeded by 1940. Nearly 50 percent owned their own homes in the Italian sections of Bloomfield and East Liberty. Blacks, in contrast, were almost exclusively renters. Even in the more affluent Homewood-Brushton less than 15 percent owned their own homes.

Length of tenure in the community, level of affluence, and job and residential stability within the community all contribute to an ability to own a home. Second-generation Poles and Italians had achieved a measure of occupational success and stability to make homeownership possible. They also felt a community attachment derived from familial ties, community services, and perhaps from the prior long-term residence to make homeownership desirable. Neighborhood lending institutions also willingly supplied mortgage funds, which made ownership possible. Blacks, conversely, had neither access to occupational success nor long-term residence. Thus, their low rate of homeownership is not surprising.

During the next two decades (1940-60) the Polish and Italian communities became less segregated, although three (Polish Hill, Southside, and Bloomfield) retained strong ethnic identities. All four became older, both in terms of residents and residential structures. Few young residents moved in to replace young couples who left or those growing older, and housing construction had almost ceased in three areas by 1920. Only East Liberty experienced any new housing after 1940. Populations declined in all four areas as expected. None of the areas was capable of absorbing new residents; thus, as children grew and started families of their own, they were forced to seek housing elsewhere. By 1960 one-fifth of the populations of Polish Hill, Bloomfield, and Southside had retired from work. One field observer noted the absence of bicycles and other children's artifacts during an on-site inspection. Catholic school populations declined, and buildings were in need of rehabilitation by 1960. Declining populations also offered a greater amount of living space per resident. Finally, the residents of all four areas became more affluent as a result of occupational improvement for some or simply steady work and rising wages for others. Homeownership became common, and, while the structures had aged, less than 10 percent in each area required major repairs.[39] In short Bloomfield, Polish Hill, and the Southside neighborhoods all remained blue-collar, ethnic neighborhoods.

East Liberty, an area in transition, had already lost a substantial portion of its Italian population and would lose considerably more in the next decade. The proportion of black residents in tract 12D increased from 13.7 percent in 1950 to 54 percent in 1960. The specific Larimer Avenue area selected for this study continued to house primarily Italians, but this changed dramatically by 1970.

If conditions, measured by the above characteristics—affluence, living space, job security—generally improved in at least three ethnic neighborhoods, they deteriorated in the black communities. The lower hill was liquidated, but it had experienced a steady decline since immigrants first arrived in the area in large numbers in the 1890s. By 1950 two-thirds of the homes investigated by the U.S. Bureau of the Census were reported as dilapidated. Unemployment continued to plague the area and less than 5 percent of the residents owned their own homes. Contemporary accounts suggest that the lower hill continued its historic role as an area of first settlement by absorbing most of the blacks who migrated to Pittsburgh in the 1940s. Thousands of blacks also left the area, and the white population almost totally abandoned the lower hill by 1950.

The upper hill neighborhood and the Homewood-Brushton areas were more fortunate, but they too experienced difficult times. Both areas grew slightly older in terms of population, but the upper hill lost population while Homewood-Brushton (and other East End areas) experienced a major in-migration. This shift in the black population marked the decline of the Hill District's importance as the major area of black concentration: in 1960, for the first time in the city's history, less than half of Pittsburgh's blacks (36 percent) resided there.

Most of the private housing in the upper hill neighborhood selected for this study was demolished in 1950 and replaced by federally sponsored, low-income housing—the Bedford Apartments. By 1960 these two- and three-bedroom apartments housed 221 families. The population, compared with the 1940 upper hill group, aged somewhat but continued to labor at semiskilled service-style occupations, and unemployment remained a serious problem. Except for housing conditions, which rapidly deteriorated, the residents of the upper hill were much like those who lived there in 1940.

Homewood-Brushton, in contrast, underwent dramatic changes. The number, the density, and the proportion of blacks all soared in a single decade. Residents came both from other Pittsburgh neighborhoods and from other cities. The total black population in tract 13C increased by 167 percent between 1950 and 1960. The white population fell by 66 percent during the same period. Schools changed from predominantly white to predominantly black, and several new black churches were erected. As in the Hill District earlier, the incoming black residents inherited a variety of community problems. A 1953 Action-Housing report noted that "Homewood-Brushton entered the 1950s with all the usual problems of an aging city neighborhood. . . . spot overcrowding, rising crime rate, heavy traffic on residential streets, a shortage of recreational facilities, empty stores, most housing in need of modernization, inadequate local governmental services and low morale."[40] Local agencies and volunteer organizations such as the Homewood Community Improvement Association attempted to correct the most glaring problems and to solicit financial and technical help from city's social agencies. The community profiles suggest that, in spite of these problems, the early black residents of Homewood-Brushton were making important gains toward neighborhood stability. An increase in homeownership from 12 percent in 1940 to 38 percent in 1950, a mild increase in the occupational level of the residents, and the development of several neighborhood associations provided stabilizing elements in the community. The massive in-migration of new blacks, triggered by the lower hill redevelopment, and the exodus of long-term white residents thus occurred at a most inopportune time. Once again blacks were faced with the prospect of building a community in a neighborhood abandoned by others as undesirable. Many of the Hill District experiences of the 1930s and 1940s would be repeated during the 1960s and 1970s.

A number of factors—historic, economic, and social—contributed to the divergent patterns of Pittsburgh's ethnic and racial neighborhoods during the second third of the twentieth century. The variations in values and traditions help explain some of the differences in neighborhood development. External forces, however, influenced the range of choices.

The topography of the city of Pittsburgh made possible the survival of ethnic enclaves. Polish Hill, Bloomfield, and the Southside all presented formidable barriers—natural or manufactured—to encroachment from the outside. Other ethnic or racial neighborhoods did not merge with these communities but remained separated by highways, hills, or railroads. The East Liberty–Larimer area, in contrast, lacked natural barriers and eventually lost its ethnic identity as black migrants "spilled over" from Homewood-Brushton in the 1950s. The Hill District's only geographic barrier, Grant's Hill, which separated the area from the central business district, was removed in 1911. Within the hill itself no natural divisions existed; thus, until the 1940s the area contained small racial or ethnic clusters but remained highy integrated. Homewood-Brushton, a relatively flat area with weak boundaries, contained clusters of Italians, blacks, Jews, and native-born Americans. As the area became a primary recipient of migrants throughout the 1930-60 period, its lack of geographic divisions prevented one group from isolating itself from another.

Geographic barriers, of course, do not make racial or ethnic segregation inevitable; they merely make it easier. The services provided by some communities made neighborhood retention desirable to the inhabitants. Bloomfield, Polish Hill, and Southside residents, for example, acted consciously to preserve the community by persisting within it even when they moved from house to house. Children who inherited the homes, moreover, frequently inhabited rather than sold the structures. Whether they also acted consciously to exclude outsiders is not clear, but the Polish areas contained neither blacks nor Italians, and Bloomfield housed no Poles nor blacks.

Housing and employment conditions, however, exercised a stronger influence on neighborhood stability and change than either ethnic institutions or the city's topography. Blacks inherited, in every neighborhood they inhabited, old, usually inferior housing from prior residents. Many homes lacked sanitation, and most needed substantial repairs. These conditions clearly induced blacks to seek better housing. That almost all rented rather than owned increased their transiency. While blacks expressed a strong desire to own their own homes, limited and sporadic incomes and an inability to secure mortgage funds reduced the available alternatives, and second and third homes were often no better than the first. Most blacks interviewed revealed a pattern of six, seven, or more residences in their adult lifetimes.

Unstable occupational situations often contributed to the residential instability. Jobs for blacks were frequently short in duration. Less than 10 percent of the 1930 sample blacks who could be traced held the same job during any ten-year period between 1930 and 1960. Chronic black unemployment accompanied a tenuous work condition, while Poles and Italians clung tenaciously to available blue-collar employment. Blacks who had moved from as far as Florida in search of work moved willingly across the city or to another city to secure the elusive position that held the promise of decent wages and human dignity. Whether their decisions were related to housing or work, most blacks were constantly on the move. The turbulence within the black neighborhood resulted in part from this transiency.

Second-generation Italians and Poles also faced difficult housing and employment conditions. Crowding, a shortage of social services, and difficult work at low wages were common to all three groups. The children of immigrants, however, inherited homes or at least neighborhoods inhabited by their parents. Buildings were old but structurally sound and inexpensive and could be made comfortable. This relative level of comfort led to greater neighborhood persistence and a more stable neighborhood, which, in turn, contributed to the inhabitants' ability to create a community and provide needed services. The latter, as so many interviewees revealed, enhanced the desire to remain in the community.

Occupational security also played an important role. Poles and Italians seldom changed employment locations, and thus they were not required to relocate to be near a new job. The ability of both groups to pass jobs along to their children also meant that second- and even third-generation Poles and Italians would find their childhood neighborhood as convenient as did their parents. Steady work and rising wages, combined with cooperative family efforts, enabled both groups to purchase homes in the neighborhood, increasing the likelihood that they would stay.

Finally, as the out-migration of Italians and the in-migration of blacks in the East Liberty area amply demonstrate, race relations remained important. Where ethnic groups, via geography or other means, could protect their own neighborhoods, they did so. When they could not, they abandoned the area. This phenomenon has occurred in most northeastern cities since World War II. Only the relatively small proportion of blacks in Pittsburgh prevented its impact from being felt more strongly. Pittsburgh contained the smallest proportion of blacks in 1960 among the ten northeastern cities whose black populations exceeded 100,000. The East Liberty, Homewood-Brushton, and earlier Hill District areas all suggest that ethnic communities in Pittsburgh continue to thrive in part because they never faced the population pressure from in-coming blacks common to Cleveland, Chicago, Detroit, and Philadelphia. Blacks, Poles, and Italians resided in separate communities in Pittsburgh, but their life experiences influenced each other.

NOTES

1. We originally intended to examine the adjustment patterns of two successive generations of Poles, blacks, and Italians in Pittsburgh between 1900 and 1960. The original 1900 sample, therefore, contained both adults and their children. The geographic instability of all three migrant groups, however, prevented any valid analysis beyond 1930. In some cases, traces beyond 1920 (1905 for the Austrian Poles) proved futile. Obviously, true second-generation studies could not be attempted from the original population sample. The U.S. aggregate census provided some useful clues to the occupational distribution of various groups over time but presented problems. The census provides a snapshot of a particular group at a particular time. For example, it enabled us to determine whether the group, as a group, had improved its occupational standing, but it told nothing about individuals within the group. Newcomers and persisters were treated alike. Ward- and tract-level data permitted us to analyze a particular section of a city in greater detail, but they, too, suffered from weaknesses. Again, newcomers and persisters were treated alike. One may, for example, determine that the relative wealth of a neighborhood is improving but not be able to determine whether the new wealth results from upward mobility or from the recent influx of affluent residents. Moreover, ward- and tract-level data often conceal important differences within these political subdivisions. Census tract divisions in Pittsburgh suffer less in this regard than most other cities, since "the wards were subdivided into census tracts by boundaries drawn along natural barriers or geographic divisions. Hillsides, ravines, business streets and other factors tending to separate one district from another were recognized wherever it was reasonably possible to do so." (U.S. Bureau of the Census, *Census Tract Tables of Population and Families: 1930* [Washington, D.C.,

1932], 2: 1.) Even when substantial barriers separate tracts, however, the data blur important distinctions within the tract. Most obvious a highly integrated tract may contain pockets of intense segregation.

2. Two other considerations also entered into the choice to include three black neighborhoods in the study. Blacks in tract 13C were somewhat more affluent and were more often second-generation residents than those in the Hill District. Omitting them would likely result in a biased picture of the patterns of blacks in Pittsburgh. In addition, we knew that tract 3C in the lower hill would disappear in the 1950s as a result of an urban redevelopment program and that many of the 3C residents migrated to 13C. Including both neighborhoods also permitted an examination of the effects of that migration on neighborhood development.

3. See, among others, Caroline Golab, *Immigrant Destinations* (Philadelphia, 1977); Kenneth Kusmer, *A Ghetto Takes Shape: Black Cleveland, 1870-1930* (Urbana, Ill., 1976); Edward Kantowicz, *Polish-American Politics in Chicago, 1888-1940* (Chicago, 1975); Thomas Kessner, *The Golden Door: Italian and Jewish Immigrant Mobility in New York City, 1880-1915* (New York, 1977); and Stanley Lieberson, *Ethnic Patterns in American Cities* (New York, 1963).

4. A. G. Moran and F. F. Stephan, "The Negro Population and Negro Families in Pittsburgh and Allegheny County," *Social Research Bulletin*, 1 (Apr. 20, 1933), 4.

5. R. L. Hill, "A View of the Hill: A Study of Experiences and Attitudes in the Hill District of Pittsburgh, Pennsylvania, 1900-1973" (Ph.D. diss., University of Pittsburgh, 1973), 238-41 (interview with Frank K.).

6. Interview with Mrs. K. by Donald Fastuca, Nov. 9, 1978. Transcript of interview is held by M. W.

7. A. L. Harris, "The New Negro Worker in Pittsburgh" (M.A. thesis, University of Pittsburgh, 1924), 17.

8. *Plat Book of Pittsburgh, Pa.* (Philadelphia, 1906).

9. The data were compiled from U.S. Census tracts for Pittsburgh, 1930, city directories, and oral interviews.

10. Several Italian interviewees recalled the presence of unrelated boarders in their homes at some time during the Depression. They insisted, however, that the incidence was only temporary, made necessary by difficult economic conditions.

11. Ella Burns Myers, "Some Italian Groups in Pittsburgh" (M.A. thesis, Carnegie Institute of Technology, 1920), 41.

12. Interviews with Stanley N., Sept. 22, 1976; Stephanie W., Mar. 24, 1976; Edward R., Sept. 10, 1976; John K., Sept. 13, 1976; Stanley E., Sept. 9, 1976, Pittsburgh Oral History Project (POHP); American Service Institute 1, "Testimony Given to Senate Sub-Committee on Housing," Dec. 13, 1957, 16-17.

13. Abraham Epstein, *The Negro Migrant in Pittsburgh* (Pittsburgh, 1918), 19.

14. Corrine Azen Krause, *Grandmothers, Mothers and Daughters: An Oral History of Ethnicity, Mental Health, and Continuity of Three Generations of Jewish, Italian and Slavic-American Women* (Pittsburgh, 1978), 83, 86.

15. Ira Reid, *Social Conditions of the Negro in the Hill District of Pittsburgh* (Pittsburgh, 1930), 57. Of 134 female workers surveyed by Reid in 1930, 62 percent performed general house work, 12 percent were maids, and 7 percent worked in laundries. A detailed survey of black women workers conducted by the National Urban League between July and August 1927 reported that black women were increasingly becoming targets of discrimination by Pittsburgh employers.

16. Hill, "A View of the Hill," 19.

17. "Negroes in Labor Unions in Pittsburgh, 1940," typewritten report of a survey conducted by the Pittsburgh Urban League, 1940, located through the offices of the Pittsburgh branch of the National Urban League. Unions with black members included journeyman barbers, typographers union, the Amalgamated Association of Iron, Steel, and Tin Workers, and two carpenters' locals.

18. See various issues of *Pittsburgh Press* and *Pittsburgh Post Gazette*, summer and fall of 1969. The struggle by the Black Construction Coalition for admittance into the city's construction unions continued for nearly six months. Street demonstrations and several mild confrontations eventually led to a compromise settlement.

19. Philip Klein, *A Social Study of Pittsburgh: Community Problems and Social Services of Allegheny County* (New York, 1937), 282; "Report of the Interracial Program at Brashear Association (May 1945)" and "Report of the Hoyt House Project, 1947," in American Service Institute Papers, file cabinet 1, Archives of Industrial Society, University of Pittsburgh.

20. Martha E. Foy, "The Negro in the Courts: A Case Study in Race Relations" (M.A. thesis, University of Pittsburgh, 1953), 88. Most cases brought to a hearing were settled before reaching the courts.

21. The black community protested vehemently the press characterization of disturbances after 1927 as race riots. See, for example, *Pittsburgh Post*, "Police with Riot Guns Patrol Hill after Race Clash," July 16, 1927; *Pittsburgh Post Gazette*, "Riots Broken Up in McKees Rocks," Aug. 27, 1932. The Pittsburgh Urban League investigated each incident and concluded that neither constituted a race riot. "The police," the league noted in the first incident, "did not have riot guns, and to their minds it was merely a 'kids' scrap.'" The incidence of such disturbances, as recorded by the league, continued to increase throughout the next decade. See letters and clipping files of the Pittsburgh branch of the National Urban League, in the basement of the league offices, Pittsburgh.

22. Interviews with Joseph B., May 13, 1976; John B., Mar. 3, 1976; John K., Sept. 13, 1976; Sadie A. Aug. 1, 1974; Jane D., Feb. 17, 1973; Viola J., Feb. 11, 1973, POHP.

23. Delmer C. Seawright, "The Effect of City Growth on the Homewood-Brushton District" (M.A. thesis, University of Pittsburgh, 1932).

24. Interview with Hezekiah M., Oct. 8, 1976; Raymond C., July 1, 1976; John K., Sept. 13, 1976, POHP; interview with Mrs. Helen C., July 26, 1978, by Beverly Thurston. Transcript of Helen C. interview is held by M.W.

25. Interview with Guy C., Dec. 13, 1978, by Noelle Calabro. Transcript

of interview is held by M.W.

26. Ibid.
27. Interviews with Stanley N., Sept. 22, 1976; Stephanie W., Mar. 24, 1976; John K., Sept. 13, 1976, POHP.
28. Interview with Dan C., July 11, 1979, POHP.
29. U.S. Bureau of the Census, Census tract data for Pittsburgh, "Median Equivalent Monthly Rental: 1930," Table 10.
30. U.S. Bureau of the Census, "Pittsburgh, Pa., by Census Tracts and Blocks, 1940," Characteristics of Housing for Census Tracts by Blocks, 1940, 9, 10, 13.
31. National Youth Administration, *Social Facts*, Bureau of Social Research, Federation of Social Agencies of Pittsburgh and Allegheny County (Pittsburgh, 1941). These data cover the entire 1930-39 period.
32. Roy Lubove, *Twentieth-Century Pittsburgh: Government, Business, and Environmental Change* (New York, 1969), 130.
33. Jacqueline Wolfe, "The Changing Pattern of Residence of the Negro in Pittsburgh" (M.A. thesis, University of Pittsburgh, 1964), 57-59.
34. Karl E. and Alma Taeuber, *Negroes in Cities: Residential Segregation and Neighborhood Change* (New York, 1972), 39.
35. U.S. Bureau of the Census. *Block statistics, Pittsburgh, Pa.* (Washington, D.C., 1940).
36. Reid, *Social Conditions of the Negro*, 32; Wiley A. Hall, "Negro Housing and Rents in the Hill District of Pittsburgh" (M.A. thesis, University of Pittsburgh, 1929).
37. Ira Reid, "The Negro in Major Industries and Building Trades of Pittsburgh" (M.A. thesis, University of Pittsburgh, 1925), 11-12.
38. National Youth Administration, *Social Facts*.
39. Reid, "The Negro in Major Industries."
40. Action Housing Inc., *First Annual Report of Homewood-Brushton Self-Help Renewal Program* (Pittsburgh, 1962), 8.

9

Occupation and Ownership

The neighborhood profiles presented in chapter 8 demonstrate the extent of change in several ethnic areas over time. Polish Hill, Bloomfield, and the Southside experienced improved occupational status as neighborhoods, although all three remained blue-collar communities. Occupational distribution in the black communities, on the other hand, remained relatively static, clustered mainly in the unskilled and semiskilled positions. Unemployment also became a chronic problem in the black community.

Neighborhood profiles reveal little about the occupational patterns of individual workers or of the generation that toiled in the city from 1930 through 1960. Black, Polish, and Italian workers who came to Pittsburgh around 1900 arrived under relatively similar circumstances. The second generation, however, began their working careers under far different conditions. Poles and Italians, usually aided by relatives or neighbors, secured jobs in the, by now, traditional industries—Poles in the metal trades; Italians in metal, construction, or other skilled trades or in petty proprietorships. Most often they joined co-ethnics, if not friends and relatives, on the job. The shop was frequently an extension of the ethnic community. Thus, the second-generation Poles and Italians built upon the occupational and residential base established by their parents. The patterns developed earlier continued to provide support from which to launch a career and an adult life of one's own. The strength of these patterns guaranteed that the experiences of the second generation would not differ markedly from that of their parents.

The continuity in both work and residence of two generations of Poles and Italians contrasted sharply with the volatile patterns exhibited by the city's migrant blacks. Black workers during the 1915-25 period, for example, made important, but temporary, inroads into industrial work in Pittsburgh. The decline of European migration coupled with increased labor demands brought on by World War I opened the doors of Pittsburgh's mills to incoming blacks. The number of black workers employed by twenty-seven major industrial firms increased by 140 percent between 1915 and 1918; seventeen of the firms had never employed blacks prior to 1916.[1]

The steel strike of 1919 presented another opportunity to blacks seeking industrial jobs, although their role as strikebreakers has been highly overestimated. Blacks, systematically excluded from all but a few labor unions, had little sympathy for striking industrial workers. Industry leaders, as one noted, looked upon the black worker as a way of "mixing up the labor force to establish a balance of power...as the Negro is more individualistic, does not like to group, and does not follow a leader as readily as some foreigners do."[2] Few black workers joined the strikers during the 1919 disruption, and many were moved from plant to plant to maintain operations. It is not clear, however, how many black workers found employment in the mills during the strike. That the number of industrially employed blacks increased only slightly between the end of the war and 1920 suggests that strikebreaking played a limited role in the job procurement process of incoming blacks.[3]

The further increase of blacks in industry, following the recession of 1920-21, underscores the conclusion that labor shortages rather than strike activities played a more important role in creating industrial opportunities for blacks. By August 1923, 17,224 blacks held jobs in twenty-seven Pittsburgh industries. Most, as one might expect, held unskilled or semiskilled jobs, yet nearly 10 percent managed to secure work as moulders, millwrights, and blowers, and eighteen of twenty-three firms had black foremen.[4] Unfortunately for them, black successes were short-lived. The Pittsburgh economy returned to more normal conditions following a brief boom in 1923, and black industrial workers felt the normalization most severely. Industrial employment among blacks fell by 55 percent in 1924. During the next six years, the number and proportion of blacks in industrial jobs rose and fell almost annually. The totals, however, never approached the high point achieved in 1923. By 1930 less than 5,000 black workers held jobs in the city's iron and steel industries and better than 90 percent were unskilled.[5] Whatever gains they achieved during the war and the period of labor strife that followed were almost totally erased.

Some scholars have attempted to explain the occupational instability of black migrants after 1930 by referring to the recency of their arrival from agricultural origins and to their unfamiliarity with industrial labor. The diversity of the Pittsburgh group suggests more complex reasons. A substantial number of blacks—perhaps as many as 50 percent—did come to Pittsburgh with limited industrial experience, but oral evidence suggests that other blacks arriving after 1930, like their predecessors, had encountered various forms of nonagricultural wage labor before reaching the city.[6] The data and interviews also suggest that the overt discrimination that influenced job acquisition before the Depression continued to frustrate black careers. Blacks, usually the last hired, were indeed the first fired. Their exclusion from labor unions denied them the limited protection provided by these organizations. Discrimination on the part of employers at the same time increased the precarious nature of their jobs. Several Pittsburgh firms declared, in response to a survey conducted by the Pittsburgh Urban League, that they had tried black workers but found them incapable of performing the required work. One employer explained that he refused to hire blacks because they "will not stick on the job."[7] The employment manager of the one steel plant seeking workers in 1923 wrote to a labor agent, "Don't send me any more niggers, I am sick and tired of them."[8] Another firm, the Central Tube Company, constructed the elaborate chart reproduced here. Black workers were considered "good" in pick-and-shovel work, in certain janitorial occupations, in those "requiring speed," and in "hot," "dusty," and "polluted atmospheres." They were categorized as unadaptable in every listed skilled position. Poles and Italians, in contrast, were listed as fair and good, respectively, in the skilled occupations.

Not surprisingy, blacks found it impossible to attain certain skilled industrial jobs such as craneman or roller. Viola J. recalled many evenings when her father complained that at the Jones and Laughlin mill he was often asked to perform "higher jobs" to replace vacationing white workers, but he was never permitted to take the test for promotion to those same tasks, even though he had already demonstrated his ability. A black millworker who became discouraged during World War II clearly articulated his frustration:

Men were leaving the plant; jobs were opening up but it seemed as if I could never get any of those jobs and it was a big disappointment. I almost got off the track. I got a little bitter for a while. When you see women move in on jobs that you thought you would have a chance to get, and they would actually put [women] on better jobs than the [black] men that had been there for years. It was discrimination. There was no question about that, and you felt kind of bad and bitter, but nobody would stick their neck out.[9]

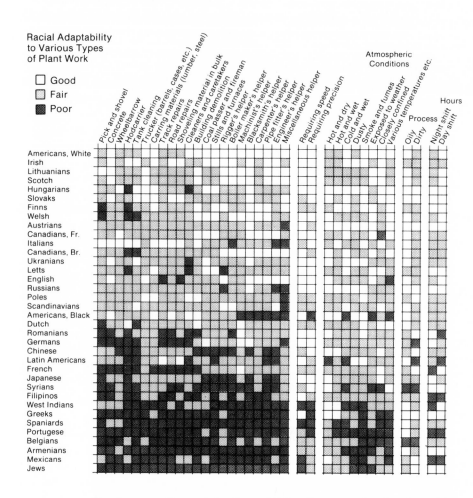

Employment Chart of the Central Tube Company, Pittsburgh, 1925

Source.   Adapted from the three-color chart located in the archives of the Pittsburgh branch of The National Urban League (uncatalogued boxes, located in
the basement of the office).

Increasing racial discrimination combined with an erratic economy clearly contributed to the occupational instability experienced by blacks after 1930. One black female recalled that her two brothers abandoned jobs as radio repairman and laborer at H. J. Heinz, respectively, to seek better careers in the U.S. army. Her sister worked successively as a waitress for a catering service and as a seamstress at Kaufmann's department store. Henry R. made a living by hanging wallpaper, "hustling" odd jobs in the Hill District, and for a time by working on the railroad. Another black male recalled losing his job as a steelworker, then attempting to operate a poolroom, and eventually turning to bartending for a living.[10]

In spite of this widespread occupational instability, blacks, while slipping occupationally, did manage to secure a modest foothold in Pittsburgh industry. Nearly 45 percent of the black male work force in 1930 clustered in manufacturing and mechanical operations—a major departure from the occupational distribution of the prior generation. The impact of the opening of industrial occupations on the black population may be seen in Table 34. Unlike their forefathers, black males now clustered in three major occupational groups. Within the categories clustering was even more evident.

Table 34. Distribution of Gainful Workers, Ten Years of Age or Older in Pittsburgh in 1930

	Males			Females		
Occupation	Native-born White	Foreign-born White	Black	Native-born White	Foreign-born White	Black
Percentage of population 10 and over working	72.2	88.7	83.2	26.6	16.0	31.5
Manufacturing and mechanical	38.4	53.0	44.7	10.2	11.9	4.0
Transportation	12.8	9.4	14.6	4.6	0.3	...
Trade	19.6	18.1	6.9	14.7	13.4	1.1
Public service	3.5	3.0	2.4	...	...	...
Professional service	7.1	3.8	2.2	15.5	7.9	1.8
Domestic and personal service	3.6	8.0	25.1	23.6	55.8	90.5
Clerical	14.0	2.9	2.4	31.0	9.3	1.8
Total no. of workers	138,570	50,551	19,198	54,758	8,235	6,923

NOTE. All data except last row are given as percentages. The data are compiled from the U.S. Bureau of the Census's listing of occupations in Pennsylvania from the 1930 census. It was not possible to differentiate "foreign-born white" into groups such as Poles and Italians— such data were not provided in the census.

Approximately three of every five black workers in the manufacturing classification held jobs in basic steel. Most were unskilled. Small groups of 100 or more also worked in the city's foundries, brick yards, or at Westinghouse Electric. Nearly two-thirds of those engaged in industrial work in 1930 held jobs in the city's largest firms, which employed between 1,000 and 10,000 persons. Thus, the majority of black males no longer worked for themselves or in small two- or three-person operations. Whatever environmental advantages—cleaner air, shorter working hours, e.g.—accrued to the earlier generation who worked out-of-doors or for small family concerns had been sacrificed for the opportunity to secure mill work.

A significant proportion (14.6 percent) of black males continued to hold jobs in transportation, but the specific types of work indicate a decline in status over the previous generation. Blacks held the majority of taxi, hack, bus, and truck driver positions in Pittsburgh at the turn of the century. By 1930 white workers held these positions. Blacks remaining in transportation worked as garbage truck driver/collectors, porters of all types, and truck helpers.

Slippage of black workers engaged in the services also occurred from generation to generation. Nearly half of the 1900 blacks were engaged in public or personal services; 21 percent of the total working population worked as barbers, hairdressers, or in similar occupations. By 1930 service work continued to occupy more than one-fourth of the population, but the jobs were more menial. Only 2 percent of the black males in the public and personal service categories held jobs such as those cited above. Only fifty were police- or firemen. The balance, more than 3,000 men, worked as porters (often a euphemism for janitor) in apartment or office buildings or in department stores. Two-thirds of the black service workers recorded in one study of 702 Pittsburgh firms worked with broom and mop. Clerical positions either in stores or in offices were almost completely closed to blacks. Less than 300 of 17,000 such positions in 1930 Pittsburgh were held by black males.[11]

Black females fared even worse than black males, holding less than 1 percent of all clerical positions. In fact, only two occupations remained open to back women: domestic servant and household laundress. Even commercial laundries—once dominated by black women—were now 90 percent white.

The deterioration in the overall occupational standing of both male and female black workers reflects the dramatic changes in the migratory process of many blacks, the increased competition for industrial work, and the growing racial antagonism in Pittsburgh. Migrants not weaned from the rural South via a series of moves to the urban North were often thrust into a highly urbanized society almost overnight. The Ebenezer Baptist Church, recognizing the trauma created by such a dramatic transition, organized a welcoming committee to greet immigrants at the various rail stations. The committee provided overnight lodging and assistance in securing permanent accommodations and work. The Pittsburgh branch of the Urban League performed similar services. Both organizations reported being overwhelmed at times due to the large number of incoming migrants.[12]

Second-generation Poles and Italians, in contrast, grew up in an urban and industrial environment. Many of the adjustments still required of the new blacks had already been made by the immigrant generation. Their children benefited from such adjustments. Life in Pittsburgh, particularly during the Depression, presented innumerable hardships, but survival, as in the case of black families, was no longer in question.

It is not possible to determine the exact occupational distribution of Poles and Italians by industry, but some rough estimates may be offered by combining data from the U.S. Census Bureau and the 1930 Pittsburgh city directory. Foreign-born males continued to cluster in the manufacturing and mechanical industries and in the trades such as retail dealers and, to some extent, salesmen. Another 10 percent held positions in transportation—mostly on the railroad—while 8 percent worked at a variety of personal service jobs. Information supplied by the 1930 Pittsburgh city directory suggests a distribution within these categories similar to that exhibited by Poles and Italians in 1900. Nearly two-thirds of the 1930 Polish workers held unskilled occupations, and most of those could be found in the city's metal industries.[13] That Poles remained clustered in metal work, however, should not obscure that as a group they were better off. Only 15 percent of all Poles in 1900 held jobs above the unskilled level; the proportion had climbed to one-third by 1930. At the beginning of the fourth decade of the century finding Poles in skilled and even low white-collar jobs was still unusual but no longer a rarity in Pittsburgh.

Second-generation Italians, like their parents, continued to be the most widely distributed and the most successful of all three groups in question. The unskilled (59 percent) from Bloomfield and East Liberty still found work on the railroad, at various utilities, in the mills, and in construction of all types. Nineteen percent, almost identical to the 1900 figure, held craft positions while approximately 10 percent held petty proprietorships or other white-collar occupations.

Even in 1930 second-generation Poles and Italians improved slightly on the occupations held by their parents. Nevertheless, they remained clustered in the same industrial categories as the early immigrant groups. The ability of both Poles and Italians to intercede successfully with employers to secure work for children, kin, or neighbors created a horizontal occupational pattern spanning both generations.

Polish parents remained vital in assisting progeny in securing jobs, an important consideration during the 1930s in Pittsburgh. The immigrant generation, of course, valued steady work and were anxious for their children to gain entrance to one of the numerous plants in Lawrenceville or on the Southside. The father of Walter K. was able to bring Walter and his two brothers to laboring positions at Phoenix Iron and Steel. One young Pole secured a job from a local Catholic newspaper through his mother who cleaned and laundered for the editor. The father of Joseph D. made arrangements for him to secure an apprenticeship with a housing contractor for three years in order to learn a trade "like they did in the old country." John K. got a job at the West Penn Hospital through his father who worked there, and Peter L. recalled that his father took him to numerous plants until he obtained a position for him at the Pittsburgh Provisions Company. Many other Poles were taken by parents or other close relatives to the Armour Meat Company to be "hamboners," to Armstrong Cork, and especially to H. J. Heinz, which employed a number of young girls. At Heppenstalls in Lawrenceville, a job was almost unobtainable unless a father or close relative was already employed. Joseph L. and John S., both of whom assumed the same job as their fathers at the plant, remembered distinctly that Heppenstalls was a "father and son deal where everyone was putting in his own son."[14]

A simultaneous process occurred in Lawrenceville, which reinforced the operation of kinship ties and parental values in securing work. Companies in the area established close ties with the local boys clubs that attempted to keep young men from joining gangs and provided recreational opportunities. Boys who became active in the club quickly learned that their participation could lead to jobs at Heppenstalls or the National Valve Company. This association emerged from the support those plants provided the clubs and from the fact that company officials served as club trustees. Frank B., the club's athletic director, became the key contact who recommended young Poles for employment when they reached an appropriate age. John S. recalled that he joined the club at age twenty-two to avoid the numerous gangs such as the Davidson and Leslie street gangs. During the 1930s the club had an "unemployment club" that offered him a place to spend his idle hours until he was given a position at Heppenstalls machine shop. Ray C. thought the entire system was like an "employment service." More important, this display of company paternalism sustained the intricate web of kinship ties that assisted young Poles in launching blue-collar careers and kept them close to the Polish community.[15]

In spite of family and neighborhood pressures, however, some alterations did occur in the occupational patterns of second-generation Poles. The aspirations of these children of immigrants shifted toward higher paying occupations, particularly after 1940. Improved prosperity brought yearnings for careers and occupations seldom considered earlier. At the same time, many Poles were reluctant to jeopardize the link to blue-collar work that existed in their neighborhoods or the contacts that kin provided. John K., for example, desired work as a salesman, but decided to enter the Armour meat plant in his neighborhood because he felt somewhat unsure of his ability in another line of work. Similarly, Edward N. aspired to be a teacher, and Stanley N. thought of becoming a civil engineer. Both chose "steady" careers close to home instead. John S. considered becoming a pharmacist but lacked confidence in his ability to complete college and assumed a job next to his father at Heppenstalls in the 1940s. A few, like Joseph B., who became an accountant, did begin to fulfill individual aspirations but this was exceptional.[16]

Italian patterns after the 1930s also exhibited remarkable similarities to those of the immigration years, as Italians continued their distinctive trait of seeking trades and small entrepreneurships as well as relying on kin for assistance. Since they had already created particular occupational clusters, it was almost inevitable that they would attempt to bring the second generation to these clusters. The association between Italians from the village of Ateleta and the Equitable Gas Company was strengthened with the maturation of the second generation. While the Ateleta club continued to provide sickness and death benefits, it also functioned as an informal employment network that provided vital contacts for construction and building trade jobs with the gas company. Families functioned in the same way. The brother of Lou G. was able to work for the Pittsburgh Railways Company because his uncle and father were employed there. His brother filled the identical position held by his father. Frank D. bought into a grocery business with assistance from his two brothers. Tom B. started a produce business with the aid of his brother, as a number of immigrants had done earlier. Following the death of his father, Amico L. left high school and relied on a cousin to obtain a construction job for him. Through useful contacts with relatives he eventually became a roofer's helper. Nicholas R. had his father, who knew the "pusher," get him employment installing street car lines for the Pittsburgh Railways. At the age of fifteen Martin T. was able to start working in the kitchen of Pittsburgh's Duquesne Club, peeling potatoes and "mopping up" because his mother had

friends there. Some Italians remained in their initial occupational endeavors, while others left voluntarily and involuntarily for other work.
In nearly all cases a career began with the aid of kin or friends during
the 1920s and 1930s.[17]

While Italians relied on relatives, they also urged their children to
acquire a trade or skill in an attempt to insure that their working-class
pursuits would provide somewhat steady remuneration and employment. Sons were admonished to do more than simply assist their parents;
they were directed to improve themselves as individuals by entering
jobs other than in factories and mills, which Poles seemed reluctant to
do. When he reached thirteen, the parents of Lou G. indicated to him
that he should learn a craft and placed him in a shoemaker's shop much
as might have been done in Italy. Lou explained his father's decision by
saying that his father insisted a trade would be necessary if he were to
find a good job.[18] Frank D. never entered high school because his parents felt it would be preferable for him to learn a "good trade." At the
age of twelve, his father took him to a tailor he knew and obtained an
apprenticeship for Frank. The father and brother of Ray L. learned barbering in Pittsburgh from Ray's uncle and grandfather. Ray's father sent
him to barbering school as well, but Ray disliked the profession and entered a mill. Ray elaborated on that decision: "My parents were most
in favor of learning a trade such as barber, blacksmith, or shoemaker. If
a person got a trade they felt you would never starve. Most of the
Italians who came, even as young people, had a trade. If you got an
education, there was still a possibility that you would have to know
someone before getting a job."[19]

Umberto B. continued the pattern by becoming a shoemaker's apprentice at age fifteen. By the time he was nineteen he was able to rely on
"paesani" to acquire a position for him through the Master Shoe Re-
building Association, an organization heavily dominated by Italians.
Dan C. recalled that his parents stressed that children would not have
to work as hard as they had upon learning a trade. At age fifteen Dan's
father told him to choose a trade. Dan had been impressed by an uncle
in Wilkinsburg who was a barber. "He had a gold watch in his pocket
and looked like a professional man," Dan vividly recalled. His parents
became convinced that barbering was an appropriate trade for their
son when the uncle told them that "you never get rich but you always
have money." After Dan completed tenth grade, his father arranged an
apprenticeship with a barber he knew on Liberty Avenue in Bloomfield. Dan worked two years without pay, eventually earning a full-time
job.[20]

The experiences of Tom B., an American born of Sicilian parentage, illustrate the continued Italian ventures into business after World War II. Tom began working at age fourteen, but failed to accumulate any capital until he started delivering moonshine in 1933. Tom and his brother used the profits from the illegal whiskey trade to finance a small fruit business that was destroyed by the 1936 flood. Undaunted, Tom and his brother repaired their one truck and began picking peaches on nearby farms and selling them in the city. Tom eventually invested his newly accumulated savings in a truck hauling company in 1947, which became a prosperous enterprise. In a similar case, Joseph A. took over his father's Bloomfield grocery business after serving time in Europe and India as a sergeant in the U.S. army during World War II. He had "always expected," he reported, "to be a grocer."[21]

The experiences of Tom B. and Joseph A., while not typical among the Italian communities, occurred with considerable regularity. The proportion who experienced striking success will become apparent shortly.

The differences between blacks and ethnics in female labor, like those of their male counterparts, remained relatively consistent over two generations. Nearly one-third of the black female population over age ten worked for wages in 1930, while only half that proportion of foreign-born females held jobs outside the home. The unstable occupational position of black males, their younger marrying ages, the higher rate of broken homes, and the inability of family and community to provide economic aid when needed, all forced black females to seek outside employment. Approximately one-half of the nearly 7,000 black women employed in 1930 also had family responsibilities. The remainder were young girls whose wages provided some economic assistance to the family. Polish and Italian females, in contrast, seldom worked outside the home. Old World cultural prohibitions against female labor remained strong among both groups. Polish and Italian women interviewed reported a reluctance on the part of their parents to permit them to work even during the worst years of the Depression. For most the ban was lifted only during World War II.

Family ties and religious practices also kept Polish and Italian women in the home. Widows, for example, almost never had to work to support themselves and surviving children. More than 90 percent of the widows from either group found in the 1930 Pittsburgh city directory lived with their adult children. Few women from either group, moreover, were ever forced to support their own families as religious taboos against divorce remained strong. Only eleven women among all Italian and Polish families in the 1930 neighborhoods were the sole support for members of their household. The overwhelming majority of Polish and

Italian working females were young and most likely unmarried. More-over, unlike their black counterparts who were excluded from all but servant and maid positions, female children of immigrants worked at a variety of positions, ranging from domestic work to sales and clerical positions. A few were teachers and nurses. Most young ethnic women, however, remained in school or worked in the family home until marriage. This prolonged period of reliance on the family, in turn, strengthened already powerful family bonds and no doubt contributed to the residential stability discussed earlier.

Thus by 1930 an occupational hierarchy and several trends were clearly evident. Italians stood at the top followed by Poles, black males, and black females. Italian and Polish women remained largely outside of the occupational structure. Second-generation Italian and Polish workers held slightly better jobs than their parents, although they remained clustered in the same industries. Blacks, scattered among a variety of occupations, made particularly significant inroads into the metal and manufacturing industries. Their skill levels (mainly unskilled and semiskilled) remained similar to the 1900 group, but they had slipped somewhat from the gains recorded between 1915 and 1925. Unemployment also became a severe problem by 1930. Black women workers stood at the bottom of the Pittsburgh occupational hierarchy in 1930. Except for a small number who were janitresses in Pittsburgh industry, black women could find work only in low-paying domestic occupations. They were almost totally excluded from jobs open to other women in Pittsburgh, such as clerical and sales positions.

As discussed earlier in this work, the Depression, World War II, the postwar economic boom and recession, racial discrimination, and other variables influenced Pittsburgh between 1930 and 1960. Many blacks left Pittsburgh to seek employment elsewhere. Others, Poles and Italians included, left during the war years and never returned. But what of those who remained in Pittsburgh during most of the thirty-year period?[22] Would the upward occupational trends of Poles and Italians continue? Would blacks continue their slide, producing an ever widening distance between second-generation immigrants and black migrants to Pittsburgh? Table 35 reveals the occupational patterns of these three groups between 1930 and 1960.

Just as families from all three groups exhibited greater residential stability during the 1930s than the 1940s or 1950s, they were also occupationally more stable. Individuals fortunate enough to hold jobs during the Depression obviously clung to them tenaciously. Occupational mobility, either up or down, occurred in only a few instances. The net movement of blacks and Poles, moreover, was downward, while those

Table 35. Net Occupational Mobility of the 1930 Neighborhood Sample in Pittsburgh between 1940 and 1960

Ethnic/Minority Group	1930 N	1940				1950				1960			
		Same	Up	Down	Net Mobility Index	Same	Up	Down	Net Mobility Index	Same	Up	Down	Net Mobility Index
Blacks	120	0.85	0.05	0.09	0.47	0.65	0.25	0.10	0.230	0.53	0.41	0.18	0.442
Southern-born blacks	64	0.83	0.08	0.08	0	0.66	0.13	0.12	0.011	0.72	0.14	0.14	0
Poles	309	0.84	0.07	0.09	0.022	0.71	0.20	0.09	0.965	0.63	0.30	0.67	0.369
Italians	162	0.78	0.16	0.06	0.132	0.63	0.31	0.06	0.400	0.50	0.48	0.02	0.920
1940 Percent Neighborhood Sample													
Blacks	102					0.76	0.21	0.02	0.247	0.69	0.28	0.03	0.349
Poles	328					0.80	0.18	0.02	0.99	0.67	0.30	0.02	0.415
Italians	79					0.792	0.18	0.03	0.198	0.63	0.33	0.04	0.444

NOTE. No discernible differences in occupations could be detected from neighborhood to neighborhood. In addition, because individual neighborhood cohorts (when out-migrants, etc., were deleted) decreased significantly, Polish, Italian, and black neighborhoods have been combined. Unemployed workers have been omitted from the sample. See ch. 5 for a description of the net mobility index. The data were compiled from the neighborhood data sample, 1930-60.

blacks identified as definitely southern-born failed to show any net movement at all. The inability of all three groups to advance becomes particularly significant when compared with their occupational movement during the early decades of the century (Table 14). Only once did even a single group experience net downward mobility. The overall pattern in every decade from 1900 through 1930 for even the most impoverished groups was upward. The picture becomes even more bleak when one considers that 18 percent of the persisting black sample, 10 percent of the Poles, and 8 percent of the Italians were unemployed at both decade intervals (1930-40). A small proportion of Italians (twenty-three men) managed to acquire better jobs during the decade, moving from unskilled to semiskilled or skilled positions. Twelve of these, however, held higher level positions in 1920 and were merely returning to their former semiskilled or skilled occupation. It seems clear, therefore, that while unemployment struck black workers particularly hard, the Depression retarded the occupational progress of all groups with nearly equal force.

Employment conditions improved dramatically during and after World War II, and all three groups took advantage of new opportunities. Italians, as might be expected, given their long history of upward mobility, experienced the greatest success. By 1960 only half of the 1930 neighborhood sample held the same job as two decade earlier. Almost all those moving managed to secure better jobs. Nearly 50 percent of the Italians remaining from the 1930 sample moved up the occupational scale—a truly impressive rate of success.

Black workers, excluding those definitely southern-born, experienced both occupational successes and failures, but their upward movement exceeded the downward mobility by more than two to one during each decade interval, 1940-60. The erratic upward-downward pattern of blacks demonstrates their continued sensitivity to the vagaries of the Pittsburgh economy and their relatively weak position in the labor market. Their impressive upward movement (25 percent between 1940 and 1960) also reflects the persistent high aspirations of this group and their willingness to take risks in the face of uncommon obstacles to achieve these successes. The almost absolute immobility of the "identified" southern-born blacks, moreover, suggests that the achievements of true second-generation Pittsburgh blacks may be strongly underestimated. The row for blacks in Table 35 includes all those who could be identified as black but who could not be identified as definitely born in the South. It no doubt also includes some born below the Mason-Dixon line. The striking immobility of the definitely southern-born blacks (row two) illustrates clearly that they had a more difficult time achieving occupational success than their northern-born counterparts. Thus, it seems likely that longevity in Pittsburgh played a significant role in the adjustment of blacks—as well as ethnics—and in turn influenced their rate of occupational success. One can only speculate regarding the number of southern-born blacks concealed in row one in this table. If their lack of occupational success even approaches the rates recorded by those definitely born in the South, the rate of success of northern-born blacks must be adjusted substantially upward.

Polish workers, consistent with the patterns established by the first generation, remained in the steel industry throughout their lives. Except for the recent southern-born black migrants, Poles demonstrated the greatest stability of all working groups, with exactly two-thirds remaining at their initial skill level after three decades. A comparison of the occupational movement of both generations shows little change from one generation to the next. Less than one-third of either group succeeded in securing a higher level occupation. This lack of success, however, should not prove too surprising, given the relatively limited occupational aspirations of Polish workers, their reluctance to risk failure in higher level job ventures, and the tendency of industrial work to retard occupational achievement. Oral interviews revealed that Poles sought job security above all else. Second-generation Poles, thrust into the job market in the midst of the Depression, again faced unemployment. If they began their careers with expanded occupational goals, interviews with second-generation Poles (discussed earlier in this chapter) suggest a hasty retreat to the safer, more limited goals of their parents.

The impressive mobility of black workers, however, must be tempered when one examines the extent of their climb. As in our analysis of first-generation workers, we may combine both unskilled and semi-skilled classifications to examine the extent of upward mobility into the skilled or white-collar classes.

The data in Table 36 reveal what we have by now come to expect. Southern-born blacks, constituting nearly three-fourths of those living in Pittsburgh in 1930, failed to move up at all; blacks not definitely born in the South moved up, but the extent of their success occurred almost totally within the blue-collar world. Crucial to this lack of success was the initial entry of blacks into the work world. The first generation, as noted earlier, began their careers in Pittsburgh in the type of occupations that Grace Anderson has labeled "occupational traps"— janitors, cleaners, porters, and other limited-opportunity service jobs. Many of the second generation also began working in service-type occupational traps. Others shifted into industrial jobs that, as we have

Table 36. Occupational Mobility from Unskilled/Semiskilled to Skilled and White-Collar Jobs in Pittsburgh, 1930-60

Ethnic/ Minority Group	N[1]	1930 Unskilled/ Semiskilled Group (%)[2]	% to Skilled			% to White Collar			% Same		
			1940	1950	1960	1940	1950	1960	1940	1950	1960
Northern-born blacks	98	80	4	14	13	0	2	6	96	84	81
Southern-born blacks	49	81	8	8	0	2	8	0	90	82	0
Poles	281	77	85	12	14	2	8	0	91	80	66
Italians	151	70	10	18	20	4	10	23	85	71	57

NOTE. The data are compiled from the sample data of 1930 neighborhoods compiled for this study.

[1]Numbers in this column omit the unemployed.

[2]The percentages in this column denote the percentage of the 1930 labor force clustered in the unskilled/semiskilled classification. Thus, 80 percent of the 98 blacks actually working were in unskilled or semiskilled jobs in 1930.

seen with Poles, also trapped workers. Second-generation blacks, in effect, escaped one occupational trap only to become enmeshed in another.

The experiences of second-generation Poles, however, indicate that occupational traps might, over time, be sprung. Unskilled or semiskilled Poles and Italians, in contrast to blacks, scored impressive gains: the proportion of Poles achieving white-collar work nearly matched the success rate of Italians. The data from which the table was developed, however, indicate that the Polish successes derived from movement within the metal industry. Sixty-eight percent of the upwardly mobile Poles attained skilled or lower-level management positions in the steel mill or other manufacturing setting. For a limited number of Poles the occupational trap of an earlier generation became a stepping-stone into the industrial white-collar world. It is significant, however, that group longevity in the mill did not act as a spring board into high level managerial positions. Not a single Pole could be found among the industrial elite in the Pittsburgh steel industry in either 1960 or 1970.

The initial work positions of Italians continued to offer opportunities for advancement through the second generation. Jobs in construction, certain services, and retail businesses frequently led to skilled trades or small proprietorships, a pattern established by the earlier immigrant generation. By 1960 nearly half of the Italians who began their careers at the bottom of the occupational ladder had risen to a skilled or white-collar position.

Black females continued to cluster in the lowest skill, lowest paying, and least desirable occupations. Even the entry of ethnic women into the labor force during and after World War II did not alter the position of the black working woman. The available data do not permit a systematic analysis of the experiences of female workers in Pittsburgh during the 1930-60 period. An examination of the census tract data, for those tracts known to contain high concentrations of blacks, Poles, or Italians, however, illustrates the continued plight of the black female worker.

The Depression and World War II removed the barriers preventing Polish and Italian women from obtaining gainful work in Pittsburgh. Once down, those barriers were not easily replaced. By 1950 working women from each group nearly equalled the proportion of employed women in the city (29.8); Italian women in Bloomfield were overrepresented in the work force by 1960. The occupations held by those women residing in the census tracts previously identified as black, Polish, or Italian clearly suggest that the ethnic women did not suffer from their late entry into the labor force (Table 37).

Black women constituted a sizeable proportion of the Pittsburgh labor force for nearly two generations. For them as a group, however, length of service meant little. At mid-century only a tiny minority held either of the white-collar jobs traditionally open to women. Less than 10 percent of the female residents of tract 5A (96 percent black) worked in clerical or sales positions. Three-fourths performed service (mostly janitress and cleaning positions) and private household (maids and cleaning) tasks. One decade later these distributions shifted upward, but only slightly. In both decades black women were highly underrepresented in the white-collar occupations and performed the bulk of the city's lowest level domestic occupations.

The dramatic downward shift in the female occupational distribution in ward 13C (Homewood-Brushton) dramatizes the plight of Pittsburgh's black population. Black women constituted only 23 percent of that tract's female population in 1950. The proportion rose to nearly 75 percent by 1960 as blacks replaced whites in the 12th and 13th wards. The occupational distribution in the area underwent a corresponding decline. By 1960 the typical female worker in either of the black neighborhoods held some type of domestic occupation.

Black women began their careers at the bottom of the occupational pile and remained there. Polish and Italian women, conversely, entered at midlevel positions and managed to move up slightly within a decade. In spite of their recent arrival on the Pittsburgh's labor scene, more than one-third of each group held white-collar jobs in 1950 and less than one-fourth performed domestic services. By 1960 both groups were

Table 37. Distribution of Female Workers in Pittsburgh
in Selected Categories, 1950 and 1960

Job Category	City of Pittsburgh	Black Census Tracts[1]		Polish Census Tracts[2]	Italian Census Tracts[3]
		5A	13C	6B 16B	8B
			1950		
Clerical	33.0	7.6	28.5	23.9	30.0
Sales	10.8	2.5	10.8	10.3	10.2
Operative	11.6	14.2	12.9	29.7	26.0
Service	16.2	41.8	19.3	20.9	13.4
Private household	7.3	33.7	8.8	2.8	4.7
			1960		
Clerical	32.3	14.4	11.2	40.2	32.9
Sales	9.7	3.8	6.3	19.5	11.5
Operative	8.2	5.4	10.5	14.7	19.7
Service	16.8	46.4	29.8	20.8	25.3
Private household	12.3	19.9	21.1	3.1	...

NOTE. The data were compiled from the U.S. Bureau of the Census, "Age, Marital Status, and Economic Characteristics by Sex, By Census Tracts," in 1950; and the U.S. Bureau of the Census. "Labor Force Characteristics of the Population by Census Tracts," in 1960—both documents specific for Pittsburgh. All data are in percentages, but the totals do not equal 100 because certain occupational categories were excluded. Three dots = not available.

[1]Census tract 13C shifted from 23 percent black in 1950 to nearly 73 percent in 1960.

[2]The column is the average between census tracts 6B and 16B.

[3]Census tract 12C (East Liberty) proved too erratic after 1950 to permit reliable estimates; data are for 8B (Bloomfield) only.

slightly overrepresented among the city's female white-collar workers while hardly any could be found in private domestic work. The proportion in all service jobs remained about 25 percent. Clearly, while the aggregate data presented in the above table obscure a number of subtleties, ethnic women suffered little disadvantage from their late entry into the labor force.[23] Black women, like their male counterparts, continued to receive the least Pittsburgh had to offer for their efforts.

The limited occupational success of Pittsburgh's black population, male and female, when combined with the condition of the neighborhoods they inherited, the exclusionary policies of the city's labor unions, the trend toward greater residential segregation, and the overt discriminatory acts, no doubt resulted in extreme frustration. Blacks were blocked at every turn. As one black respondent noted, "I came to Pittsburgh hoping for better things. It just didn't turn out that way."[24]

Second-generation Poles and Italians obviously enjoyed more success than blacks, but like their parents their successes fell within a modest range. More important, their success seemed to coincide with the reported aspirations of each group. Italians aspired to skilled occupations and small businesses, and nearly half achieved these goals by 1960. Poles, seeking economic and occupational security, likely exceeded those goals, as approximately one-third moved to skilled or white-collar positions by 1960.

All three groups, as demonstrated earlier, adopted the prevailing middle-class attitudes toward homeownership. Homes were viewed as stable elements in an uncertain world. No sacrifice seemed too great to achieve homeownership. Families worked together toward the common goal—a home of one's own—and once achieved, the home was rarely abandoned. Even in death one did not forfeit one's home, but passed it on to one's children as the traditional family legacy. But here, too, Pittsburgh's black population enjoyed less success than either second-generation Poles or Italians.

The striking disproportion in homeownership becomes immediately apparent from the data presented in Table 38. Between one-fourth and one-half of the people sampled in Polish and Italian neighborhoods owned their homes as early as 1930. Blacks, on the other hand, were almost totally renters. Only in the more affluent Homewood-Brushton section did more than 15 percent manage to acquire a home of their own. It was originally thought that the recent arrival of most of the 1930 black sample might also provide an important clue to their lower rates of homeownership. The higher rates of ownership among the upper hill and Homewood-Brushton blacks seemed to suggest that these might be second-generation blacks. Some had left the lower hill—along with their immigrant counterparts—to escape the conditions created by the influx of new immigrants during the 1916-19 migration. The availability of voter registration data enabled us to determine that one-fifth of the total black sample definitely arrived in Pittsburgh after World War I; the origin of others could not be determined. A comparison of homeownership rates of known recent arrivals with the rest of the sample confirmed our suspicion. Nearly all of the homes owned by blacks were in possession of those among the larger or earlier arriving sample. Some, of course, may have been recent arrivals, but what is certain is that among those who definitely came after 1918 homeownership was practically nonexistent. Perhaps more important, only 7 percent of the black families in all three neighborhoods owned their own homes in 1930. Their rates of homeownership clearly improved during the next several decades, but they never reached the

Table 38. Homeownership Mobility by Black, Italian, and Polish Families
in Seven Neighborhoods in Pittsburgh, 1930-60

Decade, Residence	Pittsburgh Neighborhoods						
	Polish Hill	Southside	Bloomfield	East Liberty	Lower Hill	Upper Hill	Homewood-Brushton
1930							
Own (%)	24.2	42.5	47.2	31.0	1.3	13.2	16.2
Rent (%)	75.8	57.5	52.8	69.0	98.7	86.8	83.8
N	235	146	108	123	79	53	68
1940[1]							
Own (%)	32.8	49.3	60.2	48.8	5.1	22.6	23.5
Rent (%)	67.2	50.7	39.8	51.2	94.9	77.4	76.5
N	234	146	108	123	79	53	68
1950[2]							
Own (%)	48.0	67.9	62.1	62.4	12.5	33.3	34.1
Rent (%)	52.0	32.1	37.8	37.6	87.5	66.7	65.9
N	200	134	103	109	48	33	41
1960							
Own (%)	75.0	74.7	89.8	82.0	23.3	42.1	60.0
Rent (%)	25.0	25.3	10.1	18.0	76.7	57.8	40.0
N	120	95	59	67	30	19	20

NOTE. Families are denoted by the heads in 1930, their surviving children, or widows if a death has occurred and the home was passed on and inhabited by the widow or child. These data are compiled from the sample data generated for this study.

[1]Includes only those 1930 families persisting through 1940.

[2]Families may have but did not necessarily persist in the same (1930) neighborhood through successive decades. Thus, while seven (23.3 percent) of the thirty Lower Hill residents persisted in Pittsburgh through 1960 and owned their own homes, none continue to reside in the Lower Hill area.

ownership level enjoyed by second-generation Poles and Italians.

Only a few families from any neighborhood group managed to acquire a home during the difficult decade of the 1930s. Perhaps more surprising, neither Poles, blacks, nor Italians were forced to relinquish their homes due to economic difficulties. Those who had acquired homes earlier somehow managed to retain them in spite of frequent and often prolonged unemployment. Not a single home among those in one ten-house section of Lorigan Street (Bloomfield) changed family ownership between 1918 and 1945.[25] Their ability to maintain ownership status in the face of frequent foreclosures attests to the importance each group attached to homeownership. No sacrifice proved too large to retain control of one's home.

Black homeowners from the 1930 sample who persisted through

World War II continued to own their homes during the 1950s and 1960s. Thus, while the percentage of owners increased each decade, the number remained relatively stable. Blacks who acquired their homes early retained them. Those who did not often left the city. Blacks not part of the sample evidently fared no better. Only 30 percent of all black homes in 1960 were owner-occupied.[26]

Italian and Polish homeowners in the 1930 sample, in contrast to blacks, increased in both numbers and percentages during the ensuing decades. By 1960 more than three-fourths of each sample group from all four ethnic neighborhoods owned their own homes. Among Italians in Bloomfield and Poles in Polish Hill and the Southside, the proportion of homeowners exceeded the city average of all white homeowners in 1960.[27] Both groups held somewhat better and clearly more stable jobs than did their black counterparts. The higher and more regular incomes provided by these jobs made the accumulation of mortgage money possible. The importance of the household, the joint work efforts of family members, and the duration of their stay in the city also help to explain the differences in homeownership patterns among the sample neighborhoods.

Italians and Poles considered homeowning very important. Premigration experiences underscored the value of owning land. Owners in their premigration societies found life a bit more comfortable, and ownership provided status. Repatriates almost always expressed a desire to own property upon return to their homeland. Those who remained in the United States not surprisingly expressed a similar desire.

The mechanics of homeownership were discussed earlier and need not be repeated here. It seems clear, however, that most Poles and Italians aspired to homeownership above all else. A home provided a way to keep the family unit intact and performed valuable familial and economic functions. A home was more than a surrogate for mobility or an extension of the Old World hunger for land. It was a practical solution to problems encountered by working-class families in an industrial city with a limited supply of housing. Raymond C., who lived in four homes within the six-block Polish Hill section during sixty years of his life, reported that homeownership was "utmost in my family, to raise my family in my own home ... that was the big thing."[28] Joseph K. noted that homeownership provided a guarantee against eviction. "In some cases you'd have to move—like if somebody bought the house. It used to be this way, say I own a house and a brother or daughter got married and I want to put 'em in. You [the renter] must move out ... that happened frequently ... I told my kids I don't ever want to leave."[29]

Homes were also crucial to Polish parents in assisting progeny when they married and initiated families of their own. Nearly all Poles interviewed in this study lived in their parents' homes until marriage and frequently afterwards as well. Stephanie W. lived with her mother after marriage in 1920. Although they shared only two rooms, a kitchen and a bedroom, the arrangement proved invaluable when her new husband became unemployed for an entire year. John S. moved into the downstairs portion of his father's home upon his marriage, and his parents moved upstairs. Eventually he inherited the entire house. Peter L. benefited from a similar arrangement, moving in with his father after marriage. Ultimately he received the entire home as a result of his father's plan to purchase several homes and give one to each of his children. Arrangements such as these not only eased economic burdens on young families but allowed Polish children to follow a common admonition of their parents to avoid debt at all costs.[30]

Not surprisingly, Poles and other Slavs exceeded other ethnic groups in urban America in homeownership rates by 1930.[31] Their reasons for purchasing homes were not based simply on a transfer of the premigration values toward land ownership. They were also attempting to obtain a semblance of economic security for themselves and their families.

Joint incomes, no matter how small, also helped Italian families purchase their own homes. Anna Marie P., a life-long Bloomfield resident, revealed that she and a sister quit school, at their parents' insistence, at age fourteen to go to work. Her parents needed money to pay the mortgage and chose to take the daughters out of school rather than to take in boarders.[32] In perhaps the most remarkable example of joint-work efforts, thirteen members of the family of Robert D. all contributed their earnings to help their parents buy the home in which they had resided for fifteen years.[33]

Certain benefits awaited Italian children who assisted their parents in meeting the costs of homeownership. As with Poles, Italians frequently depended upon parents to provide living space after marriage. Such support was crucial in Pittsburgh, where a housing shortage nearly always existed. Housing arrangements grew to depend upon kin as much as employment required kin assistance. Amico L., for instance, continued to live in his parents' home on Pearl Street after marriage. Amico was able to acquire not only an inexpensive living arrangement, but he helped support his mother as well. Dan C. remained with his parents after marriage until he could save a down payment for his own home. After marriage Vincent L. lived with his parents for four years. He explained that one could get some loans, but "it was difficult to pay them back." Lou G. never left his parents' home and delayed marriage until age thirty-six to assist his parents in raising brothers and sisters. When his parents died, Lou inherited the home in Bloomfield. Frank D., who remained at home until age thirty-two, recalled that his parents quietly saved all of the earnings their six children gave to them. When each child matured, the accumulated wages were returned to the children, who were able to purchase a home of their own. Frank's parents clearly did not require financial assistance from their children, yet they continued to insist that each member contribute a portion of their earnings while they remained in the family household. In a similar case, the money Dan C. turned over to his parents was returned to him when he wanted to open a barber shop.[34]

It is not surprising, therefore, that when the U.S. Senate investigated housing in Pittsburgh in 1957, it discovered that white ethnic groups, such as Italians, resisted public housing not only because of the emotional attachment to their neighborhood but because they "believe in sub-dividing their homes to make room for children when they get married."[35]

For many Poles and Italians, these joint efforts enabled them to purchase their own homes. Blacks, in contrast, recorded significantly lower rates of homeownership. That black children established their own households at an early age hindered mutual efforts toward homeownership. Both first- and second-generation blacks were forced to acquire homes as well as jobs on their own. The task, as we have seen, was almost insurmountable.

NOTES

1. Ira Reid, "The Negro in the Major Industries and Building Trades of Pittsburgh" (M.A. thesis, University of Pittsburgh, 1925), 10-11.
2. Quoted in Abraham Epstein, *The Negro Migrant in Pittsburgh* (Pittsburgh, 1918), 36.
3. Reid, "The Negro in the Major Industries," 8, 11.
4. Ibid., 19.
5. Howard D. Gould, "An Analysis of the Occupational Opportunities for Negroes in Allegheny County" (Ph.D. diss., University of Pittsburgh, 1934), 30-31.
6. Evidence of prior industrial work by black migrants after 1930 is more fragmentary than that supplied by the pre-1930 group and is more suggestive than conclusive. Two recorded cases of brothers, for example, revealed that after leaving farms in the South, they worked making railroad ties and laying track, respectively, before arriving in Pittsburgh. A small stream of blacks identified through interviews left Texas and Arkansas in the 1920s, moved to Gary, Indiana, obtained experi-

ence in steel production, and reached Pittsburgh in the 1940s. Interviews with James S., June 13, 1974; Albert C., Apr. 2, 1974; Leroy M., July 9, 1974, Pittsburgh Oral History Project (POHP).

7. Reid, "The Negro in Major Industries," 21.
8. Ibid.
9. Interviews with Viola J., Feb. 11, 1973; anonymous, Dec. 16, 1974, POHP.
10. Interviews with Sadie A., Aug. 1, 1974; Keyo L., Aug. 11, 1974; James G., Aug. 1, 1974; Albert C., Apr. 2, 1974; Henry R., Feb. 11, 1973; Ethel C., Aug. 20, 1974, POHP.
11. Gould, "Analysis of Occupational Opportunity for Negroes," 40-41.
12. Ebenezer Baptist Church records; Pittsburgh Urban League, typewritten and handwritten reports, "Travelers Aid Committee, 1919-1922," located in the basement of the office of the league.
13. Pittsburgh city directories usually recorded unskilled workers as simply "laborer," and thus it is impossible to determine the exact proportion of Poles still in mill work. However, residential locations, oral interviews, and some limited employment records all suggest a continuing heavy concentration of Poles in the metal industries. In addition, not a single piece of evidence could be found to suggest any shift in the work patterns of the city's second-generation Poles.
14. Interviews with Stanley E., Sept. 9, 1976; Edward N., Oct. 4, 1976; Walter K., May 18, 1977; Joseph A., Sept. 17, 1976; Peter L., Sept. 11, 1976; Charles W., Dec. 10, 1976; John K., Sept. 13, 1976; Joe L., May 12, 1977; John S., Sept. 30, 1976, POHP.
15. Interviews with John S., Sept. 30, 1976; Edward N., Oct. 4, 1976; Edward M., Sept. 30, 1976; Ray C., July 1, 1976, POHP.
16. Interviews with John K., Sept. 13, 1976; Edward N., Oct. 4, 1976; Stanley E., Sept. 9, 1976; John S., Sept. 30, 1976; Joseph B., May 13, 1976, POHP.
17. Interviews with Amico L., July 28, 1977; Leo G., May 11, 1977; Frank D., May 19, 1977; Tom B., July 7, 1977; Nicholas R., June 23, 1977; Martin T., Mar. 25, 1977, POHP.
18. Interview with Lou G., May 11, 1977, POHP.
19. Interview with Ray L., Aug. 24, 1977, POHP.
20. Interviews with Umberto B., Mar. 14, 1977; Dan C., July 23, 1978, POHP.
21. Interview with Tom B., July 7, 1977, POHP. Interview with Joseph A., Mar. 23, 1980, by Pamela Sopp. Transcript of Joseph A. inteview is in the possession of M.W.
22. We recognize that the careers of many members from the sample may have been interrupted by service in World War II. Without interviewing every sample member or his descendants, we have no way of knowing how pervasive this interruption may have been.
23. By postponing their entry into the labor market, ethnic women may have inadvertently increased their own career alternatives. By remaining in school, rather than working, many acquired secretarial and other skills, thus enhancing their chances for modest success once they did seek employment.
24. Interview with Henry R., Feb. 11, 1973, POHP.

25. Allegheny County, Pennsylvania, Recorder of Deeds, Deed Books, County Office Building, Pittsburgh.
26. U.S. Bureau of the Census, *Census of Population and Housing: 1960, Census Tracts* (Washington, D.C., 1962), Table H-3 (characteristics of housing units with non-white households).
27. U.S. Bureau of the Census, *Census of Population and Housing: 1960,* Table 2 (characteristics of housing units by census blocks).
28. Interview with Raymond C., July 1, 1976, POHP.
29. Interview with Joseph K., Sept. 13, 1976, POHP.
30. For statistics on Slavic homeownership, see John Bodnar, "Immigration and Modernization: Slavic Peasants in Industrial America," *Journal of Social History,* 10 (Autumn 1976), 68-69.
31. Interviews with Stephanie W., Mar. 24, 1976; Peter L., Sept. 17, 1976; Joseph B., May 13, 1976; Edward M., Sept. 30, 1976; Stanley N., Sept. 22, 1976; Francis M., Sept. 18, 1977; John S., Sept. 30, 1976, POHP.
32. Interview with Anna Marie P., July 19, 1979, POHP.
33. Interview with Robert D., Oct. 7, 1978, POHP.
34. See Susan Kleinberg, "Technology and Women's Work: The Lives of Working Class Women in Pittsburgh, 1870-1900," *Labor History,* 17 (Winter 1976), 59-60; Lewis P. Hohos, *Zlate Jubileum Kostula Sv. Matusa* (Passiac, N.J., 1955), 27. Interviews with Martin D., Mar. 16, 1977; Umberto B., Mar. 14, 1977; Dan C., Mar. 31, 1977; Nicholas R., June 23, 1977; Vincent L., Oct. 21, 1977; Lou G., May 11, 1977; Frank D., May 19, 1977, POHP.
35. "Testimony Given to the Senate Sub-Committee on Housing, December 13, 1957," copy in American Service Institute Records, file 4, Archives of Industrial Society, University of Pittsburgh. Because of this practice of subdividing, many real estate interests resisted white ethnic movement into more affluent sections of the city, just as they resisted blacks on the basis of race.

Conclusion

By the middle years of the twentieth century, blacks, Italians, and Poles could look back upon their experience in Pittsburgh with mixed results. Certainly many had not bothered to remain in the "steel city" at all. But among those who did, years of labor had generally resulted in varied measures of success and stability. Indeed, the expansion of industrial capitalism that drew them from disparate backgrounds molded them not into a unified working class but into a segmented mass with deep fissures running along occupational, neighborhood, racial, and cultural lines. While Pittsburgh differed in important respects from some cities, its heavy industrial concentration and ethnic and racial mix were quite representative of many northern, industrial centers and suggested that in the process of industrial and urban growth complex networks surfaced that defined the initial pattern of working-class employment and settlement and the lives of subsequent generations. In familial life, occupational trajectories, and the community-building process, "networks of contact"[1] structured the adjustment of blacks, Italians, and Poles and allowed the individual migrant to influence the industrial order as well as to be affected by it. These networks acted as prisms in which newcomers selectively filtered crosscurrents emanating from their past and their present to fashion what can best be described as alternative strategies of life.

Furthermore, the problem of merging newcomers from rural regions with an expanding, industrial city was so complex that the process turned on more than simply a one-dimensional factor, such as premigration culture, urban structure, or racial antipathies. To say this is not to diminish the insidious nature of racism nor temper its pernicious impact. But racism, like traditional culture, did not operate in isolation. Families and workers from various backgrounds lived out their lives in response to multiple pressures exerted by tradition, discrimination, urban structure, and industrial employment. They acclimatized themselves to an industrial city amidst the interplay of all these forces at specific times. Unless this intermeshing of forces is appreciated, a full understanding of dissimilar paths of adjustment is not possible.

When southern-born blacks, Poles, and Italians first entered Pittsburgh in significant numbers, limited skill positions were proliferating in the city's expanding iron and steel industry. Fortunately for the immigrants, foremen prized them, rather than blacks, as potential employees and allowed the Europeans to establish friend and kinship networks in the work place. Blacks were left to fend for themselves in occupational sectors that offered considerably less opportunity for long-term, stable employment.

But the changing nature of Pittsburgh's economy during the first two decades of this century cannot alone explain the initial occupational trajectories of newly arrived laborers. Each group brought similar and distinctive premigration experiences with them that shaped these initial attachments to the "steel city." Blacks arrived in the city with expectations for considerable social and economic improvement and were more likely, for instance, to send their children to school or to pursue small entrepreneurial opportunities. Italian expectations paralleled those of blacks, although a widespread acquaintance with supplemental skills in Italy caused them to stress the acquisition of a trade rather than formal education. Poles expected less upon arrival in Pittsburgh and were satisfied to obtain the industrial unskilled and semiskilled work they received. They generally thought prolonged schooling was simply an unnecessary delay in establishing their blue-collar beachheads.

While all three groups revealed strong familial associations before and during movement to the city, the behavior of respective family groups in Pittsburgh differed and did not remain unaffected by urban forces of racism, limited opportunity, and the economic structure of the city. Traditional culture operated, to be sure, when Italian families established small businesses or acquired certain skills. But it was not premigration tradition that prevented blacks from establishing kinship clusters in the work place, restricted their ability to pass occupational connections to their progeny, and consequently forced them to nurture highly individualistic patterns of child socialization. Conversely, Poles could control children much more rigidly and expect them to remain obligated to their family because urban racism (on the part of employers) and structural opportunities reinforced the mechanics of their traditional family networks. Families, in short, were malleable rather than immutable entities; they were altered but not eradicated by social change.

The consequence of this interaction between urban forces and tradition was not only disparate occupational courses for each group, but significantly different patterns of community-building. Immigrants, able to obtain job stability and homeownership, established functional neighborhoods in Bloomfield, Lawrenceville, and the Southside. Blacks, unable to create clusters in expanding or stable sectors of the city's economy, lived in neighborhoods whose service institutions were considerably more fragmented and where homeownership was not readily obtainable.

Again, tradition intersected with urban reality. Homeownership was a lower priority among blacks partially because they appeared to have considerably less familiarity with proprietorship in the South but primarily because of their inability to secure stable employment and of the high degree of entrenched absentee ownership in their neighborhoods. Poles, of course, were almost always landowners in Europe. Indeed, the growing difficulties that they were encountering in retaining their status as proprietors in Prussia (for cultural reasons) and in the Austrian and Russian areas (for cultural and economic reasons) contributed greatly to their emigration in the first place. But their quest for homeownership in Pittsburgh resulted not only from their past but also from economic pressures in Pittsburgh to gain a modest form of stability, if possible, and to provide assistance and living space for kin in subsequent generations. Many endured repeated indebtedness to obtain that end. Italians, while having somewhat less familiarity than Poles in owning European real estate, also recognized the need to secure a hedge against economic uncertainties and a shelter for themselves and relatives in a city continually short of housing and in an area with crucial services and neighbors of similar cultural backgrounds. The entire home-acquisition and community-building process for both Italians and Poles was facilitated tremendously by their ability to create kinship-occupational systems in the Pittsburgh economy.

After the 1920s Pittsburgh's industrial economy offered fewer opportunities, and many employers left the city itself. It was the distinct disadvantage of blacks that during the period from 1930 to 1960 when they experienced the largest three-decade increase ever in their population[2] that they largely retained their first-generation urban status. They were unable to rely upon a stable occupational and community base created by an earlier generation. Second-generation Poles and Italians, on the other hand, were the beneficiaries of solid, urban bases that provided adequate housing, established institutional services, and secured vital entrees into specific occupational sectors. But the differences among the groups cannot be described simply in terms of successful and unsuccessful—in fact, such terminology is grossly misleading. During the 1930s all three groups were occupationally stagnant. After 1940 Italians did make gains into skilled and small entrepreneurial areas, partially as a result of their earlier inclinations. Poles, however, remained largely in blue-collar work, although more entered skilled and supervisory roles. Patterns for blacks continued to be unstable and erratic, although some inroads were noticeable during World War II in industrial sectors closed to them a generation earlier.

The racism that flowered in other northern cities after 1930 was certainly present in Pittsburgh. But while many observers have attributed this rise in racial antipathies simply to the influx of greater numbers of blacks,[3] the answer here—as in the entire process of urbanization—seems more complicated. The greatest wave of black migration coincided not only with a slowing economy in Pittsburgh but with the emergence of entrenched ethnic occupational, residential, and familial systems. No doubt this ethnic base had been established at the expense of an earlier black generation; beachheads for the second and largest wave of blacks were sorely missed. Consequently, structural factors were present in the post-1930 city that were a product of the period of expanding industrialization and that would have hindered black adaptation significantly, whether racial animosities existed or not. This is not to excuse or minimize racial prejudice. It is only an attempt to understand that the adjustment of migrants to the industrial city was a multidimensional, historical process for Poles, Italians, and blacks. The urbanization of these people can only begin to be understood when this interactional framework is considered.

NOTES

1. Grace M. Andeson, *Networks of Contact: The Portuguese and Toronto* (Waterloo, Ontario, 1974), 86-87.
2. Joe T. Darden, *Afro-Americans in Pittsburgh: The Residential Segregation of a People* (Lexington, Mass., 1973), 7-16.
3. Kenneth L. Kusmer, *A Ghetto Takes Shape: Black Cleveland, 1870-1930* (Urbana, Ill., 1976), 175.

Appendix A

Sources and Methods

This study relied upon a variety of sources for its information. Pittsburgh city newspapers were systematically surveyed in 1900, 1915, and 1930 for all events pertaining to the ethnic/black experience during those years; other issues were examined as necessary. Records of churches, fraternal associations, and black organizations that we consulted where possible proved valuable. Other traditional sources, including a large collection of studies conducted by the University of Pittsburgh, provided important background data. These sources acted as the mortar binding together the massive collection of quantitative and oral data, and together they enabled us to tell the story of the Polish, black, and Italian experiences in twentieth-century Pittsburgh.

The 1900 manuscript census for Pittsburgh was used to identify the city's existing Polish, Italian, and black populations. A sample population was generated by selecting every fifth household headed by one of the subject groups, then recording every member of every Polish, black, or Italian family residing within that household.

Households containing four or more members of one of the subject groups, but headed by a nonmember, were also included. This technique enabled us to capture individuals or families living in boarding houses headed by "outsiders." (In reality this rarely happened, since owners of boardinghouses in Pittsburgh seldom resided with their boarders. A male Slavic boardinghouse, for example, usually listed each individual as a family head with the individual first listed being recorded as the head of the household.)

Because we wanted a true sample from 1900, individuals with common surnames were included, even though we knew they would be untraceable in subsequent years. Approximately 12 percent of the black adult males, 7 percent of the Italians, and 4 percent of the Poles fell into this category.

The total sample consisted of 6,059 individuals divided as follows:

	Black	Russian Pole	Austrian Pole	German Pole	Italian
Male	1,810	859	118	557	661
Female	925	436	47	382	264
TOTAL	2,735	1,295	165	939	925

The census provides our most accurate portrait of a population universe at a point in time. Unfortunately, as recent studies have shown, it is not without its flaws and limitations.[1] The census typically underenumerates blue-collar workers and those at the lower end of the socioeconomic spectrum. This might not prove particularly disturbing for a study of this type, since our comparisons are of three groups who resided at or near the bottom of the occupational ladder in 1900. Recent investigations by John Sharples and Ray Shortridge, however, indicate that the census takers also underenumerated selectively across racial and ethnic lines. The 1900 census, Sharples and Shortridge estimated, missed 2.5 percent of the native-born whites, 12.5 percent of the blacks, and 22.5 percent of the foreign-born whites.[2] Unfortunately, Pittsburgh has no other large body of demographic data in 1900 against which to test the accuracy of its census data. A comparison of a 10 percent sample of our sample with the names recorded in the 1900 city directory indicates only that the directory further underenumerated all three groups. The U.S. census recorded members from all three groups who were not found in the Polk's 1900 city directory for Pittsburgh. The proportion of each group missing, however, is likely misleading, since the directory canvas and the census count were conducted at different times of the year. Individuals living in Pittsburgh at the time of the census may have moved before the directory canvassers reached their households. Conversely, others may have moved into the city during the interim. It is not possible to compare particular groups from the directory with those recorded in the U.S. census, since the directory does not identify individuals by either race or ethnicity. In addition, even if this were possible, one would have to alphabetize the entire census for Pittsburgh to compare any sizeable portion of the directory with the census.

Thus it is clear that we are dealing with a highly imperfect source of data. Comparison of these data, however, with other more traditional sources suggests that they provide a representative picture of a group's position in Pittsburgh. Few members of any of the groups held high level occupations—those who had were more likely to be included in the census than their less fortunate counterparts. Thus the bias is probably slightly upward, although not by a large degree.

Individuals from the 1900 census sample were traced at five-year intervals through the Pittsburgh city directories until 1930 or until their names failed to appear in two subsequent directories. We then created parallel records for each male recorded in the 1900 census. Females were seldom listed in Pittsburgh directories, and so it proved impossible to trace their career patterns.

The questionable accuracy of these two data sets places serious burdens on the researcher. A computer enabled us to perform all sorts of complicated statistical manipulations on nearly 17,000 observations, each characterized by three or more variables. Relationships among most variables were not proven to be statistically significant, and, even if they had, the nature of the data would not enable us to accept them at face value. Their use, moreover, suggested a precision that, in fact, could not exist given the imprecise data base. Thus it was decided at the outset that we would attempt to demonstrate trends and patterns among various groups who were exposed to the industrial milieu in Pittsburgh. When viewed in conjunction with the information provided by other sources, the trends and patterns give a more accurate portrait of the experiences of these three groups than has previously been known.

ORAL INTERVIEWS

The oral history interviews used in this study were drawn from a project that began in 1974 with support from the Pennsylvania Historical and Museum Commission. Additional support from the Rockefeller Foundation and Carnegie-Mellon University allowed the project to continue until 1978 and to expand its scope to cover Italian-American families. While numerous interviewers participated in the project, the work of Peter Gottlieb, Gregory Mihalik, and William Simons was especially valuable.

The subjects interviewed for the program were generally contacted through local community organizations. Churches, fraternal clubs, and union halls were most commonly used to penetrate working-class communities on the Southside, the Hill District, Bloomfield, and

Lawrenceville. Generally, initial contacts obtained through these institutions led to recommendations of other friends, neighbors, former associates, or relatives. While such a referral system may not have met the strictest guidelines of scientific sampling, it seemed the only workable way of getting inside Pittsburgh's neighborhoods, an important consideration for scholarly outsiders.

From the start of interviewing in 1974, certain assumptions were made about the subject areas to be examined and the structure of each interview. A conscious effort was made to analyze the mechanics of moving to the city, family life, and job procurement. These areas were thought to be critical to understanding how initial attachment to the city was made. Furthermore, as other scholarship has suggested, work and family clearly dominated working-class life. Admittedly, however, certain topics, such as the relationship between parents and children, emerged from the recollections of people themselves and from the entire interviewing process rather than any predetermined set of questions.

That oral interviews can reveal unanticipated lines of inquiry caused us to establish a basic criterion for all interviews. Each interviewer was clearly instructed not to rely solely on the prepared questionnaire but to allow respondents some opportunity to raise issues of their own choosing and to discuss them at length. Such an approach acknowledged that the oral interview was a dialogue between respondent and interviewer and that the historical record could be enriched by both the memory of the participant and informed preparation of the historian.

A final consideration of oral history data is its reliability. Obviously any historical source has potential drawbacks. But the use of a prepared questionnaire (Appendix C) for part of each interview insured that respondents would be asked common questions, thus allowing for comparability and the emergence of systematic patterns in the recorded information. The patterns that did surface strengthened considerably our confidence in the results. Moreover, certain topical areas could not be probed at all without interviewing techniques and the alternative of not trying at all seemed clearly unacceptable.

SECOND-GENERATION DATA

The 1930-60 microanalysis of seven ethnic neighborhoods relied upon data generated from several sources. Our understanding of the development of ethnic neighborhoods in Pittsburgh prior to 1930 enabled us to pinpoint relatively homogeneous wards and even census tracts in

1930. A six-block square section of each of these tracts was then selected for detailed analysis. The criteria for selection of each area were: (1) at least 80 percent residential; (2) historic identification as a Polish, black, or Italian area; (3) clearly recognizable geographic boundaries; (4) at least 50 percent Polish, black, or Italian; and (5) the largest Polish, black, or Italian neighborhoods in the Pittsburgh area.

Each structure extant within the area in 1930 was identified, along with the name of the occupants, their ethnicity, occupation, ownership status, and any other available data. A linkage of parish records and voter registration records with those data provided by the 1930 directory enabled us to determine the correct nationality and/or race of each resident. Any individual who could not be positively identified as one of the subject groups was omitted from the sample. The total 1930 sample consisted of 302 Italian families distributed in 316 structures (some structures housed non-Italians), 504 Polish families in 295 structures, and 279 black families in 392 structures. Each of the 1,085 families (1,595 individuals) were traced through city directories in 1940, 1950, and 1960. New residents of each of the 1,003 structures who appeared in any of the subsequent decades became part of the decadal neighborhood profiles. Census tract and block data, oral interviews, church records, and several earlier studies supplemented these data to permit the two-way analysis of ethnic groups and neighborhood change.

HOUSING DATA

Our interest in the process and mechanics of homeownership required that we again turn to little-used nontraditional data sources. Allegheny County, like other metropolitan areas, carries a complete record of the deed transactions of property within its political boundaries. Approximately 400 structures from four of the sample neighborhoods were selected for further analysis. Deed transactions for each home were then traced from 1978 back through approximately 1890. Mortgages were also examined for the 1900-30 period. These data enabled us to determine more precisely when a neighborhood changed from one ethnic group to another, how individuals managed to acquire property, the incidence of inheriting a home from one's family, the impact of certain economic conditions, and the workings of various economic instituitons within the ethnic and black communities.

None of the above sources may be viewed as infallible. One must exercise extreme caution in their use and be wary of drawing broad generalizations. When the sources are combined, however, one may be somewhat more confident in the historical patterns they reveal. None of the sources cited here was found to be widely at variance with all the others. They all led to similar conclusions. While other facets of immigrant and black life in Pittsburgh remain to be examined, these data shed important light on the migration and urbanization of workers in a twentieth-century industrial city.

NOTES

1. The *Pittsburgh Leader,* in a highly defamatory account, perhaps best illustrated the difficulties of achieving an accurate census count. A *Leader* reporter accompanying a census enumerator in 1900 reported the following incidents:
   (a) A woman refused to answer any further questions when queried regarding the extent of a mortgage on her home.
   (b) The census enumerator determined the number of children in one black family by lining the children up and physically counting all those present.
   (c) In a German home the respondent was asked, "How many children have you?"
   "Nein," was the response.
   "Nine, are you sure its nine or ten?" The enumerator questioned.
   "Nein, Nein, Kinder mir haben nichts," explained the man filling in with well-known gestures the gap caused by poverty of speech.
   (d) In an Italian boardinghouse the lone man who could speak English provided the vital information on twenty-three boarders. Several of the boarders, the *Leader* reported, believed that the enumeration was "a scheme to make them pay money in some way or to 'do them up' in some deal." The questionable accuracy of their responses clearly generates little confidence in the U.S. census returns.
   See the *Pittsburgh Leader,* "Taking the Census among the Furreners," July 14, 1900, p. 1.
2. John Sharpless and Ray M. Shortridge, "Biased Underenumeration in Census Manuscripts: Methodological Implications," *Journal of Urban History,* 1 (Aug. 1975), 430ff.

Appendix B

Population Distribution:
Poles, Blacks, and Italians
in Pittsburgh, 1930

274

Source: Allegheny County Bureau of Social Research, 1933.

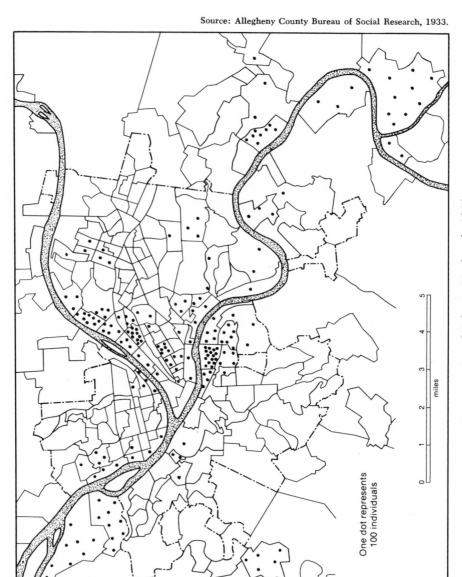

One dot represents
100 individuals

miles

Concentration of Poles in Pittsburgh, 1930.

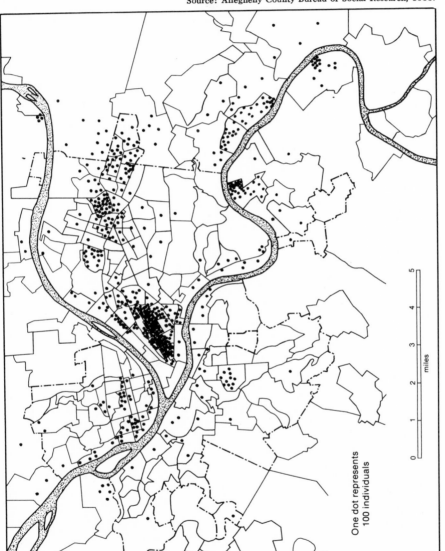

Source: Allegheny County Bureau of Social Research, 1933.

Concentration of Blacks in Pittsburgh, 1930.

One dot represents
100 individuals

0   1   2   3   4   5
miles

276

Source: Allegheny County Bureau of Social Research, 1933.

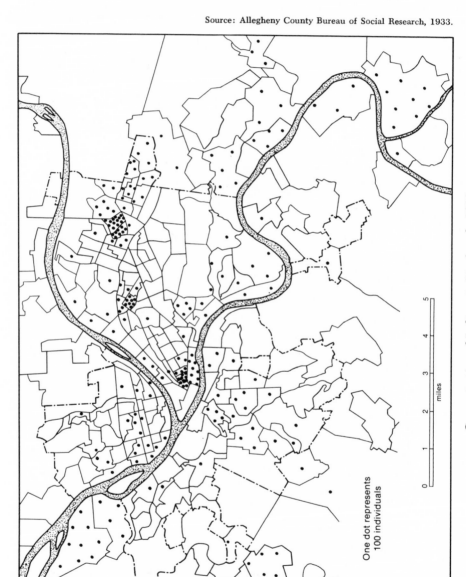

Concentration of Italians in Pittsburgh, 1930.

One dot represents
100 individuals

miles

Appendix C

Basic Oral History Questionnaire
of the Pennsylvania Historical
and Museum Commission

Main areas to be covered in interviews:

(1) *Introduction:* Basic questions to be asked at the start of each interview and required information
  (a) Name of interviewer, place, date.
  (b) Person being interviewed:
> age
> place of birth
> ethnic origin
> occupation
> religion, politics

(2) *Family history*
  (a) Birthplace of parents.
  (b) When did parents enter this area?
  (c) Why did they come to this area?
  (d) All locations parents lived before coming to this area.
  (e) Father's occupational history.
  (f) Did mother work, when, where, how long?
  (g) Who resided in household as a child (relatives, boarders, etc.)?
  (h) Port of entry (if immigrants).
  (i) Did children do any household work?
  (j) Parents' views on religion, education, values, etc.
  (k) Particular problems of being second generation.

(l)   Size of family.

(m) What do you recall of Depression days (1930s)?

(3) *Occupational history of person being interviewed*

  (a) Did you work as a child?

  (b) Did your income go to the support of your household as a child?

  (c) First adult occupation.

  (d) How long did you go to school?

  (e) Did you have to move around in search of work?

  (f) Union activities, if any.

  (g) What was your first job, last job? What were you told about blacks, foreigners, Americans?

  (h) Do you recall any strikes? What were the issues involved? What was your role? Who were the strikebreakers?

  (i) Were you ever discriminated against for any reason?

  (j) What did you think of unions? What union did you join?

  (k) Was your job hazardous? What measures were taken to insure your safety?

(4) *Career evaluations*

  (a) As a young person, what did you want to do in life?

  (b) Did you aspire to any particular job?

  (c) Was your job better than your father's?

  (d) How long did you go to school?

  (e) What was your father's last job?

  (f) Describe what you did in your work.

  (g) What job did you feel you were capable of attaining?

  (h) Did you ever want to leave your job for a better one or start a business of your own? Why?

  (i) Were you capable of a reasonable amount of control of your own career?

  (j) What opportunities were open to you for advancement in your job?

  (k) Did you feel you have earned respect? Why?

  (l) Were you successful in your career? Why?

  (m) Did your efforts benefit your children?

  (n) What are you most proud of in your life?

(5) *Family relations*

  (a) Did you feel closer to your mother or your father?

  (b) Was your relationship with your parents intimate or were they distant?

(c) Were either of your parents strict-authoritarians?
(d) Were either of your parents away at work a great deal?
(e) Were you anxious to leave your ethnic neighborhood, home?
(f) Did you have to sacrifice your own aspirations to family need (Depression)?
(g) Which of your parents wanted you to work?
(h) Which stressed education?
(i) At what age did you begin working?
(j) What percentage of your earnings did you turn over to your parents, what percentage did you keep?
(k) Did you differ with your parents on how much of your earnings you could keep?

(6) *Residential history*
(a) How many different places have you lived?
(b) Did you live in an "ethnic neighborhood"?
(c) Did you ever leave your neighborhood because of your job? Arrival of other ethnic groups?
(d) Did you live near your work?

(7) *Unstructured*
At this point interviewer should encourage the respondent to elaborate about any aspect of his life that he wants to discuss or is especially knowledgeable. He may wish to elaborate his role in politics, in a church group, in a fraternal association, or in a strike. He should be encouraged to discuss points already mentioned in the interview or which he wants to raise.

Index

A Note on the Authors

JOHN BODNAR, formerly of the Pennsylvania Historical and Museum Commission, is now associate professor of history at Indiana University, Bloomington. He received his Ph.D. from the University of Connecticut. His other works include *Immigration and Industrialization: Ethnicity in an American Mill Town, 1870-1940*, and *The Ethnic Experience in Pennsylvania* (editor). He has published articles in the *Journal of Social History*, the *Journal of American History*, and *Labor History*.

ROGER SIMON is associate professor of history at Lehigh University, Bethlehem, Pennsylvania. He has a B.A. from Rutgers University, and an M.A. and Ph.D. from the University of Wisconsin, Madison. His previous publications include *The City-Building Process: Housing and Services in New Milwaukee Neighborhoods, 1880-1910*, as well as articles in the *Journal of Urban History* and *Antioch Review*.

MICHAEL P.WEBER is associate professor of history at Carnegie-Mellon University, Pittsburgh. He has a B.A. and M.A. from Edinboro State College and received his doctorate from Carnegie-Mellon. His other works include *Social Change in an Industrial Town: Patterns of Progress in Warren, Pennsylvania, from Civil War to World War I* and *The American City* (co-author). He has published articles on urban history and occupational mobility in the *Journal of Social History*, *Pennsylvania History*, and the *Journal of American History*.